# AUTHORS
## OF THE
## 19TH CENTURY

# AUTHORS
## OF THE
# 19TH CENTURY

EDITED BY ADAM AUGUSTYN, ASSISTANT MANAGER AND
ASSISTANT EDITOR, LITERATURE

**Britannica**®
Educational Publishing

IN ASSOCIATION WITH

## ROSEN
EDUCATIONAL SERVICES

Published in 2014 by Britannica Educational Publishing (a trademark of Encyclopædia
Britannica, Inc.) in association with Rosen Educational Services, LLC

29 East 21st Street, New York, NY 10010.

Distributed exclusively by Rosen Educational Services.
For a listing of additional Britannica Educational Publishing titles, call toll free (800) 237-9932.

First Edition

Britannica Educational Publishing
J.E. Luebering: Director, Core Reference Group
Adam Augustyn: Assistant Manager, Core Reference Group
Marilyn L. Barton: Senior Coordinator, Production Control
Steven Bosco: Director, Editorial Technologies
Lisa S. Braucher: Senior Producer and Data Editor
Yvette Charboneau: Senior Copy Editor
Kathy Nakamura: Manager, Media Acquisition
Adam Augustyn, Assistant Manager and Assistant Editor, Literature

Rosen Educational Services
Hope Killcoyne: Executive Editor
Nelson Sá: Art Director
Cindy Reiman: Photography Manager
Karen Huang: Photo Researcher
Brian Garvey: Designer, Cover Design
Introduction by Joseph Kampff

**Library of Congress Cataloging-in-Publication Data**

Authors of the 19th century/edited by Adam Augustyn.—First edition.
     pages cm.—(The Britannica Guide to Authors)
Includes bibliographical references and index.
ISBN 978-1-62275-001-6 (library binding)
1. Authors—19th century--Biography. 2. Literature, Modern—19th century—History
and criticism. 3. Authorship—History—19th century. I. Augustyn, Adam, 1979- editor of
compilation.
PN451.A956 2014
809'.034—dc23

                                                                    2013001501

*Manufactured in the United States of America*

**On the cover, p.iii** : Portrait of Jane Austen, whose novels detailing middle-class life in 19th-
century England enjoy enormous popularity to this day. *Stock Montage/Archive Photos/Getty
Images*

# CONTENTS

17

91

152

*184*

*237*

*364*

# INTRODUCTION

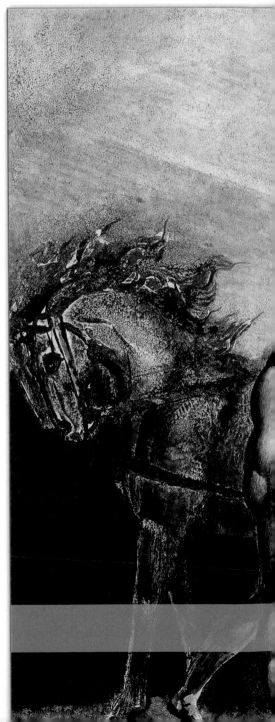

One way to approach literature written during the 19th century is to read such works while considering their authors' engagement with—or reaction to—Romanticism. Authors of the Romantic period tended to value nature and emotion over reason and order, often addressing themes of madness, illness, and death. In lieu of the abstract concerns about large-scale subjects such as truth and society found in the writings of the Enlightenment (the literary movement that preceded Romanticism), Romantic-era writers prioritized individual thoughts and personal feelings. *Authors of the 19th Century* provides a thorough, authoritative introduction to the writers of the period, individuals who addressed many important issues and themes that remain current today.

Among these men and women is the German poet, novelist, and playwright Johann Wolfgang von Goethe, who stands as arguably the

God Judging Adam, *from a folio of colour etchings by William Blake.*
DEA/G. Nimatallah/De Agostini/Getty Images

greatest early figure of European Romanticism. Goethe was educated at home before leaving, at age 16, to study law at Leipzig, where he composed some of his earliest works. Illness and emotional turmoil, brought on by unrequited love, compelled him to return to Frankfurt in 1768. After recuperating, Goethe went to Strasbourg to continue his education. There, he befriended Johann Gottfried von Herder, a prominent figure of the influential Sturm und Drang ("Storm and Stress") literary movement. Goethe experienced something of a literary transformation, as he began to view language as the expression of a national culture.

Goethe published his first novel, *Die Leiden des jungen Werthers* (*The Sorrows of Young Werther*), in 1774. The novel, which follows the emotional and intellectual disintegration of its titular antihero, earned him instant international acclaim, as well as some degree of moral censure for the story's treatment of suicide and adultery. Goethe's supreme literary achievement—and arguably one of the greatest works of European literature—is *Faust*, a tragic drama in two parts that he worked on through much of his adult life.

The English poet William Wordsworth attended primary school at Hawkshead in the bucolic Lake District, an area that no doubt influenced his affinity for nature. He then attended St. John's College, Cambridge, from 1787 to 1791, but as he put it, he "was not for that hour, nor for that place." After spending some time in France, Wordsworth moved in with his sister, the poet Dorothy Wordsworth, in 1797. This move and his subsequent acquaintance with fellow poet Samuel Taylor Coleridge inaugurated the period of great artistic production for which Wordsworth is best known.

With Coleridge, Wordsworth initiated the Romantic movement in England with their 1798 collection of poems, *Lyrical Ballads*. Although the collection contains Coleridge's most famous work, "The Rime of the Ancient Mariner," Wordsworth composed the majority of the poems that make up the volume. In the preface to the second edition of the book, Wordsworth laid out a radical agenda for Romantic poetry that would break with the poetic forms of artistic predecessors, communicating human experience in language that the common man understood and used.

The seventh of eight children, Jane Austen had extensive family connections that informed and inspired many of the central themes of her novels, which focused on everyday domestic realities. Although Austen completed her earliest works—*Sense and Sensibility*, *Pride and Prejudice*, and *Northanger Abbey*—before 1800, they went unpublished for more than 10 years. When Austen's novels began to be published anonymously after 1811, they enjoyed a wide and enthusiastic readership. Austen wrote and revised her novels vigorously until her untimely death in 1817. Both *Northanger Abbey* and *Persuasion* were published posthumously, at which time her brother revealed their author's identity to the public. In many ways, the novel as we know it today—with its frequent focus on the realistic treatment of relatable characters—begins with Austen.

Few authors can claim the immense popularity that Charles Dickens enjoyed during his lifetime. Dickens was born to a newly middle-class family in Portsmouth, England, in 1812. Although his father earned a respectable salary as a clerk in the Royal Navy pay office, he was irresponsible with money, and his debts landed him in prison in 1824. The family was ruined, and Dickens's education was cut short, as he left school to do manual labor to support his family. This early experience had a profound effect on Dickens, which one finds reflected in his writings.

Dickens's novels, such as *David Copperfield*, *Bleak House*, *A Tale of Two Cities*, and *Great Expectations*, provide a compelling portrait of Victorian-era England, featuring a large variety of memorable characters from all social strata—from the privileged to the working classes. In addition to his prodigious fiction output, Dickens is notable for his journalistic work as editor of the periodicals *Household Words* (in the 1850s) and *All the Year Round*, which he founded and ran until his death in 1870. His works, which continue to be widely read today, have been adapted for film and the stage, produced as cartoons, and trimmed down into children's books.

In Russia, Fyodor Dostoyevsky was also well regarded during his lifetime for his journalism. His true claim to fame, however, is his outstanding achievement as a novelist. Born in Moscow in 1821, Dostoyevsky was part of a family that was removed from the Russian aristocracy. Unlike Leo Tolstoy and many other prominent Russian writers of the period, Dostoyevsky often wrote under pressure to meet his next deadline and receive payment. A supporter of political reform in Russia—he was strongly opposed to serfdom—Dostoyevsky was arrested for his beliefs in 1849. After spending the next eight months in prison, he was led in front of a firing squad to be executed. Just before shots were to be fired it was revealed that the tsar had commuted the death sentence.

Subsequently, Dostoyevsky was sentenced to four years of hard labor in Siberia, an experience that greatly affected him for the rest of his life. His novel *Zapiski iz myortvogo doma* (*The House of the Dead*) is based on his time in prison; while in Siberia, he developed a belief in the dignity and fundamental goodness of commoners that came to inform all of his later writing. His longer novels *Crime and Punishment*, *The Idiot*, *The Possessed*, and *The Brothers Karamazov* have had a profound influence on much of the fiction—as well as philosophical and psychological thought—that followed.

Victor Hugo was the greatest writer of the Romantic era in France. Hugo was born in Besançon in 1802, but his father's military career caused the family to move frequently throughout his childhood. Despite the constant displacements of his youth, Hugo always returned to Paris, where he lived for much his life. He was deeply engaged in the turbulent political life of France at the time and spent nearly 20 years living in political exile. Hugo is revered in France for his poetic achievements, but in much of the rest of the world he is famous for his remarkable novels *The Hunchback of Notre-Dame* and *Les Misérables*. The latter work has been especially successful, as the epic tale of the post-Revolution French underclass has been adapted into a long-running Broadway musical and a number of films.

Often cited as the first modern poet, the French author and critic Charles Baudelaire served as a bridge between Romanticism and the subsequent Modernism movement in literature. Born in Paris in 1821, Baudelaire was the only child of a civil servant and artist, François Baudelaire, and his second wife, Caroline Defayis. His mother was much younger than her husband, who died in 1827, while Baudelaire was a child. Baudelaire loved living alone in Paris with his mother for the following 18 months and was deeply distressed when she remarried in 1828. A child of the city, he was less taken with nature than other poets of the period, choosing instead to focus on the shocking effects of urbanization on the modern consciousness. He begins "Les sept vieillards" ("The Seven Old Men") with the line, "O swarming city, city full of dreams." Although he is famous today for his poetry, particularly his masterpiece *Les Fleurs du mal* (*The Flowers of Evil*)—a controversial volume of poems that was heavily censored upon its appearance in 1857, with six of the poems banned in France until 1949 — Baudelaire spent most of his adult life working on his translations of the works of Edgar Allan Poe.

Born in Boston, Massachusetts, Poe was an important innovator of the 19th-century gothic tale. Although he published some early volumes of poetry and gained some recognition for his literary criticism, he remained relatively unknown as a writer until the publication of *The Raven and Other Poems* in 1845, which quickly brought him national fame. Poe's life was plagued with poverty that was compounded by his frequent drinking.

Poe's poetry and short stories often explore themes of terror, madness, and death with a psychological penetration that few writers have equaled. Many readers will recognize the refrain of his long, haunting poem, "The Raven" — "Quoth the raven, 'Nevermore,'" — and his short stories, such as "The Fall of the House of Usher" and "The Tell-Tale Heart," are classic works of horror. Poe's "The Murders in the Rue Morgue" is considered the first modern detective story.

While many authors have difficulty getting their work published, one of America's most beloved and accomplished poets, Emily Dickinson, seems never to have intended the majority of her nearly 1,800 poems for print. Although she shared many of them with friends and family, only 10 of Dickinson's poems were published during her lifetime. Born in 1830 to a prosperous family in Amherst, Massachusetts, Dickinson attended Amherst Academy (which would later become Amherst College) and, later, the Mount Holyoke Female Seminary. Although she excelled at Amherst, receiving particular recognition for her skills in composition, she did not finish her studies at Mount Holyoke. Whether she disliked the religious climate there, the severity of her teachers, or was simply homesick is unclear.

Nevertheless, Dickinson returned early from Mount Holyoke and rarely left her father's house in Amherst again. While many of her poems express her deep sense of spirituality, Dickinson was not attracted to organized religion, preferring instead to explore the extraordinary in everyday life through her bold and experimental verse. In the opening stanza of one of her most anthologized poems, she writes:

*Some keep the Sabbath going to Church —*
*I keep it, staying at Home —*
*With a Bobolink for a Chorister —*
*And an Orchard, for a Dome —*

The American novelist Ernest Hemingway famously wrote in 1935 that "[a]ll modern American literature comes from one book by Mark Twain called *Huckleberry Finn*." While some of Hemingway's statements are best taken with a grain of salt, it is nevertheless true that *The Adventures of Huckleberry Finn* has been profoundly influential. The novel has sometimes been purged from schools' curriculums because of its representation of the slave, Jim, and its frequent use of racially charged language. However, Twain's novelistic treatment of racism and slavery illustrates a crucial, albeit unfortunate, chapter in America's history.

The author known as Mark Twain was born Samuel Langhorne Clemens in Florida, Missouri. As he puts it, Twain was not a "literary person" until he was in his early thirties. Before establishing himself as a writer, he worked at a number of trades, the most important and satisfying of which was as a riverboat pilot on the Mississippi; that job later led to the adoption of his famous pen name ("mark twian" being a riverman's phrase for water found to be two fathoms [12 feet, or

3.7 metres] deep ). Life on the Mississippi River would figure prominently in his novels *The Adventures of Tom Sawyer* and *Huckleberry Finn*, as well as in his travel book *Life on the Mississippi.*

Many 19th-century authors included in this volume came from working-class families and worked in a number of professions while devoting the balance of their time to writing. Thus, the authors of the period worked to extend literature beyond the boundaries of the privileged domain of high culture, making it accessible to readers from a wide variety of social circumstances. The newfound attention to working-class individuals, nature, and the often harsh realities of everyday life make the 19th century one of the most informative, productive, and fascinating eras in the history of world literature.

# JOHANN WOLFGANG VON GOETHE

(b. August 28, 1749, Frankfurt am Main [Germany]—d. March 22, 1832, Weimar, Saxe-Weimar)

The German poet, playwright, novelist, scientist, statesman, theatre director, critic, and amateur artist Johann Wolfgang von Goethe is considered the greatest German literary figure of the modern era.

Goethe is the only German literary figure whose range and international standing equal those of Germany's supreme philosophers (who have often drawn on his works and ideas) and composers (who have often set his works to music). In a European perspective he appears as the central and unsurpassed representative of the Romantic movement, broadly understood. He could be said to stand in the same relation to the culture of the era that began with the Enlightenment and continues to the present day as William Shakespeare does to the culture of the Renaissance and Dante to the culture of the High Middle Ages.

## Early Years

His father, Johann Caspar Goethe (1710–82), the son of a wealthy tailor-turned-innkeeper, was a man of leisure who lived on his inherited fortune and devoted himself, after studying law in Leipzig and Strasbourg and touring Italy, France, and the Low Countries, to collecting books and paintings and to the education of his children. Goethe's

*Johann Wolfgang von Goethe, engraving by James Posselwhite, 19th century.* © Photos.com/Thinkstock

mother, Catharina Elisabeth Textor (1731–1808), was one of the daughters of Frankfurt's most senior official and was a lively woman closer in age to her son than to her husband. Goethe was the eldest of seven children, though only one other survived into adulthood, his sister Cornelia (1750–77), for whom he felt an intense affection of whose potentially incestuous nature he seems to have been aware.

In 1765 Goethe left home to study law in Leipzig. He had in almost-finished form a biblical play and a moralistic novel when he entered the university, but, after reading them to his friends, he ostentatiously burned them as unworthy of his now advanced taste and started to write erotic verse and a pastoral drama, *Die Laune des Verliebten* (1806; "The Lover's Spleen"; Eng. trans. *The Lover's Caprice*), begun in 1767. He fell in love with the daughter of an innkeeper, Käthchen Schönkopf, but she preferred someone more solid, a lawyer who eventually became deputy burgomaster of Leipzig. Goethe took revenge by starting his first mature play, *Die Mitschuldigen* (1787; "Partners in Guilt"), a verse comedy showing a woman's regrets after a year of marriage to the wrong man. His emotional state became hectic, and his health gave way—he may have suffered an attack of tuberculosis—and in September 1768 he returned home to Frankfurt without a degree. Another bout of illness then brought him apparently near death, and in the aftermath he underwent a brief conversion from freethinking to evangelical Christianity.

## Sturm und Drang

From April 1770 until August 1771 Goethe studied in Strasbourg for the doctorate. However, he had now emerged from his Christian period, and for his dissertation he chose a potentially shocking subject from ecclesiastical law concerning the nature of ancient Jewish religion. The dissertation, which questioned the status of the Ten Commandments, proved too scandalous to be accepted, as perhaps he intended, and he took instead the Latin oral examination for the licentiate in law.

Strasbourg was also the scene of an intellectual and emotional awakening that came over Goethe with something of the force of a conversion. In the winter of 1770–71 Johann Gottfried Herder, already a famous young literary intellectual, was staying in Strasbourg for an eye operation. During their long conversations in a darkened room, Goethe learned to look at language and literature in a new, almost anthropological way: as the expression of a national culture, part of the historically specific genius of a particular people, concentrated from time to time in the genius of individuals, such as Shakespeare or the anonymous authors of the Scottish border ballads or, in 16th-century Germany, Martin Luther.

In Frankfurt Goethe started a legal practice but found the new literary possibilities to which Herder had opened his mind running away with him. Written down in first draft in six weeks in the autumn of 1771, *Geschichte Gottfriedens von Berlichingen mit der eisernen Hand, dramatisirt* ("The History of Gottfried von Berlichingen with the Iron Hand, Dramatized"), later titled simply *Götz von Berlichingen*, was eventually translated by Sir Walter Scott, who was inspired by Goethe's example to think of using his own local history as the material for his novels. *Götz* was not published immediately but became known to a few friends in manuscript, and Goethe, already well-connected at the cultivated local court of Darmstadt, was asked to start reviewing for a new intellectual Frankfurt journal, the *Frankfurter Gelehrte Anzeigen* ("Frankfurt Review of Books"), which was hostile to the enlightened despotism of the German princely states, notably Prussia and Austria. He thereby effectively became part of the literary movement subsequently known as the Sturm und Drang ("Storm and Stress").

Law took up some of Goethe's time in 1773, but most of it went on literary work—the dramatic fragment *Prometheus* dates from this period—and on preparing for the private publication of a revised version of *Götz* in the summer. This publication made his name overnight, even though it was a financial disaster. In 1774 an even greater literary success brought him European notoriety. *Die Leiden des jungen Werthers* (*The Sorrows of Young Werther*), written in two months early in the year, appeared that autumn, at Michaelmas, and captured the imagination of a generation. It was almost immediately translated into French and in 1779 into English. The uncompromising concentration on the principal character's viewpoint—no one else's letters are communicated to the reader—permits the depiction from within of emotional and intellectual disintegration and partly accounts for the strength of the public reaction. Much moral outrage was generated by a work that appeared to condone both adultery and suicide, but for 35 years Goethe was known in the first instance as the author of *Werther*. He at once attracted visitors from all over Germany—among them the 17-year-old prince of Weimar, Charles Augustus (Karl August), who was about to come of age and so take over the government of his duchy and who was bowled over by the electric personality of the poet when he met him in December 1774.

The years from 1773 to 1776 were the most productive period in Goethe's life: poems and other works, mainly fragments, poured out. *Clavigo* (1774; Eng. trans. *Clavigo*), a tragedy, was written in a week, and the plays *Stella* and *Egmont* were begun. *Stella* (1776; Eng. trans. *Stella*), in a picturesque blend of realism and self-indulgence, shows a man in love with two women who finds an unconventional resolution to his conventional conflict by setting up a ménage à trois. *Egmont* (1788; Eng. trans. *Egmont*), another historical drama but formally more controlled than *Götz*, uses the theme of the war for Dutch independence from Spain (Eighty Years' War) to launch a more explicit assault on the cultural poverty of bureaucratic and military despotism. Also about this time, Goethe's privileged acquaintances first record getting a sight of the developing manuscript of his *Faust*.

## First Weimar Period

In November 1775 Goethe arrived in Weimar on the invitation of the young duke Charles Augustus. It was soon clear that more was wanted of him than supplying a passing visit from a fashionable personality. The duke bought him a cottage and garden just outside the city walls and paid for them to be restored. Six months after his arrival, Goethe was made a member of the ruling Privy Council—there were two other members, besides himself, who advised the duke—and Herder was summoned to become the primate of the duchy's Lutheran church. Although at first Goethe had few duties beyond accompanying Charles Augustus and arranging court entertainments, he soon began to accumulate more prosaic responsibilities and was, initially at least, motivated by the idea of a reformed principality governed, in accordance with Enlightenment principles, for the benefit of all its subjects and not just of the landowning nobility. In 1779 he took on the War Commission, in addition to the Mines and Highways commissions, and in 1782, when the chancellor of the duchy's Exchequer left under a cloud, he agreed to act in his place for two and a half years. This post made him virtually—though not in fact—prime minister and the principal representative of the duchy in the increasingly complex diplomatic affairs in which Charles Augustus was at the time involving himself.

*Goethe's garden house, Weimar, Ger.; detail of a photomechanical print, c. 1890–1900.* Library of Congress, Washington, D.C. (neg. no. LC-DIG-ppmsca-01163)

It was therefore essential to raise him to the nobility, and in 1782 he became "von Goethe."

Goethe was attracted to the world of the court. He liked the idea of a society of noble, self-disciplined people devoting themselves to their own culture and the improvement of the world. The reality, naturally, in no way corresponded to that ideal—the Weimar court was petty, backbiting, and snobbish—but in Charlotte von Stein, the wife of the duke's equerry, Goethe thought he saw the ideal embodied. He felt destined for her even before he met her, and, for 10 years during which they were lovers in everything except a physical sense, he allowed her to exercise over him an extraordinary fascination. In her he saw fulfilled the longing for calm after storm and stress that he expressed in his two "Wandrers Nachtlieder" ("Wanderer's Night Songs"), the second of which—*Über allen Gipfeln* ("Over All the Peaks"), written in 1780—is probably the best-known of all his poems.

With his ennoblement Goethe might be thought to have reached the pinnacle of his career. However, his literary output had begun to suffer. Until 1780 he continued to produce original and substantial works, particularly, in 1779, a prose drama in a quite new manner, *Iphigenie auf Tauris* (*Iphigenia in Tauris*), which shows the healing process he attributed to the influence of Frau von Stein in the context of an emotionally charged brother-and-sister relationship and as a profound moral and theological reeducation. Thereafter, however, he found it increasingly difficult to complete anything, and the flow of poetry, which had been getting thinner, all but dried up. He kept himself going as a writer by forcing himself to write one book of a novel, *Wilhelm Meisters theatralische Sendung* (*The Theatrical Mission of Wilhelm Meister*), each year until 1785.

Goethe was never entirely at ease in his role of Weimar courtier and official. As an avowed non-Christian, he had no spiritual director he could consult, but on several occasions he turned to the unknown powers that he usually called "das Schicksal" ("fate" or "destiny") and looked for a sign. In a state near to despair he decided to escape secretly to Italy. He would travel incognito, breaking, if only temporarily, all his ties with Weimar—even with Frau von Stein—and taking with him only the task of preparing his volumes for publication.

## Life During the French Revolution

Upon his return in June 1788 from an enlightening two-year journey to Italy, Goethe was relieved of virtually all routine administrative tasks and freed to concentrate on the task of being a poet. Goethe resolved to preserve as much as he could of the Roman atmosphere in Weimar, set about hiring artists he had met in Italy, and at once— before there was time for any second thoughts—took himself a mistress, Christiane Vulpius, the daughter of the duke's late archivist. She bore Goethe a son, August, on December 25, 1789. She was a busy and very competent housewife, but Weimar aristocratic society was merciless to her and grew suspicious of her lover. Goethe refused to undergo the church ceremony that was the only way of being legally married, and so her very existence could not formally be acknowledged. Frau von Stein suffered a kind of nervous collapse, and all but the most superficial communication between her and Goethe ceased.

The years from 1788 to 1794 were lonely years for Goethe. His household was warm and happy enough, though no second child survived from Christiane's repeated pregnancies. But outside the house, apart from Herder, who was increasingly disenchanted with Weimar, his only close friend was the duke. Personal loyalty to Charles Augustus partly explains Goethe's hostility from the start to the French Revolution, of which Herder was a vocal supporter, and his accompanying Charles Augustus on campaigns against France in 1792 and 1793. These campaigns were Goethe's first direct experience of war, and he found them a nightmare.

After the remarkable effort of completing the collected edition of his works in 1789, Goethe seems not to have known where to go next as a poet. A new prose drama, *Der Gross-Cophta* (1792; "The Grand Kofta"), was a failure on the stage in 1791. A satire on Freemasonry, it was also the first of several unsatisfactory or fragmentary attempts to deal in a literary form with recent events in France (*Der Bürgergeneral* [1793; "The Citizen-General"]; *Die Aufgeregten* [1817; "Agitation"], written in 1793; *Das*

*Mädchen von Oberkirch* [1895; "The Maid of Oberkirch"], written in 1795). As an exercise in political satire and in German equivalents of Classical metres, he put Johann Christoph Gottsched's prose translation of the medieval stories of Reynard the Fox into hexameters (*Reineke Fuchs*, written in 1793 and published the following year).

## Friendship with Schiller

In 1794 the poet and dramatist Friedrich Schiller suggested that he and Goethe should collaborate on a new journal, *Die Horen* (*The Horae*), intended to give literature a voice in an age increasingly dominated by politics. The friendship with Schiller began a new period in Goethe's life, in some ways one of the happiest and, from a literary point of view, one of the most productive, though not all that was produced was of the highest quality. In *The Horae* he published a collection of short stories, *Unterhaltungen deutscher Ausgewanderten* ("Conversations of German Émigrés"; Eng. trans. *The German Refugees*), which were found tedious, and the *Roman Elegies*, which were found scandalous, and serialized a translation of the autobiography of Florentine Mannerist artist Benvenuto Cellini, which was acceptable but unexciting. Schiller soon lost interest in the journal, which ceased publication after three years. Perhaps it had served its purpose simply by initiating the collaboration with Goethe, which was closer, longer, and on a higher level than any comparable friendship in world literature. Both profited incalculably from the relationship. Schiller provided a constant commentary while Goethe rewrote, completed, and published his novel begun nearly 20 years before, now titled *Wilhelm Meisters Lehrjahre* (1795–96; *Wilhelm Meister's Apprenticeship*).

In 1797 Goethe and Schiller wrote a series of narrative poems (soon called "ballads"). With these Goethe returned to rhymed verse on a grand scale after some 10 years of writing in Classical metres and blank verse. At the same time, he took up again his great play in rhymed verse, *Faust*, and worked on it as the mood took him over the next five years. He decided (probably in 1800) to divide it into two parts, of which the first at least could be completed soon, since it would cover all that he had so far written and required merely that certain gaps be filled.

In December 1803 Herder died, and in early 1805 Schiller and Goethe both fell seriously ill. Schiller died. Goethe recovered but felt that, with Schiller dead, he had lost "the half of my existence."

## Napoleonic Period

Goethe responded to the death of Schiller by winding up the projects that had dominated his middle years. In 1805 he started preparing a new collected edition of his literary works with the publisher Johann Friedrich Cotta, who also began the separate printing of his largest work, *Zur Farbenlehre* ("On the Theory of Colour"; Eng. trans. *Goethe's Color Theory*), and in 1806 Goethe sent to him the completed manuscript of part one of *Faust*. War, however, delayed publication of *Faust* until 1808. On October 14, 1806, Napoleon routed the Prussian armies at the Battle of Jena. Weimar, 12 miles (19 kilometres) from the battle, was subsequently occupied and sacked, though Goethe's house was spared, thanks to Napoleon's admiration for the author of *Werther*. Christiane showed great courage in keeping control of the soldiers billeted with the family, and, probably in order to secure her position in these dangerous days, Goethe formally married her in the vestry of the court church five days after the battle. In an obvious reaction against this decision finally to commit himself, Goethe shortly afterward fell briefly and passionately in love with an unremarkable young lady, Wilhelmine Herzlieb, extricating himself from the entanglement only with considerable pain.

The period after the death of Schiller and the Battle of Jena was at first a sombre one. He drew a large number of strange and threatening landscapes, began a sequel— *Wilhelm Meisters Wanderjahre* ("Wilhelm Meister's Years of Wandering"; Eng. trans. *Wilhelm Meister's Travels*), with the telling subtitle *oder, die Entsagenden* ("or, The Renunciants")— to his earlier Wilhelm Meister novel, and wrote his mysterious and tragic novel *Die Wahlverwandtschaften* (1809; *Elective Affinities*) and the related tragic fragment of a "festival play," *Pandora* (1810). At this time Goethe also composed and published the first three parts of his autobiography, *Aus meinem Leben: Dichtung und Wahrheit* (1811–13; *From My Life: Poetry and Truth*).

After the overthrow of Napoleon's dominion by allied troops at the Battle of Leipzig (1813), Goethe, who had conspicuously failed to share in the nationalist fervour of the German Wars of Liberation, was asked to write a festival play for the king of Prussia to celebrate the allies' achievement. He obliged with *Des Epimenides Erwachen* (1815; "Epimenides Awakes"), but the play shows that his feelings about the great victory were ambiguous. Alienation from the modern age is the undertone in all his work of this period.

While in Frankfurt he met Marianne Jung, just 30 years old and about to marry the 54-year-old banker Johann Jakob von Willemer; Goethe and Marianne took to writing each other love poems. Out of this game grew a new collection of lyric verse, of which the hybrid, self-consciously pseudo-Asian quality was acknowledged by Goethe in its title: *West-östlicher Divan* ("The Parliament of East and West"; Eng. trans. *Poems of the East and West*). Goethe was fleeing from the upheavals of his own time. But in 1816 he was cruelly reminded that he could not flee present reality entirely. His wife died in June, probably of epilepsy.

## Last Years

The period until 1823 was one of tidying up at the end of life. But there was no decline in Goethe's energies. He completed another collected edition with Cotta, began some more-impersonal autobiographical memoirs (*Tag- und Jahreshefte* [1830; "Journals and Annals"]), wrote a vivid account of his military experiences in 1792 and 1793 (*Campagne in Frankreich, Belagerung von Mainz* [1822; "Campaign in France, Siege of Mainz"]), rather hastily finished off *The Wanderings of Wilhelm Meister*, and brought out many of his earlier, hitherto unpublished scientific writings in a new irregular periodical (*Zur Naturwissenschaft Überhaupt* ["On Natural Science in General"]).

Goethe stayed in Weimar and its immediate surroundings for the rest of his life. It was a final stage of renunciation, an acknowledgement of the reality of passing time and strength and life. But it was also a time of extraordinary, indeed probably unparalleled literary achievement by a man of advanced age. Partly in order to secure the financial future of his family—he now had three grandchildren and could not know that they would all die without issue—he prepared a final collected edition of his works, initially in 40 volumes, the *Ausgabe letzter Hand* ("Edition of the Last Hand"). In the course of this huge task, he rewrote and greatly extended *The Wanderings of Wilhelm Meister* (1821; 2nd ed. 1829). Less a novel than a collection of stories, extracts, and reflections in which fact and fiction, the prosaic and the intensely poetic, interact unpredictably, the book is held together by a framework narrative that violates conventional expectations as deliberately as much 20th-century experimental writing. He wrote a fourth section of his autobiography *Poetry and Truth*, completing the story of his life up to his departure for Weimar in 1775; he compiled an account of his time in Rome in 1787–88, *Zweiter Römischer Aufenthalt* (1829; "Second Sojourn in Rome"); and above all he wrote part two of *Faust*, of which only a few passages had been drafted in 1800.

The year 1829 brought celebrations throughout Germany of Goethe's 80th birthday. In 1830, however, came the unexpected and terrible news that his son had died in Rome during his own Italian journey. Goethe fell seriously ill immediately but recovered. He still had work to do, and only in August 1831 did he say he could regard any life that remained to him as a "pure gift." The following spring, having caught a cold, he died of a heart attack, sitting in his armchair in the modest little bedroom beside his study.

## Faust

Work on *Faust* accompanied Goethe throughout his adult life. In its first known form, Goethe's version already contains the feature that most decisively differentiates it from its predecessors, the 16th-century German chapbooks about Faust and the puppet plays ultimately deriving from English dramatist Christopher Marlowe's adaptation of those chapbooks for the stage: the tragic story of Faust's love for a town girl, Margarete (Gretchen), and of her seduction, infanticide, and execution. This theme is entirely of Goethe's invention. This earliest manuscript version (usually called the *Urfaust*), to which Goethe probably added little after 1775, is a Sturm und Drang drama in a balladesque, sometimes mock-16th-century style— intensely poetic, both visually and verbally—in which the self-assertion of the magician Faust meets its nemesis in the Gretchen catastrophe. The precise nature of Faust's agreement with the diabolical figure Mephistopheles remains inexplicit, however.

That issue was still unresolved in the scenes Goethe wrote for the first published version, *Faust: ein Fragment* (1790), which seems to suggest that the Gretchen story was destined to become merely a subordinate episode in Faust's career through the gamut of human experience. Only in *Faust: Part One* (1808) does Goethe commit himself to his second great divergence from the traditional fable: his Faust now makes not a contract with the Devil but a wager. Faust wagers that, however much of human life the Devil shows him, he will find none of it satisfying—and if he is wrong (i.e., if he is satisfied), he is willing to give up living altogether. Faust now appears as a singularly modern figure, racing through satisfactions but condemned by his own choice to discard them all.

Goethe had always wanted to dramatize that part of the traditional story which shows Faust summoning up Helen of Troy, the quintessence of the beauty of the ancient world, and the logic of the wager required that Faust should at least taste the experience of public and political life. *Faust: Part Two* (1832) thus became an extraordinary poetic phantasmagoria, covering—as Goethe acknowledged—3,000 years of history and mingling evocations of Classical landscapes and mythological figures with literary allusions from Homer to Lord Byron and with satire of the Holy Roman Empire, the French Revolution, and the capitalism and imperialism of the 1820s. Yet it is all held together by the thematic device of the wager and by structural parallels with *Part One*, and at the end Faust is redeemed, not by his own efforts but by the intercession of Gretchen and the divine love he has known in her. *Part Two* is in a sense a poetic reckoning with Goethe's own times, with their irresistible dynamism and their alienation from his Classical ideal of fulfilled humanity. As with much of Goethe's later work, its richness, complexity, and literary daring began to be appreciated only in the 20th century.

# WILLIAM BLAKE

(b. November 28, 1757, London, England—d. August 12, 1827, London)

William Blake was an English engraver, artist, poet, and visionary and was the author of exquisite lyrics in *Songs of Innocence* (1789) and *Songs of Experience* (1794) and profound and difficult "prophecies," such as *Visions of the Daughters of Albion* (1793), *The First Book of Urizen* (1794), *Milton* (1804[–?11]), and *Jerusalem* (1804[–?20]). In the early 21st century, Blake was regarded as the earliest and most original of the Romantic poets, but in his lifetime he was generally neglected or (unjustly) dismissed as mad.

Blake was born over his father's modest hosiery shop at 28 Broad Street, Golden Square, London. His parents were James Blake (1722–84) and Catherine Wright Armitage Blake (1722–92). William Blake grew up in modest circumstances. What teaching he received as a child was at his mother's knee, as most children did. This he saw as a positive matter, later writing, "Thank God I never was sent to school/ To be Flogd into following the Style of a Fool[.]"

## Visions of Eternity

Visions were commonplaces to Blake, and his life and works were intensely spiritual. His friend the journalist Henry Crabb Robinson wrote that when Blake was four years old he saw God's head appear in a window. While still a child he also saw the Prophet Ezekiel under a tree in the fields and had a vision, according to his first biographer, Alexander Gilchrist (1828–61), of "a tree filled with angels, bright angelic wings bespangling every bough like stars." Robinson reported in his diary that Blake spoke of visions "in the ordinary unemphatic tone in which we

*Portrait of William Blake, one of the earliest poets of the Romantic movement in England.* Universal Images Group/Getty Images

speak of trivial matters....Of the faculty of Vision he spoke as One he had had from early infancy—He thinks all men partake of it—but it is lost by not being cultiv[ate]d."

He was, he wrote in 1804, "really drunk with intellectual vision whenever I take a pencil or graver into my hand." Blake's wife once said to his young friend Seymour Kirkup, "I have very little of Mr. Blake's company; he is always in Paradise."

## Blake's Religion

Blake was christened, married, and buried by the rites of the Church of England, but his creed was likely to outrage the orthodox. In *A Vision of the Last Judgment* he wrote that "the Creator of this World is a very Cruel Being," whom Blake called variously Nobodaddy and Urizen, and in his emblem book *For the Sexes: The Gates of Paradise*, he addressed Satan as "The Accuser who is The God of This World." To Robinson "He warmly declared that all he knew is in the Bible. But he understands the Bible in its spiritual sense." Blake's religious singularity is demonstrated in his poem *The Everlasting Gospel* (*c.* 1818):

> *The Vision of Christ that thou dost See*
> *Is my Visions Greatest Enemy*
>
> ...
>
> *Both read the Bible day & night*
> *But thou readst black where I read White.*

Blake loved the world of the spirit and abominated institutionalized religion, especially when it was allied with government; he wrote in his annotations to Bishop Watson's *Apology for the Bible* (1797), "all [...] codes given under pretence [sic] of divine command were what Christ pronounced them, The Abomination that maketh desolate, i.e. State Religion" and later in the same text, "The Beast & the Whore rule without control." According to his long-time friend John Thomas Smith, "He did not for the last forty years attend any place of Divine worship." For Blake, true worship was private communion with the spirit.

## Education as Artist and Engraver

From childhood Blake wanted to be an artist, at the time an unusual aspiration for someone from a family of small businessmen and Nonconformists (dissenting Protestants). His father indulged him by sending him to Henry Pars's Drawing School in the Strand, London (1767–72). The boy hoped to be apprenticed to some artist of the newly formed and flourishing English school of painting, but the fees proved to be more than the parental pocket could withstand.

The young Blake was ultimately apprenticed for 50 guineas to James Basire (1730–1802), a highly responsible and conservative line engraver who specialized in prints depicting architecture. For seven years (1772–79) Blake lived with Basire's family on Great Queen Street, near Lincoln's Inn Fields, London. He became so proficient in all aspects of his craft that Basire trusted him to go by himself to Westminster Abbey to copy the marvelous medieval monuments there for one of the greatest illustrated English books of the last quarter of the 18th century, the antiquarian Richard Gough's *Sepulchral Monuments in Great Britain* (vol. 1, 1786).

## Career as Engraver

On the completion of his apprenticeship in 1779, Blake began to work vigorously as an independent engraver. At first most of his work was copy engraving after the designs of other artists, such as the two fashion plates for the *Ladies New and Polite Pocket Memorandum-Book* (1782). Blake became so well known that he received commissions to engrave his own designs. His style of designing, however, was so extreme and unfamiliar, portraying spirits with real bodies, that one review in *The British Critic* (1796; of Gottfried August Bürger's *Leonora*) called them "distorted, absurd," and the product of a "depraved fancy."

One of the best known of Blake's designs is *Glad Day*, also called *Albion Rose* (designed 1780, engraved 1805?), depicting a naked youth dancing upon the mountaintops. Even more ambitiously, he invented a method of printing in colour, still not clearly understood, which he used in 1795 to create his 12 great folio colour prints, including *God Judging Adam* and *Newton*. The latter shows the great mathematician naked and seated on a rock at the bottom of the sea making geometric designs. These were printed in only two or three copies apiece, and some were still in his possession at his death.

More publicly visible were Blake's engravings of his enormous design of Geoffrey Chaucer's Canterbury Pilgrims (1810), his 22 folio designs for the Book of Job (1826), and his 7 even larger unfinished plates for Dante (1826–27). Though only the Chaucer sold well enough to repay its probable expenses during Blake's lifetime, these are agreed today to be among the greatest triumphs of line engraving in England, sufficient to ensure Blake's reputation as an engraver and artist even had he made no other watercolours or poems.

## Marriage to Catherine Boucher and Death of Robert Blake

In 1781 Blake fell in love with Catherine Sophia Boucher (1762–1831), the pretty, illiterate daughter of an unsuccessful market gardener from the farm village of Battersea across the River Thames from London.

Blake returned to Soho to achieve financial security to support a wife, and 12 months later, on August 18,

1782, the couple married in her family's church, Saint Mary's, Battersea, the bride signing the marriage register with an X.

It was an imprudent and highly satisfactory marriage. Blake taught Catherine to read and write (a little), to draw, to colour his designs and prints, to help him at the printing press, and to see visions as he did. She believed implicitly in his genius and his visions and supported him in everything he did with charming credulity. After his death she lived chiefly for the moments when he came to sit and talk with her.

One of the most traumatic events of Blake's life was the death of his beloved 24-year-old brother, Robert, from tuberculosis in 1787. Blake claimed that in a vision Robert taught him the secret of painting his designs and poems on copper in a liquid impervious to acid before the plate was etched and printed. This method, which Blake called "Illuminated Printing," made it possible for Blake to be his own compositor, printer, binder, advertiser, and salesman for all his published poetry thereafter, from *Songs of Innocence* to *Jerusalem* (1804[–20?]).

## Career as an Artist

While pursuing his career as an engraver, in 1779 Blake enrolled as a student in the newly founded Royal Academy of Arts; he exhibited a few pictures there, in 1780, 1784, 1785, 1799, and 1808. His greatest ambition was as an artist; according to his friend Henry Crabb Robinson, "The spirit said to him, 'Blake be an artist & nothing else. In this there is felicity.'" His materials were watercolours and paper, not the fashionable oil on canvas, and he painted subjects from the Bible and British history instead of the portraits and landscapes that were in vogue. And increasingly his subjects were his own visions.

Blake's first really important commission, which he received in about 1794, was to illustrate every page of Edward Young's popular and morbid long poem *Night Thoughts*—a total of 537 watercolours. For these he was paid £21 by the ambitious and inexperienced young bookseller Richard Edwards. From these 537 designs were to be chosen subjects for, as a promotional flyer touted, 150 engravings by Blake "in a perfectly new style of decoration, surrounding the text" for a "MAGNIFICENT" and "splendid" new edition. The first of a proposed four parts was published in 1797 with 43 plates, but it fell stillborn from the press, and no further engraving for the edition was made. Instead, most of Blake's commissions thereafter were for watercolours rather than for engravings, the majority of which were never published but only displayed on the private walls of their unostentatious owners. Blake's art and his livelihood were thus largely in the hands of a small number of connoisseurs whose commissions were often inspired as much by love for the man as by admiration for his art.

## *Blake as a Poet*

Blake's profession was engraving, and his principal avocation was painting in watercolours. But even from boyhood he wrote poetry. In the early 1780s he attended the literary and artistic salons of the bluestocking Harriet Mathew, and there he read and sang his poems. In 1783 Harriet Mathew's husband, the Rev. Anthony Stephen Mathew, and Blake's friend John Flaxman had some of these poems printed in a modest little volume of 70 pages titled *Poetical Sketches*, with the attribution on the title page reading simply, "By W.B." They gave the sheets of the book, uncut and unsewn, to Blake, in the expectation that he would sell them or at least give them away to potential patrons.

Blake, however, showed little interest in the volume, and when he died he still had uncut and unstitched copies in his possession.

But some contemporaries and virtually all succeeding critics agreed that the poems did merit "respite from oblivion." Some are merely boyish rodomontade, but some, such as *To Winter* and *Mad Song,* are exquisite. *To the Muses,* lamenting the death of music, concludes,

> *How have you left the antient love*
> *That bards of old enjoy'd in you!*
> *The languid strings do scarcely move!*
> *The sound is forc'd, the notes are few!*

Blake never published his poetry in the ordinary way. Instead, he drew his poems and their surrounding designs on copper in a liquid impervious to acid. He then etched them and, with the aid of his devoted wife, printed them, coloured them, stitched them in rough sugar-paper wrappers, and offered them for sale. He rarely printed more than a dozen copies at a time, reprinting them when his stock ran low, and no more than 30 copies of any of them survive; several are known only in unique copies, and some to which he refers no longer exist.

After experimenting with tiny plates to print his short tracts *There Is No Natural Religion* (1788) and *All Religions Are One* (1788?), Blake created the first of the poetical works for which he is chiefly remembered: *Songs of Innocence*, with 19 poems on 26 prints. The poems are written for children—in *Infant Joy* only three words have as many as two syllables—and they represent the innocent and the vulnerable, from babies to beetles, protected and fostered by powers beyond their own. In *The Chimney Sweeper,* for example,

*[...]the Angel told Tom if he'd be a good boy,*
*He'd have God for his father & never want joy.*

*And so Tom awoke and we rose in the dark*
*And got with our bags & our brushes to work.*
*Tho' the morning was cold, Tom was happy & warm.*
*So if all do their duty, they need not fear harm.*

Sustained by the vision, "Tom was happy & warm" despite the cold.

In one of the best-known lyrics, called *The Lamb*, a little boy gives to a lamb the same kind of catechism he himself had been given in church:

*Little Lamb, who made thee?*
*Dost thou know who made thee?*
*...*

*Little Lamb, I'll tell thee,*
*Little Lamb, I'll tell thee:*
*He is called by thy name,*
*For he calls himself a Lamb*

*...*
*I a child, & thou a lamb,*
*We are called by his name.*

The syllogism is simple if not simplistic: the creator of child and lamb has the same qualities as his creation.

Most of Blake's poetry embodies myths that he invented. Blake takes the inquiry about the nature of life a little further in *The Book of Thel* (1789), the first of his published myths. The melancholy shepherdess Thel asks, "Why fade these children of the spring? Born but to smile & fall." She is answered by the Lilly of the Valley (representing water), the Cloud (air), and the Clod of Clay (earth), who tell her, "we live not for ourselves," and say that they are nourished by "he that loves the lowly." Thel enters the "land unknown" and hears a "voice of sorrow":

> *"Why cannot the Ear be closed to its own destruction?*
> *Or the glistning Eye to the poison of a smile!"*

The poem concludes with the frightened Thel seeing her own grave there, shrieking, and fleeing back to her valley.

Blake's next work in Illuminated Printing, *The Marriage of Heaven and Hell* (1790?), has become one of his best known. It is a prose work in no familiar form; for instance, on the title page, no author, printer, or publisher is named. The work ends with "A Song of Liberty," which celebrates the values of those who stormed the Bastille in 1789: "Let the Priests of the Raven of dawn, no longer [...] curse the sons of joy [...] For every thing that lives is Holy."

*America, A Prophecy* (1793) and *Europe, A Prophecy* (1794) are even more daringly political, and they are boldly acknowledged on the title pages as "Printed by William Blake." In the first, Albion's Angel, representing the reactionary government of England, perceives Orc, the spirit of energy, as a "Blasphemous Demon, Antichrist, hater of Dignities," but Orc's vision is of an apocalypse that transforms the world:

> *Let the slave grinding at the mill, run out into the field,*
> *Let him look up into the heavens & laugh in the bright air;*
> *...*
> *For Empire is no more, and now the Lion & Wolf shall cease*
> *...*
> *For every thing that lives is holy*

The mental revolution seems to be accomplished, but the design for the triumphant concluding page shows not rejoicing and triumph but barren trees, bowed mourners, thistles, and serpents. Blake's designs often tell a complementary story, and the two visions must be combined in the reader's mind to comprehend the meaning of the work.

The frontispiece to *Europe* is one of Blake's best-known images: sometimes called *The Ancient of Days*, it represents a naked, bearded old man leaning out from the sun to define the universe with golden compasses. He seems a familiar image of God, but the usual notions about this deity are challenged by an image, on the facing title page, of what the God of reason has created: a coiling serpent with open mouth and forked tongue. It seems to represent how

> *Thought chang'd the infinite to a serpent; that which pitieth:*
> *To a devouring flame; and man fled from its face [...] ...*
> *Then was the serpent temple form'd, image of infinite*
> *Shut up in finite revolutions, and man became an Angel;*
> *Heaven a mighty circle turning; God a tyrant crown'd.*

This God is opposed by Orc and by Los, the imagination, and at the end of the poem Los "call'd all his sons to the strife of blood." The work's last illustration, however, is not of the heroic sons of Los storming the barricades of tyrannical reason but of a naked man carrying a fainting woman and a terrified girl from the horrors of a burning city.

In the same year as *Europe*, Blake published *Songs of Experience* and combined it with his previous lyrics to form *Songs of Innocence and of Experience Shewing the Two Contrary States of the Human Soul*. The poems of *Songs of Experience* centre on threatened, unprotected souls in despair. In *London* the speaker, shown in the design as blind, bearded, and "age-bent," sees in "every face... marks of woe," and observes that "In every voice... The mind-forg'd manacles I hear." In *The Tyger*, which answers *The Lamb* of *Innocence*, the despairing speaker asks the "Tyger burning bright" about its creator: "Did he who made the Lamb make thee?" But in the design the "deadly terrors" of the text are depicted as a small, meek animal often coloured more like a stuffed toy than a jungle beast.

Blake's most impressive writings are his enormous prophecies *Vala or The Four Zoas* (which Blake composed and revised from roughly 1796 to 1807 but never published), *Milton*, and *Jerusalem: The Emanation of the Giant Albion*. In them, his myth expands, adding to Urizen (reason) and Los (imagination) the Zoas Tharmas and Luvah. (The word *zoa* is a Greek plural meaning "living creatures.") Their primordial harmony is destroyed when each of them attempts to fix creation in a form corresponding to his own nature and genius. Blake describes his purpose, his "great task," in *Jerusalem*:

> *To open the immortal Eyes*
> *Of man inwards into the worlds of thought; into Eternity*
> *Ever expanding in the Bosom of God, the Human*
> *Imagination.*

Like the Zoa Los, Blake felt that he must "Create a System or be enslav'd by another Mans."

*Milton* concerns Blake's attempt, at Milton's request, to correct the ideas of *Paradise Lost*. The poem originated in an event in Felpham, recorded in Blake's letters, in which the spirit of Milton as a falling star entered Blake. It includes the lyric commonly called "Jerusalem" that has become a kind of alternative national anthem in Britain:

> *I will not cease from Mental Fight,*
> *Nor shall my Sword sleep in my hand:*
> *Till we have built Jerusalem,*
> *In Englands green & pleasant Land.*

## *Last Years*

Blake's last years, from 1818 to 1827, were made comfortable and productive as a result of his friendship with the artist John Linnell. Through Linnell, Blake met the physician and botanist Robert John Thornton, who commissioned Blake's woodcuts for a school text of Virgil (1821). Linnell also supported Blake with his commissions for the drawings and engravings of the *Book of Job* (published 1826) and *Dante* (1838), Blake's greatest achievements as a line engraver.

Blake died in his cramped rooms in Fountain Court, the Strand, London, on August 12, 1827. He was buried in Bunhill Fields, a burial ground for Nonconformists, but he was given the beautiful funeral service of the Church of England.

# *F*RANÇOIS-*A*UGUSTE-*R*ENÉ, VICOMTE DE *C*HATEAUBRIAND

(b. September 4, 1768, Saint-Malo, France — d. July 4, 1848, Paris)

The French author and diplomat François-Auguste-René, vicomte de (viscount of) Chateaubriand, was one of his country's first Romantic writers. He was the preeminent literary figure in France in the early 19th century and had a profound influence on the youth of his day.

The youngest child of an eccentric and impecunious noble, Chateaubriand spent his school holidays largely with his sister at the family estate at Combourg, with its half-derelict medieval castle set in ancient oak woods and wild heaths. After leaving school, he eventually became a cavalry officer.

At the beginning of the French Revolution, he refused to join the Royalists and sailed in April 1791 for the United

States, a stay memorable chiefly for his travels with fur trad-
ers and for his firsthand acquaintance with Indians in the
region around Niagara Falls. After learning of Louis XVI's
flight in June 1791, Chateaubriand felt that he owed obligations to the monarchy and returned to France. Penniless, he
married an heiress of 17 and took her to Paris, which he found
too expensive; he then left her and joined the Royalist Army.
Wounded at the siege of Thionville, he was discharged.

He went to England in May 1793. Often destitute, he supported himself by translating and teaching. In London he
began his *Essai sur les révolutions* (1797; "Essay on Revolutions"),
an emotional survey of world history in which he drew parallels between ancient and modern revolutions in the context
of France's own recent upheavals.

In 1800 Chateaubriand returned to Paris, where he
worked as a freelance journalist and continued to write his
books. A fragment of an unfinished epic appeared as *Atala*
(1801); immediately successful, it combined the simplicity of a classical idyll with the more troubled beauties of
Romanticism. Set in primitive American surroundings, the
novel tells the story of a Christian girl who has taken a vow to
remain a virgin but who falls in love with a Natchez Indian.
Torn between love and religion, she poisons herself to keep
from breaking her vow. The lush Louisiana setting and passionate tale are captured in a rich, harmonious prose style
that yields many beautiful descriptive passages.

Shortly after the death of his mother in 1798,
Chateaubriand reconciled his conflict between religion and
rationalism and returned to traditional Christianity. His
apologetic treatise extolling Christianity, *Le Génie du chris-
tianisme* (1802; "The Genius of Christianity"), won favour
both with the Royalists and with Napoleon Bonaparte, who
was just then concluding a concordat with the papacy and
restoring Roman Catholicism as the state religion in France.
In this work, Chateaubriand tried to rehabilitate Christianity

from the attacks made on it during the Enlightenment by stressing its capacity to nurture and stimulate European culture, architecture, art, and literature over the centuries. Chateaubriand's theology was weak and his apologetics illogical, but his assertion of Christianity's moral superiority on the basis of its poetic and artistic appeal proved an inexhaustible sourcebook for Romantic writers. The renewed appreciation of Gothic architecture sparked by the book is the most prominent example of this.

Napoleon rewarded Chateaubriand for his treatise by appointing him first secretary to the embassy at Rome in 1803. But in 1804, when Napoleon stunned France with the unfair trial and hasty execution of the Duke d'Enghien on a flimsy pretext of conspiracy, Chateaubriand resigned his post in protest. The most important of the books he published during the following years is the novel *René* (first published separately in 1805), which tells the story of a sister who enters a convent rather than surrender to her passion for her brother. In this thinly veiled autobiographical work Chateaubriand began the Romantic vogue for world-weary, melancholy heroes suffering from vague, unsatisfied yearnings in what came to be known as the *mal du siècle* ("the malady of the age"). On the basis of *Les Martyrs* (1809), a prose epic about early Christian martyrs in Rome, and *Itinéraire de Paris à Jérusalem* (1811), an account of his recent travels throughout the Mediterranean, Chateaubriand was elected to the French Academy in 1811.

With the restoration of the Bourbon monarchy in 1814, Chateaubriand's hopes of a political career revived. In 1815 he was made a viscount and a member of the House of Peers. His extravagant lifestyle eventually caused him financial difficulties, however, and he found his only pleasure in his liaison with Mme Récamier, who illumined the rest of his life. He began *Mémoires d'outre-tombe* (1849–50), his memoir from "beyond the tomb," written for posthumous publication and perhaps his most lasting monument. This memoir, which Chateaubriand began writing as early as 1810, is as much a history of his thoughts and sensations as it is a conventional narrative of his life from childhood into old age. The vivid picture it draws of contemporary French history, of the spirit of the Romantic epoch, and of Chateaubriand's own travels is complemented by many self-revealing passages in which the author recounts his unstinting appreciation of women, his sensitivity to nature, and his lifelong tendency toward melancholy. Chateaubriand's memoirs have proved to be his most enduring work.

After six months as ambassador to Berlin in 1821, Chateaubriand became ambassador to London in 1822. He represented France at the Congress of Verona in 1822 and served as minister of foreign affairs under the ultra-Royalist premier Joseph, Count de Villèle, until 1824. In this capacity he brought France into the war with Spain in 1823 to restore that country's Bourbon king Ferdinand VII. The campaign was a success, but its high cost diminished the prestige Chateaubriand won by it. He passed the rest of his life privately, except for a year as ambassador to Rome (1828–29).

# FRIEDRICH HÖLDERLIN

(b. March 20, 1770, Lauffen am Neckar, Württemberg [Germany] — d. June 7, 1843, Tübingen)

Johann Christian Friedrich Hölderlin was a German lyric poet who succeeded in naturalizing the forms of classical Greek verse in German and in melding Christian and classical themes.

Hölderlin was born in a little Swabian town on the River Neckar. His father died in 1772, and two years afterward his mother married the burgomaster of the town of Nürtingen, where Friedrich attended school. But his mother was again widowed, in 1779, and left alone to bring up her family—which included Friedrich, his sister Heinrike, and his half-brother Karl. His mother, a parson's daughter and a woman of simple and rather narrow piety, wanted Friedrich to enter the service of the church. Candidates for the ministry received free education, and accordingly he was sent first to the "monastery schools" (so called since pre-Reformation times) at Denkendorf and Maulbronn and subsequently (1788–93) to the theological seminary in the University of Tübingen, where he obtained his master's degree and qualified for ordination.

Hölderlin could not, however, bring himself to enter the ministry. Contemporary Protestant theology, an uneasy compromise between faith and reason, offered him no safe spiritual anchorage, while acceptance of Christian dogma was not wholly compatible with his devotion to Greek mythology, which made him see the gods of Greece as real living forces whose presence manifests itself to humans in sun and earth, sea and sky. The strain of divided allegiance remained a permanent condition of his existence. Although he did not feel called to be a Lutheran pastor, Hölderlin did have a strong sense of religious vocation; for him, being a poet meant exercising the priestly function of mediator between gods and humans.

In 1793, through Friedrich Schiller's recommendation, Hölderlin obtained the first of several posts as a tutor (in most of which he failed to give satisfaction). Schiller befriended the younger man in other ways too; in his periodical *Neue Thalia*, he published some of the poetry that Hölderlin had written, as well as a fragment of his novel *Hyperion*. This elegiac story of a disillusioned fighter for the liberation of Greece remained unfinished. Hölderlin held Schiller in great reverence; he saw him again when in 1794 he left his tutor's post in order to move to Jena. His early poems clearly reveal Schiller's influence, and several of them acclaim the new world the French Revolution had seemed to promise in its early stages: they include hymns to freedom, to humanity, to harmony, to friendship, and to nature.

In December 1795 Hölderlin accepted a post as tutor in the house of J.F. Gontard, a wealthy Frankfurt banker. Before long, Hölderlin fell deeply in love with his employer's wife, Susette, a woman of great beauty and sensibility, and his affection was returned. In a letter to his friend C.L. Neuffer (February 1797), he described their relationship as "an everlasting happy sacred friendship with a being who has really strayed into this miserable century." Susette appears in his poems and in his novel *Hyperion*, the second volume of which appeared in 1799, under the Greek name of "Diotima"—a reincarnation of the spirit of ancient Greece. Their happiness was short-lived; after a painful scene with Susette's husband, Hölderlin had to leave Frankfurt (September 1798).

Though physically and mentally shaken, Hölderlin finished the second volume of *Hyperion* and began a tragedy, *Der Tod des Empedokles* (*The Death of Empedocles*), the first version of which he nearly completed; fragments of a second and a third version have also survived. Symptoms of great nervous irritability alarmed his family and friends. Nevertheless, the years 1798–1801 were a period of intense creativity; in addition to a number of noble odes, they produced the great elegies "Menons Klagen um Diotima" ("Menon's Lament for Diotima") and "Brod und Wein" ("Bread and Wine"). In January 1801 he went to Switzerland as tutor to a family in Hauptwyl, but in April of the same year Hölderlin returned to Nürtingen.

Late in 1801 he once more accepted a post as tutor, this time at Bordeaux, France. But in May 1802, after only a few months in this position, Hölderlin suddenly left Bordeaux and traveled homeward on foot through France. On his way to Nürtingen he received news that Susette had died in June; when he arrived he was completely destitute and suffering from an advanced stage of schizophrenia. He seemed to recover somewhat as a result of the kind and gentle treatment he received at home. The poems of the period 1802–06, including "Friedensfeier" ("Celebration of Peace"), "Der Einzige" ("The Only One"), and "Patmos," products of a mind on the verge of madness, are apocalyptic visions of unique grandeur. He also completed verse translations of Sophocles' *Antigone* and *Oedipus Tyrannus*, published in 1804. In this year a devoted friend, Isaak von Sinclair, obtained for him the sinecure post of librarian to the landgrave Frederick V of Hesse-Homburg. Sinclair himself provided a modest salary, and Hölderlin improved noticeably under his care and companionship. In 1805 Sinclair (who refused to believe that Hölderlin was insane) was falsely accused of subversive activities and held in custody for five months. By the time he was released, Hölderlin had succumbed irretrievably and, after a spell in a clinic in Tübingen, was moved to a carpenter's house, where he lived for the next 36 years.

Hölderlin gained little recognition during his lifetime and was almost totally forgotten for nearly 100 years. It was not until the early years of the 20th century that he was rediscovered in Germany and that his reputation as one of the outstanding lyric poets in the German language was established in Europe. Today he is ranked among the greatest of German poets, especially admired for his uniquely expressive style: like no one before or since, he succeeded in naturalizing the forms of classical Greek verse in the German language. With passionate intensity he strove to reconcile the Christian faith with the religious spirit and beliefs of ancient Greece; he was a prophet of spiritual renewal, of "the return of the gods"—utterly dedicated to his art, hypersensitive, and therefore exceptionally vulnerable. In the end his mind gave way under the strains and frustrations of his existence.

# *WILLIAM WORDSWORTH*

(b. April 7, 1770, Cockermouth, Cumberland, England—d. April 23, 1850, Rydal Mount, Westmorland)

The English poet William Wordsworth helped launch the English Romantic movement when he wrote *Lyrical Ballads* (1798) with Samuel Taylor Coleridge.

## *Early Life and Education*

Wordsworth was born in the Lake District of northern England, the second of five children of a modestly prosperous estate manager. He lost his mother when he was 7 and his father when he was 13, upon which the orphan boys were sent off by guardian uncles to a grammar school at Hawkshead, a village in the heart of the Lake District. At Hawkshead Wordsworth received an excellent education in classics, literature, and mathematics, but the chief advantage to him there was the chance to indulge in the boyhood pleasures of living and playing in the outdoors. The natural scenery of the English lakes could terrify as well as nurture, as Wordsworth would later testify in the line "I grew up fostered alike by beauty and by fear," but its generally benign aspect gave the growing boy the confidence he articulated in one of his first important poems, "Lines Composed a Few Miles Above Tintern Abbey...," namely, "that Nature never did betray the heart that loved her."

Wordsworth moved on in 1787 to St. John's College, Cambridge. Repelled by the competitive pressures there, he elected to idle his way through the university, persuaded that he "was not for that hour, nor for that place." The most important thing he did in his college years was to devote his summer vacation in 1790 to a long walking tour through revolutionary France. There he was caught up in the passionate enthusiasm that followed the fall of the Bastille, and became an ardent republican sympathizer. Upon taking his Cambridge degree—an undistinguished "pass"—he returned in 1791 to France, where he formed a passionate attachment to a Frenchwoman, Annette Vallon. But before their child was born in December 1792, Wordsworth had to return to England and was cut off there by the outbreak of war between England and France. He was not to see his daughter Caroline until she was nine.

The three or four years that followed his return to England were the darkest of Wordsworth's life. Unprepared for any profession, rootless, virtually penniless, bitterly hostile to his own country's opposition to the French, he lived in London in the company of radicals like William Godwin and learned to feel a profound sympathy for the abandoned mothers, beggars, children, vagrants, and victims of England's wars who began to march through the sombre poems he began writing at this time. This dark period ended in 1795, when a friend's legacy made possible Wordsworth's reunion with his beloved sister Dorothy—the two were never again to live apart—and their move in 1797 to Alfoxden House, near Bristol.

*English poet William Wordsworth.* Bob Thomas/Popperfoto/ Getty Images

# The Great Decade: 1797–1808

While living with Dorothy at Alfoxden House, Wordsworth became friends with a fellow poet, Samuel Taylor Coleridge. They formed a partnership that would change both poets' lives and alter the course of English poetry.

## Coleridge and Lyrical Ballads

The partnership between Wordsworth and Coleridge, rooted in one marvelous year (1797–98) in which they "together wantoned in wild Poesy," had two consequences for Wordsworth. First it turned him away from the long poems on which he had laboured since his Cambridge days. These included poems of social protest like *Salisbury Plain*, loco-descriptive poems such as *An Evening Walk* and *Descriptive Sketches* (published in 1793), and *The Borderers*, a blank-verse tragedy exploring the psychology of guilt (and not published until 1842). Stimulated by Coleridge and under the healing influences of nature and his sister, Wordsworth began in 1797–98 to compose the short lyrical and dramatic poems for which he is best remembered by many readers. Some of these were affectionate tributes to Dorothy, some were tributes to daffodils, birds, and other elements of "Nature's holy plan," and some were portraits of simple rural people intended to illustrate basic truths of human nature.

Many of these short poems were written to a daringly original program formulated jointly by Wordsworth and Coleridge, and aimed at breaking the decorum of Neoclassical verse. These poems appeared in 1798 in a slim, anonymously authored volume entitled *Lyrical Ballads*, which opened with Coleridge's long poem "The Rime of the Ancient Mariner" and closed with Wordsworth's "Tintern Abbey." All but three of the intervening poems were Wordsworth's, and, as he declared in a preface to a second edition two years later, their object was "to choose incidents and situations from common life and to relate or describe them…in a selection of language really used by men,…tracing in them…the primary laws of our nature." Most of the poems were dramatic in form, designed to reveal the character of the speaker. The manifesto and the accompanying poems thus set forth a new style, a new vocabulary, and new subjects for poetry, all of them foreshadowing 20th-century developments.

## The Recluse *and* The Prelude

The second consequence of Wordsworth's partnership with Coleridge was the framing of a vastly ambitious poetic design that teased and haunted him for the rest of his life. Coleridge had projected an enormous poem to be called "The Brook," in which he proposed to treat all science, philosophy, and religion, but he soon laid the burden of writing this poem upon Wordsworth himself. As early as 1798 Wordsworth began to talk in grand terms of this poem, to be entitled *The Recluse*. To nerve himself up to this enterprise and to test his powers, Wordsworth began writing the autobiographical poem that would absorb him intermittently for the next 40 years, and which was eventually published in 1850 under the title *The Prelude, or, Growth of a Poet's Mind*. *The Prelude* extends the quiet autobiographical mode of reminiscence that Wordsworth had begun in "Tintern Abbey" and traces the poet's life from his school days through his university life and his visits to France, up to the year (1799) in which he settled at Grasmere.

The Recluse itself was never completed, and only one of its three projected parts was actually written; this was published in 1814 as *The Excursion* and consisted of nine long philosophical monologues spoken by pastoral characters. The first monologue (Book I) contained a version of one of Wordsworth's greatest poems, "The Ruined Cottage," composed in superb blank verse in 1797. This bleak narrative records the slow, pitiful decline of a woman whose husband had gone off to the army and never returned.

## *A Turn to the Elegiac*

In the company of Dorothy, Wordsworth spent the winter of 1798–99 in Germany, where, in the remote town of Goslar, in Saxony, he experienced the most intense isolation he had ever known. As a consequence, however, he wrote some of his most moving poetry, including the "Lucy" and "Matthew" elegies and early drafts toward *The Prelude*. Upon his return to England, Wordsworth incorporated several new poems in the second edition of *Lyrical Ballads* (1800), notably two tragic pastorals of country life, "The Brothers" and "Michael." These poems, together with the brilliant lyrics that were assembled in Wordsworth's second verse collection, *Poems, in Two Volumes* (1807), help to make up what is now recognized as his great decade, stretching from his meeting with Coleridge in 1797 until 1808.

One portion of a second part of *The Recluse* was finished in 1806, but, like *The Prelude*, was left in manuscript at the poet's death. This portion, *Home at Grasmere*, joyously celebrated Wordsworth's taking possession (in December 1799) of Dove Cottage, at Grasmere, Westmorland, where he was to reside for eight of his most productive years. In 1802, during the short-lived Peace of Amiens, Wordsworth returned briefly to France, where at Calais he met his daughter and made his peace with Annette. He then returned to England to marry Mary Hutchinson, a childhood friend, and start an English family, which had grown to three sons and two daughters by 1810.

In 1805 the drowning of Wordsworth's favorite brother, John, the captain of a sailing vessel, gave Wordsworth the strongest shock he had ever experienced. Henceforth he would produce a different kind of poetry, defined by a new sobriety, a new restraint, and a lofty, almost Miltonic elevation of tone and diction.

It is generally accepted that the quality of his verse fell off as he grew more distant from the sources of his inspiration and as his Anglican and Tory sentiments hardened into orthodoxy. Today many readers discern two Wordsworths, the young Romantic revolutionary and the aging Tory humanist, risen into what John Keats called the "Egotistical Sublime." Little of Wordsworth's later verse matches the best of his earlier years.

*Dove Cottage in Westmorland. William Wordsworth lived and worked in the cottage during some of the happiest and most productive years of his life.* **Hulton Archive/Getty Images**

In his middle period Wordsworth invested a good deal of his creative energy in odes, the best known of which is "On the Power of Sound." He also produced a large number of sonnets, most of them strung together in sequences. The most admired are the Duddon sonnets (1820), which trace the progress of a stream through Lake District landscapes and blend nature poetry with philosophic reflection in a manner now recognized as the best of the later Wordsworth.

## *Late Work*

In 1808 Wordsworth and his family moved from Dove Cottage to larger quarters in Grasmere, and five years later they settled at Rydal Mount, near Ambleside, where Wordsworth spent the remainder of his life. In 1813 he accepted the post of distributor of stamps for the county of Westmorland, an appointment that carried the salary of £400 a year. Wordsworth continued to hold back from publication *The Prelude*, *Home at Grasmere*, *The Borderers*, and *Salisbury Plain*. He did publish *Poems, in Two Volumes* in 1807; *The Excursion* in 1814, containing the only finished portions of *The Recluse*; and the collected *Poems* of 1815, which contained most of his shorter poems and two important critical essays as well. Wordsworth's other works published during middle age include *The White Doe of Rylstone* (1815), a poem about the pathetic shattering of a Roman Catholic family during an unsuccessful rebellion against Elizabeth I in 1569; a *Thanksgiving Ode* (1816); and *Peter Bell* (1819), a poem written in 1798 and then modulated in successive rewritings into an experiment in Romantic irony and the mock-heroic and coloured by the poet's feelings of affinity with his hero, a "wild and woodland rover." *The Waggoner* (1819) is another extended ballad about a North Country itinerant.

Wordsworth's last years were given over partly to "tinkering" his poems, as the family called his compulsive and persistent habit of revising his earlier poems through edition after edition. *The Prelude*, for instance, went through four distinct manuscript versions (1798–99, 1805–06, 1818–20, and 1832–39) and was published only after the poet's death in 1850. Most readers find the earliest versions of *The Prelude* and other heavily revised poems to be the best, but flashes of brilliance can appear in revisions added when the poet was in his seventies.

Wordsworth succeeded his friend Robert Southey as Britain's poet laureate in 1843 and held that post until his own death in 1850. Thereafter his influence was felt throughout the rest of the 19th century, though he was honoured more for his smaller poems, as singled out by the Victorian critic Matthew Arnold, than for his masterpiece, *The Prelude*. In the 20th century his reputation was strengthened both by recognition of his importance in the Romantic movement and by an appreciation of the darker elements in his personality and verse.

# FRIEDRICH VON SCHLEGEL

(b. March 10, 1772, Hannover, Germany—d. January 12, 1829, Dresden, Saxony)

The German writer and critic Friedrich von Schlegel was the originator of many of the philosophical ideas that inspired the early German Romantic movement. Open to every new idea, he reveals a rich store of projects and theories in his provocative *Aperçus* and *Fragmente* (contributed to the *Athenäum* and other journals); his conception of a universal, historical, and comparative literary scholarship has had profound influence.

Schlegel was a nephew of the author Johann Elias Schlegel. After studying at Göttingen and Leipzig, he became closely associated with his elder brother August Wilhelm Schlegel at Jena in the quarterly *Athenäum*. He believed that Greek philosophy and culture were essential to complete education. Influenced also by J.G. Fichte's transcendental philosophy, he developed his conception of the Romantic—that poetry should be at once philosophical and mythological, ironic and religious. But his imaginative work, a semi-autobiographical novel fragment *Lucinde* (1799), and a tragedy *Alarcos* (1802) were less successful.

In 1801 Schlegel was briefly lecturer at Jena University, but in 1802 he went to Paris with Dorothea Veit, the eldest daughter of Moses Mendelssohn and the divorced wife of Simon Veit. He married her in 1804. In Paris he studied Sanskrit, publishing *Über die Sprache und Weisheit der Indier* (1808), the first attempt at comparative Indo-Germanic linguistics and the starting point of the study of Indian languages and comparative philology. In 1808 he and his wife became Roman Catholics, and he united his concept of Romanticism with ideas of medieval Christendom. He became the ideological spokesman of the anti-Napoleonic movement for German liberation, serving in the Vienna chancellery (1809) and helping to write the appeal to the German people issued by the archduke Charles. He had already edited two periodicals on the arts, *Europa* and *Deutsches Museum*; in 1820 he became editor of the right-wing Catholic paper *Concordia*, and his attack in it on the beliefs that he had earlier cherished led to a breach with his brother.

Two series of lectures Schlegel gave in Vienna between 1810 and 1812 (*Über die neuere Geschichte*, 1811; *A Course of*

*Lectures on Modern History*, 1849 and *Geschichte der alten und neueren Literatur*, 1815; *Lectures on the History of Literature*, 1818) developed his concept of a "new Middle Ages." His collected works were first issued in 10 volumes in 1822–25, augmented to 15 volumes in 1846. His correspondence with his brother was published in 1890 and that with Dorothea was edited (1926) by J. Körner, who wrote major studies of the brothers.

# SAMUEL TAYLOR COLERIDGE

(b. October 21, 1772, Ottery St. Mary, Devonshire, England—d. July 25, 1834, Highgate, near London)

Samuel Taylor Coleridge was an English lyrical poet, critic, and philosopher. His *Lyrical Ballads*, written with William Wordsworth, heralded the English Romantic movement, and his *Biographia Literaria* (1817) is the most significant work of general literary criticism produced in the English Romantic period.

## Early Life and Works

Coleridge's father was vicar of Ottery and headmaster of the local grammar school. As a child Coleridge was already a prodigious reader, and he immersed himself to the point of morbid fascination in romances and Eastern tales such as *The Arabian Nights' Entertainments*. In 1781 his father died suddenly, and in the following year Coleridge entered Christ's Hospital in London, where he completed his secondary education. In 1791 he entered Jesus College, Cambridge. At both school and university he continued to read voraciously, particularly in works of imagination and visionary

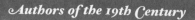

*Samuel Taylor Coleridge, detail of an oil painting by Washington Allston, 1814.* Courtesy of The National Portrait Gallery, London

philosophy, and he was remembered by his schoolmates for his eloquence and prodigious memory. In his third year at Cambridge, oppressed by financial difficulties, he went to London and enlisted as a soldier under the assumed name of Silas Tomkyn Comberbache. Despite his unfitness for the life, he remained until discovered by his friends; he was then bought out by his brothers and restored to Cambridge.

On his return, he was restless. The intellectual and political turmoil surrounding the French Revolution had set in motion intense and urgent discussion concerning the nature of society. Coleridge now conceived the design of circumventing the disastrous violence that had destroyed the idealism of the French Revolution by establishing a small society that should organize itself and educate its children according to better principles than those obtained from the society around them. A chance meeting with the poet Robert Southey led the two men to plan such a "pantisocracy" and to set up a community by the Susquehanna River in Pennsylvania. To this end Coleridge left Cambridge for good and set up with Southey as a public lecturer in Bristol. In October 1795 he married Sara Fricker, daughter of a local schoolmistress.

Shortly afterward, Southey defected from the pantisocratic scheme, leaving Coleridge married to a woman whom he did not really love. In a sense his career never fully recovered from this blow: if there is a makeshift quality about many of its later events, one explanation can be found in his constant need to reconcile his intellectual aspirations with the financial needs of his family. During this period, however, Coleridge's intellect flowered in an extraordinary manner, as he embarked on an investigation of the nature of the human mind, joined by William Wordsworth, with whom he had become acquainted in 1795. Together they entered upon one of the most influential creative periods of English literature. Coleridge's intellectual ebullience and his belief in the existence of a powerful "life consciousness" in all individuals rescued Wordsworth from the depression into which recent events had cast him and made possible the new approach to nature that characterized his contributions to *Lyrical Ballads* (which was to be published in 1798).

Coleridge, meanwhile, was developing a new, informal mode of poetry in which he could use a conversational tone and rhythm to give unity to a poem. Of these poems, the most successful is "Frost at Midnight," which begins with the description of a silent frosty night in Somerset and proceeds through a meditation on the relationship between the quiet work of frost and the quiet breathing of the sleeping baby at the poet's side, to conclude in a resolve that his child shall be brought up as a "child of nature," so that the sympathies that the poet has come to detect may be reinforced throughout the child's education.

At the climax of the poem, he touches another theme, which lies at the root of his philosophical attitude:

> *...so shalt thou see and hear*
> *The lovely shapes and sounds intelligible*
> *Of that eternal language, which thy God*
> *Utters, who from eternity doth teach*
> *Himself in all, and all things in himself.*

Coleridge's attempts to learn this "language" and trace it through the ancient traditions of mankind also led him during this period to return to the visionary interests of his schooldays: as he ransacked works of comparative religion and mythology, he was exploring the possibility that all religions and mythical traditions, with their general agreement on the unity of God and the immortality of the soul, sprang from a universal life consciousness, which was expressed particularly through the phenomena of human genius.

While these speculations were at their most intense, he retired to a lonely farmhouse near Culbone, Somersetshire, and, according to his own account, composed under the influence of laudanum the mysterious poetic fragment known as "Kubla Khan." The exotic imagery and rhythmic chant of this poem have led many critics to conclude that it should be read as a "meaningless reverie" and enjoyed merely for its vivid and sensuous qualities. An examination of the poem in the light of Coleridge's psychological and mythological interests, however, suggests that it has, after all, a complex structure of meaning and is basically a poem about the nature of human genius.

Coleridge's next notable work was "The Rime of the Ancient Mariner," composed during the autumn and winter of 1797–98. For this, his most famous poem, he drew upon the ballad form. The main narrative tells how a sailor who has committed a crime against the life principle by slaying an albatross suffers from torments, physical and mental, in which the nature of his crime is made known to him. The underlying life power against which he has transgressed is envisaged as a power corresponding to the influx of the sun's energy into all living creatures, thereby binding them together in a joyful communion. By killing the bird that hovered near the ship, the mariner has destroyed one of the links in this process. His own consciousness is consequently affected: the sun, previously glorious, is seen as a bloody sun, and the energies of the deep are seen as corrupt.

After the death of his shipmates, alone and becalmed, devoid of a sense of movement or even of time passing, the mariner is in a hell created by the absence of any link with life. Eventually, however, a chance sight of water snakes flashing like golden fire in the darkness, answered by an outpouring of love from his heart, reinitiates the creative process: he is given a brief vision of the inner unity of the universe, in which all living things hymn their source in an interchange of harmonies. Restored to his native land, he remains haunted by what he has experienced but is at least delivered from nightmare, able to see the ordinary processes of human life with a new sense of their wonder and mercifulness. These last qualities are reflected in the poem's attractive combination of vividness and sensitivity. The placing of it at the beginning of *Lyrical Ballads* was evidently intended to provide a context for the sense of wonder in common life that marks many of Wordsworth's contributions. While this volume was going through the press, Coleridge began a complementary poem, a Gothic ballad entitled "Christabel," in which he aimed to show how naked energy might be redeemed through contact with a spirit of innocent love.

## Troubled Years

Early in 1798 Coleridge had again found himself preoccupied with political issues. The French Revolutionary government had suppressed the states of the Swiss Confederation, and Coleridge expressed his bitterness at this betrayal of the principles of the Revolution in a poem entitled "France: An Ode."

At this time the brothers Josiah and Thomas Wedgwood, who were impressed by Coleridge's intelligence and promise, offered him in 1798 an annuity of £150 as a means of subsistence while he pursued his intellectual concerns. He used his new independence to visit Germany with Wordsworth and Wordsworth's sister, Dorothy. While there Coleridge attended lectures on physiology and biblical criticism at Göttingen.

On his return to England, the tensions of his marriage were exacerbated when he fell in love with Sara Hutchinson, the sister of Wordsworth's future wife, at the end of 1799. His devotion to the Wordsworths in general did little to help matters, and for some years afterward Coleridge was troubled by domestic strife, accompanied by the worsening of his health and by his increasing dependence on opium. His main literary achievements during the period included another section of "Christabel." In 1802 Coleridge's domestic unhappiness gave rise to "Dejection: An Ode," originally a longer verse letter sent to Sara Hutchinson in which he lamented the corrosive effect of his intellectual activities when undertaken as a refuge from the lovelessness of his family life.

In 1804 Coleridge accepted a post in Malta as secretary to the acting governor. The time spent in Malta was a time of personal reappraisal. Brought into direct contact with men accustomed to handling affairs of state, he had found himself lacking an equal forcefulness and felt that in consequence he often forfeited the respect of others. On his return to England he resolved to become more manly and decisive. Within a few months he had finally decided to separate from his wife and to live for the time being with the Wordsworths.

Coleridge published a periodical, *The Friend*, from June 1809 to March 1810 and ceased only when Sara Hutchinson, who had been acting as amanuensis, found the strain of the relationship too much for her and retired to her brother's farm in Wales. Coleridge, resentful that Wordsworth should apparently have encouraged his sister-in-law's withdrawal, resolved shortly afterward to terminate his working relationship with William and Dorothy Wordsworth and to settle in London again.

The period immediately following was the darkest of his life. For some time he remained in London, nursing his grievances and producing little. Opium retained its powerful hold on him, and the writings that survive from this period are redolent of unhappiness, with self-dramatization veering toward self-pity.

In spite of this, however, there also appear signs of a slow revival, principally because for the first time Coleridge knew what it was to be a fashionable figure. A course of lectures he delivered during the winter of 1811–12 attracted a large audience; for many years Coleridge had been fascinated by William Shakespeare's achievement, and his psychological interpretations of the chief characters were new and exciting to his contemporaries. During this period, Coleridge's play *Osorio*, written many years before, was produced at Drury Lane with the title *Remorse* in January 1813.

## Late Life and Works

In the end, consolation came from an unexpected source. In dejection, unable to produce extended work or break the opium habit, he spent a long period with friends in Wiltshire, where he was introduced to Archbishop Robert Leighton's commentary on the First Letter of Peter. In the writings of this 17th-century divine, he found a combination of tenderness and sanctity that appealed deeply to him and seemed to offer an attitude to life that he himself could fall back on. Christianity, hitherto one point of reference for him, now became his "official" creed.

One effect of the adoption of this basis for his intellectual and emotional life was a sense of liberation and an ability to produce large works again. He drew together a collection of his poems (published in 1817 as *Sibylline Leaves*) and wrote *Biographia Literaria* (1817), a rambling and discursive but highly stimulating and influential work in which he outlined the evolution of his thought and developed an extended critique of Wordsworth's poems.

A new dramatic piece, *Zapolya*, was also published in 1817. In the same year, Coleridge became associated for a time with the new *Encyclopaedia Metropolitana*, for which he planned a novel system of organization, outlined in his *Prospectus*. These were more settled years for Coleridge. Since 1816 he had lived in the house of James Gillman, a surgeon at Highgate, north of London. His election as a fellow of the Royal Society of Literature in 1824 brought him an annuity of £105 and a sense of recognition. The third edition of Coleridge's *Poetical Works* appeared in time for him to see it before his final illness and death in 1834.

# JANE AUSTEN

(b. December 16, 1775, Steventon, Hampshire, England—d. July 18, 1817, Winchester, Hampshire)

The English writer Jane Austen first gave the novel its distinctly modern character through her treatment of ordinary people in everyday life. Austen created the comedy of manners of middle-class life in the England of her time in her novels, *Sense and Sensibility* (1811), *Pride and Prejudice* (1813), *Mansfield Park* (1814), *Emma* (1815), and *Northanger Abbey* and *Persuasion* (published posthumously, 1817).

## Life

Jane Austen was born in the Hampshire village of Steventon, where her father, the Reverend George Austen, was rector. She was the second daughter and seventh child in a family of eight: six boys and two girls. Her closest companion throughout her life was her elder sister, Cassandra, who also remained unmarried.

Her earliest-known writings date from about 1787, and between then and 1793 she wrote a large body of material that has survived in three manuscript notebooks: *Volume the First*, *Volume the Second*, and *Volume the Third*. These contain plays, verses, short novels, and other prose and show Austen engaged in the parody of existing literary forms, notably sentimental fiction. Her passage to a more serious view of life from the exuberant high spirits and extravagances of her earliest writings is evident in *Lady Susan*, a short novel-in-letters written about 1793–94 (and not published until 1871). This portrait of a woman bent on the exercise of her own powerful mind and personality to the point of social self-destruction is, in effect, a study of frustration and of woman's fate in a society that has no use for woman's stronger, more "masculine," talents.

In 1802 it seems likely that Jane agreed to marry Harris Bigg-Wither, the 21-year-old heir of a Hampshire family, but the next morning changed her mind. There are also a number of mutually contradictory stories connecting her with someone with whom she fell in love but who died very soon after. Since Austen's novels are so deeply concerned with love and marriage, there is some point in attempting to establish the facts of these relationships. Unfortunately, the evidence is unsatisfactory and incomplete. Cassandra was a jealous guardian of her sister's private life, and after Jane's death she censored the surviving letters, destroying many and cutting up others. But Jane Austen's own novels provide indisputable evidence that their author understood the experience of love and of love disappointed.

The earliest of her novels, *Sense and Sensibility*, was begun about 1795 as a novel-in-letters called "Elinor and Marianne," after its heroines. Between October 1796 and August 1797 Austen completed the first version of *Pride and Prejudice*, then called "First Impressions." In 1797 her

*The cover of a modern-day copy of 19th-century author Jane Austen's* Sense and Sensibility. *Austen's works have proven to have a lasting power to entertain and beguile readers.* Buyenlarge/ Archive Photos/Getty Images

father wrote to offer it to a London publisher for publication, but the offer was declined. *Northanger Abbey*, the last of the early novels, was written about 1798 or 1799, probably under the title "Susan." In 1803 the manuscript of "Susan" was sold to the publisher Richard Crosby for £10. He took it for immediate publication, but, although it was advertised, unaccountably it never appeared.

Up to this time the tenor of life at Steventon rectory had been propitious for Jane Austen's growth as a novelist. This stable environment ended in 1801, however, when George Austen, then aged 70, retired to Bath with his wife and daughters. For eight years Jane had to put up with a succession of temporary lodgings or visits to relatives, in Bath, London, Clifton, Warwickshire, and, finally, Southampton, where the three women lived from 1805 to 1809. In 1804 Jane began *The Watsons* but soon abandoned it. In 1804 her dearest friend, Mrs. Anne Lefroy, died suddenly, and in January 1805 her father died in Bath.

Eventually, in 1809, Jane's brother Edward was able to provide his mother and sisters with a large cottage in the village of Chawton, within his Hampshire estate, not far from Steventon. The prospect of settling at Chawton had already given Jane Austen a renewed sense of purpose, and she began to prepare *Sense and Sensibility* and *Pride and Prejudice* for publication. She was encouraged by her brother Henry, who acted as go-between with her publishers. She was probably also prompted by her need for money. Two years later Thomas Egerton agreed to publish *Sense and Sensibility*, which came out, anonymously, in November 1811. Both of the leading reviews, the *Critical Review* and the *Quarterly Review*, welcomed its blend of instruction and amusement. Meanwhile, in 1811 Austen had begun *Mansfield Park*, which was finished in 1813 and published in 1814. By then she was an established (though anonymous) author; Egerton had published *Pride and*

*Prejudice* in January 1813, and later that year there were second editions of *Pride and Prejudice* and *Sense and Sensibility*. *Pride and Prejudice* seems to have been the fashionable novel of its season. Between January 1814 and March 1815 she wrote *Emma*, which appeared in December 1815. In 1816 there was a second edition of *Mansfield Park*, published, like *Emma*, by Lord Byron's publisher, John Murray. *Persuasion* (written August 1815–August 1816) was published posthumously, with *Northanger Abbey*, in December 1817.

The years after 1811 seem to have been the most rewarding of her life. She had the satisfaction of seeing her work in print and well reviewed and of knowing that the novels were widely read. They were so much enjoyed by the Prince Regent (later George IV) that he had a set in each of his residences; and *Emma*, at a discreet royal command, was "respectfully dedicated" to him. The reviewers praised the novels for their morality and entertainment, admired the character drawing, and welcomed the homely realism as a refreshing change from the romantic melodrama then in vogue.

For the last 18 months of her life, she was busy writing. Early in 1816, at the onset of her fatal illness, she set down the burlesque *Plan of a Novel, According to Hints from Various Quarters* (first published in 1871). Until August 1816 she was occupied with *Persuasion*, and she looked again at the manuscript of "Susan" (*Northanger Abbey*).

In January 1817 she began *Sanditon*, a robust and self-mocking satire on health resorts and invalidism. This novel remained unfinished owing to Austen's declining health. She supposed that she was suffering from bile, but the symptoms make possible a modern clinical assessment that she was suffering from Addison's disease. Her condition fluctuated, but in April she made her will, and in May she was taken to Winchester to be under the care of an expert surgeon. She died on July

18, and six days later she was buried in Winchester Cathedral.

Her authorship was announced to the world at large by her brother Henry, who supervised the publication of *Northanger Abbey* and *Persuasion*. There was no recognition at the time that regency England had lost its keenest observer and sharpest analyst; no understanding that a miniaturist (as she maintained that she was and as she was then seen), a "merely domestic" novelist, could be seriously concerned with the nature of society and the quality of its culture; no grasp of Jane Austen as a historian of the emergence of regency society into the modern world. During her lifetime there had been a solitary response in any way adequate to the nature of her achievement: Sir Walter Scott's review of *Emma* in the *Quarterly Review* for March 1816, where he hailed this "nameless author" as a masterful exponent of "the modern novel" in the new realist tradition. After her death, there was for long only one significant essay, the review of *Northanger Abbey* and *Persuasion* in the *Quarterly* for January 1821 by the theologian Richard Whately. Together, Scott's and Whately's essays provided the foundation for serious criticism of Jane Austen: their insights were appropriated by critics throughout the 19th century.

## Novels

Jane Austen's three early novels form a distinct group in which a strong element of literary satire accompanies the comic depiction of character and society.

*Sense and Sensibility* tells the story of the impoverished Dashwood sisters. Marianne is the heroine of "sensibility"—i.e., of openness and enthusiasm. She becomes infatuated with the attractive John Willoughby, who seems to be a romantic lover but is in reality an unscrupulous fortune hunter. He deserts her for an heiress, leaving her to learn a dose of "sense" in a wholly unromantic marriage with a staid and settled bachelor, Colonel Brandon, who is 20 years her senior. By contrast, Marianne's older sister, Elinor, is the guiding light of "sense," or prudence and discretion, whose constancy toward her lover, Edward Ferrars, is rewarded by her marriage to him after some distressing vicissitudes.

*Pride and Prejudice* describes the clash between Elizabeth Bennet, the daughter of a country gentleman, and Fitzwilliam Darcy, a rich and aristocratic landowner. Although Austen shows them intrigued by each other, she reverses the convention of "first impressions": "pride" of rank and fortune and "prejudice" against Elizabeth's inferiority of family hold Darcy aloof; while Elizabeth is equally fired both by the "pride" of self-respect and by "prejudice" against Darcy's snobbery. Ultimately, they come together in love and self-understanding. The intelligent and high-spirited Elizabeth was Jane Austen's own favourite among all her heroines and is one of the most engaging in English literature.

*Northanger Abbey* combines a satire on conventional novels of polite society with one on Gothic tales of terror. Catherine Morland, the unspoiled daughter of a country parson, is the innocent abroad who gains worldly wisdom: first in the fashionable society of Bath and then at Northanger Abbey itself, where she learns not to interpret the world through her reading of Gothic thrillers. Her mentor and guide is the self-assured and gently ironic Henry Tilney, her husband-to-be.

In the three novels of Jane Austen's maturity, the literary satire, though still present, is more subdued and is subordinated to the comedy of character and society.

In its tone and discussion of religion and religious duty, *Mansfield Park* is the most serious of Austen's novels. The heroine, Fanny Price, is a self-effacing and unregarded cousin cared for by the Bertram family in their country house. Fanny emerges as a true heroine whose moral strength eventually wins her complete acceptance in the Bertram family and marriage to Edmund Bertram himself, after that family's disastrous involvement with the meretricious and loose-living Crawfords.

Of all Austen's novels, *Emma* is the most consistently comic in tone. It centres on Emma Woodhouse, a wealthy, pretty, self-satisfied young woman who indulges herself with meddlesome and unsuccessful attempts at matchmaking among her friends and neighbours. After a series of humiliating errors, a chastened Emma finds her destiny in marriage to the mature and protective George Knightley, a neighbouring squire who had been her mentor and friend.

*Persuasion* tells the story of a second chance, the reawakening of love between Anne Elliot and Captain Frederick Wentworth, whom seven years earlier she had been persuaded not to marry. Now Wentworth returns from the Napoleonic Wars with prize money and the social acceptability of naval rank; he is an eligible suitor acceptable to Anne's snobbish father and his circle, and Anne discovers the continuing strength of her love for him.

# E. T. A. HOFFMANN

(b. January 24, 1776, Königsberg, Prussia [now Kaliningrad, Russia]—d. June 25, 1822, Berlin, Germany)

The German writer, composer, and painter Ernst Theodor Amadeus Hoffmann is known for his stories in which supernatural and sinister characters move in and out of men's lives, ironically revealing tragic or grotesque sides of human nature.

The product of a broken home, Hoffmann was reared by an uncle. He was educated in law and became a Prussian law officer in the Polish provinces in 1800, serving until the bureaucracy was dissolved following the defeat of Prussia by Napoleon in 1806. Hoffmann then turned to his chief interest, music, and held several positions as conductor, critic, and theatrical musical director in Bamberg and Dresden until 1814. About 1813 he changed his third baptismal name, Wilhelm, to Amadeus in homage to the composer Wolfgang Amadeus Mozart. He composed the ballet *Arlequin* (1811) and the opera *Undine* (performed in 1816) and wrote the stories in *Phantasiestücke in Callots Manier*, 4 vol. (1814–15; *Fantasy Pieces in Callot's Manner*), that established his reputation as a writer. He was appointed in 1814 to the court of appeal in Berlin, becoming councillor in 1816.

Although Hoffmann wrote two novels, *Die Elixiere des Teufels*, 2 vol. (1815–16; *The Devil's Elixir*), and *Lebens-Ansichten des Katers Murr nebst fragmentarischer Biographie des Kapellmeisters Johannes Kreisler*, 2 vol. (1820–22; "The Life and Opinions of Kater Murr, with a Fragmentary Biography of Conductor Johannes Kreisler"), and more than 50 short stories before his death from progressive paralysis, he continued to support himself as a legal official in Berlin. His later story collections, *Nachtstücke*, 2 parts (1817; *Hoffmann's Strange Stories*), and *Die Serapionsbrüder*, 4 vol. (1819–21; *The Serapion Brethren*), were popular in England, the United States, and France. Continued publication of the stories into the second half of the 20th century attested to their popularity.

In his stories Hoffmann skillfully combined wild flights of imagination with vivid and convincing examinations of human character and psychology. The weird and mysterious atmosphere of his maniacs, spectres, and automata thus intermingles with an exact and realistic narrative style. The struggle within Hoffmann between the ideal world of his art and his daily life as a bureaucrat is evident in many of his stories, in which characters are possessed by their art. His use of fantasy, ranging from fanciful fairy tales to highly suggestive stories of the macabre and supernatural, served as inspiration to several operatic composers. Richard Wagner drew on stories from *Die Serapionsbrüder* for *Die Meistersinger von Nürnberg* (1868), as did Paul Hindemith in *Cardillac* (1926) and Jacques Offenbach in *The Tales of Hoffmann* (1881), in which Hoffmann himself is the central figure. The ballet *Coppélia* (1870), by Léo Delibes, is also based on a Hoffmann story, as is Pyotr Ilyich Tchaikovsky's ballet suite, *The Nutcracker* (1892).

# HEINRICH VON KLEIST

(b. October 18, 1777, Frankfurt an der Oder, Brandenburg [now in Germany]—d. November 21, 1811, Wannsee, near Berlin)

The German dramatist Bernd Heinrich Wilhelm von Kleist is among the greatest playwrights of the 19th century. Poets of the Realist, Expressionist, Nationalist, and Existentialist movements in France and Germany saw their prototype in Kleist, a poet whose demonic genius had foreseen modern problems of life and literature.

Having grown up in military surroundings, Kleist became dissatisfied with the career of an army officer, which had been chosen for him, and resigned his commission after "the loss of seven valuable years." For a time he studied law and mathematics, but his reading of the philosophy of Immanuel Kant destroyed his faith in the value of knowledge. Despairing of reason, he decided to place his trust in emotion. The unresolved conflict between them lies at the heart of his work.

After Kleist had abandoned his studies, he went first to Paris and then to Switzerland. There he wrote his first work, the tragedy *Die Familie Schroffenstein* (1803; "The Schroffenstein Family"), which depicts pathological states with ruthless clarity. Underlying this drama of error is Kleist's recurring theme, the fallibility of human perception and the inability of the human intellect by itself to apprehend truth. At this time he was also working on the play *Robert Guiskard*, an ambitious work in which he attempted to unite ancient Sophoclean tragedy and the Shakespearean drama of character, but it would remain a fragment. He set out on a new journey and in Paris, overcome by despair, burned his manuscript of *Guiskard* (though he partially rewrote it later) and tried to volunteer for the French army. Expelled from France, he traveled to East Prussia and applied for a civil-service post in Königsberg. He resigned during training, however, and left for Dresden, where he hoped to continue writing, but was arrested by the French and imprisoned for six months as a spy.

In Dresden (1807–09) he became a member of a large circle of writers, painters, and patrons and, with the political philosopher Adam Müller, published the periodical *Phöbus*, which lasted only a few months. While he was in prison his adaptation of Molière's *Amphitryon* (published 1807) attracted some attention, and in 1808 he published *Penthesilia*, a tragic drama about the passionate love of the queen of the Amazons for Achilles. Although this play received little acclaim, it is now thought to contain some of Kleist's most powerful poetry, with the grimness of plot and intensity of feeling that have made his place unique among German poets. In March 1808 Kleist's one-act comedy in verse, *Der zerbrochene Krug* (*The Broken Pitcher*), was unsuccessfully produced by Johann Wolfgang von Goethe in Weimar. The play employs vividly portrayed rustic characters, skillful dialogue, earthy humour, and subtle realism in its depiction of the fallibility of human feeling and the flaws inherent in human justice. It ranks among the masterpieces of German dramatic comedy. Toward the end of 1808, inspired by a threatened rising against Napoleon, Kleist wrote some savage war poems and a political and patriotic tragedy, *Die Hermannsschlacht* (1821; "Hermann's Battle"), and in 1809 attempted to found a political periodical that would call all Germany to arms. Between 1810 and 1811 his *Das Käthchen von Heilbronn* (1810; *Katherine of Heilbronn*), a drama set in Swabia during the Middle Ages, was performed in Vienna, Graz, and Bamberg. But the Berlin stage remained closed to him.

Kleist also wrote eight masterly novellas, collected in *Erzählungen* (1810–11), of which *Das Erdbeben in Chili* ("The Earthquake in Chile"), *Michael Kohlhaas,* and *Die Marquise von O...* have become well-known as tales of violence and mystery. They are all characterized by an extraordinary economy, power, and vividness and by a tragic subject matter in which men are driven to the limits of their endurance by the violence of other men or of nature. Kleist's last drama, *Prinz Friedrich von Homburg* (published posthumously in 1821 by Ludwig Tieck), is a brilliant psychological drama. The play's problematical hero is Kleist's finest figure, reflecting Kleist's own conflicts between heroism and cowardice, dreaming and action.

For six months Kleist had edited the daily newspaper *Berliner Abendblätter*, and, when it ceased publication, he lost his means of livelihood. Disappointed in life and embittered by the lack of recognition accorded him by his contemporaries, particularly Goethe, he came to know an incurably sick woman, Henriette Vogel, who begged him to kill her. This gave Kleist the final incentive to end his life, and on November 21, 1811, he shot Henriette and himself on the shore of the Wannsee.

# WILLIAM HAZLITT

(b. April 10, 1778, Maidstone, Kent, England—
d. September 18, 1830, London)

The English writer William Hazlitt is best known for his humanistic essays. Lacking conscious artistry or literary pretention, his writing is noted for the brilliant intellect it reveals.

Hazlitt's childhood was spent in Ireland and North America, where his father, a Unitarian preacher, supported the American rebels. The family returned to England when William was nine, settling in Shropshire. At puberty the child became somewhat sullen and unapproachable, tendencies that persisted throughout his life. He read intensively, however, laying the foundation of his learning. Having some difficulty in expressing himself either in conversation or in writing, he turned to painting and in 1802 traveled to Paris to work in the Louvre, though war between England and France compelled his return the following year. His friends, who already included Charles Lamb, William Wordsworth, and Samuel Taylor Coleridge, encouraged his ambitions as a painter; yet in 1805 he turned to metaphysics and the study of philosophy that had attracted him earlier, publishing his first book, *On the Principles of Human Action*. In 1808 he married Sarah Stoddart, and the couple went to live at Winterslow on Salisbury Plain, which was to become Hazlitt's favourite retreat for thinking and writing.

Although he successfully completed several literary projects, by the end of 1811 Hazlitt was penniless. He then gave a course of lectures in philosophy in London and began reporting for the *Morning Chronicle*, quickly establishing himself as critic, journalist, and essayist. His collected dramatic criticism appeared as *A View of the English Stage* in 1818. He also contributed to a number of journals, among them Leigh Hunt's *Examiner*; this association led to the publication of *The Round Table*, 2 vol. (1817), 52 essays of which 40 were by Hazlitt. Also in 1817 Hazlitt published his *Characters of Shakespeare's Plays*, which met with immediate approval in most quarters. He had, however, become involved in a number of quarrels, often with his friends, resulting from the forcible expression of his views in the journals. At the same time, he made new friends and admirers (among them Percy Bysshe Shelley and John Keats) and consolidated his reputation as a lecturer, delivering courses *On the English Poets* (published 1818) and *On the English Comic Writers* (published 1819), as well as publishing a collection of political essays. His volume entitled *Lectures on the Dramatic Literature of the Age of Elizabeth* was prepared during 1819, but thereafter he devoted himself to essays for various journals, notably John Scott's *London Magazine*.

Hazlitt lived apart from his wife after the end of 1819, and they were divorced in 1822. He fell in love with the daughter of his London landlord, but the affair ended disastrously, and Hazlitt described his suffering in the strange *Liber Amoris; or, The New Pygmalion* (1823). Even so, many of his best essays were written during this difficult period and were collected in his two most famous books: *Table Talk* (1821) and *The Plain Speaker* (1826). Others were afterward edited by his son, William, as *Sketches and Essays* (1829), *Literary Remains* (1836), and *Winterslow* (1850) and by his biographer, P.P. Howe, as *New Writings* (1925–27). Hazlitt's other works during this period of prolific output included *Sketches of the Principal Picture Galleries in England* (1824), with its celebrated essay on the Dulwich gallery.

In April 1824 Hazlitt married a widow named Bridgwater. But the new wife was resented by his son, whom Hazlitt adored, and the couple separated after three years. Part of this second marriage was spent abroad, an experience recorded in *Notes of a Journey in France and Italy* (1826). In France he began an ambitious but not very successful *Life of Napoleon*, 4 vol. (1828–30), and in 1825 he published some of his most effective writing in *The Spirit of the Age*.

**English essayist William Hazlitt.** Hulton Archive/ Getty Images

His last book, *Conversations of James Northcote* (1830), recorded his long friendship with that eccentric painter.

Hazlitt's *Complete Works*, in 13 volumes, appeared in 1902–06, to be reissued, edited by P.P. Howe, in 21 volumes in 1930–34.

## *ADAM GOTTLOB OEHLENSCHLÄGER*

(b. November 14, 1779, Vesterbro, Denmark—
d. January 20, 1850, Copenhagen)

Adam Gottlob Oehlenschläger was a poet and dramatist who was a leader of the Romantic movement in Denmark and traditionally has been considered the great Danish national poet.

Oehlenschläger's father was organist and then steward at Frederiksberg castle near Copenhagen. In his youth Oehlenschläger attended a school directed by the poet Edvard Storm, a Norwegian known for patriotic poetry and drinking songs. After a short career as an actor, Oehlenschläger entered the University of Copenhagen to study law, but turned to writing. He wrote his famous poem *Guldhornene* (1802; *The Golden Horns*), about the loss of two golden horns symbolizing a union of past and present, after his meeting with the Norwegian scientist and philosopher Henrik Steffens, who was eager to spread the doctrine of German Romanticism in Denmark. The ideals of Steffens gave Oehlenschläger the courage to break with 18th-century literary traditions, and *Guldhornene* marks this turning point in Danish literature. Oehlenschläger's first volume of poetry, *Digte* (1803; "Poems"), contained not only *Guldhornene* but also *Sanct Hansaften-spil* ("A Midsummer Night's Play"); this latter work is a lyrical drama combining literary satire with poetic discourses on love and nature. His *Poetiske skrifter* (1805; "Poetic Writings") contains two long cycles of lyric poems and *Aladdin*, a poetic drama on the writer's own life, with the lamp of the story symbolizing intuitive poetic genius. Oehlenschläger was by now recognized as an important Romantic poet and an able practitioner of what Friedrich Schlegel termed *Universalpoesie*, a universal, historical, comparative approach to literature. In 1805 he received a government grant to study and travel in Germany and other countries, where he visited Goethe and the leaders of the Romantic movement.

In the historical plays published in *Nordiske Digte* (1807; "Nordic Poems"), Oehlenschläger broke somewhat with the Romantic school and turned to Nordic history and mythology for his materials. In this collection are the historical tragedy *Hakon Jarl hin Rige* ("Earl Haakon the Great"), based on that Danish national hero, and *Baldur hin Gode* ("Baldur the Good"), based on Norse mythology.

Oehlenschläger returned to Copenhagen in 1809 and became a professor of aesthetics at the university there in 1810. He subsequently wrote many other plays, but these are generally thought to be inferior to his earlier plays. The exception is his one-act tragedy *Yrsa*, which together with two cycles of poems forms one of his most outstanding works, *Helge* (1814). *Helge* came to inspire both Swedish and Finnish national epic poems, by Esaias Tegnér (*Frithiofs saga*, 1825) and Johan Ludvig Runeberg (*Kung Fjalar*, 1844), respectively. His lyric poetry has in general outlived his dramatic verse. Oehlenschläger's other significant later work is the poetic epic *Nordens guder* (1819; *The Gods of the North*), which is a sort of modern *Edda*.

# $S$TENDHAL

(b. January 23, 1783, Grenoble, France—d. March 23, 1842, Paris)

One of the most original and complex French writers of the first half of the 19th century, Stendhal is chiefly known for his works of fiction. His finest novels are *Le Rouge et le noir* (1830; *The Red and the Black*) and *La Chartreuse de Parme* (1839; *The Charterhouse of Parma*).

## Life

Stendhal is only one of the many pseudonyms Marie-Henri Beyle adopted. As a student he grew interested in literature and mathematics. In 1799 he left for Paris, ostensibly to prepare for the entrance examination to the École Polytechnique, but in reality to escape from Grenoble and from paternal rule.

His secret ambition on arriving in Paris was to become a successful playwright. But some highly placed relatives of his, the Darus, obtained an appointment for him as second lieutenant in the French military forces stationed in Italy. This led him to discover Piedmont, Lombardy, and the delights of Milan. The culture and landscape of Italy were the revelation that was to play a psychologically and thematically determining role in his life and works.

In 1802 the 19-year-old Henri Beyle was back in Paris and at work on a number of literary projects, none of which he completed. He dreamed of becoming a modern Molière, enrolled in drama classes, worked at ridding himself of his provincial accent, and fell in love with a second-rate actress (Mélanie Louason), whom he followed to Marseille. By then he was keeping a diary (posthumously published as his *Journal*) and writing other texts dealing with his intimate thoughts.

The year 1806 proved to be a turning point. Count Pierre Daru, having been appointed intendant-general of Napoleon's army, had his young protégé sent as an adjunct military commissary to the German city of Brunswick. This was the beginning of an administrative career in the French army that allowed Henri Beyle to discover parts of Germany and Austria. His army appointment gave him a direct experience of the Napoleonic regime and of Europe at war. In 1814, when the French empire fell, he decided to settle in Italy.

From the moment he took up residence in Milan, his literary vocation became irreversible. He became friends with Milanese liberals and Carbonari patriots, discovered the *Edinburgh Review*, studied music and the visual arts, and published his first books: *Vies de Haydn, de Mozart et de Métastase* (1814; *Lives of Haydn, Mozart and Metastasio*) and *Histoire de la peinture en Italie* (1817; "History of Painting in Italy"). In these early works Henri Beyle was not always above plagiarism, which was seasoned, however, with brilliant and original insights. His travel book *Rome, Naples et Florence en 1817* also appeared (a later version was published in 1826), and this was the first time he used the pseudonym of Stendhal. His political friendships compromised him in the eyes of the Austrian occupying authorities, which finally led him to leave Milan in 1821.

From 1821 to 1830, Stendhal's social and intellectual life in Paris was very active. He made a name for himself in the salons as a conversationalist and polemicist. His wit and unconventional views were much appreciated, and he had notable friendships and love affairs. In 1822 he published *De l'amour* (*On Love*), which claims to study the operations of love dispassionately and objectively, but which can be read as a hidden confession of Stendhal's emotional experiences and longings. His *Racine et Shakespeare* (1823, 1825) was one of the first Romantic manifestos to appear in France. Stendhal's literary production during this period was quite varied. In addition to his regular contributions to English journals, he published *Vie de Rossini* (1823; *Life of Rossini*); his first novel, *Armance* (1827); and the travel book *Promenades dans Rome* (1829). During this period he also wrote one of his two masterpieces, the novel *Le Rouge et le noir* (*The Red and the Black*), which appeared in 1830.

The year 1830, during which the July Revolution brought the constitutional monarch Louis-Philippe to the throne in France, marked a new turning point in Stendhal's life. He was appointed French consul in the port of Civitavecchia in the Papal States. In this small town, where he felt bored and isolated, Stendhal was occupied by endless administrative chores and found it difficult to write in a sustained manner. He sought distractions in nearby Rome, absenting himself frequently from his official duties. Lonely, aware of age and of failing health, he felt increasingly drawn to autobiography and began *Souvenirs d'égotisme* (1892; *Memoirs of an Egotist*) and *Vie de Henri Brulard* (1890; *The Life of Henri Brulard*), as well as a new and largely autobiographical novel entitled *Lucien Leuwen* (1894). All these works remained uncompleted, though they were published posthumously, and are now considered among Stendhal's finest writings.

During his consulate, Stendhal discovered in Rome unpublished accounts of crimes of passion and grim executions set in the Renaissance. They became the inspiration for stories he later published under the title of *Chroniques italiennes* ("Italian Chronicles"). But it was only in Paris, where he took up residence again during a prolonged leave (1836-1839), that Stendhal could undertake new major literary work. He composed *Mémoires d'un touriste*;

his second masterpiece, the novel *La Chartreuse de Parme* (1839; *The Charterhouse of Parma*); and began work on a new novel, *Lamiel* (1889), which he did not live long enough to complete. He died in 1842 after suffering a stroke while again on leave in Paris.

## *Works*

During Stendhal's lifetime, his reputation was largely based on his books dealing with the arts and with tourism (a term he helped introduce in France), and on his political writings and conversational wit. His unconventional views, his hedonistic inclinations tempered by a capacity for moral and political indignation, his prankish nature and his hatred of boredom—all constituted for his contemporaries a blend of provocative contradictions. But the more authentic Stendhal is to be found elsewhere, and above all in a cluster of favourite ideas: the hostility to the concept of "ideal beauty," the notion of modernity, and the exaltation of energy, passion, and spontaneity.

It was in his novels above all, and in his autobiographical writings (the interchange between these two literary activities remains a constant feature in his case), that Stendhal's thoughts are expressed most fully. But even these texts remain baffling. Their prosaic and ironic style at first glance hides the intensity of Stendhal's vision and the profundity of his views.

*Armance* (1827) is a somewhat enigmatic novel in which the hero's sexual impotence is symbolic of France's conformist and oppressive society after the Restoration. The antagonism between the individual and society is the central subject of *The Red and the Black*. This realistic novel depicts the French social order under the Second Restoration (1815–30). The story centres on a carpenter's son, Julien Sorel, a sensitive and intelligent but extremely ambitious youth who, after seeing no road to power in the military after Napoleon's fall, endeavours to make his mark in the church. Viewing himself as an unsentimental opportunist, he employs seduction as a means to advancement, first with Madame de Rênal, whose children he is employed to tutor. After then spending some time in a seminary, he leaves the provinces and goes to Paris, where he seduces the aristocratic Mathilde, the daughter of his second employer. The book ends with Julien's execution for the attempted murder of Madame de Rênal after she had jeopardized his projected marriage to Mathilde.

The title of *The Red and the Black* apparently refers to both the tensions in Julien's character and to the conflicting choice he is faced with in his quest for success: the army (symbolized by the colour red) or the church (symbolized by the colour black). A variety of other polarities tempt the ambitious young hero as he sets out with fierce determination to rise above his lowly condition: the provinces or Paris, tender love or sexual conquest, happiness through ambition and achievement or happiness through reverie and the cultivation of selfhood. Careerism, political opportunism, the climate of fear and denunciation in Restoration France, a critique of bourgeois materialistic values—all these are dealt with in a subtle and incisive manner in a novel that is based on a newspaper account of a contemporary crime of passion. Julien Sorel, the central character, is a study in psychological complexity who both attracts and repels the reader. Timid and aggressive, sensitive and ruthless, vulnerable and supremely ambitious, Julien ultimately comes to realize, in prison, the vanity of worldly success and the superior value of love and a rich inner life. *The Red and the Black* also offers delicate portraits of two feminine figures, the maternal Madame de Renal and the romantic young aristocrat Mathilde de La Mole. At every point, the novel challenges conventions and denounces the sham of societal values. As a literary achievement, it is remarkable for its blend of comedy, satire, and ironic lyricism.

The uncompleted *Lucien Leuwen* (1894) is perhaps the most autobiographical of Stendhal's novels. The memory of Métilde Dembowski hovers over the relationship between the young hero of the title and Madame de Chasteller. This biting fictional assessment of French society and politics during the reign of Louis-Philippe also describes a basic father-son conflict that corresponds to the conflicting ethos of two distinct historical periods. As it stands, despite its imperfections and uncompleted form, *Lucien Leuwen* contains some of Stendhal's finest pages of psychological and social analysis, as well as delicate evocations of a young lover's emotional states.

*The Charterhouse of Parma* is Stendhal's other masterpiece. It fuses elements of Renaissance chronicles, fictional and historical sources, recent historical events (the Napoleonic regime in Italy, the Battle of Waterloo, the Austrian occupation of Milan), and an imaginative, almost dreamlike transposition of contemporary reality into fictional terms. The novel is set mainly in the court of Parma, Italy, in the early 19th century. Fabrice del Dongo, a young aristocrat and ardent admirer of Napoleon, goes to Paris to join the French army and is present at the Battle of Waterloo. He returns thereafter to Parma and enters the church for worldly advantage under the sponsorship of his aunt, the Duchess de Sanseverina, who is the mistress of the chief minister of Parma, Count Mosca. Following an affair with an actress, Fabrice kills a rival, is imprisoned, escapes, and is pardoned. In prison Fabrice falls in love with Clélia Conti, the daughter of the citadel's governor. He continues his affair with her after she marries, and he becomes a high-ranking ecclesiastic and an admired preacher. The death of their child and then of Clélia herself causes Fabrice to retire to the Carthusian monastery, or charterhouse, of Parma, where he dies.

The incongruous yet always harmonious combination of lyricism and high comedy, of realism and dreamlike atmosphere, of *The Charterhouse of Parma* allows the author to caricaturize the petty tyranny of post-Napoleonic Europe, to question public morality, and to assert the prerogatives of love's follies. There are subtly drawn portraits of the naive and idealistic young Fabrice del Dongo (notably at the Battle of Waterloo); of his courageous and passionate aunt, the Duchess de Sanseverina; of her lover, the benevolent Machiavellian statesman Count Mosca; and of the young and innocent Clélia Conti, the daughter of Fabrice's jailer, who falls in love with the handsome prisoner. Passion in all its forms is the novel's recurrent theme. And once again, the young hero learns the deeper lessons of spirituality, love, and freedom within the liberating confines of a prison cell.

Perhaps the most remarkable aspect of *The Charterhouse of Parma* is its highly sophisticated psychology. Rejecting traditional notions of a fixed and determined psychological makeup, Stendhal never defines his characters and instead depicts individuals in the process of becoming. His literary devices (his authorial comments, the improvisational tone of his narration) seem to grant his characters the freedom to discover themselves. Various forms of freedom are Stendhal's ultimate preoccupation, which probably explains why he repeatedly explores the ambiguities of the prison image. True freedom, in the world of Stendhal, reveals itself in the context of the cell, once confinement becomes the symbol of the inner world of dreams and longings. His novels thus illustrate metaphorically the fundamental conflict between the demands of society and those of the individual.

# *WASHINGTON IRVING*

(b. April 3, 1783, New York, New York, U.S.—d. November 28, 1859, Tarrytown, New York)

Washington Irving was a writer who was called the "first American man of letters." He is best known for the short stories "The Legend of Sleepy Hollow" and "Rip Van Winkle."

The favourite and last of 11 children of an austere Presbyterian father and a genial Anglican mother, young, frail Irving grew up in an atmosphere of indulgence. He escaped a college education, which his father required of his older sons, but read intermittently at the law, notably in the office of Josiah Ogden Hoffman, with whose pretty daughter Matilda he early fell in love. He wrote a series of whimsically satirical essays over the signature of Jonathan Oldstyle, Gent., published in Peter Irving's newspaper, the *Morning Chronicle*, in 1802–03. He made several trips up the Hudson, another into Canada for his health, and took an extended tour of Europe in 1804–06.

On his return he passed the bar examination late in 1806 and soon set up as a lawyer. But during 1807–08 his chief occupation was to collaborate with his brother William and James K. Paulding in the writing of a series of 20 periodical essays entitled *Salmagundi*. Concerned primarily with passing phases of contemporary society, the essays retain significance as an index to the social milieu.

His *A History of New York...by Diedrich Knickerbocker* (1809) was a comic history of the Dutch regime in New York, prefaced by a mock-pedantic account of the world from creation onward. Its writing was interrupted in April 1809 by the sudden death of Matilda Hoffman, as grief

*Daguerrotype photographic portrait of author Washington Irving. During his lifetime Irving worked as a lawyer and lobbyist, but he is best remembered as the author of some of America's first short stories.* **Library of Congress Prints and Photographs Division**

incapacitated him. In 1811 he moved to Washington, D.C., as a lobbyist for the Irving brothers' hardware-importing firm, but his life seemed aimless for some years. He prepared an American edition of Thomas Campbell's poems, edited the *Analectic Magazine*, and acquired a staff colonelcy during the War of 1812. In 1815 he went to Liverpool to look after the interests of his brothers' firm. In London he met Sir Walter Scott, who encouraged him to renewed effort. The result was *The Sketch Book of Geoffrey Crayon, Gent* (1819–20), a collection of stories and essays that mix satire and whimsicality with fact and fiction. Most of the book's 30-odd pieces concern Irving's impressions of England, but six chapters deal with American subjects. Of these, the tales "The Legend of Sleepy Hollow" and "Rip Van Winkle" have been called the first American short stories. They are both Americanized versions of German folktales. The main character of "Rip Van Winkle" is a henpecked husband who sleeps for 20 years and awakes as an old man to find his wife dead, his daughter happily married, and America now an independent country. The tremendous success of *The Sketch Book* in both England and the United States assured Irving that he could live by his pen. In 1822 he produced *Bracebridge Hall,* a sequel to *The Sketch Book.* He traveled in Germany, Austria, France, Spain, the British Isles, and later in his own country.

Early in 1826 he accepted the invitation of Alexander H. Everett to attach himself to the American legation in Spain, where he wrote his *Columbus* (1828), followed by *The Companions of Columbus* (1831). Meanwhile, Irving had become absorbed in the legends of the Moorish past and wrote *A Chronicle of the Conquest of Granada* (1829) and *The Alhambra* (1832), a Spanish counterpart of *The Sketch Book.*

After a 17-year absence Irving returned to New York in 1832, where he was warmly received. He made a journey west and produced in rapid succession *A Tour of the Prairies* (1835), *Astoria* (1836), and *The Adventures of Captain Bonneville* (1837). Except for four years (1842–46) as minister to Spain, Irving spent the remainder of his life at his home, "Sunnyside," in Tarrytown, on the Hudson River, where he devoted himself to literary pursuits.

# BROTHERS GRIMM

Respectively, Jacob: (b. January 4, 1785, Hanau, Hesse-Kassel [Germany] — d. September 20, 1863, Berlin); Wilhelm: (b. February 24, 1786, Hanau, Hesse-Kassel [Germany] — d. December 16, 1859, Berlin)

The Brothers Grimm are famous for their classic collections of folk songs and folktales, particularly *Kinder- und Hausmärchen* (1812–22; also called *Grimm's Fairy Tales*), which led to the birth of the science of folklore.

## Beginnings and Kassel Period

Jacob and Wilhelm Grimm were the oldest in a German family of five brothers and one sister. Their father, Philipp Wilhelm, a lawyer, was town clerk in Hanau and later justiciary in Steinau, another small Hessian town, where his father and grandfather had been ministers of the Calvinistic Reformed Church. The father's death in 1796 brought social hardships to the family; the death of the mother in 1808 left 23-year-old Jacob with the responsibility of four brothers and one sister. Jacob, a scholarly type, was small and slender with sharply cut features, while Wilhelm was taller, had a softer face, and was sociable and fond of all the arts.

After attending the high school in Kassel, the brothers followed their father's footsteps and studied law at the University of Marburg (1802–06) with the intention of entering civil service. At Marburg they came under the influence of Clemens Brentano, who awakened in both a love of folk poetry, and Friedrich Karl von Savigny, cofounder of the historical school of jurisprudence, who taught them a method of antiquarian investigation that formed the real basis of all their later work. Others, too, strongly influenced the Grimms, particularly the philosopher Johann Gottfried Herder (1744–1803), with his ideas on folk poetry. Essentially, they remained individuals, creating their work according to their own principles.

In 1805 Jacob accompanied Savigny to Paris to do research on legal manuscripts of the Middle Ages; the following year he became secretary to the war office in Kassel. Because of his health, Wilhelm remained without regular employment until 1814. After the French entered in 1806, Jacob became private librarian to King Jérôme of Westphalia in 1808 and a year later *auditeur* of the Conseil d'État but returned to Hessian service in 1813 after Napoleon's defeat. As secretary to the legation, he went twice to Paris (1814–15), to recover precious books and paintings taken by the French from Hesse and Prussia. He also took part in the Congress of Vienna (September 1814– June 1815). Meantime, Wilhelm had become secretary at the Elector's library in Kassel (1814), and Jacob joined him there in 1816.

By that time the brothers had definitely given up thoughts of a legal career in favour of purely literary research. In the years to follow they lived frugally and worked steadily, laying the foundations for their lifelong interests. Their whole thinking was rooted in the social and political changes of their time and the challenge these changes held. Jacob and Wilhelm had nothing in common with the fashionable "Gothic" Romanticism of the 18th and 19th centuries. Their state of mind made them more

*Jacob* (Left) *and Wilhelm Grimm. The brothers collected folk tales from around the world, publishing the stories that are now considered classic fairy tales.* Hulton Archive/Getty Images

Realists than Romantics. They investigated the distant past and saw in antiquity the foundation of all social institutions of their days. But their efforts to preserve these foundations did not mean that they wanted to return to the past. From the beginning, the Grimms sought to include material from beyond their own frontiers—from the literary traditions of Scandinavia, Spain, the Netherlands, Ireland, Scotland, England, Serbia, and Finland.

They first collected folk songs and tales for their friends Achim von Arnim and Brentano, who had collaborated on an influential collection of folk lyrics in 1805, and the brothers examined in some critical essays the essential difference between folk literature and other writing. To them, folk poetry was the only true poetry, expressing the eternal joys and sorrows, the hopes and fears of mankind.

Encouraged by Arnim, they published their collected tales as the *Kinder- und Hausmärchen*, implying in the title that the stories were meant for adults and children alike. In contrast to the extravagant fantasy of the Romantic school's poetical fairy tales, the 200 stories of this collection (mostly taken from oral sources, though a few were from printed sources) aimed at conveying the soul, imagination, and beliefs of people through the centuries—or at a genuine reproduction of the teller's words and ways. The great merit of Wilhelm Grimm is that he gave the fairy tales a readable form without changing their folkloric character. The results were threefold: the collection enjoyed wide distribution in Germany and eventually in all parts of the globe (there are now translations in 70 languages); it became and remains a model for the collecting of folktales everywhere; and the Grimms' notes to the tales, along with other investigations, formed the basis for the science of the folk narrative and even of folklore. To this day the tales remain the earliest "scientific" collection of folktales.

The *Kinder- und Hausmärchen* was followed by a collection of historical and local legends of Germany, *Deutsche Sagen* (1816–18), which never gained wide popular appeal, though it influenced both literature and the study of the folk narrative. The brothers then published (in 1826) a translation of Thomas Crofton Croker's *Fairy Legends and Traditions of the South of Ireland*, prefacing the edition with a lengthy introduction of their own on fairy lore. At the same time, the Grimms gave their attention to the written documents of early literature, bringing out new editions of ancient texts, from both the Germanic and other languages. Wilhelm's outstanding contribution was *Die deutsche Heldensage* ("The German Heroic Tale"), a collection of themes and names from heroic legends mentioned in literature and art from the 6th to the 16th centuries, together with essays on the art of the saga.

While collaborating on these subjects for two decades (1806–26), Jacob also turned to the study of philology with an extensive work on grammar, the *Deutsche Grammatik* (1819–37). The word *deutsch* in the title does not mean strictly "German," but it rather refers to the etymological meaning of "common," thus being used to apply to all of the Germanic languages, the historical development of which is traced for the first time. He represented the natural laws of sound change (both vowels and consonants) in various languages and thus created bases for a method of scientific etymology; i.e., research into relationships between languages and development of meaning. In what was to become known as Grimm's law, Jacob demonstrated the principle of the regularity of correspondence among consonants in genetically related languages, a principle previously observed by the Dane Rasmus Rask. Jacob's work on grammar exercised an enormous influence on the contemporary study of linguistics, Germanic, Romance, and Slavic, and it remains of value and in use even now. In 1824 Jacob Grimm translated a Serbian grammar by his friend Vuk Stefanović Karadžić, writing an erudite introduction on Slavic languages and literature.

He extended his investigations into the Germanic folk-culture with a study of ancient law practices and beliefs published as *Deutsche Rechtsaltertümer* (1828), providing systematic source material but excluding actual laws. The work stimulated other publications in France, the Netherlands, Russia, and the southern Slavic countries and has not yet been superseded.

## The Göttingen Years

The quiet contentment of the years at Kassel ended in 1829, when the brothers suffered a snub—perhaps motivated politically—from the Elector of Hessen-Kassel: they were not given advancement following the death of a senior colleague. Consequently, they moved to the nearby University of Göttingen, where they were appointed librarians and professors. Jacob Grimm's *Deutsche Mythologie*, written during this period, was to be of far-reaching influence. From poetry, fairy tales, and folkloristic elements, he traced the pre-Christian faith and superstitions of the Germanic people, contrasting the beliefs to those of classical mythology and Christianity. The *Mythologie* had many successors all over Europe, but often disciples were not as careful in their judgments as Jacob had been.

Wilhelm published here his outstanding edition of Freidank's epigrams. But again fate overtook them. When Ernest Augustus, duke of Cumberland, became king of Hanover, he repealed the constitution of 1833, which he considered too liberal. Two weeks after the king's declaration, the Grimms, together with five other professors (the "Göttingen Seven"), sent a protest to the king, explaining that they felt themselves bound by oath to the old constitution. As a result they were dismissed, and three professors, including Jacob, were ordered to leave the kingdom of Hanover at once. During three years of exile in Kassel, institutions in Germany and beyond (Hamburg, Marburg, Rostock, Weimar, Belgium, France, the Netherlands, and Switzerland) tried to obtain the brothers' services.

## The Berlin Period

In 1840 they accepted an invitation from the king of Prussia, Frederick William IV, to go to Berlin, where as members of the Royal Academy of Sciences they lectured at the university. There they began work in earnest on their most ambitious enterprise, the *Deutsches Wörterbuch*, a large German dictionary intended as a guide for the user of the written and spoken word as well as a scholarly reference work. In the dictionary, all German words found in the literature of the three centuries "from Luther to Goethe" were given with their historical variants, their etymology, and their semantic development; their usage in specialized and everyday language was illustrated by quoting idioms and proverbs. Begun as a source of income in 1838 for the brothers after their dismissal from Göttingen, the work required generations of successors to bring the gigantic task to an end more than a hundred years later. Jacob lived to see the work proceed to the letter *F*, while Wilhelm finished only the letter *D*. The dictionary became an example for similar publications in other countries: Britain, France, the Netherlands, Sweden, and Switzerland. Jacob's philological research later led to a history of the German language, *Geschichte der deutschen Sprache*, in which he attempted to combine the historical study of language with the study of early history. Research into names and dialects was stimulated by Jacob Grimm's work, as were ways of writing and spelling—for example, he used roman type and advocated spelling German nouns without capital letters.

For some 20 years they worked in Prussia's capital, respected and free from financial worries. Much of importance can be found in the brothers' lectures and essays, the prefaces and reviews (*Kleinere Schriften*) they wrote in this period. In Berlin they witnessed the Revolution of 1848 and took an active part in the political strife of the succeeding years. In spite of close and even emotional ties to their homeland, the Grimms were not nationalists in the narrow sense. They maintained genuine—even political—friendships with colleagues at home and abroad, among them the jurists Savigny and Eichhorn; the historians F.C. Dahlmann, G.G. Gervinus, and Jules Michelet; and the philologists Karl Lachmann, John Mitchell Kemble, Jan Frans Willems, Vuk Karadžić, and Pavel Josef Šafařik. Nearly all academies in Europe were proud to count Jacob and Wilhelm among their members. The more robust Jacob undertook many journeys for scientific investigations, visiting France, the Netherlands, Belgium, Switzerland, Austria, Italy, Denmark, and Sweden. Jacob remained a bachelor; Wilhelm married Dorothea Wild from Kassel, with whom he had four children: Jacob (who was born and died in 1826), Herman (literary and art historian, 1828–1901), Rudolf (jurist, 1830–89), and Auguste (1832–1919). The graves of the brothers are in the Matthäikirchhof in Berlin.

# *ALESSANDRO MANZONI*

(b. March 7, 1785, Milan, Italy — d. May 22, 1873, Milan)

Alessandro Manzoni was an Italian poet and novelist whose novel *I promessi sposi* (*The Betrothed*, 1952) had immense patriotic appeal for Italians of the nationalistic Risorgimento period and is generally ranked among the masterpieces of world literature.

After Manzoni's parents separated in 1792, he spent much of his childhood in religious schools. In 1805 he joined his mother and her lover in Paris, where he moved in radical circles and became a convert to Voltairian skepticism. His anticlerical poem "Il trionfo della libertà" demonstrates his independence of thought. When his mother's lover and his father died, the former left him a comfortable income, through his mother.

In 1808 he married Henriette Blondel, a Calvinist, who soon converted to Roman Catholicism, and two years later Manzoni himself returned to Catholicism. Retiring to a quiet life in Milan and at his villa in Brusiglio, he wrote (1812–15) a series of religious poems, *Inni sacri* (1815; *The Sacred Hymns*), on the church feasts of Christmas, Good Friday, and Easter, and a hymn to Mary. The last, and perhaps the finest, of the series, "La pentecoste," was published in 1822.

During these years, Manzoni also produced the treatise *Osservazioni sulla morale cattolica* (1819; "Observations on Catholic Ethics"); an ode on the Piedmontese revolution of 1821, "Marzo 1821"; and two historical tragedies influenced by Shakespeare: *Il conte di Carmagnola* (1820), a romantic work depicting a 15th-century conflict between

Venice and Milan; and *Adelchi* (performed 1822), a richly poetic drama about Charlemagne's overthrow of the Lombard kingdom and conquest of Italy. Another ode, written on the death of Napoleon in 1821, "Il cinque maggio" (1822; "The Napoleonic Ode"), was considered by Goethe, one of the first to translate it into German, as the greatest of many written to commemorate the event.

Manzoni's masterpiece, *I promessi sposi*, 3 vol. (1825–27), is a novel set in early 17th-century Lombardy during the period of the Milanese insurrection, the Thirty Years' War, and the plague. It is a sympathetic portrayal of the struggle of two peasant lovers whose wish to marry is thwarted by a vicious local tyrant and the cowardice of their parish priest. A courageous friar takes up the lovers' cause and helps them through many adventures to safety and marriage. Manzoni's resigned tolerance of the evils of life and his concept of religion as the ultimate comfort and inspiration of humanity give the novel its moral dimension, while a pleasant vein of humour in the book contributes to the reader's enjoyment. The novel brought Manzoni immediate fame and praise from all quarters, in Italy and elsewhere.

Prompted by the patriotic urge to forge a language that would be accessible to a wide readership rather than a narrow elite, Manzoni decided to write his novel in an idiom as close as possible to contemporary educated Florentine speech. The final edition of *I promessi sposi* (1840–42), rendered in clear, expressive prose purged of all antiquated rhetorical forms, reached exactly the sort of broad audience he had aimed at, and its prose became the model for many subsequent Italian writers.

Manzoni's wife died in 1833; his second wife and most of his children also predeceased him. These calamities deepened rather than destroyed his faith. Revered by the men of his time, he was made a senator of Italy in 1860. A stroke followed the death of his oldest son in 1873, and he died that same year and was buried with a state funeral.

# GEORGE GORDON BYRON, 6TH BARON BYRON

(b. January 22, 1788, London, England—d. April 19, 1824, Missolonghi, Greece)

G eorge Gordon Byron, 6th Baron Byron—often referred to simply as Lord Byron—was a British Romantic poet and satirist whose poetry and personality captured the imagination of Europe.

## Early Life and Great Works

Byron was the son of the handsome and profligate Captain John ("Mad Jack") Byron and his second wife, Catherine Gordon, a Scots heiress. After her husband had squandered most of her fortune, Mrs. Byron took her infant son to Aberdeen, Scotland, where they lived in lodgings on a meagre income; the captain died in France in 1791. George Gordon Byron had been born with a clubfoot and early developed an extreme sensitivity to his lameness. In 1798, at age 10, he unexpectedly inherited the title and estates of his great-uncle William, the 5th Baron Byron. His mother proudly took him to England, where the boy fell in love with the ghostly halls and spacious ruins of Newstead Abbey, which had been presented to the Byrons by Henry VIII. After living at Newstead for a while, Byron was sent to school in London, and in 1801 he went to Harrow, one

*George Gordon Byron, known as Lord Byron.* © Photos.com/ Thinkstock

of England's most prestigious schools. In 1803 he fell in love with his distant cousin, Mary Chaworth, who was older and already engaged, and when she rejected him she became the symbol for Byron of idealized and unattainable love. He probably met Augusta Byron, his half sister from his father's first marriage, that same year.

In 1805 Byron entered Trinity College, Cambridge, where he piled up debts at an alarming rate and indulged in the conventional vices of undergraduates there. The signs of his incipient sexual ambivalence became more pronounced in what he later described as "a violent, though *pure*, love and passion" for a young chorister, John Edleston. In 1806 Byron had his early poems privately printed in a volume entitled *Fugitive Pieces*, and that same year he formed at Trinity what was to be a close, lifelong friendship with John Cam Hobhouse, who stirred his interest in liberal Whiggism.

Byron's first published volume of poetry, *Hours of Idleness*, appeared in 1807. A sarcastic critique of the book in *The Edinburgh Review* provoked his retaliation in 1809 with a couplet satire, *English Bards and Scotch Reviewers*, in which he attacked the contemporary literary scene. This work gained him his first recognition.

On reaching his majority in 1809, Byron took his seat in the House of Lords, and then embarked with Hobhouse on a grand tour. They sailed to Lisbon, crossed Spain, and proceeded by Gibraltar and Malta to Greece, where they ventured inland to Ioánnina and to Tepelene in Albania. In Greece Byron began *Childe Harolde's Pilgrimage*, which he continued in Athens. Byron's sojourn in Greece made a lasting impression on him. The Greeks' free and open frankness contrasted strongly with English reserve and hypocrisy and served to broaden his views of men and manners.

Byron arrived back in London in July 1811, and his mother died before he could reach her at Newstead. In

February 1812 he made his first speech in the House of Lords, a humanitarian plea opposing harsh Tory measures against riotous Nottingham weavers. At the beginning of March, the first two cantos of *Childe Harold's Pilgrimage* were published by John Murray, and Byron "woke to find himself famous." Besides furnishing a travelogue of Byron's own wanderings through the Mediterranean, the first two cantos express the melancholy and disillusionment felt by a generation weary of the wars of the post-Revolutionary and Napoleonic eras. In the poem Byron reflects upon the vanity of ambition, the transitory nature of pleasure, and the futility of the search for perfection in the course of a "pilgrimage" through Portugal, Spain, Albania, and Greece. In the wake of *Childe Harold*'s enormous popularity, Byron was lionized in Whig society.

During the summer of 1813, Byron apparently entered into intimate relations with his half sister Augusta, now married to Colonel George Leigh. He then carried on a flirtation with Lady Frances Webster as a diversion from this dangerous liaison. The agitations of these two love affairs and the sense of mingled guilt and exultation they aroused in Byron are reflected in the series of gloomy and remorseful Asian verse tales he wrote at this time: *The Giaour* (1813); *The Bride of Abydos* (1813); *The Corsair* (1814), which sold 10,000 copies on the day of publication; and *Lara* (1814).

Seeking to escape his love affairs in marriage, Byron proposed in September 1814 to Anne Isabella (Annabella) Milbanke. The marriage took place in January 1815, and Lady Byron gave birth to a daughter, Augusta Ada, in December 1815. From the start the marriage was doomed by the gulf between Byron and his unimaginative and humorless wife; and in January 1816 Annabella left Byron to live with her parents, amid swirling rumours centring on his relations with Augusta Leigh and his bisexuality.

The couple obtained a legal separation. Wounded by the general moral indignation directed at him, Byron went abroad in April 1816, never to return to England.

Byron sailed up the Rhine River into Switzerland and settled at Geneva, near Percy Bysshe Shelley and Mary Godwin, who had eloped, and Godwin's stepdaughter by a second marriage, Claire Clairmont, with whom Byron had begun an affair in England. In Geneva he wrote the third canto of *Childe Harold* (1816), which follows Harold from Belgium up the Rhine River to Switzerland. A visit to the Bernese Oberland provided the scenery for the Faustian poetic drama *Manfred* (1817), whose protagonist reflects Byron's own brooding sense of guilt and the wider frustrations of the Romantic spirit doomed by the reflection that man is "half dust, half deity, alike unfit to sink or soar."

At the end of the summer the Shelley party left for England, where Claire gave birth to Byron's illegitimate daughter Allegra in January 1817. In October Byron and Hobhouse departed for Italy. They stopped in Venice, where Byron enjoyed the relaxed customs and morals of the Italians and carried on a love affair with Marianna Segati, his landlord's wife. In May he joined Hobhouse in Rome, gathering impressions that he recorded in a fourth canto of *Childe Harold* (1818). He also wrote *Beppo*, a poem in ottava rima that satirically contrasts Italian with English manners in the story of a Venetian menage-à-trois. Back in Venice, Margarita Cogni, a baker's wife, replaced Segati as his mistress, and his descriptions of the vagaries of this "gentle tigress" are among the most entertaining passages in his letters describing life in Italy. The sale of Newstead Abbey in the autumn of 1818 for £94,500 cleared Byron of his debts, which had risen to £34,000, and left him with a generous income.

In the light, mock-heroic style of *Beppo* Byron found the form in which he would write his greatest poem, *Don Juan*, a satire in the form of a picaresque verse tale. The first two cantos of *Don Juan* were begun in 1818 and published in July 1819. Byron transformed the legendary libertine Don Juan into an unsophisticated, innocent young man who, though he delightedly succumbs to the beautiful women who pursue him, remains a rational norm against which to view the absurdities and irrationalities of the world. Upon being sent abroad by his mother from his native Sevilla (Seville), Juan survives a shipwreck en route and is cast up on a Greek island, whence he is sold into slavery in Constantinople. He escapes to the Russian army, participates gallantly in the Russians' siege of Ismail, and is sent to St. Petersburg, where he wins the favour of the empress Catherine the Great and is sent by her on a diplomatic mission to England. The poem's story, however, remains merely a peg on which Byron could hang a witty and satirical social commentary. His most consistent targets are, first, the hypocrisy and cant underlying various social and sexual conventions, and, second, the vain ambitions and pretenses of poets, lovers, generals, rulers, and humanity in general. *Don Juan* remains unfinished; Byron completed 16 cantos and had begun the 17th before his own illness and death. In *Don Juan* he was able to free himself from the excessive melancholy of *Childe Harold* and reveal other sides of his character and personality—his satiric wit and his unique view of the comic rather than the tragic discrepancy between reality and appearance.

## Later Years

Shelley and other visitors in 1818 found Byron grown fat, with hair long and turning gray, looking older than his years, and sunk in sexual promiscuity. But a chance meeting with Countess Teresa Gamba Guiccioli, who was only 19 years old and married to a man nearly three times her age, reenergized Byron and changed the course of his life. Byron followed her to Ravenna, and she later accompanied him back to Venice. Byron returned to Ravenna in January 1820 as Teresa's *cavalier servente* (gentleman-in-waiting) and won the friendship of her father and brother, Counts Ruggero and Pietro Gamba, who initiated him into the secret society of the Carbonari and its revolutionary aims to free Italy from Austrian rule. In Ravenna Byron wrote *The Prophecy of Dante*; cantos III, IV, and V of *Don Juan*; the poetic dramas *Marino Faliero*, *Sardanapalus*, *The Two Foscari*, and *Cain* (all published in 1821); and a satire on the poet Robert Southey, *The Vision of Judgment*, which contains a devastating parody of that poet laureate's fulsome eulogy of King George III.

Byron arrived in Pisa in November 1821, having followed Teresa and the Counts Gamba there after the latter had been expelled from Ravenna for taking part in an abortive uprising. He left his daughter Allegra, who had been sent to him by her mother, to be educated in a convent near Ravenna, where she died the following April. In Pisa Byron again became associated with Shelley, and in early summer of 1822 Byron went to Leghorn (Livorno), where he rented a villa not far from the sea. There in July the poet and essayist Leigh Hunt arrived from England to help Shelley and Byron edit a radical journal, *The Liberal*. Byron returned to Pisa and housed Hunt and his family in his villa. Despite the drowning of Shelley on July 8, the periodical went forward, and its first number contained *The Vision of Judgment*. At the end of September Byron moved to Genoa, where Teresa's family had found asylum.

Byron's interest in the periodical gradually waned, but he continued to support Hunt and to give manuscripts to *The Liberal*. After a quarrel with his publisher, John Murray,

Byron gave all his later work, including cantos VI to XVI of *Don Juan* (1823–24), to Leigh Hunt's brother John, publisher of *The Liberal*.

By this time Byron was in search of new adventure. In April 1823 he agreed to act as agent of the London Committee, which had been formed to aid the Greeks in their struggle for independence from the Turks. In July 1823 Byron left Genoa for Cephalonia. He sent £4,000 of his own money to prepare the Greek fleet for sea service and then sailed for Missolonghi on December 29 to join Prince Aléxandros Mavrokordátos, leader of the forces in western Greece.

Byron made efforts to unite the various Greek factions and took personal command of a brigade of Souliot soldiers, reputedly the bravest of the Greeks. But a serious illness in February 1824 weakened him, and in April he contracted the fever from which he died at Missolonghi on April 19. Deeply mourned, he became a symbol of disinterested patriotism and a Greek national hero. His body was brought back to England and, refused burial in Westminster Abbey, was placed in the family vault near Newstead. Ironically, 145 years after his death, a memorial to Byron was finally placed on the floor of the Abbey.

# JAMES FENIMORE COOPER

(b. September 15, 1789, Burlington, New Jersey, U.S.—d. September 14, 1851, Cooperstown, New York)

The first major American novelist, James Fenimore Cooper is the author of the novels of frontier adventure known as the Leatherstocking Tales, featuring the wilderness scout called Natty Bumppo, or Hawkeye. They include *The Pioneers* (1823), *The Last of the Mohicans* (1826), *The Prairie* (1827), *The Pathfinder* (1840), and *The Deerslayer* (1841).

## Early Years

Cooper's mother, Elizabeth Fenimore, was a member of a respectable New Jersey Quaker family, and his father, William, founded a frontier settlement at the source of the Susquehanna River (now Cooperstown, New York) and served as a Federalist congressman during the administrations of George Washington and John Adams. It was a most appropriate family background for a writer who, by the time of his death, was generally considered America's "national novelist."

James was but a year old when William Cooper moved his family to the primitive settlement in upstate New York. He was doubtless fortunate to be the 11th of 12 children, for he was spared the worst hardships of frontier life while he was able to benefit educationally from both the rich oral traditions of his family and a material prosperity that afforded him a gentleman's education. After private schooling in Albany, Cooper attended Yale from 1803 to 1805. Little is known of his college career other than that he was the best Latin scholar of his class and was expelled in his junior year because of a prank. Since high spirits seemed to fit him for an active life, his family allowed him to join the navy as a midshipman. But prolonged shore duty at several New York stations merely substituted naval for academic discipline. His father's death in 1809 left him financially independent, and in 1811 he married Susan De Lancy and resigned from the navy.

For 10 years after his marriage Cooper led the active but unproductive life of a dilettante, dabbling in agriculture, politics, the American Bible Society, and the Westchester militia. It was in this amateur spirit that he wrote and published his first fiction, reputedly on a challenge from his wife. *Precaution* (1820) was a plodding imitation of Jane Austen's novels of English gentry manners. It is mainly interesting today as a document in the history of American cultural colonialism and as an example of a clumsy attempt to imitate Jane Austen's investigation of the ironic discrepancy between illusion and reality. His second novel, *The Spy* (1821), was based on another British model, Sir Walter Scott's "Waverley" novels, stories of adventure and romance set in 17th- and 18th-century Scotland. But in *The Spy* Cooper broke new ground by using an American Revolutionary War setting (based partly on the experiences of his wife's British loyalist family) and by introducing several distinctively American character types. Like Scott's novels of Scotland, *The Spy* is a drama of conflicting loyalties and interests in which the action mirrors and expresses more subtle internal psychological tensions. *The Spy* soon brought him international fame and a certain amount of wealth. The latter was very welcome, indeed necessary, since his father's estate had proved less ample than had been thought, and, with the death of his elder brothers, he had found himself responsible for the debts and widows of the entire Cooper family.

## Novels

The first of the renowned Leatherstocking Tales, *The Pioneers* (1823), followed and adhered to the successful formula of *The Spy*, reproducing its basic thematic conflicts and utilizing family traditions once again. In *The Pioneers*, however, the traditions were those of William Cooper of Cooperstown, who appears as Judge Temple of Templeton, along with many other lightly disguised inhabitants of

James's boyhood village. No known prototype exists, however, for the novel's principal character—the former wilderness scout Natty Bumppo, alias Leatherstocking. The Leatherstocking of *The Pioneers* is an aged man, of rough but sterling character, who ineffectually opposes "the march of progress," namely, the agricultural frontier and its chief spokesman, Judge Temple. Fundamentally, the conflict is between rival versions of the American Eden: the "God's Wilderness" of Leatherstocking and the cultivated garden of Judge Temple. Since Cooper himself was deeply attracted to both ideals, he was able to create a powerful and moving story of frontier life. Indeed, *The Pioneers* is both the first and finest detailed portrait of frontier life in American literature; it is also the first truly original American novel.

Both Cooper and his public were fascinated by the Leatherstocking character. He was encouraged to write a series of sequels in which the entire life of the frontier scout was gradually unfolded. *The Last of the Mohicans* (1826) takes the reader back to the French and Indian wars of Natty's middle age, when he is at the height of his powers. That work was succeeded by *The Prairie* (1827) in which, now very old and philosophical, Leatherstocking dies, facing the westering sun he has so long followed. (The five novels of the series were not written in their narrative order.) Identified from the start with the vanishing wilderness and its natives, Leatherstocking was an unalterably elegiac figure, wifeless and childless, hauntingly loyal to a lost cause. This conception of the character was not fully realized in *The Pioneers*, however, because Cooper's main concern with depicting frontier life led him to endow Leatherstocking with some comic traits and make his laments, at times, little more than whines or grumbles. But in these sequels Cooper retreated stylistically from a realistic picture of the frontier in order to portray a more idyllic and romantic wilderness; by doing so he could exploit the parallels between the American Indians and the forlorn Celtic heroes of James Macpherson's pseudo-epic *Ossian*, leaving Leatherstocking intact but slightly idealized and making extensive use of Macpherson's imagery and rhetoric.

Cooper intended to bury Leatherstocking in *The Prairie*, but many years later he resuscitated the character and portrayed his early maturity in *The Pathfinder* (1840) and his youth in *The Deerslayer* (1841). These novels, in which Natty becomes the centre of romantic interest for the first time, carry the idealization process further. In *The Pathfinder* he is explicitly described as an American Adam, while in *The Deerslayer* he demonstrates his fitness as a warrior-saint by passing a series of moral trials and revealing a keen, though untutored, aesthetic sensibility.

The "Leatherstocking" tales are Cooper's great imperfect masterpiece, but he continued to write many other volumes of fiction and nonfiction. His fourth novel, *The Pilot* (1823), inaugurated a series of sea novels, which were at once as popular and influential as the "Leatherstocking" tales. And they were more authentic: such Westerners as General Lewis Cass, governor of Michigan Territory, and Mark Twain might ridicule Cooper's woodcraft, but old salts like Herman Melville and Joseph Conrad rightly admired and learned from his sea stories, in particular *The Red Rover* (1827) and *The Sea Lions* (1849). Never before in prose fiction had the sea become not merely a theatre for, but the principal actor in, moral drama that celebrated man's courage and skill at the same time that it revealed him humbled by the forces of God's nature. As developed by Cooper, and later by Melville, the sea novel became a powerful vehicle for spiritual as well as moral exploration. Not satisfied with mere fictional treatment of life at sea, Cooper also wrote a meticulously researched, highly readable *History of the Navy of the United States of America* (1839).

## Cultural and Political Involvement

Though most renowned as a prolific novelist, he did not simply retire to his study after the success of *The Spy*. Between 1822 and 1826 he lived in New York City and participated in its intellectual life, founding the Bread and Cheese Club, which included such members as the poets Fitz-Greene Halleck and William Cullen Bryant, the painter and inventor Samuel F.B. Morse, and the great Federalist judge James Kent. Like Cooper himself, these were men active in both cultural and political affairs.

Cooper's own increasing liberalism was confirmed by a lengthy stay (1826–33) in Europe, where he moved for the education of his son and four daughters. Those years coincided with a period of revolutionary ferment in Europe, and, because of a close friendship that he developed with the old American Revolutionary War hero Lafayette, he was kept well-informed about Europe's political developments. Through his novels, most notably *The Bravo* (1831), and other more openly polemical writings, he attacked the corruption and tyranny of oligarchical regimes in Europe. His active championship of the principles of political democracy (though never of social egalitarianism) coincided with a steep decline in his literary popularity in America, which he attributed to a decline in democratic feeling among the reading—i.e. the propertied—classes to which he himself belonged.

## *Return to America*

When he returned to America, he settled first in New York City and then for the remainder of his life in Cooperstown. In the gentlemanly tradition of Jefferson and Lafayette he attacked the oligarchical party of his day, in this case the Whig Party, which opposed President Andrew Jackson, the exponent of a more egalitarian form of democracy. The Whigs, however, were soon able to turn the tables on Cooper and other leading Jacksonians by employing Jackson's egalitarian rhetoric against them. Squire Cooper had made himself especially vulnerable to popular feeling when, in 1837, he refused to let local citizens picnic on a family property known as Three Mile Point. This incident led to a whole series of charges of libel, and suits and countersuits by both the Whigs and Cooper. At this time, too, agrarian riots on the estates of his old New York friends shattered his simple Jeffersonian faith in the virtue of the American farmer. All of this conflict and unrest was hard to bear, and harder still because he was writing more and earning less as the years went by. The public, which had reveled in his early forest and sea romances, was not interested in his acute political treatise, *The American Democrat* (1838), or even in such political satires as *The Monikins* (1835) or *Home As Found* (1838). And though he wrote some of his best romances—particularly the later "Leatherstocking" tales and *Satanstoe* (1845)—during the last decade of his life, profits from publishing so diminished that he gained little benefit from improved popularity. Though his circumstances were never straitened, he had to go on writing; and some of the later novels, such as *Mercedes of Castile* (1840) or *Jack Tier* (1846–48), were mere hackwork. His buoyant political optimism had largely given way to calm Christian faith, though he never lost his troubled concern for the well-being of his country.

# ALPHONSE DE LAMARTINE

(b. October 21, 1790, Mâcon, France—d. February 28, 1869, Paris)

Alphonse de Lamartine was a French poet and statesman whose lyrics in *Méditations poétiques* (1820) established him as one of the key figures in the Romantic movement in French literature.

Alphonse's father, an aristocrat, was imprisoned during the culminating phase of the French Revolution known as the Reign of Terror but was fortunate enough to escape the guillotine. Alphonse was educated at the college at Belley, which was maintained by the Jesuits though they were suppressed in France at this time.

Lamartine had wanted to enter the army or the diplomatic corps, but because France was ruled by Napoleon, whom his faithful royalist parents regarded as the usurper, they would not allow him to serve. Thus he remained idle until the Bourbon monarchy was restored in 1814, when he served in Louis XVIII's bodyguard. The following year, however, Napoleon returned from exile and attempted to rebuild his empire during the Hundred Days. Lamartine emigrated to Switzerland. After Napoleon's defeat at Waterloo and the Second Bourbon Restoration, he abandoned the military profession.

Attracted to literature, he wrote some tragedies in verse and a few elegies. By this time his health was not good, and he left for the spa of Aix-les-Bains, where, in October of 1816, on the shore of Lake Bourget, he met the brilliant but desperately ill Julie Charles. Early in 1812 Lamartine had fallen deeply in love with a young working girl named Antoniella. In 1815 he had learned of her death, and later he was to recast her as Graziella in his prose "anecdote" of that name. He now became passionately attached to Charles, who, because of her vast connections in Paris, was able to help him find a position. After her death in December 1817, Lamartine, who had already dedicated many strophes to her (notably "Le Lac"), devoted new verses to her memory (particularly "Le Crucifix").

In 1820 Lamartine married Maria Ann Birch, a young Englishwoman connected by marriage to the Churchills. The same year he published his first collection of poetry, *Méditations poétiques*, and finally joined the diplomatic corps, as secretary to the French embassy at Naples. *Méditations* was immensely successful because of its new romantic tone and sincerity of feeling. It brought to French poetry a new music; the themes were at the same time intimate and religious. If the vocabulary remained that of the somewhat faded rhetoric of the preceding century, the resonance of the sentences, the power of the rhythm, and the passion for life sharply contrasted with the often-withered poetry of the 18th century. The book was so successful that Lamartine attempted to extend it two years later with his *Nouvelles méditations poétiques* and his *Mort de Socrates*, in which his preoccupation with metaphysics first became evident. *Le Dernier Chant du pèlerinage d'Harold,* published in 1825, revealed the charm that the English poet Lord Byron exerted over him. Lamartine was elected to the French Academy in 1829, and the following year he published the two volumes of *Harmonies poétiques et religieuses*, a sort of alleluia, filled with deist—and even occasionally Christian ("L'Hymne au Christ")—enthusiasm.

That same year (1830), when Louis-Philippe acceded to the throne as constitutional monarch after the July Revolution, Lamartine abandoned his diplomatic career to enter politics. He refused to commit himself to the July Monarchy, however, and, preserving his independence, he set out to draw attention to social problems. After two unsuccessful attempts he was elected deputy in 1833. Yet he still wanted to write a poem, *Les Visions*, that he had been thinking about since 1821 and that he had conceived of as an "epic of the soul." The symbolic theme was that of a fallen angel cast out of heaven for having chosen the love of a woman and condemned to successive reincarnations until the day on which he realized that he "preferred God." Lamartine wrote the last fragment of this immense adventure first, and it appeared in 1836 as *Jocelyn*. It is the story of a young man who intended to take up the religious life but, instead, when cast out of the seminary by the Revolution, falls in love with a young girl; recalled to the order by his dying bishop, he renounces his love and becomes a "man of God," a parish priest, consecrating his life to the service of his fellow men. In 1838 Lamartine published the first fragment of this vast metaphysical poem under the appropriate title *La Chute d'un ange* ("The Fall of an Angel"). In 1832–33 he travelled to Lebanon, Syria, and the Holy Land. He had by then definitively lost the Catholic faith he had tried to recover in 1820; a further blow was the death in Beirut, on December 7, 1832, of his only remaining child, Julia. A son born in Rome in 1821 had not survived infancy.

After a collection published in 1839 under the title *Recueillements poétiques* ("Poetic Meditations"), Lamartine interrupted his literary endeavours to become more active as a politician. He was convinced that the social question, which he himself called "the question of the proletariat," was the principal issue of his time; he deplored the inhumanity of the worker's plight; he denounced the trusts and their dominant influence on governmental politics, directing against them two discourses, one in 1838, another in 1846; he held that a working-class revolution was inevitable and did not hesitate to hasten the hour, promising the authorities, in July 1847, a "revolution of scorn." In the same year he published his *Histoire des Girondins*, a history of the right, or moderate, Girondin Party during and after the French Revolution, which earned him immense popularity with the left-wing parties.

After the revolution of February 24, 1848, the Second Republic was proclaimed in Paris, and Lamartine became, in effect, head of the provisional government. The propertied classes, who were at first startled, pretended to accept the new circumstances, but they were unable to tolerate the fact that the working class possessed arms with which to defend themselves. In April 1848 Lamartine was elected to the National Assembly by 10 *départements*. The bourgeoisie, represented by the right-wing parties, thought they had elected in Lamartine a clever manipulator who could placate the proletariat, while military forces capable of establishing order, such as they conceived of it, were being reconstituted. The bourgeoisie was enraged to discover, however, that Lamartine was, indeed, as he had proclaimed himself to be, the spokesman of the working class. On June 24, 1848, he was thrown out of office and the revolt crushed.

A broken man, Lamartine entered the "twilight" of his life. He was 60 years old in 1850, and his debts were enormous, not because he had been personally extravagant but because of the allowances he gave his sisters to compensate for the total property inheritance he had received as the only male in the Lamartine family. For 20 years he struggled desperately, though in vain, against bankruptcy, publishing book after book: *Raphaël*, a transposed account of his love for Julie Charles; *Les Confidences* and *Nouvelles Confidences*, wherein he intermingled real and imaginary elements (*Graziella* is a fragment of it); novels: *Geneviève* (1851), *Antoniella, Mémoires politiques* (1863), the last work being of great historical interest; a periodical titled *Cours familiers de littérature* (1856–1868/69), in which he published such poems as "La Vigne et la maison" and "Le Désert"; some historical works that remained unequaled, including *Histoire des Constituants* (1854), *Histoire de la Restauration* (1851–52), *Histoire de la Russie, Histoire de la Turquie*. He died nearly forgotten by his contemporaries.

# FRANZ GRILLPARZER

(b. January 15, 1791, Vienna [Austria]—d. January 21, 1872, Vienna)

The Austrian dramatist Franz Grillparzer wrote tragedies that were belatedly recognized as the greatest works of the Austrian stage.

Grillparzer's father was a lawyer who died in debt in 1809; his markedly neurotic mother committed suicide 10 years later. Grillparzer studied law at the University of Vienna and spent much of his life in government service. Beginning in 1814 as a clerk in the department of revenue, he became a clerk in the treasury (1818) and later director of the treasury archives. His hopes for a higher position were never fulfilled, however, and he retired from government service in 1856.

In 1817 the first performance of Grillparzer's tragedy *Die Ahnfrau* (*The Ancestress*) evoked public interest. Previously he had written a play in blank verse, *Blanka von Castilien* (*Blanche of Castile*), that already embodied the principal idea of several later works—the contrast between a quiet, idyllic existence and a life of action. *Die Ahnfrau*, written in the trochaic Spanish verse form, has many of the outward features of the then-popular "fate tragedy" (*Schicksalsdrama*), but the characters are themselves ultimately responsible for their own destruction. A striking advance was the swiftly written tragedy *Sappho* (1818).

Here the tragic fate of Sappho, who is depicted as hetero-sexual, is attributed to her unhappy love for an ordinary man and to her inability to reconcile life and art, clearly an enduring problem for Grillparzer. Work on the trilogy *Das Goldene Vlies* (1821; *The Golden Fleece*) was interrupted by the suicide of Grillparzer's mother and by illness. This drama, with Medea's assertion that life is not worth living, is the most pessimistic of his works and offers human-ity little hope. Once more the conflict between a life of meditation and one of action seems to lead inevitably to renunciation or despair.

More satisfying, both aesthetically and emotionally, is the historical tragedy *König Ottokars Glück und Ende* (written 1823, but because of censorship difficulties not performed or published until 1825; *King Ottocar, His Rise and Fall*). Here the action is drawn from Austrian his-tory, and the rise of Rudolph of Habsburg (the first of Grillparzer's characters to avoid guilt and tragedy) is con-trasted with the fall of the tyrant Ottokar of Bohemia, so that Ottokar's fate is not presented as representative of all humanity. Grillparzer was disappointed at the reception given to this and a following play and became discour-aged by the objections of the censor. Although he loved Katharina Fröhlich (1800–79), whom he had met in the winter of 1820–21, he felt unable to marry, possibly because of a conviction that as an artist he had no right to per-sonal happiness. His misery during these years is reflected not only in his diaries but also in the impressive cycle of poems entitled *Tristia ex Ponto* (1835).

*Des Meeres und der Liebe Wellen* (1831; *The Waves of Sea and Love*), often judged to be Grillparzer's greatest trag-edy because of the degree of harmony achieved between content and form, marks a return to the classical theme in treating the story of Hero and Leander, which is, however, interpreted with a psychological insight anticipating the plays of Ibsen. Hero, the priestess, who lacks a true sense of vocation, forgets her vows in her blind passion for Leander and, when her lover is ensnared to his death, she dies of a broken heart. The following of vital instincts is shown to rob the individual of inner harmony and self-possession. *Der Traum ein Leben* (1834; *A Dream Is Life*) owes much to Grillparzer's intensive and prolonged studies of Spanish drama. This Austrian *Faust* ends happily, for the ambitious young peasant Rustan only dreams the adventures that involve him in crime and awakes to a realization of the vanity of earthly aspirations. Grillparzer's only comedy, *Weh dem, der lügt!* (1838; "Woe to Him Who Lies!"), was a failure with the public, chiefly because the theme — the hero succeeds because he tells the truth when everyone thinks he is lying — was too subtle and too serious for comic treatment.

Grillparzer wrote no more for the stage and very little at all after the 1840s. The honours that were heaped on him in old age came too late. In 1861 he was elected to Vienna's upper legislative house (Herrenhaus), his 80th birthday was the occasion for a national celebration, and his death in Vienna in 1872 was widely mourned. Three tragedies, apparently complete, were found among his papers. *Die Jüdin von Toledo* (*The Jewess of Toledo*), based on a Spanish theme, portrays the tragic infatuation of a king for a young Jewish woman. He is only brought back to a sense of his responsibilities after she has been killed at the queen's command. *Ein Bruderzwist in Habsburg* (*Family Strife in Hapsburg*), a profound and moving historical tragedy, lacks the theatrical action that would make it successful in performance and is chiefly remarkable for the portrayal of the emperor Rudolph II. Much of Grillparzer's most mature thought forms the basis of the third play, *Libussa*, in which he foresees human development beyond the rationalist stage of civilization.

Apart from his critical studies on Spanish drama and a posthumous autobiography, Grillparzer's finest prose work is *Der arme Spielmann* (1848), the story of a poor musician who cheerfully accepts life's failures and dies through his efforts to help others.

Grillparzer's work looks back to the great Classical and Romantic achievements and the painful evolution from the disillusionment of idealism to a compromise with reality. Grillparzer was unusually gifted not only as a dramatic poet but also as a playwright capable of creating dramas suitable for performance. Unlike his great predecessors, Goethe and Schiller, he distinguishes between the speech of the cultured person and that of the uneducated. He also introduces colloquialisms, humour, and elements from the popular farce. Although the central dramatic conflict of Grillparzer's plays is often rooted in his personal problems, it is presented objectively. Grillparzer's solution is renunciation rather than acceptance. He undoubtedly suffered from the censorship and repression imposed by the Metternich regime, but it is probable that his unhappiness originated principally in an inability to resolve his own difficulties of character.

# PERCY BYSSHE SHELLEY

(b. August 4, 1792, Field Place, near Horsham, Sussex, England—d. July 8, 1822, at sea off Livorno, Tuscany [Italy])

Percy Bysshe Shelley was an English Romantic poet whose passionate search for personal love and social justice was gradually channeled from overt actions into poems that rank with the greatest in the English language.

Shelley was the heir to rich estates acquired by his grandfather, Bysshe (pronounced "Bish") Shelley. Timothy

Shelley, the poet's father, was a weak, conventional man who was caught between an overbearing father and a rebellious son. The young Shelley was educated at Syon House Academy (1802–04) and then at Eton (1804–10), where he resisted physical and mental bullying by indulging in imaginative escapism and literary pranks. Between the spring of 1810 and that of 1811, he published two Gothic novels and two volumes of juvenile verse. In the fall of 1810 Shelley entered University College, Oxford, where he enlisted his fellow student Thomas Jefferson Hogg as a disciple. But in March 1811, University College expelled both Shelley and Hogg for refusing to admit Shelley's authorship of *The Necessity of Atheism*. Hogg submitted to his family, but Shelley refused to apologize to his.

Late in August 1811, Shelley eloped with Harriet Westbrook, the younger daughter of a London tavern owner; by marrying her, he betrayed the acquisitive plans of his grandfather and father, who tried to starve him into submission but only drove the strong-willed youth to rebel against the established order. Early in 1812, Shelley, Harriet, and her older sister Eliza Westbrook went to Dublin, where Shelley circulated pamphlets advocating political rights for Roman Catholics, autonomy for Ireland, and freethinking ideals. The couple traveled to Lynmouth, Devon, where Shelley issued more political pamphlets, and then to North Wales, where they spent almost six months in 1812–13.

Lack of money finally drove Shelley to moneylenders in London, where in 1813 he issued *Queen Mab*, his first major poem—a nine-canto mixture of blank verse and lyric measures that attacks the evils of the past and present (commerce, war, the eating of meat, the church, monarchy, and marriage) but ends with resplendent hopes for humanity when freed from these vices. In June 1813 Harriet Shelley gave birth to their daughter Ianthe, but a year later Shelley fell in love with Mary Wollstonecraft Godwin, daughter of William Godwin and his first wife, *née* Mary Wollstonecraft. Against Godwin's objections, Shelley and Mary Godwin eloped to France on July 27, 1814, taking with them Mary's stepsister Jane (later "Claire") Clairmont. Following travels through France, Switzerland, and Germany, they returned to London, where they were shunned by the Godwins and most other friends. Shelley dodged creditors until the birth of his son Charles (born to Harriet, November 30, 1814), his grandfather's death (January 1815), and provisions of Sir Bysshe's will forced Sir Timothy to pay Shelley's debts and grant him an annual income.

Settling near Windsor Great Park in 1815, Shelley read the classics with Hogg and another friend, Thomas Love Peacock. He also wrote *Alastor; or The Spirit of Solitude*, a blank-verse poem, published with shorter poems in 1816, that warns idealists (like Shelley himself) not to abandon "sweet human love" and social improvement for the vain pursuit of evanescent dreams. By mid-May 1816, Shelley, Mary, and Claire Clairmont hurried to Geneva to intercept Lord Byron, with whom Claire had begun an affair. During this memorable summer, Shelley composed the poems "Hymn to Intellectual Beauty" and "Mont Blanc," and Mary began her novel *Frankenstein*. Shelley's party returned to England in September, settling in Bath. Late in the year, Harriet Shelley drowned herself in London, and on December 30, 1816, Shelley and Mary were married with the Godwins' blessing. But a Chancery Court decision declared Shelley unfit to raise Ianthe and Charles (his children by Harriet), who were placed in foster care at his expense.

In March 1817 the Shelleys settled near Peacock at Marlow, where Shelley wrote his twelve-canto romance-epic *Laon and Cythna; or, The Revolution of the Golden City* and Mary Shelley finished *Frankenstein*. They compiled *History of a Six Weeks' Tour* jointly from the letters and journals of their trips to Switzerland, concluding with "Mont Blanc." In November, *Laon and Cythna* was suppressed by its printer and publisher, who feared that Shelley's idealized tale of a peaceful national revolution, bloodily suppressed by a league of king and priests, violated the laws against blasphemous libel. After revisions, it was reissued in 1818 as *The Revolt of Islam*.

Because Shelley's health suffered from the climate and his financial obligations outran his resources, the Shelleys and Claire Clairmont went to Italy, where Byron was residing. They reached Milan in April 1818 and proceeded to Pisa and Leghorn (Livorno). That summer, at Bagni di Lucca, Shelley translated Plato's *Symposium* and wrote his own essay "On Love." He also completed a modest poem entitled *Rosalind and Helen*, in which he imagines his destiny in the poet-reformer "Lionel," who—imprisoned for radical activity—dies young after his release.

Thus far, Shelley's literary career had been politically oriented. *Queen Mab*, the early poems first published in 1964 as *The Esdaile Notebook*, *Laon and Cythna*, and most of his prose works were devoted to reforming society; and even *Alastor, Rosalind and Helen*, and the personal lyrics voiced the concerns of an idealistic reformer who is disappointed or persecuted by an unreceptive society. But in Italy, far from the daily irritations of British politics, Shelley deepened his understanding of art and literature and, unable to reshape the world to conform to his vision, he concentrated on embodying his ideals within his poems. His aim became, as he wrote in "Ode to the West Wind," to make his words "Ashes and sparks" as from "an unextinguished hearth," thereby transforming subsequent generations and, through them, the world.

In August 1818, Shelley and Byron again met in Venice; the Shelleys remained there or at Este through October 1818. During their stay, little Clara Shelley (b. 1817) became ill and died. In "Lines Written Among the Euganean Hills" (published with *Rosalind and Helen*), Shelley writes how visions arising from the beautiful landscape seen from a hill near Este had revived him from despair to hopes for the political regeneration of Italy, thus transforming the scene into "a green isle.../ In the deep wide sea of Misery." He also began *Julian and Maddalo*—in which Byron ("Maddalo") and Shelley debate human nature and destiny—and drafted Act I of *Prometheus Unbound*. In November 1818 the Shelleys traveled through Rome to Naples, where they remained until the end of February 1819.

Settling next at Rome, Shelley continued *Prometheus Unbound* and outlined *The Cenci*, a tragedy on the Elizabethan model based on a case of incestuous rape and patricide in sixteenth-century Rome. He completed this drama during the summer of 1819 near Leghorn, where the Shelleys fled in June after their other child, William Shelley (b. 1816), died from malaria. Memorable characters, classic five-act structure, powerful and evocative language, and moral ambiguities still make *The Cenci* theatrically effective. Even so, it is a less notable achievement than *Prometheus Unbound: A Lyrical Drama*, which Shelley completed at Florence in the autumn of 1819, near the birth of Percy Florence Shelley, Mary Shelley's only surviving child. Both plays appeared about 1820.

In *Prometheus* Shelley inverts the plot of a lost play by Aeschylus in a poetic masterpiece that combines supple blank verse with a variety of complex lyric measures. In Act I, Prometheus, tortured on Jupiter's orders for having given mankind the gift of moral freedom, recalls his earlier curse of Jupiter and forgives him ("I wish no living thing to suffer pain"). By eschewing revenge, Prometheus, who embodies the moral will, can be reunited with his beloved Asia, a spiritual ideal transcending humanity; her love prevents him from becoming another tyrant when Jupiter is overthrown by the mysterious power known as Demogorgon. Act II traces Asia's awakening and journey toward Prometheus, beginning with her descent into the depths of nature to confront and question Demogorgon. Act III depicts the overthrow of Jupiter and the union of Asia and Prometheus, who—leaving Jupiter's throne vacant—retreat to a cave from which they influence the world through ideals embodied in the creative arts. The end of the act describes the renovation of both human society and the natural world. Act IV opens with joyful lyrics by spirits who describe the benevolent transformation of the human consciousness that has occurred. Next, other spirits hymn the beatitude of humanity and nature in this new millennial age; and finally, Demogorgon returns to provide spells with which moral freedom can be restored, should the fragile state of grace be lost.

*Prometheus Unbound*, which was the keystone of Shelley's poetic achievement, was written after he had been chastened by "sad reality" but before he began to fear that he had failed to reach an audience. Published with it were some of the poet's finest and most hopeful shorter poems, including "Ode to Liberty," "Ode to the West Wind," "The Cloud," and "To a Sky-Lark."

While completing *Prometheus Unbound* and *The Cenci*, Shelley reacted to news of the Peterloo Massacre (August 1819) in England by writing *The Masque of Anarchy* and several radical songs that he hoped would rouse the British people to active but nonviolent political protest. Later in 1819 he sent to England *Peter Bell the Third*, which joins literary satire of William Wordsworth's *Peter Bell* to attacks on corruptions in British society, and he drafted

*A Philosophical View of Reform*, his longest (though incomplete) prose work, urging moderate reform to prevent a bloody revolution that might lead to new tyranny. Too radical to be published during Shelley's lifetime, *The Masque of Anarchy* appeared after the reformist elections of 1832, *Peter Bell the Third* and the political ballads in 1839–40, and *A Philosophical View of Reform* not until 1920.

After moving to Pisa in 1820, Shelley was stung by hostile reviews into expressing his hopes more guardedly. His "Letter to Maria Gisborne" in heroic couplets and "The Witch of Atlas" in ottava rima (both 1820; published 1824) combine the mythopoeic mode of *Prometheus Unbound* with the urbane self-irony that had emerged in *Peter Bell the Third*, showing Shelley's awareness that his ideals might seem naive to others. Late that year, *Oedipus Tyrannus; or, Swellfoot the Tyrant*, his satirical drama on the trial for adultery of Caroline (estranged wife of King George IV), appeared anonymously but was quickly suppressed. In 1821, however, Shelley reasserted his uncompromising idealism. *Epipsychidion* (in couplets) mythologizes his infatuation with Teresa ("Emilia") Viviani, a convent-bound young admirer, into a Dantesque fable of how human desire can be fulfilled through art. His essay *A Defence of Poetry* (published 1840) eloquently declares that the poet creates humane values and imagines the forms that shape the social order: thus each mind recreates its own private universe, and "Poets are the unacknowledged legislators of the World." *Adonais*, a pastoral elegy in Spenserian stanzas, commemorates the death of John Keats by declaring that, while we "decay/ Like corpses in a charnel," the creative spirit of Adonais, despite his physical death, "has outsoared the shadow of our night."

The verse drama *Hellas* (published 1822) celebrates the Greek revolution against Turkish rule and reiterates the political message of *Laon and Cythna* — that the struggle for human liberty can be neither totally defeated nor fully realized, since the ideal is greater than its earthly embodiments.

After Byron's arrival in Pisa late in 1821, Shelley, inhibited by his presence, completed only a series of urbane, yet longing lyrics—most addressed to Jane Williams—during the early months of 1822. After the Shelleys and Edward and Jane Williams moved to Lerici, Shelley began "The Triumph of Life," a dark fragment on which he was at work until he sailed to Leghorn to welcome his friend Leigh Hunt, who had arrived to edit a periodical called *The Liberal*. Shelley and Edward Williams drowned on July 8, 1822, when their boat sank during the stormy return voyage to Lerici.

# JOHN KEATS

(b. October 31, 1795, London, England—d. February 23, 1821, Rome, Papal States [Italy])

The English Romantic lyric poet John Keats devoted his short life to the perfection of a poetry marked by vivid imagery, great sensuous appeal, and an attempt to express a philosophy through classical legend.

## Youth

The son of a livery-stable manager, John Keats received relatively little formal education. His father died in 1804, and his mother remarried almost immediately. Throughout his life Keats had close emotional ties to his sister, Fanny, and his two brothers, George and Tom. After the breakup of their mother's second marriage, the

Keats children lived with their widowed grandmother at Edmonton, Middlesex. John attended a school at Enfield, two miles away, that was run by John Clarke, whose son Charles Cowden Clarke did much to encourage Keats's literary aspirations. At school Keats was noted as a pugnacious lad and was decidedly "not literary," but in 1809 he began to read voraciously. After the death of the Keats children's mother in 1810, their grandmother put the children's affairs into the hands of a guardian, Richard Abbey. At Abbey's instigation John Keats was apprenticed to a surgeon at Edmonton in 1811. He broke off his apprenticeship in 1814 and went to live in London, where he worked as a dresser, or junior house surgeon, at Guy's and St. Thomas' hospitals. His literary interests had crystallized by this time, and after 1817 he devoted himself entirely to poetry. From then until his early death, the story of his life is largely the story of the poetry he wrote.

## Early Works

Charles Cowden Clarke had introduced the young Keats to the poetry of Edmund Spenser and the Elizabethans, and these were his earliest models. His first mature poem is the sonnet *On First Looking Into Chapman's Homer* (1816), which was inspired by his excited reading of George Chapman's classic 17th-century translation of the *Iliad* and the *Odyssey*. Clarke also introduced Keats to the journalist and contemporary poet Leigh Hunt, and Keats made friends in Hunt's circle with the young poet John Hamilton Reynolds and with the painter Benjamin Haydon. Keats's first book, *Poems*, was published in March 1817 and was written largely under "Huntian" influence. This is evident in the relaxed and rambling sentiments evinced and in Keats's use of a loose form of the heroic couplet and light rhymes. The most interesting poem in this volume is *Sleep and Poetry*, the middle section of which contains a prophetic view of Keats's own poetical progress. He sees himself as, at present, plunged in the delighted contemplation of sensuous natural beauty but realizes that he must leave this for an understanding of "the agony and strife of human hearts."

In 1817 Keats left London briefly for a trip to the Isle of Wight and Canterbury and began work on *Endymion*, his first long poem. On his return to London he moved into lodgings in Hampstead with his brothers. *Endymion* appeared in 1818. This work is divided into four 1,000-line sections, and its verse is composed in loose rhymed couplets. The poem narrates a version of the Greek legend of the moon goddess Diana's (or Cynthia's) love for Endymion, a mortal shepherd, but Keats puts the emphasis on Endymion's love for Diana rather than on hers for him. Keats transformed the tale to express the widespread Romantic theme of the attempt to find in actuality an ideal love that has been glimpsed heretofore only in imaginative longings. The poem equates Endymion's original romantic ardour with a more universal quest for a self-destroying transcendence in which he might achieve a blissful personal unity with all creation. Keats, however, was dissatisfied with the poem as soon as it was finished.

## Personal Crisis

In the summer of 1818 Keats went on a walking tour in the Lake District (of northern England) and Scotland with his friend Charles Brown, and his exposure and overexertions on that trip brought on the first symptoms of the tuberculosis of which he was to die. On his return to London a brutal criticism of his early poems appeared in *Blackwood's Magazine*, followed by a similar

*Portraits of the Romantic poet John Keats and his fiancée, Fanny Brawne, on display in Keats's former London home, in 2009.* Peter Macdiarmid/Getty Images

attack on *Endymion* in the *Quarterly Review*. Contrary to later assertions, Keats met these reviews with a calm assertion of his own talents, and he went on steadily writing poetry.

But there were family troubles. Keats's brother Tom had been suffering from tuberculosis for some time, and in the autumn of 1818 the poet nursed him through his last illness. About the same time, he met Fanny Brawne, a near neighbour in Hampstead, with whom he soon fell hopelessly and tragically in love. After Tom's death (George had already gone to America), Keats moved into Wentworth Place with Brown; and in April 1819 Brawne and her mother became his next-door neighbours. About October 1819 Keats became engaged to Fanny.

# The Year 1819

Keats had written *Isabella,* an adaptation of the story of the *Pot of Basil* in Giovanni Boccaccio's *Decameron*, in 1817–18, soon after the completion of *Endymion*, and again he was dissatisfied with his work. It was during the year 1819 that all his greatest poetry was written—*Lamia, The Eve of St. Agnes*, the great odes (*On Indolence, On a Grecian Urn, To Psyche, To a Nightingale, On Melancholy*, and *To Autumn*), and the two versions of *Hyperion*. This poetry was composed under the strain of illness and his growing love for Brawne; and it is an astonishing body of work, marked by careful and considered development, technical, emotional, and intellectual. *Isabella*, which Keats himself called "a weak-sided poem," contains some of the emotional weaknesses of *Endymion*; but *The Eve of St. Agnes* may be considered the perfect culmination of Keats's earlier poetic style. Written in the first flush of his meeting with Brawne, it conveys an atmosphere of passion and excitement in its description of the elopement of a pair of youthful lovers. Written in Spenserian stanzas, the poem presents its theme with unrivaled delicacy but displays no marked intellectual advance over Keats's earlier efforts. *Lamia* is another narrative poem and is a deliberate attempt to reform some of the technical weaknesses of *Endymion*. Keats makes use in this poem of a far tighter and more disciplined couplet, a firmer tone, and more controlled description.

The odes are Keats's most distinctive poetic achievement. They are essentially lyrical meditations on some object or quality that prompts the poet to confront the conflicting impulses of his inner being and to reflect upon his own longings and their relations to the wider world around him. All the odes were composed between March and June 1819 except *To Autumn*, which is from September. The internal debates in the odes centre on the dichotomy of eternal, transcendent ideals and the transience and change of the physical world. This subject was forced upon Keats by the painful death of his brother and his own failing health, and the odes highlight his struggle for self-awareness and certainty through the liberating powers of his imagination. In the *Ode to a Nightingale* a visionary happiness in communing with the nightingale and its song is contrasted with the dead weight of human grief and sickness, and the transience of youth and beauty—strongly brought home to Keats in recent months by his brother's death. The song of the nightingale is seen as a symbol of art that outlasts the individual's mortal life. This theme is taken up more distinctly in the *Ode on a Grecian Urn*. The figures of the lovers depicted on the Greek urn become for him the symbol of an enduring but unconsummated passion that subtly belies the poem's celebrated conclusion, "Beauty is truth, truth beauty,—that is all ye know on earth, and all ye need to know." The *Ode on Melancholy* recognizes that sadness is the inevitable concomitant of human passion and happiness; the transience of joy and desire is an inevitable aspect of the natural process. But the rich, slow movement of this and the other odes suggests an enjoyment of such intensity and depth that it makes the moment eternal. *To Autumn* is essentially the record of such an experience. Autumn is seen not as a time of decay but as a season of complete ripeness and fulfillment, a pause in time when everything has reached fruition, and the question of transience is hardly raised. These poems, with their rich and exquisitely sensuous detail and their meditative depth, are among the greatest achievements of Romantic poetry. With them should be mentioned the ballad *La Belle Dame sans merci*, of about the same time, which reveals the obverse and destructive side of the idyllic love seen in *The Eve of St. Agnes*.

Keats's fragmentary poetic epic, *Hyperion*, exists in two versions, the second being a revision of the first with the addition of a long prologue in a new style, which makes it into a different poem. *Hyperion* was begun in the autumn of 1818, and all that there is of the first version was finished by April 1819. In September Keats wrote to Reynolds that he had given up *Hyperion*, but he appears to have continued working on the revised edition, *The Fall of Hyperion*, during the autumn of 1819. The two versions of *Hyperion* cover the period of Keats's most intense experience, both poetical and personal. The poem is his last attempt, in the face of increasing illness and frustrated love, to come to terms with the conflict between absolute value and mortal decay that appears in other forms in his earlier poetry. The epic's subject is the supersession of the earlier Greek gods, the Titans, by the later Olympian gods. Keats's desire to write something unlike the luxuriant wandering of *Endymion* is clear, and he thus consciously attempts to emulate the epic loftiness of John Milton's *Paradise Lost*. The poem opens with the Titans already fallen, like Milton's fallen angels, and Hyperion, the sun god, is their one hope of further resistance, like Milton's Satan. There are numerous Miltonisms of style, but these are subdued in the revised version, as Keats felt unhappy with them; and the basis of the writing is revealed after all as a more austere and disciplined version of Keats's own manner.

The second version of *Hyperion* is one of the most remarkable pieces of writing in Keats's work; the blank verse has a new energy and rapidity, and the vision is presented with a spare grandeur, rising to its height in the epiphany of the goddess Moneta, who reveals to the dreamer the function of the poet in the world. It is his duty to separate himself from the mere dreamer and to share in the sufferings of humankind. The theme is not new to Keats—it appears in his earliest poetry—but it is here realized far more intensely. Yet with the threat of approaching death upon him, Keats could not advance any further in the direction that he foresaw as the right one, and the poem remains a fragment.

## Last Years

There is no more to record of Keats's poetic career. The poems *Isabella*, *Lamia*, *The Eve of St. Agnes*, and *Hyperion* and the odes were all published in the famous 1820 volume, the one that gives the true measure of his powers. It appeared in July, by which time Keats was evidently doomed. He had been increasingly ill throughout 1819, and by the beginning of 1820 the evidence of tuberculosis was clear. His friends Brown, the Hunts, and Brawne and her mother nursed him assiduously through the year. When Keats was ordered south for the winter, Joseph Severn undertook to accompany him to Rome. They sailed in September 1820, and from Naples they went to Rome, where in early December Keats had a relapse. Faithfully tended by Severn to the last, he died in Rome.

# ALFRED-VICTOR, COUNT DE VIGNY

(b. March 27, 1797, Loches, France—d. September 17, 1863, Paris)

The poet, dramatist, and novelist Alfred-Victor, count de (count of) Vigny, was the most philosophical of the French Romantic writers.

Vigny was born into an aristocratic family that had been reduced to modest circumstances by the French Revolution. His father, a 60-year-old retired soldier at the time of his son's birth, was a veteran of the Seven

Years' War, and his maternal grandfather, the Marquis de Baraudin, had served as commodore in the royal navy. Vigny grew up in Paris and took preparatory studies for the École Polytechnique at the Lycée Bonaparte, where he conceived an "inordinate love for the glory of bearing arms," a passion common to the young men of his generation. Attached to the monarchy by family tradition, he became a second lieutenant in the king's guard when the Bourbons returned to power in 1814 and when he was only 17 years old.

## Romantic Works

Though he was promoted to first lieutenant in 1822 and to captain the following year, the military profession, limited to garrison duty rather than pursued on the battlefield, bored the young officer, who preferred the adventures of a literary career. After several leaves of absence, he abandoned military life in 1827. In the meantime, he had published his first poem, "Le Bal," in 1820. Two years later his first collection of verse was published as *Poèmes*, along with contributions to Victor Hugo's politically conservative literary periodical *La Muse Française*. Salons and reviews in Paris hailed the birth of a poet who combined grace with a strength and depth that was totally Romantic. Vigny's expanded version of *Poèmes* under the title *Poèmes antiques et modernes* (1826) was also a success.

Vigny, however, was not content to excel merely in poetry, and he revealed his narrative talent in *Cinq-Mars* (1826), a historical novel centred around the conspiracy of Louis XIII's favourite, the Marquis de Cinq-Mars, against the Cardinal de Richelieu. *Cinq-Mars* was the first important historical novel in French, and it derived much of its popularity at the time from the enormous vogue of the novels of Sir Walter Scott. Vigny also showed a typically

Romantic interest in William Shakespeare, freely adapting *Othello* (*Le More de Venise*, first performed 1829) as well as *The Merchant of Venice* (*Shylock*, 1829). During these years Vigny was regarded as a literary leader of the Romantic movement in France. The Romantic poet Alphonse de Lamartine recognized his talents, and Hugo and Charles Sainte-Beuve treated him as a friend. Vigny and the writer Delphine Gay, the "muse of the country" as she was called—for her beauty as well as her literary talents—formed a striking couple before his marriage in February 1825 to Lydia Bunbury, daughter of a wealthy Englishman.

## *Maturity and Disillusionment*

By 1830 Vigny's temperament had become more sombre. The July Revolution engendered in him a political pessimism inspired by the repeated faults of the French monarchy, an issue that had become evident already in *Cinq-Mars*. As a point of honour he, like Chateaubriand, sought to remain faithful to the monarchy, but he did not conceal the fact that the cause of the Bourbon king Charles X was worth no more than that of Louis-Philippe, who had been placed on the throne by the moneyed bourgeoisie. He searched unsuccessfully for a political creed and studied every shade of opinion without giving his allegiance to any. From this time on he closely followed current affairs, grasping them with a clarity that was at times prophetic, though his overt political activity remained erratic.

He acknowledged his disillusionment as early as 1831 in "Paris," a poem of a new genre that he termed *élévations*. He felt all the more tormented, for he could no longer count on the religious faith of his childhood. His feelings on this score are evident in another poem (1832) in which he contemplated suicide: "And God? Such were the times, they no longer thought about Him." The only thing left for him to doubt was love itself, a trauma he painfully experienced in the course of his liaison (1831–38) with the actress Marie Dorval, for whom he was to create the role of Kitty Bell in the play *Chatterton* in 1835. He accused Dorval of deceiving him and of having maintained an overaffectionate friendship with the writer George Sand. His relationship with Dorval left Vigny profoundly embittered.

In *Stello* (1832) Vigny put together a series of *consultations*, or dialogues, between two symbolic figures: Doctor Noir (the Black Doctor), who represents Vigny's own intellect; and Stello, who represents the poet's desire for an active part in the public arena. In seeking to preserve Stello from the dangers of his imprudent enthusiasm, Doctor Noir tells him three anecdotes. In these three short stories Vigny examines the poet in his dealings with political authority: the levity of Louis XV condemns Nicolas Gilbert to die in privation; the fanaticism of the republican tyrant Robespierre leads André Chénier to the scaffold; the egoism of William Beckford, lord mayor of London, provokes the suicide of the poet Thomas Chatterton; all political regimes inflict on the poet the harshness of "perpetual ostracism." What then is this evil malaise? Vigny questions himself on the nature of it. He submits Stello to a sort of psychoanalytic examination, as confided to Doctor Noir. After having listened to Stello, the doctor prescribes a remedy of "separating poetic life from political life" and advises the poet against direct involvement in politics in order to preserve the dignity of his art and escape the horrible cruelties that characterize every kind of fanaticism.

Vigny adapted the part of *Stello* dealing with the suicide of Chatterton into a prose drama in three acts, *Chatterton* (1835). In presenting the last moments of Chatterton's life, he exalts the nobility and suffering of a misunderstood genius in a pitiless and materialistic society. The triumph of Vigny's career as a playwright, *Chatterton* remains one of the best Romantic dramas. It is far superior to *La Maréchale d'Ancre* (first performed 1831) and expresses Vigny's melancholy genius more seasonably than does his spiritual comedy *Quitte pour la peur* (first performed 1833).

Vigny's novel *Servitude et grandeur militaires* (1835; "Servitude and Military Greatness"; Eng. trans. *The Military Necessity*) is also a *consultation*. The book's three stories, linked by personal comment, deal with the dignity and suffering of the soldier, who is obliged by his profession to kill yet who is condemned by it to passive obedience as well. The first and third stories in this volume are Vigny's masterpieces in prose, and the third story's portrait of Captain Renaud, an old Napoleonic soldier, is a profound portrait of human greatness. Vigny began another ambitious *consultation* dealing with the religious prophet, but only one story, *Daphné* (published 1912), about the Roman emperor Julian the Apostate, survives.

Vigny's *consultations* enlarged upon his philosophy, formulated theories about the fate of man, and defined the principles that he thought should govern human conduct. To give these ideas the finish they required, he turned again, between 1838 and his death, to poetry, slowly composing the 11 poems that were later collected under the title *Les Destinées* (1864). The early poems are very pessimistic, but the later ones are increasingly confident affirmations of the imperishable nature of human spiritual powers.

In middle age Vigny gradually withdrew into a curious silence and retired, according to the famous expression of Sainte-Beuve, to an "ivory tower." He rarely went out, preferring the calm of his country manor to the excitement of Paris. In 1841 he stood as a candidate to the Académie Française, but he was elected only in 1845, after five checks, and was received there with a perfidious speech by Count Molé. His wife, Lydia, whose longtime invalidism had caused him constant anxiety, died in 1862, and Vigny himself died of cancer of the stomach after much suffering the following year. He left several unedited works whose posthumous publication enhanced his reputation: *Les Destinées*, *Le Journal d'un poète* (1867), *Daphné*, and *Mémoires inédits* (1958).

# MARY WOLLSTONECRAFT SHELLEY

(b. August 30, 1797, London, England—d. February 1, 1851, London)

The English Romantic novelist Mary Wollstonecraft Shelley is best known as the author of *Frankenstein*. The only daughter of William Godwin and Mary Wollstonecraft, she met the young poet Percy Bysshe Shelley in 1812 and eloped with him to France in July 1814. The couple were married in 1816, after Shelley's first wife had committed suicide. After her husband's death in 1822, she returned to England and devoted herself to publicizing Shelley's writings and to educating their only surviving child, Percy Florence Shelley. She published her late husband's *Posthumous Poems* (1824); she also edited his *Poetical Works* (1839), with long and invaluable notes, and his prose works. Her *Journal* is a rich source of Shelley biography, and her letters are an indispensable adjunct.

Mary Shelley's best-known book is *Frankenstein; or, The Modern Prometheus* (1818, revised 1831), a text that is part Gothic novel and part philosophical novel; it is also often considered an early example of science fiction. It narrates the dreadful consequences that arise after a scientist has artificially created a human being. (The man-made monster in this novel inspired a similar creature in numerous American horror films.) She wrote several other novels, including *Valperga* (1823), *The Fortunes of Perkin Warbeck* (1830), *Lodore* (1835), and *Falkner* (1837); *The Last Man* (1826), an account of the future destruction of the human race by a plague, is often ranked as her best work. Her travel book *History of a Six Weeks' Tour* (1817) recounts the continental tour she and Shelley took in 1814 following their elopement and then recounts their summer near Geneva in 1816.

Late 20th-century publications of her casual writings include *The Journals of Mary Shelley, 1814–1844* (1987), edited by Paula R. Feldman and Diana Scott-Kilvert, and *Selected Letters of Mary Wollstonecraft Shelley* (1995), edited by Betty T. Bennett.

# *HEINRICH HEINE*

(b. December 13, 1797, Düsseldorf, Prussia [Germany] — d. February 17, 1856, Paris, France)

Christian Johann Heinrich Heine was a German poet whose international literary reputation and influence were established by the *Buch der Lieder* (1827; *The Book of Songs*), frequently set to music, though the more sombre poems of his last years are also highly regarded.

## Life

Heine was born of Jewish parents. His father was a handsome and kindly but somewhat ineffectual merchant; his mother was fairly well educated for her time and sharply ambitious for her son. Much of Heine's early life, however, was influenced by the financial power of his uncle Salomon Heine, a millionaire Hamburg banker who endeavoured to trade generosity for obedience and with whom Heine remained on an awkward and shifting footing for many years. After he had been educated in the Düsseldorf Lyceum, an unsuccessful attempt was undertaken to make a businessman of him, first in banking, then in retailing. Eventually, his uncle was prevailed upon to finance a university education, and Heine attended the universities of Bonn, Göttingen, Berlin, and Göttingen again, where he finally took a degree in law with absolutely minimal achievement in 1825. In that same year, in order to open up the possibility of a civil service career, closed to Jews at that time, he converted to Protestantism with little enthusiasm and some resentment. He never practiced law, however, nor held a position in government service; and his student years had been primarily devoted not to the studies for which his uncle had been paying but to poetry, literature, and history.

## Early Works

Heine's pre-university years are rather obscure, but during this period he apparently conceived an infatuation for one, and possibly both, of his uncle's daughters, neither of whom had the slightest notion of mortgaging her future to a dreamy and incompetent cousin. Out of the emotional desolation of this experience arose, over a period of years, the poems eventually collected in *The Book of Songs*. The sound of Romantic poetry was firmly lodged in Heine's ear; but the Romantic faith, the hope for a poeticization of life and the world to overcome the revolution, alienation, and anxiety of the times, was not in his heart. Thus, he became the major representative of the post-Romantic crisis in Germany, a time overshadowed by the stunning achievements of Goethe, Schiller, and the Romantics but increasingly aware of the inadequacy of this tradition to the new stresses and upheavals of a later age. The most consistent characteristic of Heine's thought and writing throughout his career is a taut and ambiguous tension between "poesy," as he called the artistic sensibility, and reality. His love poems, though they employ Romantic materials, are at the same time suspicious of them and of the feelings they purportedly represent. They are bitter-sweet and self-ironic, displaying at the same time poetic virtuosity and a skepticism about poetic truth; their music is now liquid, now discordant, and the collection as a whole moves in the direction of desentimentalization and a new integration of the poet's self-regard in the awareness of his artistic genius.

The steady growth of Heine's fame in the 1820s was accelerated by a series of experiments in prose. In the fall of 1824, in order to relax from his hated studies in Göttingen, he took a walking tour through the Harz Mountains and wrote a little book about it, fictionalizing his modest adventure and weaving into it elements both of his poetic imagination and of sharp-eyed social comment. "Die Harzreise" ("The Harz Journey") became the first piece of what were to be four volumes of *Reisebilder* (1826–31; *Pictures of Travel*); the whimsical amalgam of its fact and fiction, autobiography, social criticism, and literary polemic was widely imitated by other writers in subsequent years. Some of the pieces were drawn from a journey to England Heine made in 1827 and a trip to Italy in 1828, but the finest of them, "Ideen. Das Buch Le Grand" (1827; "Ideas. The Book Le Grand"), is a journey into the self, a wittily woven fabric of childhood memory, enthusiasm for Napoleon, ironic sorrow at unhappy love, and political allusion.

## *Later Life and Works*

When the July Revolution of 1830 occurred in France, Heine did not, like many of his liberal and radical contemporaries, race to Paris at once but continued his more or less serious efforts to find some sort of paying position in Germany. In the spring of 1831 he finally went to Paris, where he was to live for the rest of his life. He had originally been attracted by the new Saint-Simonian religion (a socialistic ideology according to which the state should own all property and the worker should be entitled to share according to the quality and amount of his work); it inspired in him hopes for a modern doctrine that would overcome the repressive ideologies of the past and put what he variously called spiritualism and sensualism, or Nazarenism (adherence to Judeo-Christian ideals) and Hellenism (adherence to ancient Greek ideals), into a new balance for a happier human society. His critical concern with political and social matters deepened as he watched the development of limited democracy and a capitalist order in the France of the citizen-king, Louis-Philippe. He wrote a series of penetrating newspaper articles about the new order in France, which he collected in book form as *Französische Zustände* (1832; "French Affairs") and followed with two studies of German culture, *Die Romantische Schule* (1833–35; *The Romantic School*) and "Zur Geschichte der Religion und Philosophie in Deutschland" (1834–35; "On the History of Religion and Philosophy in Germany"), in which he mounted a criticism of Germany's present and recent past and argued the long-range revolutionary potential of the German heritage of the Reformation, the Enlightenment, and modern critical philosophy. The books were conceived with a French audience in mind and were originally published in French. In 1840–43 he wrote another series of newspaper articles about French life, culture, and politics, which he reedited and published as *Lutezia*, the ancient Roman name for Paris, in 1854.

During these years, then, Heine's attention turned from "poesy" to writing of contemporary relevance. His second volume of poems, *Neue Gedichte* (1844; *New Poems*), illustrates the change. The first group, "Neuer Frühling" ("New Spring," written mostly in 1830/31), is a more mannered reprise of the love poems of *Buch der Lieder*, and the volume also contains some ballad poetry, a genre in which Heine worked all his life. But the second group, "Verschiedene" ("Varia"), is made up of short cycles of sour poems about inconstant relationships with the blithe girls of Paris; the disillusioning tone of the poems was widely misunderstood and held against him. Another section is called "Zeitgedichte" ("Contemporary Poems"), a group of harsh verses of political satire. Several of these were written for Karl Marx's newspaper *Vorwärts* ("Forward"). Heine had become acquainted with the young Marx at the end of 1843, and it was at this time that he produced, after a visit to his family in Germany, a long verse satire, *Deutschland, Ein Wintermärchen* (1844; *Germany, a Winter's Tale*), a stinging attack on reactionary conditions in Germany. Though Heine remained on good, if not intimate, terms with Marx in later years, he never was much taken with Communism, which did not fit his ideal of a revolution of joy and sensuality. About the time that he met Marx, he also wrote another long poem, *Atta Troll. Ein Sommernachtstraum* (1843–45; *Atta Troll, a Midsummer Night's Dream*), a comic spoof of radical pomposity and the clumsiness of contemporary political verse.

Heine's early years in Paris were his happiest. From an outcast in the society of his own rich uncle, he was transformed into a leading literary personality, and he became acquainted with many of the prominent people of his time. In 1834 he found in an uneducated shopgirl, Crescence Eugénie Mirat, whom for some reason he called "Mathilde," a loyal if obstreperous mistress. He married her in 1841. But troubles were soon hard upon him. His critical and satirical writings brought him into grave difficulties with the German censorship, and, at the end of 1835, the Federal German Diet tried to enforce a nation-wide ban on all his works. He was surrounded by police spies, and his voluntary exile became an imposed one. In 1840 Heine wrote a witty but ill-advised book on the late Ludwig Börne (1786–1837), the leader of the German radicals in Paris, in which Heine attempted to defend his own more subtle stand against what he thought of as the shallowness of political activism; but the arrogance and ruthlessness of the book alienated all camps.

Though never destitute, Heine was always out of money; and when his uncle died in 1844, all but disinheriting him, he began, under the eyes of all Europe, a violent struggle for the inheritance, which was settled with the grant of a right of censorship over his writings to his uncle's family; in this way, apparently, the bulk of Heine's memoirs was lost to posterity. The information, revealed after the French Revolution of 1848, that he had been receiving a secret pension from the French government, further embarrassed him.

The worst of his sufferings, however, were caused by his deteriorating health. An apparently venereal disease began to attack one part of his nervous system after another, and from the spring of 1848 he was confined to his "mattress-grave," paralyzed, tortured with spinal cramps, and partially blind. Heine returned again to "poesy." With sardonic evasiveness he abjured his faith in the divinity of man and acknowledged a personal God in order to squabble with him about the unjust governance of the world. His third volume of poems, *Romanzero* (1851), is full of heartrending laments and bleak glosses on the human condition; many of these poems are now regarded as among his finest. A final collection, *Gedichte 1853 und 1854* (*Poems 1853 and 1854*), is of the same order. After nearly eight years of torment, Heine died and was buried in the Montmartre Cemetery.

# HONORÉ DE BALZAC

(b. May 20, 1799, Tours, France—d. August 18, 1850, Paris)

The French literary artist Honoré de Balzac produced a vast number of novels and short stories collectively called *La Comédie humaine* (*The Human Comedy*). He helped to establish the traditional form of the novel and is generally considered to be one of the greatest novelists of all time.

## Early Career

Balzac's father was a man of southern peasant stock who worked in the civil service for 43 years under Louis XVI and Napoleon. Honoré's mother came from a family of prosperous Parisian cloth merchants. His sister Laure (later de Surville) was his only childhood friend, and she became his first biographer.

Balzac was sent to school at the Collège des Oratoriens at Vendôme from age 8 to 14. At Napoleon's downfall his family moved from Tours to Paris, where he went to school for two more years and then spent three years as a lawyer's clerk. During this time he already aimed at a literary career, but as the writer of *Cromwell* (1819) and other tragic plays he was utterly unsuccessful.

He then began writing novels filled with mystic and philosophical speculations before turning to the production of potboilers—gothic, humorous, historical novels—written under composite pseudonyms. Then he tried a business career as a publisher, printer, and owner of a typefoundry, but disaster soon followed. In 1828 he was narrowly saved from bankruptcy and was left with debts of more than 60,000 francs. From then on his life was to be one of mounting debts and almost incessant toil. He returned to writing with a new mastery, and his literary apprenticeship was over.

Two works of 1829 brought Balzac to the brink of success. *Les Chouans*, the first novel he felt enough confidence about to have published under his own name, is a historical novel about the Breton peasants called Chouans who took part in a royalist insurrection against Revolutionary France in 1799. The other, *La Physiologie du mariage* (*The Physiology of Marriage*), is a humorous and satirical essay on the subject of marital infidelity, encompassing both its causes and its cure. The six stories in his *Scènes de la vie privée* (1830; "Scenes from Private Life") further increased his reputation.

From this point forward Balzac spent much of his time in Paris. He began to frequent some of the best-known Parisian salons of the day and redoubled his efforts to set himself up as a dazzling figure in society. To most people he seemed full of exuberant vitality, talkative, jovial and robustious, egoistic, credulous, and boastful. He adopted for his own use the armorial bearings of an ancient noble family with which he had no connection and assumed the honorific particle *de*. He was avid for fame, fortune, and love but was above all conscious of his own genius. He also began to have love affairs with fashionable or aristocratic women at this time, finally gaining that firsthand understanding of mature women that is so evident in his novels.

Between 1828 and 1834 Balzac led a tumultuous existence, spending his earnings in advance as a dandy and
man-about-town. A fascinating raconteur, he was fairly
well received in society. In 1832 Balzac became friendly
with Éveline Hanska, a Polish countess who was married
to an elderly Ukrainian landowner. She, like many other
women, had written to Balzac expressing admiration of
his writings. They met twice in Switzerland in 1833—the
second time in Geneva, where they became lovers—and
again in Vienna in 1835. They agreed to marry when her
husband died, and so Balzac continued to conduct his
courtship of her by correspondence; the resulting *Lettres
à l'étrangère* ("Letters to a Foreigner"), which appeared
posthumously (4 vol., 1889–1950), are an important
source of information for the history both of Balzac's life
and of his work.

To clear his debts and put himself in a position to marry
Madame Hanska now became Balzac's great incentive. He
was at the peak of his creative power. In the period 1832–
35 he produced more than 20 works, including the novels
*Le Médecin de campagne* (1833; *The Country Doctor*), *Eugénie
Grandet* (1833), *L'Illustre Gaudissart* (1833; *The Illustrious
Gaudissart*), and *Le Père Goriot* (1835), one of his masterpieces. Among the shorter works were *Le Colonel Chabert*
(1832), *Le Curé de Tours* (1832; *The Vicar of Tours*), the trilogy of stories entitled *Histoire des treize* (1833–35; *History
of the Thirteen*), and *Gobseck* (1835). Between 1836 and 1839
he wrote *Le Cabinet des antiques* (1839), the first two parts
of another masterpiece, *Illusions perdues* (1837–43; *Lost
Illusions*), *César Birotteau* (1837), and *La Maison Nucingen*
(1838; *The Firm of Nucingen*). Between 1832 and 1837 he also
published three sets of *Contes drolatiques* (*Droll Stories*).
These stories, Rabelaisian in theme, are written with great
verve and gusto in an ingenious pastiche of 16th-century
language. During the 1830s he also wrote a number of

philosophical novels dealing with mystical, pseudoscientific, and other exotic themes. Among these are *La Peau de chagrin* (1831; *The Wild Ass's Skin*), *Le Chef-d'oeuvre inconnu* (1831; *The Unknown Masterpiece*), *Louis Lambert* (1834), *La Recherche de l'absolu* (1834; *The Quest of the Absolute*), and *Séraphîta* (1834–35).

In all these varied works Balzac emerged as the supreme observer and chronicler of contemporary French society. These novels are unsurpassed for their narrative drive, their large casts of vital, diverse, and interesting characters, and their obsessive interest in and examination of virtually all spheres of life: the contrast between provincial and metropolitan manners and customs; the commercial spheres of banking, publishing, and industrial enterprise; the worlds of art, literature, and high culture; politics and partisan intrigue; romantic love in all its aspects; and the intricate social relations and scandals among the aristocracy and the haute bourgeoisie.

No theme is more typically Balzacian than that of the ambitious young provincial fighting for advancement in the competitive world of Paris. He was especially attracted by the theme of the individual in conflict with society: the adventurer, the scoundrel, the unscrupulous financier, and the criminal. He was both fascinated and appalled by the French social system of his time, in which the bourgeois values of material acquisitiveness and gain were steadily replacing what he viewed as the more stable moral values of the old-time aristocracy.

These topics provided material largely unknown, or unexplored, by earlier writers of French fiction. The individual in Balzac's stories is continually affected by the pressure of material difficulties and social ambitions, and he may expend his tremendous vitality in ways Balzac views as socially destructive and self-destructive. Linked with this idea of the potentially destructive power of passionate will, emotion, and thought is Balzac's peculiar notion of a vital fluid concentrated inside the person, a store of energy that he may husband or squander as he desires, thereby lengthening or shortening his vital span. Indeed, a supremely important feature in Balzac's characters is that most are spendthrifts of this vital force, a fact that explains his monomaniacs who are both victim and embodiment of some ruling passion; avarice, as in the main character of *Gobseck*, a usurer gloating over his sense of power, or the miserly father obsessed with riches in *Eugénie Grandet*; excessive paternal affection, as in the idolatrous Learlike father in *Le Père Goriot*; feminine vindictiveness, as evidenced in *La Cousine Bette* and a half-dozen other novels; the mania of the art collector, as in *Le Cousin Pons*; the artist's desire for perfection, as in *Le Chef-d'oeuvre inconnu*; the curiosity of the scientist, as in the fanatical chemist of *La Recherche de l'absolu*; or the vaulting and frustrated ambition of the astonishingly resourceful criminal mastermind Vautrin in *Illusions perdues* and *Splendeurs et misères des courtisanes*. Once such an obsession has gained a hold, Balzac shows it growing irresistibly in power and blinding the person concerned to all other considerations.

## La Comédie Humaine

The year 1834 marks a climax in Balzac's career, for by then he had become totally conscious of his great plan to group his individual novels so that they would comprehend the whole of contemporary society in a diverse but unified series of books. There were to be three general categories of novels: *Études analytiques* ("Analytic Studies"), dealing with the principles governing human life and society; *Études philosophiques* ("Philosophical Studies"), revealing the causes determining human action; and *Études de moeurs* ("Studies of Manners"), showing the effects of those causes, and themselves to be divided into six kinds of *scènes*—private, provincial, Parisian, political, military, and country life. This entire project resulted in a total of 12 volumes (1834–37). By 1837 Balzac had written much more, and by 1840 he had hit upon a Dantesque title for the whole: *La Comédie humaine*. He negotiated with a consortium of publishers for an edition under this name, 17 volumes of which appeared between 1842 and 1848, including a famous foreword written in 1842. In 1845, having new works to include and many others in project, he began preparing for another complete edition. A "definitive edition" was published, in 24 volumes, between 1869 and 1876. The total number of novels and novellas comprised in the *Comédie humaine* is roughly 90.

Also in 1834 the idea of using "reappearing characters" matured. Balzac was to establish a pool of characters from which he would constantly and repeatedly draw, thus adding a sense of solidarity and coherence to the *Comédie humaine*. A certain character would reappear—now in the forefront, now in the background, of different fictions—in such a way that the reader

*French novelist Honoré de Balzac in an 1842 daguerreotype by noted French photographer Louis-Auguste Bisson 1845.* Apic/Hulton Archive/Getty Images

could gradually form a full picture of him. Balzac's use of this device places him among the originators of the modern novel cycle. In the end, the total number of named characters in the *Comédie humaine* is estimated to have reached 2,472, with a further 566 unnamed characters.

In January 1842 Balzac learned of the death of Wenceslas Hanski. He now had good expectations of marrying Éveline, but there were many obstacles, not the least being his inextricable indebtedness. She in fact held back for many years, and the period of 1842–48 shows Balzac continuing and even intensifying his literary activity in the frantic hope of winning her, though he had to contend with increasing ill health.

Balzac produced many notable works during the early and mid-1840s. These include the masterpieces *Une Ténébreuse Affaire* (1841; *A Shady Business*), *La Rabouilleuse* (1841–42; *The Black Sheep*), *Ursule Mirouët* (1841), and one of his greatest works, *Splendeurs et misères des courtisanes* (1843–47; *A Harlot High and Low*). Balzac's last two masterpieces were *La Cousine Bette* (1847; *Cousin Bette*) and *Le Cousin Pons* (1847; *Cousin Pons*).

In the autumn of 1847 Balzac went to Madame Hanska's château at Wierzchownia and remained there until February 1848. He returned again in October to stay, mortally sick, until the spring of 1850. Then at last Éveline relented. They were married in March and proceeded to Paris, where Balzac lingered on miserably for the few months before his death.

Balzac is regarded as the creator of realism in the novel. He is also acknowledged as having helped to establish the technique of the traditional novel, in which consequent and logically determined events are narrated by an all-seeing observer (the omniscient narrator) and characters are coherently presented. Balzac had exceptional powers of observation and a photographic memory, but he also had a sympathetic, intuitive capacity to understand and describe other people's attitudes, feelings, and motivations. He was bent on illustrating the relation between cause and effect, between social background and character. His ambition was to "compete with the civil register," exactly picturing his contemporaries in their class distinctions and occupations. In this he succeeded, but he went even further in his efforts to show that the human spirit has power over men and events—to become, as he has been called, "the Shakespeare of the novel."

# ALEKSANDR PUSHKIN

(b. May 26 [June 6, New Style], 1799, Moscow, Russia—d. January 29 [February 10], 1837, St. Petersburg)

The Russian poet, novelist, dramatist, and short-story writer Aleksandr Pushkin has often been considered his country's greatest poet and the founder of modern Russian literature.

## The Early Years

Pushkin's father came of an old boyar family; his mother was a granddaughter of Abram Hannibal, who, according to family tradition, was an Abyssinian princeling bought as a slave at Constantinople (Istanbul) and adopted by Peter the Great, whose comrade in arms he became. Like many aristocratic families in early 19th-century Russia, Pushkin's parents adopted French culture, and he and his brother and sister learned to talk and to read in French. They were left much to the care of their maternal grandmother, who told Aleksandr, especially, stories of his ancestors in Russian. During summers at his grandmother's estate near Moscow he talked to the peasants and spent hours alone, living in the dream world of a precocious, imaginative child. He read widely in his father's library and gained stimulus from the literary guests who came to the house.

In 1811 Pushkin entered the newly founded Imperial Lyceum at Tsarskoye Selo (later renamed Pushkin) and while there began his literary career with the publication (1814, in *Vestnik Evropy*, "The Messenger of Europe") of his verse epistle "To My Friend, the Poet." In his early verse, he followed the style of his older contemporaries, the Romantic poets K.N. Batyushkov and V.A. Zhukovsky, and of the French 17th- and 18th-century poets, especially the Vicomte de Parny.

While at the Lyceum he also began his first completed major work, the romantic poem *Ruslan i Lyudmila* (1820; *Ruslan and Ludmila*), written in the style of the narrative poems of Ludovico Ariosto and Voltaire but with an old Russian setting and making use of Russian folklore. The poem flouted accepted rules and genres and was violently attacked by both of the established literary schools of the day, Classicism and Sentimentalism. It brought Pushkin fame, however, and Zhukovsky presented his portrait to the poet with the inscription "To the victorious pupil from the defeated master."

## St. Petersburg

In 1817 Pushkin accepted a post in the foreign office at St. Petersburg, where he was elected to Arzamás, an exclusive literary circle founded by his uncle's friends. Pushkin also joined the Green Lamp association, which, though founded (in 1818) for discussion of literature and history, became a clandestine branch of a secret society, the Union of Welfare. In his political verses and epigrams, widely circulated in manuscript, he made himself the spokesman for the ideas and aspirations of those who were to take part in the Decembrist rising of 1825, the unsuccessful culmination of a Russian revolutionary movement in its earliest stage.

## Exile in the South

For these political poems, Pushkin was banished from St. Petersburg in May 1820 to a remote southern province. Sent first to Yekaterinoslav (now Dnipropetrovsk, Ukraine), he was there taken ill and, while convalescing, traveled in the northern Caucasus and later to the Crimea. The impressions he gained provided material for his "southern cycle" of romantic narrative poems: *Kavkazsky plennik* (1820–21; *The Prisoner of the Caucasus*), *Bratya razboyniki* (1821–22; *The Robber Brothers*), and *Bakhchisaraysky fontan* (1823; *The Fountain of Bakhchisaray*).

Although this cycle of poems confirmed the reputation of the author of *Ruslan and Ludmila* and Pushkin was hailed as the leading Russian poet of the day and as the leader of the romantic, liberty-loving generation of the 1820s, he himself was not satisfied with it. In May 1823 he started work on his central masterpiece, the novel in verse *Yevgeny Onegin* (1833), on which he continued to work intermittently until 1831. In it he returned to the idea of presenting a typical figure of his own age but in a wider setting and by means of new artistic methods and techniques.

*Yevgeny Onegin* unfolds a panoramic picture of Russian life. The characters it depicts and immortalizes—Onegin, the disenchanted skeptic; Lensky, the romantic, freedom-loving poet; and Tatyana, the heroine, a profoundly affectionate study of Russian womanhood: a "precious ideal," in the poet's own words—are typically Russian and are shown in relationship to the social and environmental forces by which they are molded. Although formally the work resembles Lord Byron's *Don Juan*, Pushkin rejects Byron's subjective, romanticized treatment in favour of objective description and shows his hero not in exotic surroundings but at the heart of a Russian way of life. Thus, the action begins at St. Petersburg, continues on a provincial estate, then switches to Moscow, and finally returns to St. Petersburg.

Pushkin had meanwhile been transferred first to Kishinyov (1820–23; now Chişinău, Moldova) and then to Odessa (1823–24). His bitterness at continued exile is expressed in letters to his friends—the first of a collection of correspondence that became an outstanding and enduring monument of Russian prose. At Kishinyov, a remote outpost in Moldavia, he devoted much time to writing, though he also plunged into the life of a society engaged in amorous intrigue, hard drinking, gaming, and violence. He fought several duels, and eventually the count asked for his discharge. Pushkin, in a letter to a friend intercepted by the police, had stated that he was now taking "lessons in pure atheism." This finally led to his being again exiled to his mother's estate of Mikhaylovskoye, near Pskov, at the other end of Russia.

## At Mikhaylovskoye

Although the two years at Mikhaylovskoye were unhappy for Pushkin, they were to prove one of his most productive periods. Alone and isolated, he embarked on a close study of Russian history; he came to know the peasants on the estate and interested himself in noting folktales and songs. During this period the specifically Russian features of his poetry became steadily more marked. His ballad "Zhenikh"

(1825; "The Bridegroom"), for instance, is based on motifs from Russian folklore; and its simple, swift-moving style, quite different from the brilliant extravagance of *Ruslan and Ludmila* or the romantic, melodious music of the "southern" poems, emphasizes its stark tragedy.

In 1824 he published *Tsygany* (*The Gypsies*), begun earlier as part of the "southern cycle." At Mikhaylovskoye, too, he wrote the provincial chapters of *Yevgeny Onegin*; the poem *Graf Nulin* (1827; "Count Nulin"), based on the life of the rural gentry; and, finally, one of his major works, the historical tragedy *Boris Godunov* (1831).

The latter marks a break with the Neoclassicism of the French theatre and is constructed on the "folk-principles" of William Shakespeare's plays, especially the histories and tragedies, plays written "for the people" in the widest sense and thus universal in their appeal. Written just before the Decembrist rising, it treats the burning question of the relations between the ruling classes, headed by the tsar, and the masses; it is the moral and political significance of the latter, "the judgment of the people," that Pushkin emphasizes. Set in Russia in a period of political and social chaos on the brink of the 17th century, its theme is the tragic guilt and inexorable fate of a great hero—Boris Godunov, son-in-law of Malyuta Skuratov, a favourite of Ivan the Terrible, and here presented as the murderer of Ivan's little son, Dmitri. The development of the action on two planes, one political and historical, the other psychological, is masterly and is set against a background of turbulent events and ruthless ambitions. The play owes much to Pushkin's reading of early Russian annals and chronicles, as well as to Shakespeare, who, as Pushkin said, was his master in bold, free treatment of character, simplicity, and truth to nature. Pushkin's ability to create psychological and dramatic unity, despite the episodic construction, and to heighten the dramatic tension by economy of language, detail, and characterization make this outstanding play a revolutionary event in the history of Russian drama.

## *Return from Exile*

After the suppression of the Decembrist uprising of 1825, the new tsar Nicholas I, aware of Pushkin's immense popularity and knowing that he had taken no part in the Decembrist "conspiracy," allowed him to return to Moscow in the autumn of 1826. During a long conversation between them, the tsar met the poet's complaints about censorship with a promise that in the future he himself would be Pushkin's censor and told him of his plans to introduce several pressing reforms from above and, in particular, to prepare the way for liberation of the serfs.

Pushkin saw that without the support of the people, the struggle against autocracy was doomed. He considered that the only possible way of achieving essential reforms was from above, "on the tsar's initiative," as he had written in "Derevnya." This is the reason for his persistent interest in the age of reforms at the beginning of the 18th century and in the figure of Peter the Great, the "tsar-educator," whose example he held up to the present tsar in the poem "Stansy" (1826; "Stanzas"), in *The Negro of Peter the Great*, in the historical poem *Poltava* (1829), and in the poem *Medny vsadnik* (1837; *The Bronze Horseman*).

After returning from exile, Pushkin found himself in an awkward and invidious position. The tsar's censorship proved to be even more exacting than that of the official censors, and his personal freedom was curtailed. Not only was he put under secret observation by the police but he was openly supervised by its chief, Count Benckendorf. The anguish of his spiritual isolation at this time is reflected in a cycle of poems about the poet and the mob (1827–30) and in the unfinished *Yegipetskiye nochi* (1835; *Egyptian Nights*).

Yet it was during this period that Pushkin's genius came to its fullest flowering. His art acquired new dimensions, and almost every one of the works written between 1829 and 1836 opened a new chapter in the history of Russian literature. He spent the autumn of 1830 at his family's Nizhny Novgorod estate, Boldino, and these months are the most remarkable in the whole of his artistic career. During them he wrote the four so-called "little tragedies"—*Skupoy rytsar* (1836; *The Covetous Knight*), *Motsart i Salyeri* (1831; *Mozart and Salieri*), *Kamenny gost* (1839; *The Stone Guest*), and *Pir vo vremya chumy* (1832; *Feast in Time of the Plague*)—the five short prose tales collected as *Povesti pokoynogo Ivana Petrovicha Belkina* (1831; *Tales of the Late Ivan Petrovich Belkin*); the comic poem of everyday lower-class life *Domik v Kolomne* (1833; "A Small House in Kolomna"); and many lyrics in widely differing styles, as well as several critical and polemical articles, rough drafts, and sketches.

## Last Years

In 1831 Pushkin married Natalya Nikolayevna Goncharova and settled in St. Petersburg. Once more he took up government service and was commissioned to write a history of Peter the Great. Three years later he received the rank of *Kammerjunker* (gentleman of the emperor's bedchamber), partly because the tsar wished Natalya to have the entrée to court functions. Without abandoning poetry altogether, he turned increasingly to prose. Alongside the theme of Peter the Great, the motif of a popular peasant rising acquired growing importance in his work, as is shown by the unfinished satirical *Istoriya sela Goryukhina* (1837; *The History of the Village of Goryukhino*), the unfinished novel *Dubrovsky* (1841), *Stseny iz rytsarskikh vremen* (1837; *Scenes from the Age of Chivalry*), and finally, the most important of his prose works, the historical novel of the Pugachov Rebellion, *Kapitanskaya dochka* (1836; *The Captain's Daughter*), which had been preceded by a historical study of the rebellion, *Istoriya Pugachova* (1834; "A History of Pugachov").

Meanwhile, both in his domestic affairs and in his official duties, his life was becoming more intolerable. In court circles he was regarded with mounting suspicion and resentment, and his repeated petitions to be allowed to resign his post, retire to the country, and devote himself entirely to literature were all rejected. Finally, in 1837, Pushkin was mortally wounded defending his wife's honour in a duel forced on him by influential enemies.

# *Victor Hugo*

(b. February 26, 1802, Besançon, France—d. May 22, 1885, Paris)

The poet, novelist, and dramatist Victor-Marie Hugo was the most important of the French Romantic writers. Though regarded in France as one of that country's greatest poets, he is better known abroad for such novels as *Notre-Dame de Paris* (1831) and *Les Misérables* (1862).

## *Early Years*

Victor was the third son of Joseph-Léopold-Sigisbert Hugo, a major and, later, general in Napoleon's army. His childhood was coloured by his father's constant traveling with the imperial army and by the disagreements that soon alienated his parents from one another.

*Victor Hugo, photograph by Nadar (Gaspard-Félix Tournachon).*
Archives Photographiques, Paris

His mother's royalism and his father's loyalty to successive governments—the Convention, the Empire, the Restoration—reflected their deeper incompatibility. It was a chaotic time for Victor, continually uprooted from Paris to set out for Elba or Naples or Madrid, yet always returning to Paris with his mother, whose royalist opinions he initially adopted. The fall of the empire gave him, from 1815 to 1818, a time of uninterrupted study at the Pension Cordier and the Lycée Louis-le-Grand, after which he graduated from the law faculty at Paris.

From 1816, at least, Hugo had conceived ambitions other than the law. He was already filling notebooks with verses, translations—particularly from Virgil—two tragedies, a play, and elegies. Encouraged by his mother, Hugo founded a review, the *Conservateur Littéraire* (1819–21), in which his own articles on the poets Alphonse de Lamartine and André de Chénier stand out. His mother died in 1821, and a year later Victor married a childhood friend, Adèle Foucher, with whom he had five children. In that same year he published his first book of poems, *Odes et poésies diverses*, whose royalist sentiments earned him a pension from Louis XVIII.

In 1823 he published his first novel, *Han d'Islande*, which in 1825 appeared in an English translation as *Hans of Iceland*. In 1824 he published a new verse collection, *Nouvelles Odes*, and followed it two years later with an exotic romance, *Bug-Jargal* (Eng. trans. *The Slave King*). In 1826 he also published *Odes et ballades*, an enlarged edition of his previously printed verse, the latest of these poems being brilliant variations on the fashionable Romantic modes of mirth and terror. The youthful vigour of these poems was also characteristic of another collection, *Les Orientales* (1829), which appealed to the Romantic taste for Asian local colour.

Hugo emerged as a true Romantic, however, with the publication in 1827 of his verse drama *Cromwell*. The subject of this play, with its near-contemporary overtones, is that of a national leader risen from the people who seeks to be crowned king. But the play's reputation rested largely on the long, elaborate preface, in which Hugo proposed a doctrine of Romanticism that for all its intellectual moderation was extremely provocative. He demanded a verse drama in which the contradictions of human existence—good and evil, beauty and ugliness, tears and laughter—would be resolved by the inclusion of both tragic and comic elements in a single play.

## Success

The defense of freedom and the cult of an idealized Napoleon in such poems as the ode "À la Colonne" and "Lui" brought Hugo into touch with the liberal group of writers on the newspaper *Le Globe*, and his move toward liberalism was strengthened by the French king Charles X's restrictions on the liberty of the press as well as by the censor's prohibiting the stage performance of his play *Marion de Lorme* (1829), which portrays the character of Louis XIII unfavourably. Hugo immediately retorted with *Hernani*, the first performance of which, on February 25, 1830, gained victory for the young Romantics over the Classicists in what came to be known as the battle of *Hernani*. In this play Hugo extolled the Romantic hero in the form of a noble outlaw at war with society, dedicated to a passionate love and driven on by inexorable fate. The actual impact of the play owed less to the plot than to the sound and beat of the verse, which was softened only in the elegiac passages spoken by Hernani and Doña Sol.

While Hugo had derived his early renown from his plays, he gained wider fame in 1831 with his historical novel *Notre-Dame de Paris* (Eng. trans. *The Hunchback of Notre-Dame*), an evocation of life in medieval Paris during the reign of Louis XI. The novel condemns a society that, in the persons of Frollo the archdeacon and Phoebus the soldier, heaps misery on the hunchback Quasimodo and the gypsy girl Esmeralda. The theme touched the public consciousness more deeply than had that of his previous novel, *Le Dernier Jour d'un condamné* (1829; *The Last Days of a Condemned*), the story of a condemned man's last day, in which Hugo launched a humanitarian protest against the death penalty. While *Notre-Dame* was being written, Louis-Philippe, a constitutional king, had been brought to power by the July Revolution. Hugo composed a poem in honour of this event, *Dicté aprés juillet 1830*. It was a fore-runner of much of his political verse.

Four books of poems came from Hugo in the period of the July Monarchy: *Les Feuilles d'automne* (1831; "Autumn Leaves"), intimate and personal in inspiration; *Les Chants du crépuscule* (1835; *Songs of Twilight*), overtly political; *Les Voix intérieures* (1837; "Inner Voices"), both personal and philosophical; and *Les Rayons et les ombres* (1840; "Sunlight and Shadows"), in which the poet, renewing these different themes, indulges his gift for colour and picturesque detail.

So intense was Hugo's creative activity during these years that he also continued to pour out plays. There were two motives for this: first, he needed a platform for his political and social ideas, and, second, he wished to write parts for a young and beautiful actress, Juliette Drouet, with whom he had begun a liaison in 1833. Juliette had little talent and soon renounced the stage in order to devote herself exclusively to him, becoming the discreet and faithful companion she was to remain until her death in 1883. The first of these plays was another verse drama, *Le Roi s'amuse* (1832; Eng. trans. *The King's Fool*). Three prose plays followed: *Lucrèce Borgia* and *Marie Tudor* in 1833 and *Angelo, tyran de Padoue* ("Angelo, Tyrant of Padua") in 1835. *Ruy Blas*, a play in verse, appeared in 1838 and was followed by *Les Burgraves* in 1843.

Hugo's literary achievement was recognized in 1841 by his election, after three unsuccessful attempts, to the French Academy and by his nomination in 1845 to the Chamber of Peers. From this time he almost ceased to publish, partly because of the demands of society and political life but also as a result of personal loss: his daughter Léopoldine, recently married, was accidentally drowned with her husband in September 1843. Hugo's intense grief found some mitigation in poems that later appeared in *Les Contemplations*, a volume that he divided into "Autrefois" and "Aujourd'hui," the moment of his daughter's death being the mark between yesterday and today. He found relief above all in working on a new novel, which became *Les Misérables*, published in 1862 after work on it had been set aside for a time and then resumed.

With the Revolution of 1848, Hugo was elected a deputy for Paris in the Constituent Assembly and later in the Legislative Assembly. He supported the successful candidacy of Prince Louis-Napoléon for the presidency that year. The more the president evolved toward an authoritarianism of the right, however, the more Hugo moved toward the assembly's left. When in December 1851 a coup d'état took place, which eventually resulted in the Second Empire under Napoleon III, Hugo made one attempt at resistance and then fled to Brussels.

## Exile

Hugo's exile lasted until the return of liberty and the reconstitution of the republic in 1870. Enforced at the beginning, exile later became a voluntary gesture and, after the amnesty of 1859, an act of pride. He remained in Brussels for a year until, foreseeing expulsion, he took refuge on British territory. He first established himself on the island of Jersey, in the English Channel, where he remained from 1852 to 1855. When he was expelled from there, he moved to the neighbouring island of Guernsey. During this exile of nearly 20 years he produced the most extensive part of all his writings and the most original.

Immersed in politics as he was, Hugo devoted the first writings of his exile to satire and recent history: *Napoléon le Petit* (1852), an indictment of Napoleon III, and *Histoire d'un crime*, a day-by-day account of Louis Bonaparte's coup. Hugo's return to poetry was an explosion of wrath: *Les Châtiments* (1853; "The Punishments"). This collection of poems unleashed his anger against the new emperor and, on a technical level, freed him from his remaining classical prejudices and enabled him to achieve the full mastery of his poetic powers.

Despite the satisfaction he derived from his political poetry, Hugo wearied of its limitations and, turning back to the unpublished poems of 1840–50, set to work on the volume of poetry entitled *Les Contemplations* (1856). This work contains the purest of his poetry—the most moving because the memory of his dead daughter is at the centre of the book, the most disquieting, also, because it transmits the haunted world of a thinker. In poems such as "Pleurs dans la nuit" and "La Bouche d'ombre," he reveals a tormented mind that struggles between doubt and faith in its lonely search for meaning and significance.

Hugo's apocalyptic approach to reality was the source of two epic or metaphysical poems, *La Fin de Satan* ("The End of Satan") and *Dieu* ("God"), both of them confrontations of the problem of evil. Written between 1854 and 1860, they were not published until after his death because his publisher preferred the little epics based on history and legend contained in the first installment (1859) of the gigantic epic poem *La Légende des siècles* (*The Legend of the Centuries*), whose second and third installments appeared in 1877 and 1883, respectively. The many poems that make up this epic display all his spiritual power without sacrificing his exuberant capacity to tell a story.

After the publication of three long books of poetry, Hugo returned to prose and took up his abandoned novel, *Les Misérables*. Its extraordinary success with readers of every type when it was published in 1862 brought him instant popularity in his own country, and its speedy translation into many languages won him fame abroad. The novel's name means "the wretched," or "the outcasts," but English translations generally carry the French title. The story centres on the convict Jean Valjean, a victim of society who has been imprisoned for 19 years for stealing a loaf of bread. A hardened and astute criminal upon his release, he eventually softens and reforms, becoming a successful industrialist and mayor of a northern town. Yet he is stalked obsessively by the detective Javert for an impulsive, regretted former crime, and Jean Valjean eventually sacrifices himself for the sake of his adopted daughter, Cosette, and her husband, Marius. *Les Misérables* is a vast panorama of Parisian society and its underworld, and it contains many famous episodes and passages, among them a chapter on the Battle of Waterloo and the description of Jean Valjean's rescue of Marius by means of a flight through the sewers of Paris. The story line of *Les Misérables* is basically that of a detective story, but by virtue of its characters, who are sometimes a little larger than life yet always vital and engaging, and by its re-creation of the swarming Parisian underworld, the main theme of humankind's ceaseless combat with evil clearly emerges.

## Last Years

The defeat of France in the Franco-German War and the proclamation of the Third Republic in 1871 brought Hugo back to Paris. He became a deputy in the National Assembly (1871) but resigned the following month. Though he still fought for his old ideals, he no longer possessed the same energies. The trials of recent years had aged him, and there were more to come: in 1868 he had lost his wife, Adèle, a profound sadness to him; in 1871 one son died, as did another in 1873. Though increasingly detached from life around him, the poet of *L'Année terrible* (1872), in which he recounted the siege of Paris during the "terrible year" of 1870, had become a national hero and a living symbol of republicanism in France. In 1878 Hugo was stricken by cerebral congestion, but he lived on for some years in the Avenue d'Eylau, renamed Avenue Victor-Hugo on his 80th birthday. In 1885, two years after the death of his faithful companion Juliette, Hugo died and was given a national funeral. His body lay in state under the Arc de Triomphe and was buried in the Panthéon.

# ALEXANDRE DUMAS, PÈRE

(b. July 24, 1802, Villers-Cotterêts, Aisne, France—d. December 5, 1870, Puys, near Dieppe)

Alexandre Dumas, père, was one of the most prolific and most popular French authors of the 19th century. Without ever attaining indisputable literary merit, Dumas succeeded in gaining a great reputation first as a dramatist and then as a historical novelist, especially for such works as *The Count of Monte Cristo* and *The Three*

*Musketeers*. His memoirs, which, with a mixture of candour, mendacity, and boastfulness, recount the events of his extraordinary life, also provide a unique insight into French literary life during the Romantic period. He was the father (*père*) of the dramatist and novelist Alexandre Dumas, called Dumas *fils*.

Dumas's father, Thomas-Alexandre Davy de La Pailleterie—born out of wedlock to the marquis de La Pailleterie and Marie Cessette Dumas, a black slave of Santo Domingo—was a common soldier under the ancien régime who assumed the name Dumas in 1786. He later became a general in Napoleon's army. The family fell on hard times, however, especially after General Dumas's death in 1806, and the young Alexandre went to Paris to attempt to make a living as a lawyer. He managed to obtain a post in the household of the Duke d'Orléans, the future King Louis-Philippe, but tried his fortune in the theatre. He made contact with the actor François-Joseph Talma and with the young poets who were to lead the Romantic movement.

Dumas's plays, when judged from a modern viewpoint, are crude, brash, and melodramatic, but they were received with rapture in the late 1820s and early 1830s. *Henri III et sa cour* (1829) portrayed the French Renaissance in garish colours; *Napoléon Bonaparte* (1831) played its part in making a legend of the recently dead emperor; and in *Antony* (1831) Dumas brought a contemporary drama of adultery and honour to the stage.

Though he continued to write plays, Dumas next turned his attention to the historical novel, often working with collaborators (especially Auguste Maquet). Considerations of probability or historical accuracy generally were ignored, and the psychology of the characters was rudimentary. Dumas's main interest was the creation of an exciting story set against a colourful background of history, usually the 16th or 17th century.

The best known of his works are *Les Trois Mousquetaires* (published 1844, performed 1845; *The Three Musketeers*), a romance about four swashbuckling heroes in the age of Cardinal Richelieu; *Vingt ans après* (1845; "Twenty Years After"); *Le Comte de Monte Cristo* (1844–45; *The Count of Monte Cristo*); *Dix ans plus tard ou le Vicomte de Bragelonne* (1848–50; "Ten Years Later; or, The Vicomte de Bragelonne"); and *La Tulipe noire* (1850; "The Black Tulip").

When success came, Dumas indulged his extravagant tastes and consequently was forced to write more and more rapidly in order to pay his creditors. He tried to make money by journalism and with travel books but with little success.

The unfinished manuscript of a long-lost novel, *Le Chevalier de Sainte-Hermine* (*The Last Cavalier*), was discovered in the Bibliothèque Nationale in Paris in the late 1980s and first published in 2005.

# RALPH WALDO EMERSON

(b. May 25, 1803, Boston, Massachusetts, U.S.—d. April 27, 1882, Concord, Massachusetts)

The American lecturer, poet, and essayist Ralph Waldo Emerson was the leading exponent of New England Transcendentalism.

The son of the Reverend William Emerson, a Unitarian clergyman and friend of the arts, Ralph Waldo Emerson inherited the profession of divinity, which had attracted all his ancestors in direct line from Puritan days. The family of his mother, Ruth Haskins, was strongly Anglican, and among influences on Emerson were such Anglican writers and thinkers as Ralph Cudworth, Robert Leighton, Jeremy Taylor, and Samuel Taylor Coleridge.

On May 12, 1811, Emerson's father died, leaving the son largely to the intellectual care of Mary Moody Emerson, his aunt, who took her duties seriously. In 1812 Emerson entered the Boston Public Latin School, where his juvenile verses were encouraged and his literary gifts recognized. In 1817 he entered Harvard College, where he began his journals.

## Early Work and Personal Doctrine

Emerson graduated in 1821 and taught school while preparing for part-time study in the Harvard Divinity School. Though he was licensed to preach in the Unitarian community in 1826, illness slowed the progress of his career, and he was not ordained to the Unitarian ministry at the Second Church, Boston, until 1829. There he began to win fame as a preacher, and his position seemed secure.

In 1829 he also married Ellen Louisa Tucker. When she died of tuberculosis in 1831, his grief drove him to question his beliefs and his profession. But in the previous few years Emerson had already begun to question Christian doctrines. His older brother William, who had gone to Germany, had acquainted him with the new biblical criticism and the doubts that had been cast on the historicity of miracles. Emerson's own sermons, from the first, had been unusually free of traditional doctrine and were instead a personal exploration of the uses of spirit, showing an idealistic tendency and announcing his personal doctrine of self-reliance and self-sufficiency. Indeed, his sermons had divested Christianity of all external or historical supports and made its basis one's private intuition of the universal moral law and its test a life of virtuous accomplishment. Unitarianism had little appeal to him by now, and in 1832 he resigned from the ministry.

## *Mature Life and Works*

When Emerson left the church, he was in search of a more certain conviction of God than that granted by the historical evidences of miracles. He wanted his own revelation—i.e., a direct and immediate experience of God. When he left his pulpit he journeyed to Europe. In Paris he saw Antoine-Laurent de Jussieu's collection of natural specimens arranged in a developmental order that confirmed his belief in man's spiritual relation to nature. In England he paid memorable visits to Samuel Taylor Coleridge, William Wordsworth, and Thomas Carlyle. At home once more in 1833, he began to write *Nature* and established himself as a popular and influential lecturer. By 1834 he had found a permanent dwelling place in Concord, Massachusetts, and in the following year he married Lydia Jackson and settled into the kind of quiet domestic life that was essential to his work.

The 1830s saw Emerson become an independent literary man. During this decade his own personal doubts and difficulties were increasingly shared by other intellectuals. Before the decade was over his personal manifestos—*Nature*, "The American Scholar," and the divinity school *Address*—had rallied together a group that came to be called the Transcendentalists, of which he was popularly acknowledged the spokesman. Emerson helped initiate Transcendentalism by publishing anonymously in Boston in 1836 a little book of 95 pages entitled *Nature*. Having found the answers to his spiritual doubts, he formulated his essential philosophy, and almost everything he ever wrote afterward was an extension, amplification, or amendment of the ideas he first affirmed in *Nature*.

Emerson's religious doubts had lain deeper than his objection to the Unitarians' retention of belief in the historicity of miracles. He was also deeply unsettled by Newtonian physics' mechanistic conception of the universe and by the Lockean psychology of sensation that he had learned at Harvard. Emerson felt that there was no place for free will in the chains of mechanical cause and effect that rationalist philosophers conceived the world as being made up of. This world could be known only through the senses rather than through thought and intuition; it determined men physically and psychologically; and yet it made them victims of circumstance, beings whose superfluous mental powers were incapable of truly ascertaining reality.

Emerson reclaimed an idealistic philosophy from this dead end of 18th-century rationalism by once again asserting the human ability to transcend the materialistic world of sense experience and facts and become conscious of the all-pervading spirit of the universe and the potentialities of human freedom. God could best be found by looking inward into one's own self, one's own soul, and from such an enlightened self-awareness would in turn come freedom of action and the ability to change one's world according to the dictates of one's ideals and conscience. Human spiritual renewal thus proceeds from the individual's intimate personal experience of his own portion of the divine "oversoul," which is present in and permeates the entire creation and all living things, and which is accessible if only a person takes the trouble to look for it. Emerson enunciates how "reason," which to him denotes the intuitive awareness of eternal truth, can be relied upon in ways quite different from one's

*Ralph Waldo Emerson, a poet and essayist who was at the forefront of the Transcendental movement in 19th-century New England.* Otto Herschan/Hulton Archive/Getty Images

reliance on "understanding"—i.e., the ordinary gathering of sense-data and the logical comprehension of the material world. Emerson's doctrine of self-sufficiency and self-reliance naturally springs from his view that the individual need only look into his own heart for the spiritual guidance that has hitherto been the province of the established churches. The individual must then have the courage to be himself and to trust the inner force within him as he lives his life according to his intuitively derived precepts.

Obviously these ideas are far from original, and it is clear that Emerson was influenced in his formulation of them by his previous readings of Neoplatonist philosophy, the works of Coleridge and other European Romantics, the writings of Emmanuel Swedenborg, Hindu philosophy, and other sources. What set Emerson apart from others who were expressing similar Transcendentalist notions were his abilities as a polished literary stylist able to express his thought with vividness and breadth of vision. His philosophical exposition has a peculiar power and an organic unity whose cumulative effect was highly suggestive and stimulating to his contemporary readers' imaginations.

In a lecture entitled "The American Scholar" (August 31, 1837), Emerson described the resources and duties of the new liberated intellectual that he himself had become. This address was in effect a challenge to the Harvard intelligentsia, warning against pedantry, imitation of others, traditionalism, and scholarship unrelated to life. Emerson's "Address at Divinity College," Harvard University, in 1838 was another challenge, this time directed against a lifeless Christian tradition, especially Unitarianism as he had known it. He dismissed religious institutions and the divinity of Jesus as failures in man's attempt to encounter deity directly through the moral principle or through an intuited sentiment of virtue. This address alienated many, left him with few opportunities to preach, and resulted in his being ostracized by Harvard for many years. Young disciples, however, joined the informal Transcendental Club (founded in 1836) and encouraged him in his activities.

In 1840 he helped launch *The Dial*, first edited by Margaret Fuller and later by himself, thus providing an outlet for the new ideas Transcendentalists were trying to present to America. Though short-lived, the magazine provided a rallying point for the younger members of the school. From his continuing lecture series, he gathered his *Essays* into two volumes (1841, 1844), which made him internationally famous. In his first volume of *Essays* Emerson consolidated his thoughts on moral individualism and preached the ethics of self-reliance, the duty of self-cultivation, and the need for the expression of self. The second volume of *Essays* shows Emerson accommodating his earlier idealism to the limitations of real life; his later works show an increasing acquiescence to the state of things, less reliance on self, greater respect for society, and an awareness of the ambiguities and incompleteness of genius.

His *Representative Men* (1849) contained biographies of Plato, Swedenborg, Montaigne, Shakespeare, Napoleon, and Goethe. In *English Traits* he gave a character analysis of a people from which he himself stemmed. *The Conduct of Life* (1860), Emerson's most mature work, reveals a developed humanism together with a full awareness of man's limitations. It may be considered as partly confession. Emerson's collected *Poems* (1846) were supplemented by others in *May-Day* (1867), and the two volumes established his reputation as a major American poet.

By the 1860s Emerson's reputation in America was secure, for time was wearing down the novelty of his rebellion as he slowly accommodated himself to society. He continued to give frequent lectures, but the writing he did after 1860 shows a waning of his intellectual powers. A new generation knew only the old Emerson and had absorbed his teaching without recalling the acrimony it had occasioned. Upon his death in 1882 Emerson was transformed into the Sage of Concord, shorn of his power as a liberator and enrolled among the worthies of the very tradition he had set out to destroy.

Emerson's voice and rhetoric sustained the faith of thousands in the American lecture circuits between 1834 and the American Civil War. He served as a cultural middleman through whom the aesthetic and philosophical currents of Europe passed to America, and he led his countrymen during the burst of literary glory known as the American renaissance (1835–65). As a principal spokesman for Transcendentalism, the American tributary of European Romanticism, Emerson gave direction to a religious, philosophical, and ethical movement that above all stressed belief in the spiritual potential of every man.

# NATHANIEL HAWTHORNE

(b. July 4, 1804, Salem, Massachusetts, U.S. — d. May 19, 1864, Plymouth, New Hampshire)

The American novelist and short-story writer Nathaniel Hawthorne was a master of the allegorical and symbolic tale. One of the greatest fiction writers in American literature, he is best known for *The Scarlet Letter* (1850) and *The House of the Seven Gables* (1851).

## Early Years

Hawthorne's ancestors had lived in Salem since the 17th century. His earliest American ancestor, William Hathorne (Nathaniel added the *w* to the name when he began to write), was a magistrate who had sentenced a Quaker woman to public whipping. He had acted as a staunch defender of Puritan orthodoxy, with its zealous advocacy of a "pure," unaffected form of religious worship, its rigid adherence to a simple, almost severe, mode of life, and its conviction of the "natural depravity" of "fallen" man. Hawthorne was later to wonder whether the decline of his family's prosperity and prominence during the 18th century, while other Salem families were growing wealthy from the lucrative shipping trade, might not be a retribution for this act and for the role of William's son John as one of three judges in the Salem witchcraft trials of 1692. When Nathaniel's father—a ship's captain—died during one of his voyages, he left his young widow without means to care for her two girls and young Nathaniel, aged four. She moved in with her affluent brothers, the Mannings. Hawthorne grew up in their house in Salem and, for extensive periods during his teens, in Raymond, Maine, on the shores of Sebago Lake. He returned to Salem in 1825 after four years at Bowdoin College, in Brunswick, Maine. Hawthorne did not distinguish himself as a young man. Instead, he spent nearly a dozen years reading and trying to master the art of writing fiction.

## First Works

In college Hawthorne had excelled only in composition and had determined to become a writer. Upon graduation, he had written an amateurish novel, *Fanshawe*, which he published at his own expense—only to decide that it was unworthy of him and to try to destroy all copies. Hawthorne, however, soon found his own voice, style, and subjects, and within five years of his graduation he had published such impressive and distinctive stories as *The Hollow of the Three Hills* and *An Old Woman's Tale*. By 1832, *My Kinsman, Major Molineux* and *Roger Malvin's Burial*, two of his greatest tales—and among the finest in the language—had appeared. *Young Goodman Brown,* perhaps the greatest tale of witchcraft ever written, appeared in 1835.

His increasing success in placing his stories brought him a little fame. Unwilling to depend any longer on his uncles' generosity, he turned to a job in the Boston Custom House (1839–40) and for six months in 1841 was a resident at the agricultural cooperative Brook Farm, in West Roxbury, Massachusetts. Even when his first signed book, *Twice-Told Tales,* was published in 1837, the work had brought gratifying recognition but no dependable income. By 1842, however, Hawthorne's writing had brought him a sufficient income to allow him to marry Sophia Peabody; the couple rented the Old Manse in Concord and began a happy three-year period that Hawthorne would later record in his essay *The Old Manse.*

The presence of some of the leading social thinkers and philosophers of his day, such as Ralph Waldo Emerson, Henry Thoreau, and Bronson Alcott, in Concord made the village the centre of the philosophy of Transcendentalism, which encouraged man to transcend the materialistic world of experience and facts and become conscious of the pervading spirit of the universe and the potentialities for human freedom. Hawthorne welcomed the companionship of his Transcendentalist neighbours, but he had little to say to them. Artists and intellectuals never inspired his full confidence, but he thoroughly enjoyed the visit of his old college friend and classmate Franklin

Pierce, later to become president of the United States. At the Old Manse, Hawthorne continued to write stories, with the same result as before: literary success, monetary failure. His new short-story collection, *Mosses from an Old Manse*, appeared in 1846.

## Return to Salem

A growing family and mounting debts compelled the Hawthornes' return in 1845 to Salem, where Nathaniel was appointed surveyor of the Custom House by the Polk administration (Hawthorne had always been a loyal Democrat and pulled all the political strings he could to get this appointment). Three years later the presidential election brought the Whigs into power under Zachary Taylor, and Hawthorne lost his job; but in a few months of concentrated effort, he produced his masterpiece, *The Scarlet Letter.* The bitterness he felt over his dismissal is apparent in *The Custom House* essay prefixed to the novel. *The Scarlet Letter* tells the story of two lovers kept apart by the ironies of fate, their own mingled strengths and weaknesses, and the Puritan community's interpretation of moral law, until at last death unites them under a single headstone. The book made Hawthorne famous and was eventually recognized as one of the greatest of American novels.

Determined to leave Salem forever, Hawthorne moved to Lenox, located in the mountain scenery of the Berkshires in western Massachusetts. There he began work on *The House of the Seven Gables* (1851), the story of the Pyncheon family, who for generations had lived under a curse until it was removed at last by love.

At Lenox he enjoyed the stimulating friendship of Herman Melville, who lived in nearby Pittsfield. This friendship, although important for the younger writer and his work, was much less so for Hawthorne. Melville praised

Hawthorne extravagantly in a review of his *Mosses from an Old Manse*, and he also dedicated *Moby Dick* to Hawthorne. But eventually Melville came to feel that the friendship he so ardently pursued was one-sided. Later he was to picture the relationship with disillusion in his introductory sketch to *The Piazza Tales* and depicted Hawthorne himself unflatteringly as "Vine" in his long poem *Clarel*.

In the autumn of 1851 Hawthorne moved his family to another temporary residence, this time in West Newton, near Boston. There he quickly wrote *The Blithedale Romance,* which was based on his disenchantment with Brook Farm. Then he purchased and redecorated Bronson Alcott's house in Concord, the Wayside. *Blithedale* was disappointingly received and did not produce the income Hawthorne had expected. He was hoping for a lucrative political appointment that would bolster his finances; in the meantime, he wrote a campaign biography of his old friend Franklin Pierce. When Pierce won the presidency, Hawthorne was in 1853 rewarded with the consulship in Liverpool, Lancashire, a position he hoped would enable him in a few years to leave his family financially secure.

## Last Years

The remaining 11 years of Hawthorne's life were, from a creative point of view, largely anticlimactic. He performed his consular duties faithfully and effectively until his position was terminated in 1857, and then he spent a year and a half sight-seeing in Italy. Determined to produce yet another romance, he finally retreated to a seaside town in England and quickly produced *The Marble Faun*. In writing it, he drew heavily upon the experiences and impressions he had recorded in a notebook kept during his Italian tour to give substance to an allegory of the Fall of man, a theme that had usually been assumed in his earlier works but that now received direct and philosophic treatment.

Back in the Wayside once more in 1860, Hawthorne devoted himself entirely to his writing but was unable to make any progress with his plans for a new novel. The drafts of unfinished works he left are mostly incoherent and show many signs of a psychic regression, already fore-shadowed by his increasing restlessness and discontent of the preceding half dozen years. Some two years before his death he began to age very suddenly. His hair turned white, his handwriting changed, he suffered frequent nosebleeds, and he took to writing the figure "64" com-pulsively on scraps of paper. He died in his sleep on a trip in search of health with his friend Pierce.

## *Major Novels*

The main character of *The Scarlet Letter* is Hester Prynne, a young married woman who has borne an illegitimate child while living away from her husband in a village in Puritan New England. The husband, Roger Chillingworth, arrives in New England to find his wife pilloricd and made to wear the letter A (meaning adulteress) in scarlet on her dress as a punishment for her illicit affair and for her refusal to reveal the name of the child's father. Chillingworth becomes obsessed with finding the identity of his wife's former lover. He learns that Hester's paramour is a saintly young minister, Arthur Dimmesdale, and Chillingworth then proceeds to revenge himself by mentally tormenting the guilt-stricken young man. Hester herself is revealed to be a compassionate and splendidly self-reliant hero-ine who is never truly repentant for the act of adultery committed with the minister; she feels that their act was consecrated by their deep love for each other. In the end Chillingworth is morally degraded by his monomaniac pursuit of revenge, and Dimmesdale is broken by his own sense of guilt and publicly confesses his adultery before dying in Hester's arms. Only Hester can face the future optimistically, as she plans to ensure the future of her beloved little girl by taking her to Europe.

*The House of the Seven Gables* is a sombre study in hereditary sin based on the legend of a curse pronounced on Hawthorne's own family by a woman condemned to death during the witchcraft trials. The greed and arrogant pride of the novel's Pyncheon family down the generations is mirrored in the gloomy decay of their seven-gabled mansion, in which the family's enfeebled and impoverished poor relations live. At the book's end the descendant of a family long ago defrauded by the Pyncheons lifts his ancestors' curse on the mansion and marries a young niece of the family.

In *The Marble Faun* a trio of expatriate American art students in Italy become peripherally involved to varying degrees in the murder of an unknown man; their contact with sin transforms two of them from innocents into adults now possessed of a mature and critical awareness of life's complexity and possibilities.

# HANS CHRISTIAN ANDERSEN

(b. April 2, 1805, Odense, near Copenhagen, Denmark—d. August 4, 1875, Copenhagen)

Hans Christian Andersen was a unique master of the literary fairy tale whose stories are famous throughout the world; he is also the author of plays, novels, poems, travel books, and several autobiographies. While many of

*Danish writer Hans Christian Andersen was prodigious in several different literary forms, including plays, novels, and poems. He is best known, however, as the author of popular fairy tales.* Hulton Archive/Getty Images

these works are almost unknown outside Denmark, his fairy tales are among the most frequently translated works in all literary history.

Andersen was born in a slum and had a difficult battle breaking through the rigid class structure of his time. The first significant help came from Jonas Collin, one of the directors of the Royal Theatre in Copenhagen, to which Andersen had gone as a youth in the vain hope of winning fame as an actor. Collin raised money to send him to school. Although school was an unhappy experience for Andersen because of an unpleasant headmaster, it allowed him to be admitted to the University of Copenhagen in 1828.

The next year Andersen produced what is considered his first important literary work, *Fodrejse fra Holmens Kanal til Østpynten af Amager i aarene 1828 og 1829* (1829; "A Walk from Holmen's Canal to the East Point of the Island of Amager in the Years 1828 and 1829"), a fantastic tale in the style of the German Romantic writer E.T.A. Hoffmann. This work was an immediate success. He then turned to playwriting. After some unsuccessful attempts, he achieved recognition for *Mulatten* (1840; "The Mulatto"), a play portraying the evils of slavery. The theatre, however, was not to become his field, and for a long time Andersen was regarded primarily as a novelist. Most of his novels are autobiographical; among the best-known are *Improvisatoren* (1835; *The Improvisatore*), *O.T.* (1836; *OT: A Danish Romance*), and *Kun en spillemand* (1837; *Only a Fiddler*).

Andersen's first book of tales, *Eventyr, fortalte for børn* (1835; "Tales, Told for Children"), included stories such as "The Tinderbox," "Little Claus and Big Claus," "The Princess and the Pea," and "Little Ida's Flowers." Two further installments of stories made up the first volume of *Eventyr* (1837); a second volume was completed in 1842, and to these was added *Billedbog uden billeder* (1840; *A Picture-book Without Pictures*). New collections appeared in 1843, 1847, and 1852. The genre was expanded in *Nye eventyr og historier* (1858–72; "New Fairy Tales and Stories").

These collections broke new ground in both style and content. A real innovator in his method of telling tales, Andersen used the idioms and constructions of the spoken language, thus breaking with literary tradition. While some of his tales exhibit an optimistic belief in the ultimate triumph of goodness and beauty (e.g., "The Snow Queen"), others are deeply pessimistic and end unhappily. Indeed, one reason for Andersen's great appeal to both children and adults is that he was not afraid of introducing feelings and ideas that were beyond a child's immediate comprehension, yet he remained in touch with the child's perspective. He combined his natural storytelling abilities and great imaginative power with universal elements of folk legend to produce a body of fairy tales that relates to many cultures.

It may also be noted that part of what makes some of the tales so compelling is Andersen's identification with the unfortunate and the outcast. A strong autobiographical element runs through his sadder tales; throughout his life he perceived himself as an outsider, and, despite the international recognition he received, he never felt completely accepted. He suffered deeply in some of his closest personal relationships.

From 1831 to 1873 Andersen spent a good deal of his time traveling throughout Europe, Asia Minor, and Africa, and his impressions are recorded in a number of travel books, notably, *En digters bazar* (1842; *A Poet's Bazaar*), *I Sverrig* (1851; *Pictures of Sweden*), and *I Spanien* (1863; *In Spain*). Because Andersen rarely destroyed anything he wrote, his diaries and thousands of his letters are extant.

# ELIZABETH BARRETT BROWNING

(b. March 6, 1806, near Durham, Durham, England—d. June 29, 1861, Florence, Italy)

Elizabeth Barrett Browning was an English poet whose reputation rests chiefly upon her love poems, *Sonnets from the Portuguese* and *Aurora Leigh*, now considered an early feminist text. Her husband was Robert Browning.

Elizabeth was the eldest child of Edward Barrett Moulton (later Edward Moulton Barrett). Most of her girlhood was spent at a country house within sight of the Malvern Hills, in Worcestershire, where she was extraordinarily happy. At the age of 15, however, she fell seriously ill, probably as the result of a spinal injury, and her health was permanently affected. In 1832 the family moved to Sidmouth, Devon, and in 1836 they moved to London, where, in 1838, they took up residence at 50 Wimpole Street.

In London she contributed to several periodicals, and her first collection, *The Seraphim and Other Poems*, appeared in 1838. For reasons of health, she spent the next three years in Torquay, Devon, but after the death by drowning of her brother, Edward, she developed an almost morbid terror of meeting anyone apart from a small circle of intimates.

Her name, however, was well known in literary circles, and in 1844 her second volume of poetry, *Poems, by E. Barrett Barrett*, was enthusiastically received. In January 1845 she received from the poet Robert

Browning a telegram: "I love your verses with all my heart, dear Miss Barrett. I do, as I say, love these books with all my heart—and I love you too." In early summer the two met. Their courtship (whose daily progress is recorded in their letters) was kept a close secret from Elizabeth's despotic father, of whom she stood in some fear. *Sonnets from the Portuguese* (1850) records her reluctance to marry, but their wedding had taken place on September 12, 1846. Her father knew nothing of it, and Elizabeth continued to live at home for a week.

The Brownings then left for Pisa. (When Barrett died in 1856, Elizabeth was still unforgiven.) While in Pisa she wrote *The Runaway Slave at Pilgrim's Point* (Boston, 1848; London, 1849), a protest against slavery in the United States. The couple then settled in Florence, where their only child, Robert Wiedemann Barrett, was born in 1849. In 1851 and in 1855 the couple visited London; during the second visit, Elizabeth completed her most ambitious work, *Aurora Leigh* (1857), a long blank-verse poem telling the complicated and melodramatic love story of a young girl and a misguided philanthropist. This work did not impress most critics, though it was a huge popular success.

During the last years of her life, Mrs. Browning developed an interest in spiritualism and the occult, but her energy and attention were chiefly taken up by an obsession, to a degree that alarmed her closest friends, with Italian politics. *Casa Guidi Windows* (1851) had been a deliberate attempt to win sympathy for the Florentines, and she continued to believe in the integrity of Napoleon III. In *Poems Before Congress* (1860), the poem *A Curse for a Nation* was mistaken for a denunciation of England, whereas it was aimed at U.S. slavery.

In the summer of 1861 Mrs. Browning suffered a severe chill and died. She was buried in Florence.

# HENRY WADSWORTH LONGFELLOW

(b. February 27, 1807, Portland, Massachusetts [now in Maine],
U.S.—d. March 24, 1882, Cambridge, Massachusetts)

Henry Wadsworth Longfellow was the most popular American poet in the 19th century.

Longfellow attended private schools and the Portland Academy. He graduated from Bowdoin College in 1825. At college he was attracted especially to Sir Walter Scott's romances and Washington Irving's *Sketch Book*, and his verses appeared in national magazines. He was so fluent in translating that on graduation he was offered a professorship in modern languages provided that he would first study in Europe.

On the continent he learned French, Spanish, and Italian but refused to settle down to a regimen of scholarship at any university. In 1829 he returned to the United States to be a professor and librarian at Bowdoin. He wrote and edited textbooks, translated poetry and prose, and wrote essays on French, Spanish, and Italian literature, but he felt isolated. When he was offered a professorship at Harvard, with another opportunity to go abroad, he accepted and set forth for Germany in 1835. On this trip he visited England, Sweden, and the Netherlands. In 1835, saddened by the death of his first wife, whom he had married in 1831, he settled at Heidelberg, where he fell under the influence of German Romanticism.

In 1836 Longfellow returned to Harvard and settled in the famous Craigie House, which was later given to him as a wedding present when he remarried in 1843. His travel sketches, *Outre-Mer* (1835), did not succeed.

In 1839 he published *Voices of the Night*, which contained the poems "Hymn to the Night," "The Psalm of Life," and "The Light of the Stars" and achieved immediate popularity. That same year Longfellow published *Hyperion*, a romantic novel idealizing his European travels. In 1841 his *Ballads and Other Poems*, containing such favourites as "The Wreck of the Hesperus" and "The Village Blacksmith," swept the nation. The anti-slavery sentiments he expressed in *Poems on Slavery* (1842), however, lacked the humanity and power of John Greenleaf Whittier's denunciations on the same theme. Longfellow was more at home in *Evangeline* (1847), a narrative poem that reached almost every literate home in the United States. It is a sentimental tale of two lovers separated when British soldiers expel the Acadians (French colonists) from what is now Nova Scotia. The lovers, Evangeline and Gabriel, are reunited years later as Gabriel is dying.

Longfellow presided over Harvard's modern-language program for 18 years and then left teaching in 1854. In 1855, using Henry Rowe Schoolcraft's two books on the Indian tribes of North America as the base and the trochaic metrics of the Finnish epic *Kalevala* as his medium, he fashioned *The Song of Hiawatha* (1855). Its appeal to the public was immediate. Hiawatha is an Ojibwa Indian who, after various mythic feats, becomes his people's leader and marries Minnehaha before departing for the Isles of the Blessed. Both the poem and its singsong metre have been frequent objects of parody.

Longfellow's long poem *The Courtship of Miles Standish* (1858) was another great popular success. But the death in 1861 of his second wife after she accidentally set her dress on fire plunged him into melancholy. Driven by the need for spiritual relief, he translated the *Divine Comedy* of Dante Alighieri, producing one of the most notable translations to that time, and wrote six sonnets on Dante that are among his finest poems.

The *Tales of a Wayside Inn*, modeled roughly on Geoffrey Chaucer's *Canterbury Tales* and published in 1863, reveals his narrative gift. The first poem, "Paul Revere's Ride," became a national favourite. Written in anapestic tetrameter meant to suggest the galloping of a horse, this folk ballad recalls a hero of the American Revolution and his famous "midnight ride" to warn the Americans about the impending British raid on Concord, Massachusetts. Though its account of Revere's ride is historically inaccurate, the poem created an American legend. Longfellow published in 1872 what he intended to be his masterpiece, *Christus: A Mystery*, a trilogy dealing with Christianity from its beginning. He followed this work with two fragmentary dramatic poems, "Judas Maccabaeus" and "Michael Angelo." But his genius was not dramatic, as he had demonstrated earlier in *The Spanish Student* (1843). Long after his death in 1882, however, these neglected later works were seen to contain some of his most effective writing.

During his lifetime Longfellow was loved and admired both at home and abroad. In 1884 he was honoured by the placing of a memorial bust in Poets' Corner of Westminster Abbey in London, the first American to be so recognized. Sweetness, gentleness, simplicity, and a romantic vision shaded by melancholy are the characteristic features of Longfellow's poetry. He possessed great metrical skill, but he failed to capture the American spirit like his great contemporary Walt Whitman, and his work generally lacks emotional depth and imaginative power. Some years after Longfellow's death a violent reaction set in against his verse as critics dismissed his conventional high-minded sentiments and the gentle strain of Romanticism that he had made so popular. This harsh critical assessment, which tried to reduce him to the status of a mere hearthside rhymer, was perhaps as unbalanced as the adulation he had received during his lifetime. Some of Longfellow's sonnets and other lyrics are still among the finest in American poetry, and *Hiawatha*, "The Wreck of the Hesperus," *Evangeline*, and "Paul Revere's Ride" have become inseparable parts of the American heritage. Longfellow's immense popularity helped raise the status of poetry in his country, and he played an important part in bringing European cultural traditions to American audiences.

# EDGAR ALLAN POE

(b. January 19, 1809, Boston, Massachusetts, U.S.—d. October 7, 1849, Baltimore, Maryland)

The American short-story writer, poet, critic, and editor Edgar Allan Poe is famous for his cultivation of mystery and the macabre. His tale *The Murders in the Rue Morgue* (1841) initiated the modern detective story, and the atmosphere in his tales of horror is unrivaled in American fiction. His *The Raven* (1845) numbers among the best-known poems in the national literature.

## Life

Poe was the son of the English-born actress Elizabeth Arnold Poe and David Poe, Jr., an actor from Baltimore. After his mother died in Richmond, Virginia, in 1811, he was taken into the home of John Allan, a Richmond merchant (presumably his godfather), and of his childless wife. He was later taken to Scotland and England (1815–20), where he was given a classical education that was continued in Richmond. For 11 months in 1826 he attended

*Edgar Allan Poe.* U.S. Signal Corps/National Archives, Washington, D.C.

the University of Virginia, but his gambling losses at the university so incensed his guardian that he refused to let him continue, and Poe returned to Richmond to find his sweetheart, (Sarah) Elmira Royster, engaged. He went to Boston, where in 1827 he published a pamphlet of youthful Byronic poems, *Tamerlane, and Other Poems*. Poverty forced him to join the army under the name of Edgar A. Perry, but, on the death of Poe's foster mother, John Allan purchased his release from the army and helped him get an appointment to the U.S. Military Academy at West Point. Before going, Poe published a new volume at Baltimore, *Al Aaraaf, Tamerlane, and Minor Poems* (1829). He successfully sought expulsion from the academy, where he was absent from all drills and classes for a week. He proceeded to New York City and brought out a volume of *Poems*, containing several masterpieces, some showing the influence of John Keats, Percy Bysshe Shelley, and Samuel Taylor Coleridge. He then returned to Baltimore, where he began to write stories. In 1833 his *MS. Found in a Bottle* won $50 from a Baltimore weekly, and by 1835 he was in Richmond as editor of the *Southern Literary Messenger*. There he made a name as a critical reviewer and married his young cousin Virginia Clemm, who was only 13. Poe seems to have been an affectionate husband and son-in-law.

Poe was dismissed from his job in Richmond, apparently for drinking, and went to New York City. Drinking was in fact to be the bane of his life. To talk well in a large company he needed a slight stimulant, but a glass of sherry might start him on a spree; and, although he rarely succumbed to intoxication, he was often seen in public when he did. This gave rise to the conjecture that Poe was a drug addict, but according to medical testimony he had a brain lesion. While in New York City in 1838 he published a long prose narrative, *The Narrative of Arthur Gordon Pym*, combining (as so often in his tales) much factual material with the wildest fancies. It is considered one inspiration of Herman Melville's *Moby Dick*. In 1839 he became coeditor of *Burton's Gentleman's Magazine* in Philadelphia. There a contract for a monthly feature stimulated him to write *William Wilson* and *The Fall of the House of Usher,* stories of supernatural horror. The latter contains a study of a neurotic now known to have been an acquaintance of Poe, not Poe himself.

Later in 1839 Poe's *Tales of the Grotesque and Arabesque* appeared (dated 1840). He resigned from *Burton's* about June 1840 but returned in 1841 to edit its successor, *Graham's Lady's and Gentleman's Magazine*, in which he printed the first detective story, *The Murders in the Rue Morgue*. In 1843 his *The Gold-Bug* won a prize of $100 from the Philadelphia *Dollar Newspaper*, which gave him great publicity. In 1844 he returned to New York, wrote *The Balloon-Hoax* for the *Sun*, and became subeditor of the *New York Mirror* under N.P. Willis, thereafter a lifelong friend. In the *New York Mirror* of January 29, 1845, appeared, from advance sheets of the *American Review*, his most famous poem, *The Raven,* which gave him national fame at once. Poe then became editor of the *Broadway Journal*, a short-lived weekly, in which he republished most of his short stories, in 1845. During this last year the now-forgotten poet Frances Sargent Locke Osgood pursued Poe. Virginia did not object, but "Fanny's" indiscreet writings about her literary love caused great scandal. His *The Raven and Other Poems* and a selection of his *Tales* came out in 1845, and in 1846 Poe moved to a cottage at Fordham (now part of New York City), where he wrote for *Godey's Lady's Book* (May–October 1846) *The Literati of New York City*—gossipy sketches on personalities of the day, which led to a libel suit.

Poe's wife, Virginia, died in January 1847. The following year he went to Providence, Rhode Island, to woo Sarah Helen Whitman, a poet. There was a brief engagement. Poe had close but platonic entanglements with Annie Richmond and with Sarah Anna Lewis, who helped him financially. He composed poetic tributes to all of them. In 1848 he also published the lecture *Eureka,* a transcendental "explanation" of the universe, which has been hailed as a masterpiece by some critics and as nonsense by others. In 1849 he went south, had a wild spree in Philadelphia, but got safely to Richmond, where he finally became engaged to Elmira Royster, by then the widowed Mrs. Shelton, and spent a happy summer with only one or two relapses. He enjoyed the companionship of childhood friends and an unromantic friendship with a young poet, Susan Archer Talley.

Poe had some forebodings of death when he left Richmond for Baltimore late in September. There he died, although whether from drinking, heart failure, or other causes was still uncertain in the 21st century. He was buried in Westminster Presbyterian churchyard in Baltimore.

## *Appraisal*

Poe's work owes much to the concern of Romanticism with the occult and the satanic. It owes much also to his own feverish dreams, to which he applied a rare faculty of shaping plausible fabrics out of impalpable materials. With an air of objectivity and spontaneity, his productions are closely dependent on his own powers of imagination and an elaborate technique. His keen and sound judgment as an appraiser of contemporary literature, his idealism and musical gift as a poet, his dramatic art as a storyteller, considerably appreciated in his lifetime, secured him a prominent place among universally known men of letters.

The outstanding fact in Poe's character is a strange duality. The wide divergence of contemporary judgments on the man seems almost to point to the coexistence of two persons in him. With those he loved he was gentle and devoted. Others, who were the butt of his sharp criticism, found him irritable and self-centred and went so far as to accuse him of lack of principle. Was it, it has been asked, a double of the man rising from harrowing nightmares or from the haggard inner vision of dark crimes or from appalling graveyard fantasies that loomed in Poe's unstable being?

Much of Poe's best work is concerned with terror and sadness, but in ordinary circumstances the poet was a pleasant companion. He talked brilliantly, chiefly of literature, and read his own poetry and that of others in a voice of surpassing beauty. He admired Shakespeare and Alexander Pope. He had a sense of humour, apologizing to a visitor for not keeping a pet raven. If the mind of Poe is considered, the duality is still more striking. On one side, he was an idealist and a visionary. His yearning for the ideal was both of the heart and of the imagination. His sensitivity to the beauty and sweetness of women inspired his most touching lyrics (*To Helen, Annabel Lee, Eulalie, To One in Paradise*) and the full-toned prose hymns to beauty and love in *Ligeia* and *Eleonora*. In *Israfel* his imagination carried him away from the material world into a dreamland. This Pythian mood was especially characteristic of the later years of his life.

More generally, in such verses as *The Valley of Unrest, Lenore, The Raven, For Annie*, and *Ulalume* and in his prose tales, his familiar mode of evasion from the universe of common experience was through eerie thoughts, impulses, or fears. From these materials he drew the startling effects of his tales of death (*The Fall of the House of Usher, The Masque of the Red Death, The Facts in the Case of M. Valdemar, The Premature Burial, The Oval Portrait, Shadow*), his tales of wickedness and crime (*Berenice, The Black Cat, William Wilson, The Imp of the Perverse, The Cask of Amontillado, The Tell-Tale Heart*), his tales of survival after dissolution (*Ligeia, Morella, Metzengerstein*), and his tales of fatality (*The Assignation, The Man of the Crowd*). Even when he does not hurl his characters into the clutch of mysterious forces or onto the untrodden paths of the beyond, he uses the anguish of imminent death as the means of causing the nerves to quiver (*The Pit and the Pendulum*), and his grotesque invention deals with corpses and decay in an uncanny play with the aftermath of death.

On the other side, Poe is conspicuous for a close observation of minute details, as in the long narratives and in many of the descriptions that introduce the tales or constitute their settings. Closely connected with this is his power of ratiocination. He prided himself on his logic and carefully handled this real accomplishment so as to impress the public with his possessing still more of it than he had; hence the would-be feats of thought reading, problem unraveling, and cryptography that he attributed to his Legrand and Dupin. This suggested to him the analytical tales, which created the detective story, and his science fiction tales.

The same duality is evinced in his art. He was capable of writing angelic or weird poetry, with a supreme sense of rhythm and word appeal, or prose of sumptuous beauty and suggestiveness, with the apparent abandon of compelling inspiration; yet he would write down a problem of morbid psychology or the outlines of an unrelenting plot in a hard and dry style. In Poe's masterpieces the double contents of his temper, of his mind, and of his art are fused into a oneness of tone, structure, and movement, the more effective, perhaps, as it is compounded of various elements.

As a critic, Poe laid great stress upon correctness of language, metre, and structure. He formulated rules for the short story, in which he sought the ancient unities: i.e., the short story should relate a complete action and take place within one day in one place. To these unities he added that of mood or effect. He was not extreme in these views, however. He praised longer works and sometimes thought allegories and morals admirable if not crudely presented. Poe admired originality, often in work very different from his own, and was sometimes an unexpectedly generous critic of decidedly minor writers.

Poe's genius was early recognized abroad. No one did more to persuade the world and, in the long run, the United States, of Poe's greatness than the French poets Charles Baudelaire and Stéphane Mallarmé. Indeed his role in French literature was that of a poetic master model and guide to criticism. French Symbolism relied on his *The Philosophy of Composition,* borrowed from his imagery, and used his examples to generate the modern theory of "pure poetry."

#

(b. March 19 [March 31, New Style], 1809, Sorochintsy, near Poltava, Ukraine, Russian Empire [now in Ukraine]—d. February 21 [March 4], 1852, Moscow, Russia)

Nikolay Gogol was a Ukrainian-born Russian humorist, dramatist, and novelist, whose novel *Myortvye dushi* (*Dead Souls*) and whose short story "Shinel" ("The Overcoat") are considered the foundations of the great 19th-century tradition of Russian realism.

## Youth and Early Fame

The Ukrainian countryside, with its colourful peasantry, its Cossack traditions, and its rich folklore, constituted the background of Gogol's boyhood. A member of the petty Ukrainian gentry, Gogol was sent at the age of 12 to the high school at Nezhin. There he distinguished himself by his biting tongue, his contributions of prose and poetry to a magazine, and his portrayal of comic old men and women in school theatricals. In 1828 he went to St. Petersburg, hoping to enter the civil service, but soon discovered that without money and connections he would have to fight hard for a living. He even tried to become an actor, but his audition was unsuccessful. In this predicament he remembered a mediocre sentimental-idyllic poem he had written in the high school. Anxious to achieve fame as a poet, he published it at his own expense, but its failure was so disastrous that he burned all the copies and thought of emigrating to the United States. He embezzled the money his mother had sent him for payment of the mortgage on her farm and took a boat to the German port of Lübeck. He did not sail but briefly toured Germany. Whatever his reasons for undertaking such an irresponsible trip, he soon ran out of money and returned to St. Petersburg, where he got an ill-paid government post.

In the meantime Gogol wrote occasionally for periodicals, finding an escape in childhood memories of the Ukraine. He committed to paper what he remembered of the sunny landscapes, peasants, and boisterous village lads, and he also related tales about devils, witches, and other demonic or fantastic agents that enliven Ukrainian folklore. Romantic stories of the past were thus intermingled with realistic incidents of the present. Such was the origin of his eight narratives, published in two volumes in 1831–32 under the title *Vechera na khutore bliz Dikanki* (*Evenings on a Farm near Dikanka*). Written in a lively and at times colloquial prose, these works contributed something fresh and new to Russian literature. In addition to the author's whimsical inflection, they abounded in genuine folk flavour, including numerous Ukrainian words and phrases, all of which captivated the Russian literary world.

## Mature Career

The young author became famous overnight. Among his first admirers were the poets Aleksandr Pushkin and Vasily Zhukovsky, both of whom he had met before. This esteem was soon shared by the writer Sergey Aksakov and the critic Vissarion Belinsky, among others. Having given up his second government post, Gogol was now teaching history in a boarding school for girls. In 1834 he was appointed assistant professor of medieval history at St. Petersburg University, but he felt inadequately equipped for the position and left it after a year. Meanwhile, he prepared energetically for the publication of his next two books, *Mirgorod* and *Arabeski* (*Arabesques*), which appeared in 1835. The four stories constituting *Mirgorod* were a continuation of the *Evenings*, but they revealed a strong gap between Gogol's romantic escapism and his otherwise pessimistic attitude toward life. Such a splendid narrative of the Cossack past as "Taras Bulba" certainly provided an escape from the present. But "Povest o tom, kak possorilsya Ivan Ivanovich s Ivanom Nikiforovichem" ("Story of the Quarrel Between Ivan Ivanovich and Ivan Nikiforovich") was, for all its humour, full of bitterness about the meanness and vulgarity of existence. Even the idyllic motif of Gogol's "Starosvetskiye pomeshchiki" ("Old-World Landowners") is undermined with satire, for the mutual affection of the aged couple is marred by gluttony, their ceaseless eating for eating's sake.

The aggressive realism of a romantic who can neither adapt himself to the world nor escape from it, and is therefore all the more anxious to expose its vulgarity and evil, predominates in Gogol's Petersburg stories printed (together with some essays) in the second work, *Arabesques*. In one of these stories, "Zapiski sumasshedshego" ("Diary of a Madman"), the hero is an utterly frustrated office drudge who finds compensation in megalomania and ends in a lunatic asylum. In another, "Nevsky prospekt" ("Nevsky Prospect"), a tragic romantic dreamer is contrasted to an adventurous vulgarian, while in the revised finale of "Portret" ("The Portrait") the author stresses his conviction that evil is ineradicable in this world. In 1836 Gogol published in Pushkin's *Sovremennik* ("The Contemporary") one of his gayest satirical stories, "Kolyaska" ("The Coach"). In the same periodical also appeared his amusingly caustic surrealist tale, "Nos" ("The Nose"). Gogol's association with Pushkin was of great value because he always trusted his friend's taste and criticism; moreover, he received from Pushkin the themes for his two principal works, the play *Revizor* (*The Government Inspector*, sometimes titled *The Inspector General*), and *Dead Souls*, which were important not only to Russian literature but also to Gogol's further destiny.

A great comedy, *The Government Inspector* mercilessly lampoons the corrupt bureaucracy under Nicholas I. Having mistaken a well-dressed windbag for the dreaded incognito inspector, the officials of a provincial town bribe and banquet him in order to turn his attention away from the crying evils of their administration. But during the triumph, after the bogus inspector's departure, the arrival of the real inspector is announced—to the horror of those concerned. It was only by a special order of the tsar that the first performance of this comedy of indictment and "laughter through tears" took place on April 19, 1836. Yet the hue and cry raised by the reactionary press and officialdom was such that Gogol left Russia for Rome, where he remained, with some interruptions, until 1842. The atmosphere he found in Italy appealed to his taste and to his somewhat patriarchal—not to say primitive—religious propensity. The religious painter Aleksandr Ivanov, who worked in Rome, became his close friend. He also met a number of traveling Russian aristocrats and often saw the émigrée princess Zinaida Volkonsky, a convert to Roman Catholicism, in whose circle religious themes were much discussed. It was in Rome, too, that Gogol wrote most of his masterpiece, *Dead Souls*.

This comic novel, or "epic," as the author labeled it, reflects feudal Russia, with its serfdom and bureaucratic iniquities. Chichikov, the hero of the novel, is a polished swindler who, after several reverses of fortune, wants to get rich quick. His bright but criminal idea is to buy from various landowners a number of their recently deceased serfs (or "souls," as they were called in Russia) whose deaths have not yet been registered by the official census and are therefore regarded as still being alive. The landowners are only too happy to rid themselves of the fictitious property on which they continue to pay taxes until the next census. Chichikov intends to pawn the "souls" in a bank and, with the money thus raised, settle down in a distant region as a respectable gentleman. The provincial townsmen of his first stop are charmed by his polite manners; he approaches several owners in the district who are all willing to sell the "souls" in question, knowing full well the fraudulent nature of the deal. The sad conditions of Russia, in which serfs used to be bought and sold like cattle, are evident throughout the grotesquely humorous transactions. The landowners, one more queer and repellent than the last, have become nicknames known to every

Russian reader. When the secret of Chichikov's errands begins to leak out, he hurriedly leaves the town.

*Dead Souls* was published in 1842, the same year in which the first edition of Gogol's collected works was published. The edition included, among his other writings, a sprightly comedy titled *Zhenitba* (*Marriage*) and the story "The Overcoat." The latter concerns a humble scribe who, with untold sacrifices, has acquired a smart overcoat; when robbed of it he dies of a broken heart. The tragedy of this insignificant man was worked out with so many significant trifles that, years later, Fyodor Dostoyevsky was to exclaim that all Russian realists had come "from under Gogol's greatcoat." The apex of Gogol's fame was, however, *Dead Souls*. The democratic intellectuals of Belinsky's brand saw in this novel a work permeated with the spirit of their own liberal aspirations. Its author was all the more popular because after Pushkin's tragic death Gogol was now looked upon as the head of Russian literature. Gogol, however, began to see his leading role in a perspective of his own. Having witnessed the beneficent results of the laughter caused by his indictments, he was sure that God had given him a great literary talent in order to make him not only castigate abuses through laughter but also to reveal to Russia the righteous way of living in an evil world. He therefore decided to continue *Dead Souls* as a kind of *Divine Comedy* in prose; the already published part would represent the *Inferno* of Russian life, and the second and third parts (with Chichikov's moral regeneration) would be its *Purgatorio* and *Paradiso*.

## Creative Decline

Unfortunately, having embarked upon such a soul-saving task, Gogol noticed that his former creative capacity was deserting him. He worked on the second part of his novel for more than 10 years but with meagre results. In drafts of four chapters and a fragment of the fifth found among his papers, the negative and grotesque characters are drawn with some intensity, whereas the virtuous types he was so anxious to exalt are stilted and devoid of life. This lack of zest was interpreted by Gogol as a sign that, for some reason, God no longer wanted him to be the voice exhorting his countrymen to a more worthy existence. In spite of this he decided to prove that at least as teacher and preacher—if not as artist—he was still able to set forth what was needed for Russia's moral and worldly improvement. This he did in his ill-starred *Bybrannyye mesta iz perepiski s druzyami* (1847; *Selected Passages from Correspondence with My Friends*), a collection of 32 discourses eulogizing not only the conservative official church but also the very powers that he had so mercilessly condemned only a few years before. It is no wonder that the book was fiercely attacked by his one-time admirers, most of all by Belinsky, who in an indignant letter called him "a preacher of the knout, a defender of obscurantism and of darkest oppression." Crushed by it all, Gogol saw in it a further proof that, sinful as he was, he had lost God's favour forever. He increased his prayers and his ascetic practices; in 1848 he even made a pilgrimage to Palestine, but in vain. Despite a few bright moments he began to wander from place to place like a doomed soul. Finally he settled in Moscow, where he came under the influence of a fanatical priest, Father Matvey Konstantinovsky, who seems to have practiced on Gogol a kind of spiritual sadism. Ordered by him, Gogol burned the presumably completed manuscript of the second volume of *Dead Souls* on Febuary 24 (Febuary 11, O.S.), 1852. Ten days later he died, on the verge of semimadness.

# ALFRED, LORD TENNYSON

(b. August 6, 1809, Somersby, Lincolnshire, England—d. October 6, 1892, Aldworth, Surrey)

The English poet Alfred Tennyson, 1st Baron Tennyson of Aldworth and Freshwater, is often regarded as the chief representative of the Victorian age in poetry.

Tennyson was the fourth of 12 children, born into an old Lincolnshire family, his father a rector. Alfred, with two of his brothers, Frederick and Charles, was sent in 1815 to Louth grammar school—where he was unhappy. Alfred was precocious, and before his teens he had composed in the styles of Alexander Pope, Sir Walter Scott, and John Milton.

## Early Work

To Tennyson's youth belongs *The Devil and the Lady*, a collection of previously unpublished poems published posthumously in 1930. The poems show an astonishing understanding of Elizabethan dramatic verse. Lord Byron was a dominant influence on the young Tennyson.

In 1824 the health of Tennyson's father began to break down, and he took refuge in drink. Alfred, though depressed by unhappiness at home, continued to write, collaborating with Frederick and Charles in *Poems by Two Brothers* (1826; dated 1827). His contributions (more than half the volume) are mostly in fashionable styles of the day.

In 1827 Alfred and Charles joined Frederick at Trinity College, Cambridge. There Alfred made friends with Arthur Hallam, the gifted son of the historian Henry

Hallam. This was the deepest friendship of Tennyson's life. The friends became members of the Apostles, an exclusive undergraduate club of earnest intellectual interests. Tennyson's reputation as a poet increased at Cambridge. In 1829 he won the chancellor's gold medal with a poem called *Timbuctoo*. In 1830 *Poems, Chiefly Lyrical* was published. In the same year Tennyson, Hallam, and other Apostles went to Spain to help in the unsuccessful revolution against Ferdinand VII. In the meantime, Hallam had become attached to Tennyson's sister Emily but was forbidden by her father to correspond with her for a year.

In 1831 Tennyson's father died. Alfred's misery was increased by his grandfather's discovery of his father's debts. He left Cambridge without taking a degree, and his grandfather made financial arrangements for the family. In the same year, Hallam published a eulogistic article on *Poems, Chiefly Lyrical* in *The Englishman's Magazine*. He went to Somersby in 1832 as the accepted suitor of Emily.

In 1832 Tennyson published another volume of his poems (dated 1833), including "The Lotos-Eaters," "The Palace of Art," and "The Lady of Shalott." Among them was a satirical epigram on the critic Christopher North (pseudonym of the Scottish writer John Wilson), who had attacked *Poems, Chiefly Lyrical* in *Blackwood's Magazine*. Tennyson's sally prompted a scathing attack on his new volume in the *Quarterly Review*. The attacks distressed Tennyson, but he continued to revise his old poems and compose new ones.

In 1833 Hallam's engagement was recognized by his family, but while on a visit to Vienna in September he died suddenly. The shock to Tennyson was severe. It came at a depressing time; three of his brothers, Edward, Charles, and Septimus, were suffering from mental illness, and the bad reception of his own work added to the gloom. Yet it was in this period that he wrote some of his most characteristic work: "The Two Voices" (of which the original title, significantly, was "Thoughts of a Suicide"), "Ulysses," "St. Simeon Stylites," and, probably, the first draft of "Morte d'Arthur." To this period also belong some of the poems that became constituent parts of *In Memoriam*, celebrating Hallam's death, and lyrics later worked into *Maud*.

In May 1836 his brother Charles married Louisa Sellwood of Horncastle, and at the wedding Alfred fell in love with her sister Emily. For some years the lovers corresponded, but Emily's father disapproved of Tennyson because of his bohemianism, addiction to port and tobacco, and liberal religious views; and in 1840 he forbade the correspondence. Meanwhile the Tennysons had left Somersby and were living a rather wandering life nearer London.

## Major Literary Work

In 1842 Tennyson published *Poems*, in two volumes, one containing a revised selection from the volumes of 1830 and 1832, the other, new poems. The new poems included "Morte d'Arthur," "The Two Voices," "Locksley Hall," and "The Vision of Sin" and other poems that reveal a strange naïveté, such as "The May Queen," "Lady Clara Vere de Vere," and "The Lord of Burleigh." The new volume was not on the whole well received. But the grant to him at this time, by the prime minister, Sir Robert Peel, of a pension of £200 helped to alleviate his financial worries. In 1847 he published his first long poem, *The Princess,* a singular anti-feminist fantasia.

The year 1850 marked a turning point. Tennyson resumed his correspondence with Emily Sellwood, and their engagement was renewed and followed by marriage. Meanwhile, Edward Moxon offered to publish the elegies on Hallam that Tennyson had been composing over the years. They appeared, at first anonymously, as *In Memoriam* (1850), which had a great success with both reviewers and the public, won him the friendship of Queen Victoria, and helped bring about, in the same year, his appointment as poet laureate.

*In Memoriam* is a vast poem of 131 sections of varying length, with a prologue and epilogue. Inspired by the grief Tennyson felt at the untimely death of his friend Hallam, the poem touches on many intellectual issues of the Victorian Age as the author searches for the meaning of life and death and tries to come to terms with his sense of loss. Most notably, *In Memoriam* reflects the struggle to reconcile traditional religious faith and belief in immortality with the emerging theories of evolution and modern geology. The verses show the development over three years of the poet's acceptance and understanding of his friend's death and conclude with an epilogue, a happy marriage song on the occasion of the wedding of Tennyson's sister Cecilia.

After his marriage, which was happy, Tennyson's life became more secure and outwardly uneventful. There were two sons: Hallam

*Alfred, Lord Tennyson.* Encyclopædia Britannica, Inc.

and Lionel. The times of wandering and unsettlement ended in 1853, when the Tennysons took a house, Farringford, in the Isle of Wight.

Tennyson's position as the national poet was confirmed by his *Ode on the Death of the Duke of Wellington* (1852)—though some critics at first thought it disappointing—and the famous poem on the charge of the Light Brigade at Balaklava, published in 1855 in *Maud and Other Poems. Maud* itself, a strange and turbulent "monodrama," provoked a storm of protest; many of the poet's admirers were shocked by the morbidity, hysteria, and bellicosity of the hero. Yet *Maud* was Tennyson's favourite among his poems.

A project that Tennyson had long considered at last issued in *Idylls of the King* (1859), a series of 12 connected poems broadly surveying the legend of King Arthur from his falling in love with Guinevere to the ultimate ruin of his kingdom. The poems concentrate on the introduction of evil to Camelot because of the adulterous love of Lancelot and Queen Guinevere, and on the consequent fading of the hope that had at first infused the Round Table fellowship. *Idylls of the King* had an immediate success, and Tennyson, who loathed publicity, had now acquired a sometimes embarrassing public fame. The *Enoch Arden* volume of 1864 perhaps represents the peak of his popularity. New Arthurian *Idylls* were published in *The Holy Grail, and Other Poems* in 1869 (dated 1870).

In 1874 Tennyson decided to try his hand at poetic drama. *Queen Mary* appeared in 1875, and an abridged version was produced at the Lyceum in 1876 with only moderate success. It was followed by *Harold* (1876; dated 1877), *Becket* (not published in full until 1884), and the "village tragedy" *The Promise of May*, which proved a failure at the Globe in November 1882. This play—his only prose work—shows Tennyson's growing despondency and resentment at the religious, moral, and political tendencies of the age. He had already caused some sensation by publishing a poem called "Despair" in *The Nineteenth Century* (November 1881). A more positive indication of Tennyson's later beliefs appears in "The Ancient Sage," published in *Tiresias and Other Poems* (1885). Here the poet records his intimations of a life before and beyond this life.

Tennyson accepted a peerage (after some hesitation) in 1884. In 1886 he published a new volume containing "Locksley Hall Sixty Years After," consisting mainly of imprecations against modern decadence and liberalism and a retraction of the earlier poem's belief in inevitable human progress.

In 1889 Tennyson wrote the famous short poem "Crossing the Bar," during the crossing to the Isle of Wight. In the same year he published *Demeter and Other Poems*, which contains the charming retrospective "To Mary Boyle," "The Progress of Spring," a fine lyric written much earlier and rediscovered, and "Merlin and the Gleam," an allegorical summing-up of his poetic career. In 1892 his play *The Foresters* was successfully produced in New York City. Despite ill health, he was able to correct the proofs of his last volume, *The Death of Oenone, Akbar's Dream, and Other Poems* (1892).

# WILLIAM MAKEPEACE THACKERAY

(b. July 18, 1811, Calcutta, India—d. December 24, 1863, London, England)

William Makepeace Thackeray was an English novelist whose reputation rests chiefly on *Vanity Fair* (1847–48), a novel of the Napoleonic period in England,

and *The History of Henry Esmond, Esq.* (1852), set in the early 18th century.

## Life

Thackeray was the only son of Richmond Thackeray, an administrator in the East India Company. His father died in 1815, and in 1816 Thackeray was sent home to England. His mother joined him in 1820, having married (1817) an engineering officer with whom she had been in love before she met Richmond Thackeray. After attending several grammar schools Thackeray went in 1822 to Charterhouse, the London public (private) school, where he led a rather lonely and miserable existence.

He was happier while studying at Trinity College, Cambridge (1828–30). In 1830 he left Cambridge without taking a degree, and during 1831–33 he studied law at the Middle Temple, London. He then considered painting as a profession; his artistic gifts are seen in his letters and many of his early writings, which are amusingly and energetically illustrated. All his efforts at this time have a dilettante air, understandable in a young man who, on coming of age in 1832, had inherited £20,000 from his father. He soon lost his fortune, however, through gambling and unlucky speculations and investments. In 1836, while studying art in Paris, he married a penniless Irish girl, and his stepfather bought a newspaper so that he could remain there as its correspondent. After the paper's failure (1837) he took his wife back to Bloomsbury, London, and became a hardworking and prolific professional journalist.

Of Thackeray's three daughters, one died in infancy (1839); and in 1840, after her last confinement, Mrs. Thackeray became insane. She never recovered and long survived her husband, living with friends in the country. Thackeray was, in effect, a widower, relying much on club life and gradually giving more and more attention to his daughters, for whom he established a home in London in 1846. The serial publication in 1847–48 of his novel *Vanity Fair* brought Thackeray both fame and prosperity, and from then on he was an established author on the English scene.

Thackeray's one serious romantic attachment in his later life, to Jane Brookfield, can be traced in his letters. She was the wife of a friend of his Cambridge days, and during Thackeray's "widowerhood," when his life lacked an emotional centre, he found one in the Brookfield home. Henry Brookfield's insistence in 1851 that his wife's passionate but platonic friendship with Thackeray should end was a grief greater than any the author had known since his wife's descent into insanity.

Thackeray tried to find consolation in travel, lecturing in the United States on *The English Humorists of the 18th Century* (1852–53; published 1853) and on *The Four Georges* (1855–56; published 1860). But after 1856 he settled in London. He stood unsuccessfully for Parliament in 1857, quarreled with Dickens, formerly a friendly rival, in the so-called "Garrick Club Affair" (1858), and in 1860 founded *The Cornhill Magazine*, becoming its editor. After he died in 1863, a commemorative bust of him was placed in Westminster Abbey.

## Early Writings

The 19th century was the age of the magazine, which had been developed to meet the demand for family reading among the growing middle class. In the late 1830s Thackeray became a notable contributor of articles on varied topics to *Fraser's Magazine*, *The New Monthly Magazine*, and, later, to *Punch*. His work was unsigned or written under such pen names as Mr. Michael Angelo Titmarsh, Fitz-Boodle, The Fat Contributor, or Ikey Solomons. He collected the best of these early writings in *Miscellanies*, 4 vol. (1855–57). These include *The Yellowplush Correspondence*, the memoirs and diary of a young cockney footman written in his own vocabulary and style; *Major Gahagan* (1838–39), a fantasy of soldiering in India; *Catherine* (1839–40), a burlesque of the popular "Newgate novels" of romanticized crime and low life, and itself a good realistic crime story; *The History of Samuel Titmarsh and the Great Hoggarty Diamond* (1841), which was an earlier version of the young married life described in *Philip*; and *The Luck of Barry Lyndon* (1844; revised as *The Memoirs of Barry Lyndon*, 1856), which is a historical novel and his first full-length work. *Barry Lyndon* is an excellent, speedy, satirical narrative until the final sadistic scenes and was a trial run for the great historical novels, especially *Vanity Fair*. *The Book of Snobs* (1848) is a collection of articles that had appeared successfully in *Punch* (as "The Snobs of England, by One of Themselves," 1846–47). It consists of sketches of London characters and displays Thackeray's virtuosity in quick character-drawing. *The Rose and the Ring*, Thackeray's Christmas book for 1855, remains excellent entertainment, as do some of his verses; like many good prose writers, he had a facility in writing light verse and ballads.

## Mature Writings

With *Vanity Fair* (1847–48), the first work published under his own name, Thackeray adopted the system of publishing a novel serially in monthly parts that had been so successfully used by Dickens. Set in the second decade of the 19th century, the period of the Regency, the novel deals mainly with the interwoven fortunes of two contrasting women, Amelia Sedley and Becky Sharp. The latter, an unprincipled adventuress, is the leading personage and is perhaps the most memorable character Thackeray created. Subtitled "A Novel Without a Hero," the novel is deliberately antiheroic: Thackeray states that in this novel his object is to "indicate...that we are for the most part... foolish and selfish people...all eager after vanities."

The wealthy, wellborn, passive Amelia Sedley and the ambitious, energetic, scheming, provocative, and essentially amoral Becky Sharp, daughter of a poor drawing master, are contrasted in their fortunes and reactions to life, but the contrast of their characters is not the simple one between moral good and evil—both are presented with dispassionate sympathy. Becky is the character around whom all the men play their parts in an upper middle-class and aristocratic background. Amelia marries George Osborne, but George, just before he is killed at the Battle of Waterloo, is ready to desert his young wife for Becky, who has fought her way up through society to marriage with Rawdon Crawley, a young officer of good family. Crawley, disillusioned, finally leaves Becky, and in the end virtue apparently triumphs, Amelia marries her lifelong admirer, Colonel Dobbin, and Becky settles down to genteel living and charitable works.

The rich movement and colour of this panorama of early 19th-century society make *Vanity Fair* Thackeray's greatest achievement; the narrative skill, subtle characterization, and descriptive power make it one of the outstanding novels of its period. But *Vanity Fair* is more than a portrayal and imaginative analysis of a particular society. Throughout we are made subtly aware of the ambivalence of human motives, and so are prepared for Thackeray's conclusion: "Ah! *Vanitas Vanitatum!* Which of us is happy in this world? Which of us has his desire, or having it, is satisfied?" It is its tragic irony that makes *Vanity Fair* a lasting and insightful evaluation of human ambition and experience.

Successful and famous, Thackeray went on to exploit two lines of development opened up in *Vanity Fair*: a gift for evoking the London scene and for writing historical novels that demonstrate the connections between past and present. He began with the first, writing *The History of Pendennis* (1848–50), which is partly fictionalized auto-biography. In it, Thackeray traces the youthful career of Arthur Pendennis—his first love affair, his experiences at "Oxbridge University," his working as a London journalist, and so on—achieving a convincing portrait of a much-tempted young man.

Turning to the historical novel, Thackeray chose the reign of Queen Anne for the period of *The History of Henry Esmond, Esq.*, 3 vol. (1852). Some critics had thought that *Pendennis* was a formless, rambling book. In response, Thackeray constructed *Henry Esmond* with great care, giving it a much more formal plot structure. The story, narrated by Esmond, begins when he is 12, in 1691, and ends in 1718. Its complexity of incident is given unity by Beatrix and Esmond, who stand out against a back-ground of London society and the political life of the time. Beatrix dominates the book. Seen first as a charm-ing child, she develops beauty combined with a power that is fatal to the men she loves. One of Thackeray's great creations, she is a heroine of a new type, emotion-ally complex and compelling, but not a pattern of virtue. Esmond, a sensitive, brave, aristocratic soldier, falls in love with her but is finally disillusioned. Befriended as an orphan by Beatrix's parents, Lord and Lady Castlewood, Henry initially adores Lady Castlewood as a mother and eventually, in his maturity, marries her.

Written in a pastiche of 18th-century prose, the novel is one of the best evocations in English of the atmosphere of a past age. It was not well received, however—Esmond's marriage to Lady Castlewood was criticized. George Eliot called it "the most uncomfortable book you can imagine." But it has come to be accepted as a notable English historical novel.

Thackeray returned to the contemporary scene in his novel *The Newcomes* (1853–55). This work is essentially a detailed study of prosperous middle-class society and is centred upon the family of the title. Col. Thomas Newcome returns to London from India to be with his son Clive. The unheroic but attractive Clive falls in love with his cousin Ethel, but the love Clive and Ethel have for each other is fated to be unhappily thwarted for years because of worldly considerations. Clive marries Rose Mackenzie; the selfish, greedy, cold-hearted Barnes Newcome, Ethel's father and head of the family, intrigues against Clive and the Colonel; and the Colonel invests his fortune imprudently and ends as a pensioner in an almshouse. Rose dies in childbirth, and the narrative ends with the Colonel's death. This deathbed scene, described with deep feeling that avoids sentimentality, is one of the most famous in Victorian fiction. In a short epilogue Thackeray tells us that Clive and Ethel eventually marry—but this, he says, is a fable.

*The Virginians* (1857–59), Thackeray's next novel, is set partly in America and partly in England in the latter half of the 18th century and is concerned mostly with the vicissitudes in the lives of two brothers, George and Henry Warrington, who are the grandsons of Henry Esmond, the hero of his earlier novel. Thackeray wrote two other serial novels, *Lovel the Widower* (1860) and *The Adventures of Philip* (1861–62). He died after having begun writing the novel *Denis Duval*.

# CHARLES DICKENS

(b. February 7, 1812, Portsmouth, Hampshire, England—d. June 9, 1870, Gad's Hill, near Chatham, Kent)

The English novelist Charles Dickens is generally considered to be the greatest of the Victorian era. His many volumes include such works as *A Christmas Carol, David Copperfield, Bleak House, A Tale of Two Cities, Great Expectations*, and *Our Mutual Friend.*

Dickens enjoyed a wider popularity than had any previous author during his lifetime. Much in his work could appeal to simple and sophisticated, to the poor and to the queen, and technological developments as well as the qualities of his work enabled his fame to spread worldwide very quickly. His long career saw fluctuations in the reception and sales of individual novels, but none of them was negligible or uncharacteristic or disregarded, and, though he is now admired for aspects and phases of his work that were given less weight by his contemporaries, his popularity has never ceased and his present critical standing is higher than ever before. The most abundantly comic of English authors, he was much more than a great entertainer. The range, compassion, and intelligence of his apprehension of his society and its shortcomings enriched his novels and made him both one of the great forces in 19th-century literature and an influential spokesman of the conscience of his age.

## Early Years

Dickens left Portsmouth in infancy. His happiest childhood years were spent in Chatham (1817–22), an area to which he often reverted in his fiction. From 1822 he lived in London, until, in 1860, he moved permanently to a country house, Gad's Hill, near Chatham. His origins were middle class, if of a newfound and precarious respectability; one grandfather had been a domestic servant, and the other an embezzler. His father, a clerk in the navy pay office, was well paid, but his extravagance and ineptitude often brought the family to financial embarrassment or disaster. In 1824 the family reached bottom. Charles, the eldest son, had been withdrawn from school and was now set to manual work in a factory, and his father went to prison for debt. These shocks deeply affected Charles. Though abhorring this brief descent into the working class, he began to gain that sympathetic knowledge of its life and privations that informed his writings.

His schooling, interrupted and unimpressive, ended at 15. He became a clerk in a solicitor's office, then a shorthand reporter in the lawcourts, and finally, like other members of his family, a parliamentary and newspaper reporter. These years left him with a lasting affection for journalism and contempt both for the law and for Parliament. His coming to manhood in the reformist 1830s, and particularly his working on the Liberal Benthamite *Morning Chronicle* (1834–36), greatly affected his political outlook.

## *Beginning of Literary Career*

Much drawn to the theatre, Dickens nearly became a professional actor in 1832. In 1833 he began contributing stories and descriptive essays to magazines and newspapers; these attracted attention and were reprinted as *Sketches by "Boz"* (February 1836). The same month, he was invited to provide a comic serial narrative to accompany engravings by a well-known artist; seven weeks later the first installment of *Pickwick Papers* appeared. Within a few months *Pickwick* was the rage and Dickens the most popular author of the day. During 1836 he also wrote two plays and a pamphlet on a topical issue (how the poor should be allowed to enjoy the Sabbath) and, resigning from his newspaper job, undertook to edit a monthly magazine, *Bentley's Miscellany*, in which he serialized *Oliver Twist* (1837–39). Already the first of his nine surviving children had been born; he had married (in April 1836) Catherine, eldest daughter of a respected Scottish journalist and man of letters, George Hogarth.

For several years his life continued at this intensity. Finding serialization congenial and profitable, he repeated the *Pickwick* pattern of 20 monthly parts in *Nicholas Nickleby* (1838–39); then he experimented with shorter weekly installments for *The Old Curiosity Shop* (1840–41) and *Barnaby Rudge* (1841). Exhausted at last, he then took a five-month vacation in America, touring strenuously and receiving quasi-royal honours as a literary celebrity but offending national sensibilities by protesting against the absence of copyright protection. A radical critic of British institutions, he had expected more from "the republic of my imagination," but he found more vulgarity and sharp practice to detest than social arrangements to admire. Some of these feelings appear in *American Notes* (1842) and *Martin Chuzzlewit* (1843–44).

## First Novels

His writing during these prolific years was remarkably various and, except for his plays, resourceful. *Pickwick* began as high-spirited farce and contained many conventional comic butts and traditional jokes; like other early works, it was manifestly indebted to the contemporary theatre, the 18th-century English novelists, and a few foreign classics, notably *Don Quixote*. But, besides giving new life to old stereotypes,

*Pickwick* displayed, if sometimes in embryo, many of the features that were to be blended in varying proportions throughout his fiction: attacks, satirical or denunciatory, on social evils and inadequate institutions; topical references; an encyclopaedic knowledge of London (always his pre-dominant fictional locale); pathos; a vein of the macabre; a delight in the demotic joys of Christmas; a pervasive spirit of benevolence and geniality; inexhaustible powers of char-acter creation; a wonderful ear for characteristic speech, often imaginatively heightened; a strong narrative impulse; and a prose style that, if here overdependent on a few comic mannerisms, was highly individual and inventive. Rapidly improvised and written only weeks or days ahead of its serial publication, *Pickwick* contains weak and jejune passages and is an unsatisfactory whole—partly because Dickens was rapidly developing his craft as a novelist while writing and publishing it. What is remarkable is that a first novel, written in such circumstances, not only established him overnight and created a new tradition of popular literature but also survived, despite its crudi-ties, as one of the best-known novels in the world.

## Oliver Twist *and Others*

Dickens's self-assurance and artistic ambitious-ness appeared in *Oliver Twist*, where he rejected the temptation to repeat the successful *Pickwick*

*Mr. Bumble and Mrs. Corney, illustration by George Cruikshank for Charles Dickens's* Oliver Twist. *Mary Evans Picture Library*

formula. Though containing much comedy still, *Oliver Twist* is more centrally concerned with social and moral evil (the workhouse and the criminal world). The novel culminates in the murder of Nancy by her cruel boyfriend, Bill Sikes, and the thieving ringleader Fagin's last night in the condemned cell at Newgate. The latter episode was memorably depicted in George Cruikshank's engraving. One could argue that the imaginative potency of Dickens's characters and settings owes much, indeed, to his original illustrators (Cruikshank for *Sketches by "Boz"* and *Oliver Twist*, "Phiz" [Hablot K. Browne] for most of the other novels until the 1860).

The currency of his fiction owed much, too, to its being so easy to adapt into effective stage versions. The theatre was often a subject of his fiction, too, as in the Crummles troupe in *Nicholas Nickleby*. This novel reverted to the *Pickwick* shape and atmosphere, though the indictment of the brutal Yorkshire schools (Dotheboys Hall) continued the important innovation in English fiction seen in *Oliver Twist*—the spectacle of the lost or oppressed child as an occasion for pathos and social criticism. This was amplified in *The Old Curiosity Shop*, where the death of Little Nell was found overwhelmingly powerful at the time, though a few decades later it became a byword for "Victorian sentimentality." In *Barnaby Rudge* he attempted another genre, the historical novel. Like his later attempt in this kind, *A Tale of Two Cities*, it was set in the late 18th century and presented with great vigour and understanding (and some ambivalence of attitude) the spectacle of large-scale mob violence.

To create an artistic unity out of the wide range of moods and materials included in every novel, with often several complicated plots involving scores of characters, was made even more difficult by Dickens's writing and publishing them serially. In *Martin Chuzzlewit* he tried "to resist the temptation of the current Monthly Number, and to keep a steadier eye upon the general purpose and design" (1844 Preface). Its American episodes had, however, been unpremeditated; he suddenly decided to boost the disappointing sales by some America-baiting and to revenge himself against insults and injuries from the American press. A concentration on "the general purpose and design" was more effective in the next novel, *Dombey and Son* (1846–48).

## The Christmas Books

The experience of writing shorter, and unserialized, Christmas books helped Dickens obtain greater coherence. *A Christmas Carol*, suddenly conceived and written in a few weeks, was the first of these Christmas books (a new literary genre thus created incidentally). Tossed off while he was amply engaged in writing *Chuzzlewit*, it was an extraordinary achievement—the one great Christmas myth of modern literature. Dickens's view of life was later to be described or dismissed as "Christmas philosophy," and he himself spoke of "*Carol* philosophy" as the

Illustration from an undated edition of Charles Dickens's A Christmas Carol. © Photos.com/Thinkstock

basis of a projected work. His "philosophy," never very elaborated, involved more than wanting the Christmas spirit to prevail throughout the year, but his great attachment to Christmas (in his family life as well as his writings) is indeed significant and has contributed to his popularity.

Further Christmas books, essays, and stories followed annually (except in 1847) through 1867. None equalled the *Carol* in potency, though some achieved great immediate popularity.

## Renown

Dickens was very much a public figure, actively and centrally involved in his world, and a man of confident presence. He was reckoned the best after-dinner speaker of the age; other superlatives he attracted included his having been the best shorthand reporter on the London press and his being the best amateur actor on the stage. Later he became one of the most successful periodical editors and the finest dramatic recitalist of the day.

Privately in these early years, he was both domestic and social. To his many children, he was a devoted and delightful father, at least while they were young; relations with them proved less happy during their adolescence. Apart from periods in Italy (1844–45) and Switzerland and France (1846–47), he still lived in London, moving from an apartment in Furnival's Inn to larger houses as his income and family grew. Here he entertained his many friends, most of them popular authors, journalists, actors, or artists, though some came from the law and other professions or from commerce and a few from the aristocracy. He enjoyed society that was unpretentious and conversation that was genial and sensible but not too intellectualized or exclusively literary.

*Dombey and Son* (1846–48) was a crucial novel in his development, a product of more thorough planning and maturer thought. Using railways prominently and effectively, it was very up-to-date, though the questions posed included such perennial moral and religious challenges as are suggested by the child Paul's first words in the story: "Papa, what's money?" Some of the corruptions of money and pride of place and the limitations of "respectable" values are explored, virtue and human decency being discovered most often (as elsewhere in Dickens) among the poor, humble, and simple. *David Copperfield* (1849–50) has been described as a "holiday" from these larger social concerns and most notable for its childhood chapters. Largely for this reason and for its autobiographical interest, it has always been among his most popular novels and was Dickens's own "favourite child." In Micawber the novel presents one of the "Dickens characters" whose imaginative potency extends far beyond the narratives in which they figure; Pickwick and Sam Weller, Mrs. Gamp and Mr. Pecksniff, and Scrooge are some others.

## *Middle Years*

Dickens's journalistic ambitions at last found a permanent form in *Household Words* (1850–59) and its successor, *All the Year Round* (1859–88). Popular weekly miscellanies of fiction, poetry, and essays on a wide range of topics, these had substantial and increasing circulations, reaching 300,000 for some of the Christmas numbers. Dickens contributed some serials—the lamentable *Child's History of England* (1851–53), *Hard Times* (1854), *A Tale of Two Cities* (1859), and *Great Expectations* (1860–61)—and essays, some of which were collected in *Reprinted Pieces* (1858) and *The Uncommercial Traveller* (1861, later amplified). Particularly in 1850–52 and during the Crimean War, he contributed many items on current political and social affairs; in later years he wrote less—much less on politics—and the magazine was less political, too. Other distinguished novelists contributed serials, including Mrs. Gaskell, Wilkie Collins, Charles Reade, and Bulwer Lytton.

The contents of the magazine are revealing in relation to Dickens's novels. He took responsibility for all the opinions expressed (for articles were anonymous) and selected and amended contributions accordingly; thus, comments on topical events and so on may generally be taken as representing his opinions, whether or not he wrote them. No English author of comparable status has devoted 20 years of his maturity to such unremitting editorial work, and the weeklies' success was due not only to his illustrious name but also to his practical sagacity and sustained industry.

## Novels

The novels of these years, *Bleak House* (1852–53), *Hard Times* (1854), and *Little Dorrit* (1855–57), were much "darker" than their predecessors. Presenting a remarkably inclusive and increasingly sombre picture of contemporary society, they were inevitably often seen at the time as fictionalized propaganda about ephemeral issues. They are much more than this, though it is never easy to state how Dickens's imagination transformed their many topicalities into an artistically coherent vision that transcends their immediate historical context. Similar questions are raised by his often basing fictional characters, places, and institutions on actual originals. He once spoke of his mind's taking "a fanciful photograph" of a scene, and there is a continual interplay between photographic realism and "fancy" (or imagination).

In the novels of the 1850s, he was politically more despondent, emotionally more tragic. The satire is harsher, the humour less genial and abundant, the "happy endings" more subdued than in the early fiction. Technically, the later novels are more coherent, plots being more fully related to themes, and themes being often expressed through a more insistent use of imagery and symbols (grim symbols, too, such as the fog in *Bleak House* or the prison in *Little Dorrit*). His art here is more akin to poetry than to what is suggested by the photographic or journalistic comparisons. "Dickensian" characterization continues in the sharply defined and simplified grotesque or comic figures, such as Chadband in *Bleak House* or Mrs. Sparsit in *Hard Times*, but large-scale figures of this type are less frequent (the Gamps and Micawbers belong to the first half of his career).

Dickens became more concerned with "the great final secret of all life"—a phrase from *Little Dorrit*, where the spiritual dimension of his work is most overt. Critics disagree as to how far so worldly a novelist succeeded artistically in enlarging his view to include the religious. These novels, too, being manifestly an ambitious attempt to explore the prospects of humanity at this time, raise questions, still much debated, about the intelligence and profundity of his understanding of society.

## Public Readings

Dickens valued his public's affection, not only as a stimulus to his creativity and a condition for his commercial success but also as a substitute for the love he could not find at home. He had been toying with the idea of turning paid reader since 1853, when he began giving occasional readings in aid of charity. The paid series began in April 1858, the immediate impulse being to find some energetic distraction from his marital unhappiness. But the readings drew on more permanent elements in him and his art: his remarkable histrionic talents, his love of theatricals and of seeing and delighting an audience, and the eminently performable nature of his fiction. Moreover, he could earn more by reading than by writing, and more certainly; it was easier to force himself to repeat a performance than create a book.

His initial repertoire consisted entirely of Christmas books but was soon amplified by episodes from the novels and magazine Christmas stories. A performance usually consisted of two items; of the 16 eventually performed, the most popular were "The Trial from *Pickwick*" and the *Carol*. Comedy predominated, though pathos was important in the repertoire, and horrifics were startlingly introduced in the last reading he devised, "Sikes and Nancy," with which he petrified his audiences and half killed himself. Intermittently, until shortly before his death, he gave seasons of readings in London and embarked upon hard-working tours through the provinces and (in 1867–68) the United States. Altogether he performed about 471 times. No important author (at least, according to reviewers, since Homer) and no English author since who has had anything like his stature has devoted so much time and energy to this activity. The only comparable figure is his contemporary, Mark Twain, who acknowledged Dickens as the pioneer.

## Last Years

Tired and ailing though he was, Dickens remained inventive and adventurous in his final novels. *A Tale of Two Cities* (1859) was an experiment, relying less than before on characterization, dialogue, and humour. An exciting and compact narrative, it lacks too many of his strengths to count among his major works. *Great Expectations* (1860–61) resembles *Copperfield* in being a first-person narration and in drawing on parts of Dickens's personality and experience. Compact like its predecessor, it

*Charles Dickens.* © Photos.com/Thinkstock

lacks the panoramic inclusiveness of *Bleak House, Little Dorrit*, and *Our Mutual Friend*, but, though not his most ambitious, it is his most finely achieved novel. The hero Pip's mind is explored with great subtlety, and his development through a childhood and youth beset with hard tests of character is traced critically but sympathetically. Various "great expectations" in the book prove ill founded—a comment as much on the values of the age as on the characters' weaknesses and misfortunes. *Our Mutual Friend* (1864–65), a large, inclusive novel, continues this critique of monetary and class values. London is now grimmer than ever before, and the corruption, complacency, and superficiality of "respectable" society are fiercely attacked. How the unfinished *Edwin Drood* (1870) would have developed is uncertain. Here again Dickens left panoramic fiction to concentrate on a limited private action. It would have been his most elaborate treatment of the themes of crime, evil, and psychological abnormality that recur throughout his novels; a great celebrator of life, he was also obsessed with death.

His health remained precarious after the punishing American tour and was further impaired by his addiction to giving the strenuous "Sikes and Nancy" reading. His farewell reading tour was abandoned when, in April 1869, he collapsed. He began writing another novel and gave a short farewell season of readings in London. He died suddenly in June 1870, and was buried in Westminster Abbey.

# ROBERT BROWNING

(b. May 7, 1812, London, England—d. December 12, 1889, Venice, Italy)

A major English poet of the Victorian age, Robert Browning is noted for his mastery of dramatic monologue and psychological portraiture.

The son of a clerk in the Bank of England in London, Browning received only a slight formal education, although his father gave him a grounding in Greek and

Latin. In 1828 he attended classes at the University of London but left after half a session. Apart from a journey to St. Petersburg in 1834 with George de Benkhausen, the Russian consul general, and two short visits to Italy in 1838 and 1844, he lived with his parents in London until 1846, first at Camberwell and after 1840 at Hatcham. During this period (1832–46) he wrote his early long poems and most of his plays.

Browning's first published work, *Pauline: A Fragment of a Confession* (1833, anonymous), although formally a dramatic monologue, embodied many of his own adolescent passions and anxieties. Although it received some favourable comment, it was attacked by John Stuart Mill, who condemned the poet's exposure and exploitation of his own emotions and his "intense and morbid self-consciousness." It was perhaps Mill's critique that determined Browning never to confess his own emotions again in his poetry but to write objectively. In 1835 he published *Paracelsus* and in 1840 *Sordello*, both poems dealing with men of great ability striving to reconcile the demands of their own personalities with those of the world. *Paracelsus* was well received, but *Sordello*, which made exacting demands on its reader's knowledge, was almost universally declared incomprehensible.

Encouraged by the actor Charles Macready, Browning devoted his main energies for some years to verse drama, a form that he had already adopted for *Strafford* (1837). Between 1841 and 1846, in a series of pamphlets under the general title of *Bells and Pomegranates*, he published seven more plays in verse, including *Pippa Passes* (1841), *A Blot in the 'Scutcheon* (produced in 1843), and *Luria* (1846). These, and all his earlier works except *Strafford*, were printed at his family's expense. Although Browning enjoyed writing for the stage, he was not successful in the theatre, since his strength lay in depicting, as he had himself observed of *Strafford*, "Action in Character, rather than Character in Action."

By 1845 the first phase of Browning's life was near its end. In that year he met Elizabeth Barrett. In her *Poems* (1844) Barrett had included lines praising Browning, who wrote to thank her (January 1845). In May they met and soon discovered their love for each other. Barrett had, however, been for many years an invalid, confined to her room and thought incurable. Her father, moreover, was a dominant and selfish man, jealously fond of his daughter, who in turn had come to depend on his love. When her doctors ordered her to Italy for her health and her father refused to allow her to go, the lovers, who had been corresponding and meeting regularly, were forced to act. They were married secretly in September 1846; a week later they left for Pisa.

Throughout their married life, although they spent holidays in France and England, their home was in Italy, mainly at Florence, where they had a flat in Casa Guidi. Their income was small, although after the birth of their son, Robert, in 1849 Mrs. Browning's cousin John Kenyon made them an allowance of £100 a year, and on his death in 1856 he left them £11,000.

Browning produced comparatively little poetry during his married life. Apart from a collected edition in 1849 he published only *Christmas-Eve and Easter-Day* (1850), an examination of different attitudes toward Christianity, perhaps having its immediate origin in the death of his mother in 1849; an introductory essay (1852) to some spurious letters of Shelley, Browning's only considerable work in prose and his only piece of critical writing; and *Men and Women* (1855). This was a collection of 51 poems — dramatic lyrics such as "Memorabilia," "Love Among the Ruins," and "A Toccata of Galuppi's"; the great monologues such as "Fra Lippo Lippi," "How It Strikes a Contemporary," and "Bishop Blougram's Apology"; and a very few poems in which implicitly ("By the Fireside") or explicitly ("One Word More") he broke his rule and spoke of himself and of his love for his wife. *Men and Women*, however, had no great sale, and many of the reviews were unfavourable and unhelpful. Disappointed for the first time by the reception of his work, Browning in the following years wrote little, sketching and modeling in clay by day and enjoying the society of his friends at night. At last Mrs. Browning's health, which had been remarkably restored by her life in Italy, began to fail. On June 29, 1861, she died in her husband's arms. In the autumn he returned slowly to London with his young son.

His first task on his return was to prepare his wife's *Last Poems* for the press. At first he avoided company, but gradually he accepted invitations more freely and began to move in society. Another collected edition of his poems was called for in 1863, but *Pauline* was not included. When his next book of poems, *Dramatis Personae* (1864)— including "Abt Vogler," "Rabbi Ben Ezra," "Caliban upon Setebos," and "Mr. Sludge, 'The Medium' "—reached two editions, it was clear that Browning had at last won a measure of popular recognition.

In 1868–69 he published his greatest work, *The Ring and the Book*, based on the proceedings in a murder trial in Rome in 1698. Grand alike in plan and execution, it was at once received with enthusiasm, and Browning was established as one of the most important literary figures of the day. For the rest of his life he was much in demand in London society. He spent his summers with friends in France, Scotland, or Switzerland or, after 1878, in Italy.

The most important works of his last years, when he wrote with great fluency, were the long narrative or dramatic poems, often dealing with contemporary themes, such as *Prince Hohenstiel-Schwangau* (1871), *Fifine at the Fair* (1872), *Red Cotton Night-Cap Country* (1873), *The Inn Album* (1875), and the two series of *Dramatic Idyls* (1879 and 1880). He wrote a number of poems on classical subjects, including *Balaustion's Adventure* (1871) and *Aristophanes' Apology* (1875). In addition to many collections of shorter poems—*Pacchiarotto and How He Worked in Distemper* (1876), *Jocoseria* (1883), *Ferishtah's Fancies* (1884), and *Asolando: Fancies and Facts* (1889)—Browning published toward the end of his life two books of unusually personal origin—*La Saisiaz* (1878), at once an elegy for his friend Anne Egerton-Smith and a meditation on mortality, and *Parleyings with Certain People of Importance in Their Day* (1887), in which he discussed books and ideas that had influenced him since his youth.

While staying in Venice in 1889, Browning caught cold, became seriously ill, and died on December 12. He was buried in Westminster Abbey.

# HENDRIK CONSCIENCE

(b. December 3, 1812, Antwerp, Belgium—d. September 10, 1883, Elsene)

The Belgian romantic novelist Hendrik Conscience so dominated the birth and development of the Flemish novel that it was said he "taught his people to read."

Conscience's father was French, his mother Flemish. He spent some of his early years as an assistant teacher (1828–30), took part in the uprising of July 1830 (which resulted in the independence of Belgium), and served in the Belgian army from 1831 to 1836. After falling under the spell of the Kempen, a quiet region of pinewoods and heather north of Antwerp, he was introduced to

French romanticism and began to write French verse. Demobilized in 1836, he entered the literary and artistic life of Antwerp. He was fascinated by his country's Flemish past and wrote in Dutch (or Flemish, as it is often known). *In't wonderjaar* (1837; "In the Year of Miracles"), a series of historical scenes centred on the eventful year 1566, when the Calvinists of the Spanish Netherlands revolted against the Spanish Catholic rule. With *De leeuw van Vlaanderen* (1838; *The Lion of Flanders*), the passionate epic of the revolt of the Flemish towns against France and the victory of the Flemish militia at the Battle of the Golden Spurs (1302), he not only created the Flemish novel but wrote an outstanding historical novel in the tradition of Sir Walter Scott.

After 1840, while supporting himself as a clerk and taking an active part in local politics (he was a gifted orator), Conscience turned more and more to an idyllic realism and wrote novels and tales about urban and rural life. These works, which have been criticized for their sentimentality and moralizing, include *Wat een moeder lijden kan* (1844; *What a Mother Can Endure*), *Houten Clara* (1850; *Wooden Clara*), and *De arme edelman* (1851; *The Poor Gentleman*), as well as the village idylls *Blinde Rosa* (1850; *Blind Rosa*), *De loteling* (1850; *The Conscript*), and *Rikke-tikke-tak* (first published serially, 1845; as a book, 1851; Eng. trans., *Ricketicketack*). At the same time his historical novels (e.g., *Jacob van Artevelde*; 1849) took a more definite shape. He was at the height of his genius, and his works became internationally known through translations into several languages. Having abandoned politics, he became district commissioner at Kortrijk in 1856 and curator of the Wiertz Museum in Brussels in 1868. But his spendthrift manner and expensive household led him to write prolifically, sometimes to the detriment of his style. Among the many books of this last period are *Het goudland* (1862; "The

Land of Gold"), the first Flemish adventure novel, and *De kerels van Vlaanderen* (1871; "The Boys of Flanders"), another historical novel. The publication of his 100th book in 1881 led to mass tributes to him in Brussels, and in 1883 the city of Antwerp erected a statue in his honour.

Conscience was a key figure in the literary and national Flemish renaissance of the 19th century. His vivid narratives, imagination, and rich sensibility compensate for the impurities of his language and his didacticism.

# *M*IKHAIL *L*ERMONTOV

(b. October 3 [October 15, New Style], 1814, Moscow, Russia—d. July 15 [July 27], 1841, Pyatigorsk)

Mikhail Lermontov was the leading Russian Romantic poet and the author of the novel *Geroy nashego vremeni* (1840; *A Hero of Our Time*), which was to have a profound influence on later Russian writers.

Lermontov was the son of Yury Petrovich Lermontov, a retired army captain, and Mariya Mikhaylovna, *née* Arsenyeva. At the age of three he lost his mother and was brought up by his grandmother, Yelizaveta Alekseyevna Arsenyeva, on her estate in Penzenskaya province. Russia's abundant natural beauty, its folk songs and tales, its customs and ceremonies, the hard forced labour of the serfs, and stories and legends of peasant mutinies all had a great influence in developing the future poet's character. Because the child was often ill, he was taken to spas in the Caucasus on three occasions, where the exotic landscapes created lasting impressions on him.

In 1827 he moved with his grandmother to Moscow, and, while attending a boarding school for children of the nobility (at Moscow University), he began to write poetry and also studied painting. In 1828 he wrote the poems *Cherkesy* ("Circassians") and *Kavkazsky plennik* ("Prisoner of the Caucasus") in the vein of the English Romantic poet Lord Byron, whose influence then predominated over young Russian writers. Two years later his first verse, *Vesna* ("Spring"), was published. The same year he entered Moscow University, then one of the liveliest centres of culture and ideology, where such democratically minded representatives of nobility as Aleksandr Herzen, Nikolay Platonovich Ogaryov, and others studied. Students ardently discussed political and philosophical problems, the hard fate of serf peasantry, and the recent Decembrist uprising. In this atmosphere he wrote many lyrical verses, longer, narrative poems, and dramas. His drama *Stranny chelovek*

(1831; "A Strange Man") reflected the attitudes current among members of student societies: hatred of the despotic tsarist regime and of serfdom. In 1832, after clashing with a reactionary professor, Lermontov left the university and went to St. Petersburg, where he entered the cadet school. Upon his graduation in 1834 with the rank of subensign (or cornet), Lermontov was

*Russian author Mikhail Lermontov.* **Library of Congress Prints and Photographs Division**

appointed to the Life-Guard Hussar Regiment stationed at Tsarskoye Selo (now Pushkin), close to St. Petersburg. As a young officer, he spent a considerable portion of his time in the capital, and his critical observations of aristocratic life there formed the basis of his play *Maskarad* ("Masquerade"). During this period his deep—but unreciprocated—attachment to Varvara Lopukhina, a sentiment that never left him, was reflected in *Knyaginya Ligovskaya* ("Duchess Ligovskaya") and other works.

Lermontov was greatly shaken in January 1837 by the death of the great poet Aleksandr Pushkin in a duel. He wrote an elegy that expressed the nation's love for the dead poet, denouncing not only his killer but also the court aristocracy, whom he saw as executioners of freedom and the true culprits of the tragedy. As soon as the verses became known to the court of Nicholas I, Lermontov was arrested and exiled to a regiment stationed in the Caucasus. Travel to new places, meetings with Decembrists (in exile in the Caucasus), and introduction to the Georgian intelligentsia— to the outstanding poet Ilia Chavchavadze, whose daughter had married a well-known Russian dramatist, poet, and diplomatist, Aleksandr Sergeyevich Griboyedov—as well as to other prominent Georgian poets in Tiflis (now Tbilisi) broadened his horizon. Attracted to the nature and poetry of the Caucasus and excited by its folklore, he studied the local languages and translated and polished the Azerbaijanian story "Ashik Kerib." Caucasian themes and images occupy a strong place in his poetry and in the novel *Geroy nashego vremeni*, as well as in his sketches and paintings.

As a result of zealous intercession by his grandmother and by the influential poet V.A. Zhukovsky, Lermontov was allowed to return to the capital in 1838. His verses began to appear in the press: the romantic poem *Pesnya pro tsarya Ivana Vasilyevicha, molodogo oprichnika i udalogo kuptsa Kalashnikova* (1837; "A Song About Tsar Ivan Vasilyevich, His

Young Bodyguard, and the Valiant Merchant Kalashnikov"), the realistic satirical poems *Tambovskaya kaznacheysha* (1838; "The Tambov Paymaster's Wife") and *Sashka* (written 1839, published 1862), and the romantic poem *Demon*. Soon Lermontov became popular; he was called Pushkin's successor and was lauded for having suffered and been exiled because of his libertarian verses. Writers and journalists took an interest in him, and fashionable ladies were attracted to him. He made friends among the editorial staff of *Otechestvennye zapiski*, the leading magazine of the Western-oriented intellectuals, and in 1840 he met the prominent progressive critic V.G. Belinsky, who envisioned him as the great hope of Russian literature. Lermontov had arrived among the circle of St. Petersburg writers.

At the end of the 1830s, the principal directions of his creative work had been established. His freedom-loving sentiments and his bitterly skeptical evaluation of the times in which he lived are embodied in his philosophical lyric poetry ("Duma" ["Thought"], "Ne ver sebye..." ["Do Not Trust Yourself..."]) and are interpreted in an original fashion in the romantic and fantastic images of his Caucasian poems, *Mtsyri* (1840) and *Demon*, on which the poet worked for the remainder of his life. Finally, Lermontov's mature prose showed a critical picture of contemporary life in his novel *Geroy nashego vremeni*, containing the sum total of his reflections on contemporary society and the fortunes of his generation. The hero, Pechorin, is a cynical person of superior accomplishments who, having experienced everything else, devotes himself to experimenting with human situations. This realistic novel, full of social and psychological content and written in prose of superb quality, played an important role in the development of Russian prose.

In February 1840 Lermontov was brought to trial before a military tribunal for his duel with the son of the French ambassador at St. Petersburg—a duel used as a pretext for punishing the recalcitrant poet. On the instructions of Nicholas I, Lermontov was sentenced to a new exile in the Caucasus, this time to an infantry regiment that was preparing for dangerous military operations. Soon compelled to take part in cavalry sorties and hand-to-hand battles, he distinguished himself in the heavy fighting at Valerik River, which he describes in "Valerik" and in the verse "Ya k vam pishu..." ("I Am Writing to You..."). The military command made due note of the great courage and presence of mind displayed by the officer-poet.

As a result of persistent requests by his grandmother, Lermontov was given a short leave in February 1841. He spent several weeks in the capital, continuing work on compositions he had already begun and writing several poems noted for their maturity of thought and talent ("Rodina" ["Motherland"], "Lyubil i ya v bylye gody" ["And I Was in Love"]. Lermontov devised a plan for publishing his own magazine, planned new novels, and sought Belinsky's criticism. But he soon received an order to return to his regiment and left, full of gloomy forebodings. During this long journey he experienced a flood of creative energy: his last notebook contains such masterpieces of Russian lyric poetry as "Utes" ("The Cliff"), "Spor" ("Argument"), "Svidanye" ("Meeting"), "Listok" ("A Leaf"), "Net, ne tebya tak pylko ya lyublyu" ("No, It Was Not You I Loved So Fervently"), "Vykhozhu odin ya na dorogu..." ("I go to the Road Alone..."), and "Prorok" ("Prophet"), his last work.

On the way to his regiment, Lermontov lingered on in the health resort city of Pyatigorsk for treatment. There he met many fashionable young people from St. Petersburg, among whom were secret ill-wishers who knew his reputation in court circles. Some of the young people feared his tongue, while others envied his fame. An atmosphere of intrigue, scandal, and hatred grew up around him. Finally, a quarrel was provoked between Lermontov and another officer, N.S. Martynov; the two fought a duel that ended in the poet's death. He was buried two days later in the municipal cemetery, and the entire population of the city gathered at his funeral. Later, Lermontov's coffin was moved to the Tarkhana estate, and on April 23, 1842, he was buried in the Arsenyev family vault.

# *Anthony Trollope*

(b. April 24, 1815, London, England—d. December 6, 1882, London)

Anthony Trollope was an English novelist whose popular success concealed until long after his death the nature and extent of his literary merit. A series of books set in the imaginary English county of Barsetshire remains his best loved and most famous work, but he also wrote convincing novels of political life as well as studies that show great psychological penetration. One of his greatest strengths was a steady, consistent vision of the social structures of Victorian England, which he re-created in his books with unusual solidity.

Trollope grew up as the son of a sometime scholar, barrister, and failed gentleman farmer. He was unhappy at the great public schools of Winchester and Harrow. Adolescent awkwardness continued until well into his 20s. The years 1834–41 he spent miserably as a junior clerk in the General Post Office, but he was then transferred as a postal surveyor to Ireland, where he began to enjoy a social life. In 1844 he married Rose Heseltine, an Englishwoman, and set up house at Clonmel, in Tipperary. He then embarked upon a literary career that leaves a dominant impression of immense energy and versatility.

*The Warden* (1855) was his first novel of distinction, a penetrating study of the warden of an old people's home who is attacked for making too much profit from a charitable sinecure. During the next 12 years Trollope produced five other books set, like *The Warden*, in Barsetshire: *Barchester Towers* (1857), *Doctor Thorne* (1858), *Framley Parsonage* (1861), *The Small House at Allington* (1864), and *The Last Chronicle of Barset* (serially 1866–67; 1867). *Barchester Towers* is the funniest of the series; *Doctor Thorne* perhaps the best picture of a social system based on birth and the ownership of land; and *The Last Chronicle*, with its story of the sufferings of the scholarly Mr. Crawley, an underpaid curate of a poor parish, the most pathetic.

The Barsetshire novels excel in memorable characters, and they exude the atmosphere of the cathedral community and of the landed aristocracy.

In 1859 Trollope moved back to London, resigning from the civil service in 1867 and unsuccessfully standing as a Liberal parliamentary candidate in 1868. Before then, however, he had produced some 18 novels apart from the Barsetshire group. He wrote mainly before breakfast at a fixed rate of 1,000 words an hour. Outstanding among works of that period were *Orley Farm* (serially, 1861–62; 1862), which made use of the traditional plot of a disputed will, and *Can You Forgive Her?* (serially, 1864–65; 1865), the first of his political novels, which introduced Plantagenet Palliser, later duke of Omnium, whose saga was to stretch over many volumes down to *The Duke's Children* (serially, 1879–80; 1880), a subtle study of the dangers and difficulties of marriage. In the political novels Trollope is less concerned with political ideas than with the practical working of the system—with the mechanics of power.

In about 1869 Trollope's last, and in some respects most interesting, period as a writer began. Traces of his new style are to be found in the slow-moving *He Knew He Was Right* (serially, 1868–69; 1869), a subtle account of a rich man's jealous obsession with his innocent wife. Purely psychological studies include *Sir Harry Hotspur of Humblethwaite* (serially, 1870; 1871) and *Kept in the Dark* (1882). Some of the later works, however, were sharply satirical: *The Eustace Diamonds* (serially, 1871–73; 1873), a study of the influence of money on sexual relationships; *The Way We Live Now* (serially, 1874–75; 1875), remarkable for its villain-hero, the financier Melmotte; and *Mr. Scarborough's Family* (posthumously, 1883), which shows what can happen when the rights of property are wielded by a man of nihilistic temperament intent upon his legal rights.

Trollope's final years were spent in the seclusion of a small Sussex village, where he worked on in the face of gradually diminishing popularity, failing health, and increasing melancholy. He was in London when he died, having been stricken there with paralysis.

# KAWATAKE MOKUAMI

(b. March 1, 1816, Edo [now Tokyo], Japan—d. January 22, 1893, Tokyo)

The versatile and prolific Japanese dramatist Kawatake Mokuami was the last great Kabuki playwright of the Tokugawa period (1603–1867).

Growing up in Edo and originally known as Yoshimura Yoshisaburō, he became a pupil of the Kabuki playwright Tsuruya Namboku V and wrote many kinds of plays during a long apprenticeship. He became the chief playwright for the Kawarasaki Theatre in 1843. During his 40s, Kawatake established his reputation writing *sewamono*, domestic plays featuring the lives of ordinary townspeople, and *shiranamimono*, picaresque plays portraying the lives of thieves and other minor criminals. He wrote many such plays for the noted actor Ichikawa Kodanji IV until the latter's death in 1866.

Following the Meiji Restoration (1868), Kawatake began producing *katsurekimono*, or modified versions of traditional history plays (*jidaimono*), emphasizing factual accuracy in his works. He also pioneered in the production of a new kind of domestic play known as *zangirimono*, which explicitly describes the modernization and Westernization of early Meiji society. When he ostensibly retired from active playwriting in 1881, he relinquished his stage name of Kawatake Shinshichi II and adopted the name Kawatake Mokuami. He continued to write dance dramas after his retirement, including works derived from Noh theatre.

Kawatake was one of the most prolific of all dramatists. Of his more than 360 plays, about 130 are domestic plays, 90 are historical plays, and 140 are dance dramas. His plays are still performed frequently and constitute almost half of those currently in the Kabuki repertoire. They are especially notable for powerful lyrical passages recited to a musical accompaniment, which serves to intensify the mood of the dramatic situation. The plays also draw appeal from their exact and realistic portrayals of characters from the lower social classes and from their explicit love scenes.

# CHARLOTTE BRONTË

(b. April 21, 1816, Thornton, Yorkshire, England—d. March 31, 1855, Haworth, Yorkshire)

The English novelist Charlotte Brontë is noted for *Jane Eyre* (1847), a strong narrative of a woman in conflict with her natural desires and social condition. The novel gave new truthfulness to Victorian fiction. She later wrote *Shirley* (1849) and *Villette* (1853).

## Life

Her father was Patrick Brontë (1777–1861), an Anglican clergyman. Irish-born, he had changed his name from the more commonplace Brunty. After serving in several parishes, he moved with his wife, Maria Branwell Brontë, and their six small children to Haworth amid the Yorkshire moors in 1820, having been awarded a rectorship there. Soon after, Mrs. Brontë and the two eldest children (Maria and Elizabeth) died, leaving the father to care for the remaining three girls — Charlotte, Emily, and Anne — and a boy, Patrick Branwell. Their upbringing was aided by an aunt, Elizabeth Branwell, who left her native Cornwall and took up residence with the family at Haworth.

In 1824 Charlotte and Emily, together with their elder sisters before their deaths, attended Clergy Daughters' School at Cowan Bridge, near Kirkby Lonsdale, Lancashire. The fees were low, the food unattractive, and the discipline harsh. Charlotte condemned the school (perhaps exaggeratedly) long years afterward in *Jane Eyre*, under the thin disguise of Lowood; and the principal, the Rev. William Carus Wilson, has been accepted as the counterpart of Mr. Naomi Brocklehurst in the novel.

Charlotte and Emily returned home in June 1825, and for more than five years the Brontë children learned and played there, writing and telling romantic tales for one another and inventing imaginative games played out at home or on the desolate moors.

In 1831 Charlotte was sent to Miss Wooler's school at Roe Head, near Huddersfield, where she stayed a year and made some lasting friendships; her correspondence with one of her friends, Ellen Nussey, continued until her death,

*Author Charlotte Brontë, the eldest of three sisters who had novels published in 19th-century England.* Apic/Hulton Archive/Getty Images

and has provided much of the current knowledge of her life. In 1832 she came home to teach her sisters but in 1835 returned to Roe Head as a teacher. She wished to improve her family's position, and this was the only outlet that was offered to her unsatisfied energies. Branwell, moreover, was to start on his career as an artist, and it became necessary to supplement the family resources. The work, with its inevitable restrictions, was uncongenial to Charlotte. She fell into ill health and melancholia and in the summer of 1838 terminated her engagement.

In 1839 Charlotte declined a proposal from the Rev. Henry Nussey, her friend's brother, and some months later one from another young clergyman. At the same time Charlotte's ambition to make the practical best of her talents and the need to pay Branwell's debts urged her to spend some months as governess with the Whites at Upperwood House, Rawdon. Branwell's talents for writing and painting, his good classical scholarship, and his social charm had engendered high hopes for him; but he was fundamentally unstable, weak willed, and intemperate. He went from job to job and took refuge in alcohol and opium.

Meanwhile his sisters had planned to open a school together, which their aunt had agreed to finance, and in February 1842 Charlotte and Emily went to Brussels as pupils to improve their qualifications in French and acquire some German. The talent displayed by both brought them to the notice of Constantin Héger, a fine teacher and a man of unusual perception. After a brief trip home upon the death of her aunt, Charlotte returned to Brussels as a pupil-teacher. She stayed there during 1843 but was lonely and depressed. Her friends had left Brussels, and Madame Héger appears to have become jealous of her. The nature of Charlotte's attachment to Héger and the degree to which she understood herself have been much discussed. His was the most interesting mind she had yet met, and he had perceived and evoked her latent talents. His strong and eccentric personality appealed both to her sense of humour and to her affections. She offered him an innocent but ardent devotion, but he tried to repress her emotions. The letters she wrote to him after her return may well be called love letters. When, however, he suggested that they were open to misapprehension, she stopped writing and applied herself, in silence, to disciplining her feelings. However they are interpreted, Charlotte's experiences at Brussels were crucial for her development. She received a strict literary training, became aware of the resources of her own nature, and gathered material that served her, in various shapes, for all her novels.

In 1844 Charlotte attempted to start a school that she had long envisaged in the parsonage itself, as her father's failing sight precluded his being left alone. Prospectuses were issued, but no pupils were attracted to distant Haworth.

In the autumn of 1845 Charlotte came across some poems by Emily, and this led to the publication of a joint volume of *Poems by Currer, Ellis and Acton Bell* (1846), or Charlotte, Emily, and Anne; the pseudonyms were assumed to preserve secrecy and avoid the special treatment that they believed reviewers accorded to women. The book was issued at their own expense. It received few reviews and only two copies were sold. Nevertheless, a way had opened to them, and they were already trying to place the three novels they had written. Charlotte failed to place *The Professor: A Tale* but had, however, nearly finished *Jane Eyre: An Autobiography*, begun in August 1846 in Manchester, where she was staying with her father, who had gone there for an eye operation. When Smith, Elder and Company, declining *The Professor*, declared themselves willing to consider a three-volume novel with more action and excitement in it, she completed and submitted it at once. *Jane Eyre* was accepted, published less than eight weeks later (on October 16, 1847), and had an immediate success, far greater than that of the books that her sisters published the same year.

The months that followed were tragic ones. Branwell died in September 1848, Emily in December, and Anne in May 1849. Charlotte completed *Shirley: A Tale* in the empty parsonage, and it appeared in October. In the following years Charlotte went three times to London as the guest of her publisher; there she met the novelist William Makepeace Thackeray and sat for her portrait by George Richmond. She stayed in 1851 with the writer Harriet Martineau and also visited her future biographer, Mrs. Elizabeth Gaskell, in Manchester and entertained her at Haworth. *Villette* came out in January 1853. Meanwhile, in 1851, she had declined a third offer of marriage, this time from James Taylor, a member of Smith, Elder and Company. Her father's curate, Arthur Bell Nicholls (1817–1906), an Irishman, was her fourth suitor. It took some months to win her father's consent, but they were married on June 29, 1854, in Haworth church. They spent their honeymoon in Ireland and then returned to Haworth, where her husband had pledged himself to continue as curate to her father. He did not share his wife's intellectual life, but she was happy to be loved for herself and to take up her duties as his wife. She began another book, *Emma*, of which some pages remain. Her pregnancy, however, was accompanied by exhausting sickness, and she died in 1855.

## Jane Eyre *and other novels*

Charlotte's first novel, *The Professor* (published posthumously, 1857), shows her sober reaction from the indulgences of her girlhood. Told in the first person by an English tutor in Brussels, it is based on Charlotte's experiences there, with a reversal of sexes and roles. The necessity of her genius, reinforced by reading her sister Emily's *Wuthering Heights*, modified this restrictive self-discipline; and, though there is plenty of satire and dry, direct phrasing in *Jane Eyre*, its success was the fiery conviction with which it presented a thinking, feeling woman, craving for love but able to renounce it at the call of impassioned self-respect and moral conviction. The book's narrator and main character, Jane Eyre, is an orphan and is governess to the ward of Mr. Rochester, the Byronic and enigmatic employer with whom she falls in love. Her love is reciprocated, but on the wedding morning it comes out that Rochester is already married and keeps his mad and depraved wife in the attics of his mansion. Jane leaves him, suffers hardship, and finds work as a village schoolmistress. When Jane learns, however, that Rochester has been maimed and blinded while trying vainly to rescue his wife from the burning house that she herself had set afire, Jane seeks him out and marries him. There are melodramatic naïvetés in the story, and Charlotte's elevated rhetorical passages do not much appeal to modern taste, but she maintains her hold on the reader. The novel is subtitled *An Autobiography* and is written in the first person; but, except in Jane Eyre's impressions of Lowood, the autobiography is not Charlotte's. Personal experience is fused with suggestions from widely different sources, and the Cinderella theme may well come from Samuel Richardson's *Pamela*. The action is carefully motivated, and apparently episodic sections, like the return to Gateshead Hall, are seen to be necessary to the full expression of Jane's character and the working out of the threefold moral theme of love, independence, and forgiveness.

In her novel *Shirley*, Charlotte avoided melodrama and coincidences and widened her scope. Setting aside Maria Edgworth and Sir Walter Scott as national novelists, *Shirley* is the first regional novel in English, full of shrewdly depicted local material—Yorkshire characters, church and chapel, the cloth workers and machine breakers of her father's early manhood, and a sturdy but rather embittered feminism.

In *Villette* she recurred to the Brussels setting and the first-person narrative, disused in *Shirley*; the characters and incidents are largely variants of the people and life at the Pension Héger. Against this background she set the ardent heart, deprived of its object, contrasted with the woman happily fulfilled in love.

The influence of Charlotte's novels was much more immediate than that of *Wuthering Heights*. Charlotte's combination of romance and satiric realism had been the mode of nearly all the women novelists for a century. Her fruitful innovations were the presentation of a tale through the sensibility of a child or young woman, her lyricism, and the picture of love from a woman's standpoint.

# HENRY DAVID THOREAU

(b. July 12, 1817, Concord, Massachusetts, U.S.—d. May 6, 1862, Concord)

The American essayist, poet, and practical philosopher Henry David Thoreau is renowned for having lived the doctrines of Transcendentalism as recorded in his masterwork, *Walden* (1854), and for having been a vigorous advocate of civil liberties, as evidenced in the essay "Civil Disobedience" (1849).

## Early Life

Thoreau was born in 1817 in Concord, Massachusetts. Though his family moved the following year, they returned in 1823. Even when he grew ambivalent about the village after reaching manhood, it remained his world, for he never grew ambivalent about its lovely setting of woodlands, streams, and meadows. Little distinguished his family. He was the third child of a feckless small businessman named John Thoreau and his bustling, talkative wife, Cynthia Dunbar Thoreau. His parents sent him in 1828 to Concord Academy, where he impressed his teachers and so was permitted to prepare for college. Upon graduating from the academy, he entered Harvard University in 1833. There he was a good student, but he was indifferent to the rank system and preferred to use the school library for his own purposes. Graduating in the middle ranks of the class of 1837, Thoreau searched for a teaching job and secured one at his old grammar school in Concord. But he was no disciplinarian, and he resigned after two shaky weeks, after which he worked for his father in the family pencil-making business. In June 1838 he started a small school with the help of his brother John. Despite its progressive nature, it lasted for three years, until John fell ill.

A canoe trip that he and John took along the Concord and Merrimack rivers in 1839 confirmed in him the opinion that he ought to be not a schoolmaster but a poet of nature. As the 1840s began, Thoreau took up the profession of poet. He struggled to stay in it and succeeded throughout the decade, only to falter in the 1850s.

## Friendship with Emerson

Sheer chance made his entrance to writing easier, for he came under the benign influence of the essayist and poet Ralph Waldo Emerson, who had settled in Concord during Thoreau's sophomore year at Harvard. By the autumn of 1837, they were becoming friends. Emerson sensed in Thoreau a true disciple—that is, one with so much

Emersonian self-reliance that he would still be his own man. Thoreau saw in Emerson a guide, a father, and a friend.

With his magnetism Emerson attracted others to Concord. Out of their heady speculations and affirmatives came New England Transcendentalism. In retrospect it was one of the most significant literary movements of 19th-century America, with at least two authors of world stature, Thoreau and Emerson, to its credit. Essentially it combined romanticism with reform. It celebrated the individual rather than the masses, emotion rather than reason, nature rather than man. Transcendentalism conceded that there were two ways of knowing, through the senses and through intuition, but asserted that intuition transcended tuition. Similarly, the movement acknowledged that matter and spirit both existed. It claimed, however, that the reality of spirit transcended the reality of matter. Transcendentalism strove for reform yet insisted that reform begin with the individual, not the group or organization.

## Literary Career

In Emerson's company Thoreau's hope of becoming a poet looked not only proper but feasible. Late in 1837, at Emerson's suggestion, he began keeping a journal that covered thousands of pages before he scrawled the final entry two months before his death. He soon polished some of his old college essays and composed new and better ones as well. He wrote some poems—a good many, in fact—for several years. Captained by Emerson, the Transcendentalists started a magazine, *The Dial*; the inaugural issue, dated July 1840, carried Thoreau's poem "Sympathy" and his essay on the Roman poet Aulus Persius Flaccus.

*The Dial* published more of Thoreau's poems and then, in July 1842, the first of his outdoor essays, "Natural

*Essayist and poet Henry David Thoreau lived the life he expounded in his writings.* Hulton Archive/Getty Images

History of Massachusetts." Though disguised as a book review, it showed that a nature writer of distinction was in the making. Then followed more lyrics, and fine ones, such as "To the Maiden in the East," and another nature essay, remarkably felicitous, "A Winter Walk." *The Dial* ceased publication with the April 1844 issue, having published a richer variety of Thoreau's writing than any other magazine ever would.

In 1840 Thoreau fell in love with and proposed marriage to an attractive visitor to Concord named Ellen Sewall. She accepted his proposal but then immediately broke off the engagement at the insistence of her parents. He remained a bachelor for life. During two periods, 1841–43 and 1847–48, he stayed mostly at the Emersons' house. In spite of Emerson's hospitality and friendship, however, Thoreau grew restless; his condition was accentuated by grief over the death in January 1842 of his brother John, who died of lockjaw after cutting his finger. Later that year he became a tutor in the Staten Island household of Emerson's brother, William, while trying to cultivate the New York literary market. Thoreau's literary activities went indifferently, however, and the effort to conquer New York failed. Confirmed in his distaste for city life and disappointed by his lack of success, he returned to Concord in late 1843.

## *Move to Walden Pond*

Back in Concord Thoreau rejoined his family's business, making pencils and grinding graphite. By early 1845 he felt more restless than ever, until he decided to take up an idea of a Harvard classmate who had once built a waterside hut in which one could loaf or read. In the spring Thoreau picked a spot by Walden Pond, a small glacial lake located 2 miles (3 km) south of Concord on land Emerson owned.

Early in the spring of 1845, Thoreau, then 27 years old, began to chop down tall pines with which to build the foundations of his home on the shores of Walden Pond. From the outset the move gave him profound satisfaction. Once settled, he restricted his diet for the most part to the fruit and vegetables he found growing wild and the beans he planted. When not busy weeding his bean rows and trying to protect them from hungry woodchucks or occupied with fishing, swimming, or rowing, he spent long hours observing and recording the local flora and fauna, reading, and writing *A Week on the Concord and Merrimack Rivers* (1849). He also made entries in his journals, which he later polished and included in *Walden*. Much time, too, was spent in meditation.

Out of such activity and thought came *Walden*, a series of 18 essays describing Thoreau's experiment in basic living and his effort to set his time free for leisure. Several of the essays provide his original perspective on the meaning of work and leisure and describe his experiment in living as simply and self-sufficiently as possible, while in others Thoreau describes the various realities of life at Walden Pond: his intimacy with the small animals he came in contact with; the sounds, smells, and look of woods and water at various seasons; the music of wind in telegraph wires — in short, the felicities of learning how to fulfill his desire to live as simply and self-sufficiently as possible. The physical act of living day by day at Walden Pond is what gives the book authority, while Thoreau's command of a clear, straightforward but elegant style helped raise it to the level of a literary classic.

Thoreau stayed for two years at Walden Pond (1845–47). In the summer of 1847 Emerson invited him to stay with his wife and children again, while Emerson himself went to Europe. Thoreau accepted, and in September 1847 he left his cabin forever.

Midway in his Walden sojourn Thoreau had spent a night in jail. On an evening in July 1846 he encountered Sam Staples, the constable and tax gatherer. Staples asked him amiably to pay his poll tax, which Thoreau had omitted paying for several years. He declined, and Staples locked him up. The next morning a still-unidentified lady, perhaps his aunt, Maria, paid the tax. Thoreau reluctantly emerged, did an errand, and then went huckleberrying. A single night, he decided, was enough to make his point that he could not support a government that endorsed slavery and waged an imperialist war against Mexico. His defense of the private, individual conscience against the expediency of the majority found expression in his most famous essay, "Civil Disobedience," which was first published in May 1849 under the title "Resistance to Civil Government." The essay received little attention until the 20th century, when it found an eager audience. To many, its message still sounds timely: there is a higher law than the civil one, and the higher law must be followed even if a penalty ensues. So does its consequence: "Under a government which imprisons any unjustly, the true place for a just man is also a prison."

## Later Life and Works

When Thoreau left Walden, he had passed the peak of his career, and his life lost much of its illumination. Slowly his Transcendentalism drained away as he became a surveyor in order to support himself. He collected botanical specimens for himself and reptilian ones for Harvard, jotting down their descriptions in his journal. He established himself in his neighbourhood as a sound man with rod and transit, and he spent more of his time in the family business; after his father's death he took it over entirely. Thoreau made excursions to the Maine woods, to Cape

Cod, and to Canada, using his experiences on the trips as raw material for three series of magazine articles: "Ktaadn [sic] and the Maine Woods," in *The Union Magazine* (1848); "Excursion to Canada," in *Putnam's Monthly* (1853); and "Cape Cod," in *Putnam's* (1855). These works present Thoreau's zest for outdoor adventure and his appreciation of the natural environment that had for so long sustained his own spirit.

As Thoreau became less of a Transcendentalist he became more of an activist—above all, a dedicated abolitionist. As much as anyone in Concord, he helped to speed fleeing slaves north on the Underground Railroad. He lectured and wrote against slavery, with "Slavery in Massachusetts," a lecture delivered in 1854, as his hardest indictment. In the abolitionist John Brown he found a father figure beside whom Emerson paled; the fiery old fanatic became his ideal. By now Thoreau was in poor health, and when Brown's raid on Harpers Ferry failed and he was hanged, Thoreau suffered a psychic shock that probably hastened his own death. He died, apparently of tuberculosis, in 1862.

# EMILY BRONTË

(b. July 30, 1818, Thornton, Yorkshire, England—d. December 19, 1848, Haworth, Yorkshire)

The English novelist and poet Emily Brontë produced but one novel, *Wuthering Heights* (1847), a highly imaginative novel of passion and hate set on the Yorkshire moors. Emily was perhaps the greatest of the three Brontë sisters, but the record of her life is extremely meagre, for she was silent and reserved and left no correspondence of interest, and her single novel darkens rather than solves the mystery of her spiritual existence.

## Life

Her father, Patrick Brontë (1777–1861), an Irishman, held a number of curacies: Hartshead-cum-Clifton, Yorkshire, was the birthplace of his elder daughters, Maria and Elizabeth (who died young), and nearby Thornton that of Emily and her siblings Charlotte, Patrick Branwell, and Anne. In 1820 their father became rector of Haworth, remaining there for the rest of his life.

After the death of their mother in 1821, the children were left very much to themselves in the bleak moorland rectory. The children were educated, during their early life, at home, except for a single year that Charlotte and Emily spent at the Clergy Daughters' School at Cowan Bridge in Lancashire. In 1835, when Charlotte secured a teaching position at Miss Wooler's school at Roe Head, Emily accompanied her as a pupil but suffered from homesickness and remained only three months. In 1838 Emily spent six exhausting months as a teacher in Miss Patchett's school at Law Hill, near Halifax, and then resigned.

To keep the family together at home, Charlotte planned to keep a school for girls at Haworth. In February 1842 she and Emily went to Brussels to learn foreign languages and school management at the Pension Héger. Although Emily pined for home and for the wild moorlands, it seems that in Brussels she was better appreciated than Charlotte. Her passionate nature was more easily understood than Charlotte's decorous temperament. In October, however, when her aunt died, Emily returned permanently to Haworth.

In 1845 Charlotte came across some poems by Emily, and this led to the discovery that all three sisters—Charlotte, Emily, and Anne—had written verse. A year later they

*English author Emily Brontë. She published a book of verse with her sisters, but the novel* Wuthering Heights *is considered her crowning literary achievment.* Hulton Archive/Getty Images

published jointly a volume of verse, *Poems by Currer, Ellis and Acton Bell*, the initials of these pseudonyms being those of the sisters; it contained 21 of Emily's poems, and a consensus of later criticism has accepted the fact that Emily's verse alone reveals true poetic genius. The venture cost the sisters about £50 in all, and only two copies were sold.

By midsummer of 1847 Emily's *Wuthering Heights* and Anne's *Agnes Grey* had been accepted for joint publication by J. Cautley Newby of London, but publication of the three volumes was delayed until the appearance of their sister Charlotte's *Jane Eyre*, which was immediately and hugely successful. *Wuthering Heights*, when published in December 1847, did not fare well; critics were hostile, calling it too savage, too animal-like, and clumsy in construction. Only later did it come to be considered one of the finest novels in the English language.

Soon after the publication of her novel, Emily's health began to fail rapidly. She had been ill for some time, but now her breathing became difficult, and she suffered great pain. She died of tuberculosis in December 1848.

## Wuthering Heights

Emily Brontë's work on *Wuthering Heights* cannot be dated, and she may well have spent a long time on this intense, solidly imagined novel. It is distinguished from other novels of the period by its dramatic and poetic presentation, its abstention from all comment by the author, and its unusual structure. It recounts in the retrospective narrative of an onlooker, which in turn includes shorter narratives, the impact of the waif Heathcliff on the two families of Earnshaw and Linton in a remote Yorkshire district at the end of the 18th century. Embittered by abuse and by the marriage of Cathy Earnshaw—who shares his stormy nature and whom he loves—to the gentle and prosperous Edgar Linton,

Heathcliff plans a revenge on both families, extending into the second generation. Cathy's death in childbirth fails to set him free from his love-hate relationship with her, and the obsessive haunting persists until his death; the marriage of the surviving heirs of Earnshaw and Linton restores peace.

Sharing her sisters' dry humour and Charlotte's violent imagination, Emily diverges from them in making no use of the events of her own life and showing no preoccupation with a spinster's state or a governess's position. Working, like them, within a confined scene and with a small group of characters, she constructs an action, based on profound and primitive energies of love and hate, which proceeds logically and economically, making no use of such coincidences as Charlotte relies on, requiring no rich romantic similes or rhetorical patterns, and confining the superb dialogue to what is immediately relevant to the subject. The sombre power of the book and the elements of brutality in the characters affronted some 19th-century opinion. Its supposed masculine quality was adduced to support the claim, based on the memories of her brother Branwell's friends long after his death, that he was author or part author of it. While it is not possible to clear up all the minor puzzles, neither the external nor the internal evidence offered is substantial enough to weigh against Charlotte's plain statement that Emily was the author.

# IVAN TURGENEV

(b. October 28 [November 9, New Style], 1818, Oryol, Russia—d. August 22 [September 3], 1883, Bougival, near Paris, France)

Ivan Turgenev was a Russian novelist, poet, and playwright, whose major works include the short-story collection *A Sportsman's Sketches* (1852) and the novels *Rudin* (1856), *Home of the Gentry* (1859), *On the Eve* (1860), and *Fathers and Sons* (1862). These works offer realistic, affectionate portrayals of the Russian peasantry and penetrating studies of the Russian intelligentsia who were attempting to move the country into a new age. Turgenev poured into his writings not only a deep concern for the future of his native land but also an integrity of craft that has ensured his place in Russian literature. The many years that he spent in western Europe were due in part to his personal and artistic stand as a liberal between the reactionary tsarist rule and the spirit of revolutionary radicalism that held sway in contemporary artistic and intellectual circles in Russia.

## Early Life and Works

Turgenev was the second son of a retired cavalry officer and a wealthy mother who owned the extensive estate of Spasskoye-Lutovinovo. The dominant figure of his mother throughout his boyhood and early manhood probably provided the example for the dominance exercised by the heroines in his major fiction. The Spasskoye estate itself came to have a twofold meaning for the young Turgenev, as an island of gentry civilization in rural Russia and as a symbol of the injustice he saw inherent in the servile state of the peasantry. Against the Russian social system Turgenev was to take an oath of perpetual animosity, which was to be the source of his liberalism and the inspiration for his vision of the intelligentsia as people dedicated to their country's social and political betterment.

Turgenev was to be the only Russian writer with avowedly European outlook and sympathies. Though he was given an education of sorts at home, in Moscow schools, and at the universities of both Moscow and St.

Petersburg, Turgenev tended to regard his education as having taken place chiefly during his plunge "into the German sea" when he spent the years 1838 to 1841 at the University of Berlin. He returned home as a confirmed believer in the superiority of the West and of the need for Russia to follow a course of Westernization.

Though Turgenev had composed derivative verse and a poetic drama, *Steno* (1834), in the style of the English poet Lord Byron, the first of his works to attract attention was a long poem, *Parasha*, published in 1843. The potential of the author was quickly appreciated by the critic Vissarion Belinsky, who became Turgenev's close friend and mentor. Belinsky's conviction that literature's primary aim was to reflect the truth of life and to adopt a critical attitude toward its injustices became an article of faith for Turgenev. Despite the influence of Belinsky, he remained a writer of remarkable detachment, possessed of a cool and sometimes ironic objectivity.

Turgenev was not a man of grand passions, although the love story was to provide the most common formula for his fiction, and a love for the renowned singer Pauline Viardot, whom he first met in 1843, was to dominate his entire life. His relation with Viardot usually has been considered platonic, yet some of his letters, often as brilliant in their observation and as felicitous in their manner as anything he wrote, suggest the existence of a greater intimacy. Generally, though, they reveal him as the fond and devoted admirer, in which role he was for the most part content. He never married, though in 1842 he had had an illegitimate daughter by a peasant woman at Spasskoye; he later entrusted the upbringing of the child to Viardot.

During the 1840s, Turgenev wrote more long poems, including *A Conversation*, *Andrey*, and *The Landowner*, and some criticism. Having failed to obtain a professorship at the University of St. Petersburg and having abandoned work in the government service, he began to publish short works in prose. These were studies in the "intellectual-without-a-will" so typical of his generation. The most famous was "The Diary of a Superfluous Man" (1850), which supplied the epithet "superfluous man" for so many similar weak-willed intellectual protagonists in Turgenev's work as well as in Russian literature generally.

Simultaneously, he tried his hand at writing plays, some, like *A Poor Gentleman* (1848), rather obviously imitative of the Russian master Nikolay Gogol. Of these, *The Bachelor* (1849) was the only one staged at this time, the others falling afoul of the official censors. Others of a more intimately penetrating character, such as *One May Spin a Thread Too Finely* (1848), led to the detailed psychological studies in his dramatic masterpiece, *A Month in the Country* (1855). This was not staged professionally until 1872. Without precedent in the Russian theatre, it required for its appreciation by critics and audiences the prior success after 1898 of the plays of Anton Chekhov at the Moscow Art Theatre. It was there in 1909, under the great director Konstantin Stanislavsky, that it was revealed as one of the major works of the Russian theatre.

## Sketches of Rural Life

Before going abroad in 1847, Turgenev left in the editorial offices of the literary journal *Sovremennik* ("The Contemporary") a short study, "Khor and Kalinych," of two peasants whom he had met on a hunting trip in the Oryol region. It was published with the subtitle "From a Hunter's Sketches," and it had an instantaneous success. From it was to grow the short-story cycle *A Sportsman's Sketches*, first published in 1852, that brought him lasting fame. Many of the sketches portrayed various types of landowners or episodes, drawn from his experience, of the life of the manorial, serf-owning Russian gentry. Far more significant are the sketches that tell of Turgenev's encounters with peasants during his hunting trips. Amid evocative descriptions of the countryside, Turgenev's portraits suggest that, though the peasants may be "children of nature" who seek the freedom offered by the beauty of their surroundings, they are always circumscribed by the fact of serfdom.

Turgenev could never pretend to be much more than an understanding stranger toward the peasants about whom he wrote, yet through his compassionate, lucid observation, he created portraits of enormous vitality and wide impact. Not only did they make the predominantly upper class reading public aware of the human qualities of the peasantry, but they also may have been influential in provoking the sentiment for reform that led eventually to the emancipation of the serfs in 1861.

When the first collected edition of his sketches appeared, after appearing separately in various issues of the *Sovremennik*, Turgenev was arrested, detained for a month in St. Petersburg, then given 18 months of enforced residence at Spasskoye. The ostensible pretext for such official harrassment was an obituary of Gogol, which he had published against censorship regulations. But his criticism of serfdom in the *Sketches*, certainly muted in tone by any standards and explicit only in his references to the landowners' brutality toward their peasants, was sufficient to cause this temporary martyrdom for his art.

## First Novels

Although Turgenev wrote "Mumu," a remarkable exposure of the cruelties of serfdom, while detained in St. Petersburg, his work was evolving toward such extended character studies as *Yakov Pasynkov* (1855) and the subtle if pessimistic examinations of the contrariness of love found in "Faust" and "A Correspondence" (1856). Time and national events, moreover, were impinging upon him. With the defeat of Russia in the Crimean War (1854–56), Turgenev's own generation, "the men of the forties," began to belong to the past. The two novels that he published during the 1850s—*Rudin* (1856) and *Home of the Gentry* (1859)—are permeated by a spirit of ironic nostalgia for the weaknesses and futilities so manifest in this generation of a decade earlier.

The novel *On the Eve* (1860) deals with the problem facing the younger intelligentsia on the eve of the Crimean War and refers also to the changes awaiting Russia on the eve of the emancipation of the serfs in 1861. Although it has several successful minor characters and some powerful scenes, its treatment of personal relations, particularly of love, demonstrates Turgenev's profound pessimism toward such matters. Such pessimism became increasingly marked in Turgenev's view of life. It seems that there could be no real reconciliation between the liberalism of Turgenev's generation and the revolutionary aspirations of the younger intelligentsia. Turgenev himself could hardly fail to feel a sense of personal involvement in this rupture.

Turgenev's greatest novel, *Fathers and Sons* (1862), grew from this sense of involvement and yet succeeded in illustrating, with remarkable balance and profundity, the issues that divided the generations. The hero, Bazarov, is the most powerful of Turgenev's creations. A nihilist, denying all laws save those of the natural sciences, uncouth and forthright in his opinions, he is nonetheless susceptible to love and by that token doomed to unhappiness. In sociopolitical terms he represents the victory of the nongentry revolutionary intelligentsia over the gentry intelligentsia to which Turgenev belonged. In artistic terms he is a triumphant example of objective portraiture, and in the poignancy of his death he approaches tragic stature. The miracle of the novel as a whole is Turgenev's superb mastery of his theme, despite his personal hostility toward Bazarov's antiaestheticism, and his success in endowing all the characters with a quality of spontaneous life. Yet at the novel's first appearance the radical younger generation attacked it bitterly as a slander, and the conservatives condemned it as too lenient in its exposure of nihilism.

## Self-Exile and Fame

Always touchy about his literary reputation, Turgenev reacted to the almost unanimously hostile reception given to *Fathers and Sons* by leaving Russia. He took up residence in Baden-Baden in southern Germany, to which resort Viardot had retired. Quarrels with Leo Tolstoy and Fyodor Dostoyevsky, the other leading Russian writers of the time, and his general estrangement from the Russian literary scene made him an exile in a very real sense. His only novel of this period, *Smoke* (1867), set in Baden-Baden, is infused with a satirically embittered tone that makes caricatures of both the left and the right wings of the intelligentsia. The love story is deeply moving, but both this emotion and the political sentiments are made to seem ultimately no more lasting and real than the smoke of the title.

The Franco-German War of 1870–71 forced the Viardots to leave Baden-Baden, and Turgenev followed them, first to London and then to Paris. He now became an honoured ambassador of Russian culture in the Paris of the 1870s. The writers George Sand, Gustave Flaubert, the Goncourt brothers, the young Émile Zola, and Henry James were only a few of the many illustrious contemporaries with whom he corresponded and who sought his company. He was elected vice president of the Paris international literary congress in 1878, and in 1879 he was awarded an honorary degree by the University of Oxford. In Russia he was feted on his annual visits.

The literary work of this final period combined nostalgia for the past—eloquently displayed in such beautiful pieces as "A Lear of the Steppes" (1870), "Torrents of Spring" (1872), and "Punin and Baburin" (1874)—with stories of a quasi-fantastic character—"The Song of Triumphant Love" (1881) and "Klara Milich" (1883). Turgenev's final novel, *Virgin Soil* (1877), was designed to recoup his literary reputation in the eyes of the younger generation. Its aim was to portray the dedication and self-sacrifice of young populists who hoped to sow the seeds of revolution in the virgin soil of the Russian peasantry. Despite its realism and his efforts to give the war topicality, it is the least successful of his novels. His last major work, *Poems in Prose*, is remarkable chiefly for its wistfulness and for its famous eulogy to the Russian language.

# WALT WHITMAN

(b. May 31, 1819, West Hills, Long Island, New York, U.S.—d. March 26, 1892, Camden, New Jersey)

Walt Whitman was an American poet, journalist, and essayist whose verse collection *Leaves of Grass* is a landmark in the history of American literature.

Whitman was born into a family that settled in North America in the first half of the 17th century. In 1823 Walter Whitman, Sr., moved his growing family to Brooklyn, which was enjoying a boom. There he speculated in real estate and built cheap houses for artisans, but he was a poor manager and had difficulty in providing for his family, which increased to nine children.

Walt, the second child, attended public school in Brooklyn, began working at the age of 12, and learned the printing trade. He was employed as a printer in Brooklyn and New York City, taught in country schools on Long Island, and became a journalist. At the age of 23 he edited a daily newspaper in New York, and in 1846 he became editor of the *Brooklyn Daily Eagle*, a fairly important newspaper of the time. Discharged from the *Eagle* early in 1848 because of his support for the Free Soil faction of the Democratic Party, he went to New Orleans, Louisiana, where he worked for three months on the *Crescent* before returning to New York via the Mississippi River and the Great Lakes. After another abortive attempt at Free Soil journalism, he built houses and dabbled in real estate in New York from about 1850 until 1855.

## Early Work

Whitman had spent a great deal of his first 36 years walking and observing in New York City and Long Island. During these years he had also read extensively at home and in the New York libraries, and he began experimenting with a new style of poetry. While a schoolteacher, printer, and journalist he had published sentimental stories and poems in newspapers and popular magazines, but they showed almost no literary promise.

By the spring of 1855 Whitman had enough poems in his new style for a thin volume. Unable to find a publisher, he sold a house and printed the first edition of *Leaves of Grass* at his own expense. Though little appreciated upon its appearance, *Leaves of Grass* was warmly praised by the poet and essayist Ralph Waldo Emerson, who wrote to Whitman on receiving the poems that it was "the most extraordinary piece of wit and wisdom" America had yet contributed.

Whitman continued practicing his new style of writing in his private notebooks, and in 1856 the second edition of *Leaves of Grass* appeared. This collection contained revisions of the poems of the first edition and a new one, the "Sun-down Poem" (later to become "Crossing Brooklyn Ferry"). The second edition was also a financial failure, and once again Whitman edited a daily newspaper, the *Brooklyn Times*, but was unemployed by the summer of 1859. In 1860 a Boston publisher brought out the third edition of *Leaves of Grass*, greatly enlarged and rearranged, but the outbreak of the American Civil War bankrupted the firm. The 1860 volume contained the "Calamus" poems, which record a personal crisis of some intensity in Whitman's life, an apparent homosexual love affair (whether imagined or real is unknown), and "Premonition" (later entitled "Starting from Paumanok"), which records the violent emotions that often drained the poet's strength. "A Word out of the Sea" (later entitled "Out of the Cradle Endlessly Rocking") evoked some sombre feelings, as did "As I Ebb'd with the Ocean of Life." "Chants Democratic," "Enfans d'Adam," "Messenger Leaves," and "Thoughts" were more in the poet's earlier vein.

## Civil War Years

After the outbreak of the Civil War in 1861, Whitman's brother was wounded at Fredericksburg, and Whitman went there in 1862, staying some time in the camp, then taking a temporary post in the paymaster's office in Washington. He spent his spare time visiting wounded and dying soldiers in the Washington hospitals, spending his scanty salary on small gifts for Confederate and Unionist soldiers alike and offering his usual "cheer and magnetism" to try to alleviate some of the mental depression and bodily suffering he saw in the wards.

In January 1865 he became a clerk in the Department of the Interior; in May he was promoted but in June was dismissed because the secretary of the Interior thought that *Leaves of Grass* was indecent. Whitman then obtained a post in the attorney general's office, largely through the efforts of his friend, the journalist William O'Connor, who wrote a vindication of Whitman in *The Good Gray Poet* (published in 1866), which aroused sympathy for the victim of injustice.

In May 1865 a collection of war poems entitled *Drum Taps* showed Whitman's readers a new kind of poetry, moving from the oratorical excitement with which he had greeted the falling-in and arming of the young men at the beginning of the Civil War to a disturbing awareness of what war really meant. "Beat! Beat! Drums!" echoed the bitterness of the Battle of Bull Run, and "Vigil Strange I Kept on the Field One Night" had a new awareness of suffering, no less effective for its quietly plangent quality. The *Sequel to Drum Taps*, published in the autumn of 1865, contained his great elegy on President Abraham Lincoln, "When Lilacs Last in the Dooryard Bloom'd." His horror at the death of democracy's first "great martyr chief" was matched by his revulsion from the barbarities of war. Whitman's prose descriptions of the Civil War, published later in *Specimen Days & Collect* (1882–83), are no less effective in their direct, moving simplicity.

## Later Life

The fourth edition of *Leaves of Grass*, published in 1867, contained much revision and rearrangement. Apart from the poems collected in *Drum Taps*, it contained eight new poems, and some poems had been omitted. In the late 1860s Whitman's work began to receive greater recognition. O'Connor's *The Good Gray Poet* and John Burroughs's *Notes on Walt Whitman as Poet and Person* (1867) were followed in 1868 by an expurgated English edition of Whitman's poems prepared by William Michael Rossetti, the English man of letters.

Whitman was ill in 1872, probably as a result of long-experienced emotional strains related to his sexual ambiguity; in January 1873 his first stroke left him partly paralyzed. By May he had recovered sufficiently to travel to his brother's home in Camden, New Jersey, where his mother was dying. Her subsequent death he called "the great cloud" of his life. He thereafter lived with his brother in Camden, and his post in the attorney general's office was terminated in 1874.

Whitman's health recovered sufficiently by 1879 for him to make a visit to the West. In 1881 James R. Osgood published a second Boston edition of *Leaves of Grass*, and the Society for the Suppression of Vice claimed it to be immoral. Because of a threatened prosecution, Osgood gave the plates to Whitman, who, after he had published an author's edition, found a new publisher, Rees Welsh of Philadelphia, who was shortly succeeded by David McKay. *Leaves of Grass* had now reached the form in which it was henceforth to be published. Newspaper publicity had created interest in the book, and it sold better than any previous edition. As a result, Whitman was able to buy a modest little cottage in Camden, where he spent the rest of his life. He had many new friends, among them Horace Traubel, who recorded his talk and wrote his biography. *The Complete Poems and Prose* was published in 1888, along with the eighth edition of *Leaves of Grass*. The ninth, or "authorized," edition appeared in 1892, the year of Whitman's death.

## Leaves of Grass

Walt Whitman is known primarily for *Leaves of Grass*, though his prose volume *Specimen Days* contains some fine realistic descriptions of Civil War scenes. But *Leaves of Grass* is actually more than one book. During Whitman's lifetime it went through nine editions, each with its own distinct virtues and faults. Whitman compared the finished book to a cathedral long under construction, and on another occasion to a tree, with its cumulative rings of growth. Both metaphors are misleading, however, because he did not construct his book unit by unit or by successive layers but constantly altered titles, diction, and even motifs and shifted poems—omitting, adding, separating, and combining.

Under the influence of the Romantic movement in literature and art, Whitman held the theory that the chief function of the poet was to express his own personality in his verse. The first edition of *Leaves of Grass* also appeared during the most nationalistic period in American literature, when critics were calling for a literature commensurate with the size, natural resources, and potentialities of the North American continent. Whitman declared in his 1855 preface, "Here are the roughs and beards and space and ruggedness and nonchalance that the soul loves." In *Leaves of Grass* he addressed the citizens of the United States, urging them to be large and generous in spirit, a new race nurtured in political liberty, and possessed of united souls and bodies.

It was partly in response to nationalistic ideals and partly in accord with his ambition to cultivate and express his own personality that the "I" of Whitman's poems asserted a mythical strength and vitality. For the frontispiece to the first edition, Whitman used a picture of himself in work clothes, posed nonchalantly with cocked hat and hand in trouser pocket, as if illustrating a line in his leading poem, "Song of Myself": "I cock my hat as I please indoors and out." In this same poem he also characterized himself as:

*Walt Whitman, an American, one of the roughs,*
*a kosmos,*

*Disorderly fleshy and sensual...eating drink-*
*ing and breeding,*
*...Divine am I inside and out, and I make*
*holy whatever I touch or am touched from...*

From this time on throughout his life Whitman attempted to dress the part and act the role of the shaggy, untamed poetic spokesman of the proud young nation. For the expression of this persona he also created a form of free verse without rhyme or metre, but abounding in oratorical rhythms and chanted lists of American place-names and objects. He learned to handle this primitive, enumerative style with great subtlety and was especially successful in creating empathy of space and movement, but to most of his contemporaries it seemed completely "unpoetic." Both the content and the style of his verse also caused Whitman's early biographers, and even the poet himself, to confuse the symbolic self of the poems with their physical creator. In reality Whitman was quiet, gentle, courteous; neither "rowdy" (a favourite word) nor lawless. In sexual conduct he may have been unconventional, though no one is sure, but it is likely that the six illegitimate children he boasted of in extreme old age were begotten by his imagination. He did advocate greater sexual freedom and tolerance, but sex in his poems is also symbolic—of natural innocence, "the procreant urge of the world," and of the regenerative power of nature. In some of his poems the poet's own erotic emotions may have confused him, but in his greatest, such as parts of "Song of Myself" and all of "Out of the Cradle Endlessly Rocking," sex is spiritualized.

Whitman's greatest theme is a symbolic identification of the regenerative power of nature with the deathless divinity of the soul. His poems are filled with a religious faith in the processes of life, particularly those of fertility, sex, and the "unflagging pregnancy" of nature: sprouting grass, mating birds, phallic vegetation, the maternal ocean, and planets in formation ("the journey-work of stars"). The poetic "I" of *Leaves of Grass* transcends time and space, binding the past with the present and intuiting the future, illustrating Whitman's belief that poetry is a form of knowledge, the supreme wisdom of mankind.

# HERMAN MELVILLE

(b. August 1, 1819, New York City, New York, U.S.—d. September 28, 1891, New York City)

The American novelist, short-story writer, and poet Herman Melville is best known for his novels of the sea, including his masterpiece, *Moby Dick* (1851).

Melville's heritage and youthful experiences were perhaps crucial in forming the conflicts underlying his artistic vision. He was the third child of Allan and Maria Gansevoort Melvill, in a family that was to grow to four boys and four girls. His forebears had been among the Scottish and Dutch settlers of New York and had taken leading roles in the American Revolution and in the fiercely competitive commercial and political life of the new country.

In 1826 Allan Melvill wrote of his son as being "backward in speech and somewhat slow in comprehension...of a docile and amiable disposition." In that same year, scarlet fever left the boy with permanently weakened eyesight, but he attended Male High School. When the family import business collapsed in 1830, the family returned to Albany, where Herman enrolled briefly in Albany Academy. Allan Melvill died in 1832, leaving his family in desperate straits. The eldest son, Gansevoort, assumed responsibility for the family and took over his father's felt and fur business. Herman joined him after two years as a bank clerk and some months working on the farm of his uncle, Thomas Melvill, in Pittsfield, Massachusetts. About this time, Herman's branch of the family altered the spelling of its name. Though finances were precarious, Herman attended Albany Classical School in 1835 and became an active member of a local debating society. A teaching job in Pittsfield made him unhappy, however, and after three months he returned to Albany.

## *Wanderings and Voyages*

Young Melville had already begun writing, but the remainder of his youth became a quest for security. A comparable pursuit in the spiritual realm was to characterize much of his writing. The crisis that started Herman on his wanderings came in 1837, when Gansevoort went bankrupt and the family moved to nearby Lansingburgh (later Troy). In what was to be a final attempt at orthodox employment, Herman studied surveying at Lansingburgh Academy to equip himself for a post with the Erie Canal project. When the job did not materialize, Gansevoort arranged for Herman to ship out as cabin boy on the *St. Lawrence*, a merchant ship sailing in June 1839 from New York City for Liverpool. The summer voyage did not dedicate Melville to the sea, and on his return his family was dependent still on the charity of relatives. After a grinding search for work, he taught briefly in a school that closed without paying him. His uncle Thomas, who had left Pittsfield for Illinois, apparently had no help to offer when the young man followed him west. In January 1841 Melville sailed on the whaler *Acushnet*, from New Bedford, Massachusetts, on a voyage to the South Seas.

In June 1842 the *Acushnet* anchored in the Marquesas Islands in present-day French Polynesia. Melville's adventures here, somewhat romanticized, became the subject of his first novel, *Typee* (1846). In July Melville and a companion jumped ship and, according to *Typee*, spent about four months as guest-captives of the reputedly cannibalistic Typee people. Actually, in August he was registered in the crew of the Australian whaler "Lucy Ann." Whatever its precise correspondence with fact, however, *Typee* was faithful to the imaginative impact of the experience on Melville. Despite intimations of danger, Melville represented the exotic valley of the Typees as an idyllic sanctuary from a hustling, aggressive civilization.

Although Melville was down for a 120th share of the whaler's proceeds, the voyage had been unproductive. He joined a mutiny that landed the mutineers in a Tahitian jail, from which he escaped without difficulty. On these events and their sequel, Melville based his second book, *Omoo* (1847). Lighthearted in tone, with the mutiny shown as something of a farce, it describes Melville's travels through the islands, accompanied by Long Ghost, formerly the ship's doctor, now turned drifter. The carefree roving confirmed Melville's bitterness against colonial and, especially, missionary debasement of the native Tahitian peoples.

These travels, in fact, occupied less than a month. In November he signed as a harpooner on his last whaler, the *Charles & Henry*, out of Nantucket, Massachusetts. Six months later he disembarked at Lahaina, in the Hawaiian Islands. Somehow he supported himself for more than three months; then in August 1843 he signed as an ordinary seaman on the frigate *United States*, which in October 1844 discharged him in Boston.

## The Years of Acclaim

Melville rejoined a family whose prospects had much improved. Gansevoort, who after James K. Polk's victory in the 1844 presidential elections had been appointed secretary to the U.S. legation in London, was gaining political renown. Encouraged by his family's enthusiastic reception of his tales of the South Seas, Melville wrote them down.

*Typee* provoked immediate enthusiasm and outrage, and then a year later *Omoo* had an identical response. Gansevoort, dead of a brain disease, never saw his brother's career consolidated, but the bereavement left Melville head of the family and the more committed to writing to support it. Another responsibility came with his marriage in August 1847 to Elizabeth Shaw, daughter of the chief justice of Massachusetts. He tried unsuccessfully for a job in the U.S. Treasury Department, the first of many abortive efforts to secure a government post.

In 1847 Melville began a third book, *Mardi* (1849), and became a regular contributor of reviews and other pieces to a literary journal. He enjoined his publisher not to call him "the author of *Typee* and *Omoo*," for his third book was to be different. When it appeared, public and critics alike found its wild, allegorical fantasy and medley of styles incomprehensible. Concealing his disappointment at the book's reception, Melville quickly wrote *Redburn* (1849) and *White-Jacket* (1850) in the manner expected of him. In October 1849 Melville sailed to England to resolve his London publisher's doubts about *White-Jacket*. He also visited the Continent, kept a journal, and arrived back in America in February 1850. The critics acclaimed *White-Jacket*, and its powerful criticism of abuses in the U.S. Navy won it strong political support. But both novels, however much they seemed to revive the Melville of *Typee*, had passages of profoundly questioning melancholy. It was not the same Melville who wrote them. A fresh imaginative influence was supplied by Nathaniel Hawthorne's *Scarlet Letter*, a novel deeply exploring good and evil in the human being, which Melville read in the spring of 1850.

*Herman Melville, etching after a portrait by Joseph O. Eaton.*
Library of Congress, Washington, D.C. (Digital File Number:
cph 3c35949)

That summer, Melville bought a farm, which he christened "Arrowhead," near Hawthorne's home at Pittsfield, and the two men became neighbours physically as well as in sympathies.

Melville had promised his publishers for the autumn of 1850 the novel first entitled *The Whale*, finally *Moby Dick*. His delay in submitting it was caused less by his early-morning chores as a farmer than by his explorations into the unsuspected vistas opened for him by Hawthorne. Their relationship reanimated Melville's creative energies. On his side, it was dependent, almost mystically intense—"an infinite fraternity of feeling," he called it. To the cooler, withdrawn Hawthorne, such depth of feeling so persistently and openly declared was uncongenial. The two men gradually drew apart.

*Moby Dick* was published in London in October 1851 and a month later in America. It brought its author neither acclaim nor reward. Basically its story is simple. Captain Ahab pursues the white whale, Moby Dick, which finally kills him. At that level, it is an intense, superbly authentic narrative of whaling. In the perverted grandeur of Captain Ahab and in the beauties and terrors of the voyage of the "Pequod," however, Melville dramatized his deeper concerns: the equivocal defeats and triumphs of the human spirit and its fusion of creative and murderous urges. In his private afflictions, Melville had found universal metaphors.

Increasingly a recluse to the point that some friends feared for his sanity, Melville embarked almost at once on *Pierre* (1852). It was an intensely personal work, revealing the sombre mythology of his private life framed in terms of a story of an artist alienated from his society. In it can be found the humiliated responses to poverty that his youth supplied him plentifully and the hypocrisy he found beneath his father's claims to purity and faithfulness.

When published, it was another critical and financial disaster. Only 33 years old, Melville saw his career in ruins. Near breakdown, and having to face in 1853 the disaster of a fire at his New York publishers that destroyed most of his books, Melville persevered with writing.

*Israel Potter*, plotted before his introduction to Hawthorne and his work, was published in 1855, but its modest success, clarity of style, and apparent simplicity of subject did not indicate a decision by Melville to write down to public taste. His contributions to *Putnam's Monthly Magazine*—*Bartleby the Scrivener* (1853), "The Encantadas" (1854), and "Benito Cereno" (1855)—reflected the despair and the contempt for human hypocrisy and materialism that possessed him increasingly.

In 1856 Melville set out on a tour of Europe and the Levant to renew his spirits. The most powerful passages of the journal he kept are in harmony with *The Confidence-Man* (1857), a despairing satire on an America corrupted by the shabby dreams of commerce. This was the last of his novels to be published in his lifetime.

## *The Years of Withdrawal*

Melville abandoned the novel for poetry, but the prospects for publication were not favourable. With two sons and daughters to support, Melville sought government patronage. A consular post he sought in 1861 went elsewhere. On the outbreak of the Civil War, he volunteered for the Navy, but was again rejected. He had apparently returned full cycle to the insecurity of his youth, but an inheritance from his father-in-law brought some relief and "Arrowhead," increasingly a burden, was sold. By the end of 1863, the family was living in New York City. The war was much on his mind and furnished the subject of his first volume of verse, *Battle-Pieces and Aspects of the War*

(1866), published privately. Four months after it appeared, an appointment as a customs inspector on the New York docks finally brought him a secure income.

His second collection of verse, *John Marr, and Other Sailors; With Some Sea-Pieces*, appeared in 1888, again privately published. By then he had been in retirement for three years, assisted by legacies from friends and relatives. His new leisure he devoted, he wrote in 1889, to "certain matters as yet incomplete." Among them was *Timoleon* (1891), a final verse collection. More significant was the return to prose that culminated in his last work, the novel *Billy Budd*, which remained unpublished until 1924. Provoked by a false charge, the sailor Billy Budd accidentally kills the satanic master-at-arms. In a time of threatened mutiny he is hanged, going willingly to his fate. Evil has not wholly triumphed, and Billy's memory lives on as an emblem of good. Here there is, if not a statement of being reconciled fully to life, at least the peace of resignation. The manuscript ends with the date April 19, 1891. Five months later Melville died. His life was neither happy nor, by material standards, successful. By the end of the 1840s he was among the most celebrated of American writers, yet his death evoked but a single obituary notice.

In the internal tensions that put him in conflict with his age lay a strangely 20th-century awareness of the deceptiveness of realities and of the instability of personal identity. Yet his writings never lost sight of reality. His symbols grew from such visible facts, made intensely present, as the dying whales, the mess of blubber, and the wood of the ship, in *Moby Dick*. For Melville, as for Shakespeare, man was ape and essence, inextricably compounded; and the world, like the "Pequod," was subject to "two antagonistic influences... one to mount direct to heaven, the other to drive yawingly to some horizontal goal." It was Melville's triumph that he endured, recording his vision to the end. After the years of neglect, modern criticism has secured his reputation with that of the great American writers.

# GEORGE ELIOT

(b. November 22, 1819, Chilvers Coton, Warwickshire, England—
d. December 22, 1880, London)

George Eliot (a pseudonym of Marian Cross, *née* Evans) was an English Victorian novelist who developed the method of psychological analysis characteristic of modern fiction. Her major works include *Adam Bede* (1859), *The Mill on the Floss* (1860), *Silas Marner* (1861), *Middlemarch* (1871–72), and *Daniel Deronda* (1876).

## Early Years

Evans was born on an estate of her father's employer. She went as a boarder to Mrs. Wallington's School at Nuneaton (1828–32), where she came under the influence of Maria Lewis, the principal governess, who inculcated a strong evangelical piety in the young girl. At her last school (1832–35), conducted by the daughters of the Baptist minister at Coventry, her religious ardour increased. She dressed severely and engaged earnestly in good works. The school gave her a reading knowledge of French and Italian, and, after her mother's death had compelled her to return home to keep house for her father, he let her have lessons in Latin and German. In 1841 she moved with her father to Coventry.

There she became acquainted with a prosperous ribbon manufacturer, Charles Bray, a self-taught freethinker who campaigned for radical causes. His brother-in-law,

Charles Hennell, was the author of *An Inquiry Concerning the Origin of Christianity* (1838), a book that precipitated Evans's break with orthodoxy that had been long in preparation. Various books on the relation between the Bible and science had instilled in her keen mind the very doubts they were written to dispel. In 1842 she told her father that she could no longer go to church. The ensuing storm raged for several months before they reached a compromise, leaving her free to think what she pleased so long as she appeared respectably at church, and she lived with him until his death in 1849.

The Brays and the Hennells quickly drew her from extreme provincialism, introducing her to many ideas in violent disagreement with her Tory father's religious and political views. When Charles Hennell married in 1843, she took over from his wife the translating of D.F. Strauss's *Das Leben Jesu kritisch bearbeitet*, which was published anonymously as *The Life of Jesus Critically Examined*, 3 vol. (1846), and had a profound influence on English rationalism.

She spent the winter of 1849–50 at Geneva, reading extensively while living with the family of François d'Albert Durade, who painted a portrait of her. Like those by Mrs. Bray (1842) and Sir Frederic Burton (1865), all in the National Portrait Gallery, it shows her with light brown hair, gray-blue eyes, and a very fair complexion. Returning to Coventry, she spent the rest of 1850 with the Brays, pondering how to live on the £100 a year left by her father. After John Chapman, the publisher of *The Life of Jesus Critically Examined*, got her a chance to review R.W. Mackay's *The Progress of the Intellect* in *The Westminster Review* (January 1851), she decided to settle in London as a freelance writer, and in January 1851 she went to board with the Chapmans at 142, Strand.

## Life with George Henry Lewes

Soon after her arrival in London, Mrs. Chapman and the children's governess, who was also John Chapman's mistress, became jealous of Marian, as she now signed her name, and after 10 weeks she returned to Coventry in tears. Doubtless her feelings were strongly attracted to the magnetic Chapman, whose diary supplies this information, but there is no evidence that she was ever his mistress. A few months later he bought *The Westminster Review*, and Evans, contrite at the domestic complications she had unwittingly caused, returned to London. For three years, until 1854, she served as subeditor of *The Westminster*, which under her influence enjoyed its most brilliant run since the days of John Stuart Mill. At the Chapmans' evening parties she met many notable literary figures in an atmosphere of political and religious radicalism. Across the Strand lived the subeditor of *The Economist*, Herbert Spencer, whose *Social Statics* (1851) Chapman had just published. Evans shared many of Spencer's interests and saw so much of him that it was soon rumoured that they were engaged. Though he did not become her husband, he introduced her to the two men who did.

George Henry Lewes was the most versatile of Victorian journalists. In 1841 he had married Agnes Jervis, by whom he had four sons. In 1850 Lewes and a friend, the journalist Thornton Leigh Hunt, founded a radical weekly called *The Leader*, for which he wrote the literary and theatrical sections. In April 1850, two weeks after the first number appeared, Agnes Lewes gave birth to a son whose father was Thornton Hunt. Lewes, being a man of liberal views, had the child registered as Edmund Lewes and remained on friendly terms with his wife and Hunt. But after she bore Hunt a second child in October 1851,

Lewes ceased to regard her as his wife, though, having condoned the adultery, he was precluded from suing for divorce. At this moment of dejection, his home hopelessly broken, he met Marian Evans. They consulted about articles and went to plays and operas that Lewes reviewed for *The Leader*. Convinced that his break with Agnes was irrevocable, Evans determined to live openly with Lewes as his wife. In July 1854, after the publication of her translation of Feuerbach's *Essence of Christianity*, they went to Germany together. In all but the legal form it was a marriage, and it continued happily until Lewes's death in 1878. "Women who are content with light and easily broken ties," she told Mrs. Bray, "do *not* act as I have done. They obtain what they desire and are still invited to dinner."

## *Major Works*

At Weimar and Berlin she wrote some of her best essays for *The Westminster* and translated Spinoza's *Ethics* (still unpublished), while Lewes worked on his groundbreaking life of Goethe. By his pen alone he had to support his three surviving sons at school in Switzerland as well as Agnes, whom he gave £100 a year, which was continued until her death in 1902. She had four children by Hunt, the last born in 1857, all registered under Lewes's name. The few friends who knew the facts agreed that toward Agnes his conduct was more than generous, but there was a good deal of malicious gossip about the "strong-minded woman" who had "run off with" her husband. Evans's deepest regret was that her act isolated her from her family in Warwickshire. She turned to early memories and, encouraged by Lewes, wrote a story about a childhood episode in Chilvers Coton parish. Published in *Blackwood's Magazine* (1857) as *The Sad Fortunes of the Reverend Amos Barton*, it was an instant success. Two more tales, *Mr. Gilfil's Love-Story* and *Janet's Repentance*, also based on local events, appeared serially in the same year, and Blackwood republished all three as *Scenes of Clerical Life*, 2 vol. (1858), under the pseudonym George Eliot.

*Adam Bede*, 3 vol. (1859), her first long novel, she described as "a country story—full of the breath of cows and the scent of hay." Its masterly realism—"the faithful representing of commonplace things"—brought to English fiction the same truthful observation of minute detail that Ruskin was commending in the Pre-Raphaelites. The book is rich in humour. The germ of the plot was an anecdote her Methodist aunt told of visiting a girl condemned for child murder. But what was new in English fiction was the combination of deep human sympathy and rigorous moral judgment. *Adam Bede* went through eight printings within a year, and Blackwood doubled the £800 paid for it and returned the copyright.

In *The Mill on the Floss*, 3 vol. (1860), she returned again to the scenes of her early life. The first half of the book, with its remarkable portrayal of childhood, is irresistibly appealing, and throughout there are scenes that reach a new level of psychological subtlety.

At this time historical novels were in vogue, and during their visit to Florence in 1860 Lewes suggested Savonarola as a good subject. George Eliot grasped it enthusiastically and began to plan *Romola* (1862–63). First, however, she wrote *Silas Marner* (1861), which had thrust itself between her and the Italian material. Its brevity and perfection of form made this story of the weaver whose lost gold is replaced by a strayed child the best known of her books, though it has suffered unfairly from being forced on generations of schoolchildren. *Romola* was planned as a serial for *Blackwood's*, until an offer of £10,000 from *The Cornhill Magazine* induced George Eliot to desert her old publisher; but rather than divide the book into the 16 installments the editor wanted, she accepted £3,000 less, an evidence of artistic integrity few writers would have shown. It was published in 14 parts between July 1862 and August 1863.

George Eliot's next two novels are laid in England at the time of agitation for passage of the Reform Bill. In *Felix Holt, the Radical*, 3 vol. (1866), she drew the election riot from recollection of one she saw at Nuneaton in December 1832. The initial impulse of the book was not the political theme but the tragic character of Mrs. Transome, who was one of her greatest triumphs. The intricate plot popular taste then demanded now tells against the novel. *Middlemarch* (8 parts, 1871–72) is by general consent George Eliot's masterpiece. Under her hand the novel had developed from a mere entertainment into a highly intellectual form of art. Every class of Middlemarch society is depicted from the landed gentry and clergy to the manufacturers and professional men, the shopkeepers, publicans, farmers, and labourers. Several strands of plot are interwoven to reinforce each other by contrast and parallel. Yet the story depends not on close-knit intrigue but on showing the incalculably diffusive effect of the unhistoric acts of those who "lived faithfully a hidden life and rest in unvisited tombs."

*Daniel Deronda* (8 parts, 1876), in which George Eliot comes nearest the contemporary scene, is built on the contrast between Mirah Cohen, a poor Jewish girl, and the upper class Gwendolen Harleth, who marries for money and regrets it. The less convincingly realized hero, Daniel, after discovering that he is Jewish, marries Mirah and departs for Palestine to establish a home for his nation. The picture of the Cohen family evoked grateful praise from Jewish readers. But the best part of *Daniel Deronda* is the keen analysis of Gwendolen's character, which seems to many critics the peak of George Eliot's achievement.

## *Final Years*

In 1863 the Leweses bought the Priory, 21, North Bank, Regent's Park, where their Sunday afternoons became a brilliant feature of Victorian life. There on November 30, 1878, Lewes died. For nearly 25 years he had fostered her genius and managed all the practical details of life, which now fell upon her. Most of all she missed the encouragement that alone made it possible for her to write. For months she saw no one but his son Charles Lee Lewes; she devoted herself to completing the last volume of his *Problems of Life and Mind* (1873–79) and founded the George Henry Lewes Studentship in Physiology at Cambridge. For some years her investments had been in the hands of John Walter Cross (1840–1924), a banker introduced to the Leweses by Herbert Spencer. Cross's mother had died a week after Lewes. Drawn by sympathy and the need for advice, George Eliot soon began to lean on him for affection too. On May 6, 1880, they were married in St. George's, Hanover Square. Cross was 40; she was in her 61st year. After a wedding trip in Italy they returned to her country house at Witley before moving to 4, Cheyne Walk, Chelsea, where she died in December.

# CHARLES BAUDELAIRE

(b. April 9, 1821, Paris, France—d. August 31, 1867, Paris)

Charles-Pierre Baudelaire was a French poet, translator, and literary and art critic whose reputation rests primarily on *Les Fleurs du mal* (1857; *The Flowers of Evil*), which was perhaps the most important and influential poetry collection published in Europe in the 19th century.

## Early Life

Baudelaire was the only child of François Baudelaire and his much younger second wife, Caroline Defayis, whom he married in 1819. Having begun his career as a priest, François had abandoned holy orders in 1793 and ultimately became a prosperous middle-ranking civil servant. A painter and poet of modest talent, he introduced his son to art, or what the younger Baudelaire would later call his greatest, most consuming, and earliest of passions, "the cult of images." His father died in February 1827, and for some 18 months thereafter Baudelaire and his mother lived together on the outskirts of Paris in conditions that he would always remember. This "verdant paradise of childhood loves" abruptly ended in November 1828 when Caroline married Jacques Aupick, a career soldier who rose to the rank of general and who later served as French ambassador to the Ottoman Empire and Spain before becoming a senator under the Second Empire.

In 1831 Aupick was posted to Lyons, and Baudelaire began his education at the Collège Royal there in 1832 before transferring, on the family's return to Paris in 1836, to the prestigious Lycée Louis-le-Grand. Baudelaire showed promise as a student and began to write his earliest poems, but to his masters he seemed an example of precocious depravity, adopting what they called "affectations unsuited to his age." He also developed a tendency to moods of intense melancholy, and he became aware that he was solitary by nature. Regular acts of indiscipline led to his being expelled from the school after a trivial incident in April 1839. After passing his *baccalauréat* examinations while enrolled at the Collège Saint-Louis,

*Charles Baudelaire, photograph by Étienne Carjat, 1863.* Courtesy of the Bibliothèque Nationale, Paris

Baudelaire became a nominal student of law at the École de Droit while in reality leading a "free life" in the Latin Quarter. There he made his first contacts in the literary world and also contracted the venereal disease that would eventually kill him.

In an attempt to wean his stepson from such disreputable company, Aupick sent him on a protracted voyage to India in June 1841, but Baudelaire effectively jumped ship in Mauritius and, after a few weeks there and in Réunion, returned to France in February 1842. The voyage had deepened and enriched his imagination, however, and his brief encounter with the tropics would endow his writing with an abundance of exotic images and sensations and an everlasting theme of nostalgic reverie.

Baudelaire came into his inheritance in April 1842 and rapidly proceeded to dissipate it on the lifestyle of a dandified man of letters, spending freely on clothes, books, paintings, expensive food and wines, and, not least, hashish and opium. It was shortly after returning from the South Seas that Baudelaire met Jeanne Duval, who, first as his mistress and then, after the mid-1850s, as his financial charge, was to dominate his life for the next 20 years. Jeanne would inspire Baudelaire's most anguished and sensual love poetry, her perfume and, above all, her magnificent flowing black hair provoking such masterpieces of the exotic-erotic imagination as *La Chevelure* ("The Head of Hair").

Baudelaire's continuing extravagance exhausted half his fortune in two years, and he also fell prey to cheats and moneylenders, thus laying the foundation for an accumulation of debt that would cripple him for the rest of his life. In September 1844 his family imposed on him a legal arrangement that restricted his access to his inheritance and effectively made of him a legal minor.

## Early Writings

Baudelaire had returned from the South Seas in 1842 determined as never before to become a poet. From then until 1846 he probably composed the bulk of the poems that make up the first edition (1857) of *Les Fleurs du mal*. Baudelaire first established himself in the Parisian cultural milieu not as a poet but as an art critic with his reviews of the Salons of 1845 and 1846. Inspired by the example of the Romantic painter Eugène Delacroix, he elaborated in his *Salons* a wide-ranging theory of modern painting, with painters being urged to celebrate and express the "heroism of modern life." In January 1847 Baudelaire published a novella entitled *La Fanfarlo* whose hero, or antihero, Samuel Cramer, is widely, if simplistically, seen as a self-portrait of the author as he agonizedly oscillates between desire for the maternal and respectable Madame de Cosmelly and the erotic actress-dancer of the title.

## Maturity and Decline

In 1847 Baudelaire had discovered the work of Edgar Allan Poe. Overwhelmed by what he saw as the almost preternatural similarities between the American writer's thought and temperament and his own, he embarked upon the task of translation that was to provide him with his most regular occupation and income for the rest of his life. His translation of Poe's *Mesmeric Revelation* appeared as early as July 1848, and thereafter translations appeared regularly in reviews before being collected in book form in *Histoires extraordinaires* (1856; "Extraordinary Tales") and *Nouvelles Histoires extraordinaires* (1857; "New Extraordinary Tales"), each preceded by an important critical introduction by Baudelaire. These were followed by *Les Aventures d'Arthur*

*Gordon Pym* (1857), *Eurêka* (1864), and *Histoires grotesques et sérieuses* (1865; "Grotesque and Serious Tales"). Baudelaire also began studying the work of the conservative theorist Joseph de Maistre, who, together with Poe, impelled his thought in an increasingly antinaturalist and antihumanist direction. From the mid-1850s Baudelaire would regard himself as a Roman Catholic, though his obsession with original sin and the Devil remained unaccompanied by faith in God's forgiveness and love, and his Christology was impoverished to the point of nonexistence.

Between 1852 and 1854 Baudelaire addressed a number of poems to Apollonie Sabatier, celebrating her, despite her reputation as a high-class courtesan, as his madonna and muse, and in 1854 he had a brief liaison with the actress Marie Daubrun. In the meantime Baudelaire's growing reputation as Poe's translator and as an art critic at last enabled him to publish some of his poems. In June 1855 the *Revue des deux mondes* published a sequence of 18 of his poems under the general title of *Les Fleurs du mal*. The poems, which Baudelaire had chosen for their original style and startling themes, brought him notoriety. The following year Baudelaire signed a contract with the publisher Poulet-Malassis for a full-length poetry collection to appear with that title. When the first edition of *Les Fleurs du mal* was published in June 1857, 13 of its 100 poems were immediately arraigned for offences to religion or public morality. After a one-day trial on August 20, 1857, six of the poems were ordered to be removed from the book on the grounds of obscenity, with Baudelaire incurring a fine of 300 (later reduced to 50) francs. The six poems were first republished in Belgium in 1866 in the collection *Les Épaves* ("Wreckage"), and the official ban on them would not be revoked until 1949. Owing largely to these circumstances, *Les Fleurs du mal* became a byword for depravity, morbidity, and obscenity, and the legend of Baudelaire as the doomed dissident and pornographic poet was born.

## The Last Years

The failure of *Les Fleurs du mal,* from which he had expected so much, was a bitter blow to Baudelaire, and the remaining years of his life were darkened by a growing sense of failure, disillusionment, and despair. After publishing his earliest experiments in prose poetry, he set about preparing a second edition of *Les Fleurs du mal.* In 1859, while living with his mother at Honfleur on the Seine River estuary, where she had retired after Aupick's death in 1857, Baudelaire produced in rapid succession a series of poetic masterpieces beginning with *Le Voyage* in January and culminating in what is widely regarded as his greatest single poem, *Le Cygne* ("The Swan"), in December. At the same time, he composed two of his most provocative essays in art criticism, the *Salon de 1859* and *Le Peintre de la vie moderne* ("The Painter of Modern Life"). In February 1861 a second, and greatly enlarged and improved, edition of *Les Fleurs du mal* was published by Poulet-Malassis.

In 1861 Baudelaire made an ill-advised and unsuccessful attempt to gain election to the French Academy. In 1862 Poulet-Malassis was declared bankrupt; Baudelaire was involved in his publisher's failure, and his financial difficulties became desperate. Abandoning verse poetry as his medium, Baudelaire now concentrated on writing prose poems, a sequence of 20 of which was published in *La Presse* in 1862. In April 1864 he left Paris for Brussels in the hope of persuading a Belgian publisher to publish his complete works. He would remain in Belgium, increasingly embittered and impoverished, until the summer of 1866, when, following a collapse in the Church of Saint-Loup at Namur, he was stricken with paralysis and aphasia from which he would never recover. Baudelaire died at age 46 in the Paris nursing home in which he had been confined for the last year of his life.

# Les Fleurs du mal

Baudelaire's poetic masterpiece, the 1861 edition of *Les Fleurs du mal*, consists of 126 poems arranged in six sections of varying length. A prefatory poem makes it clear that Baudelaire's concern is with the general human predicament of which his own is representative. The collection may best be read in the light of the concluding poem, *Le Voyage,* as a journey through self and society in search of some impossible satisfaction that forever eludes the traveler.

The first section, entitled "Spleen et idéal," opens with a series of poems that dramatize contrasting views of art, beauty, and the artist, who is depicted alternately as martyr, visionary, performer, pariah, and fool. The focus then shifts to sexual and romantic love, with the first-person narrator of the poems oscillating between extremes of ecstasy ("idéal") and anguish ("spleen") as he attempts to find fulfillment through a succession of women whom it is possible, if simplistic, to identify with Jeanne Duval, Apollonie Sabatier, and Marie Daubrun. Each set of love poems describes an erotic cycle that leads from intoxication through conflict and revulsion to an eventual ambivalent tranquillity born of memory and the transmutation of suffering into art. Yet the attempt to find plenitude through love comes in the end to nothing, and "Spleen et idéal" ends with a sequence of anguished poems, several of them entitled "Spleen," in which the self is shown imprisoned within itself, with only the certainty of suffering and death before it.

The second section, "Tableaux parisiens," was added to the 1861 edition and describes a 24-hour cycle in the life of the city through which the Baudelairean traveler, now metamorphosed into a flaneur (idle man-about-town), moves in quest of deliverance from the miseries of self, only to find at every turn images of suffering and isolation that remind him all too pertinently of his own. The section includes some of Baudelaire's greatest poems, most notably *Le Cygne,* where the memory of a swan stranded in total dereliction near the Louvre becomes a symbol of an existential condition of loss and exile transcending time and space. His quest is predictably to no avail for, as the final section, entitled *La Mort,* reveals, his journey is an everlasting, open-ended odyssey that, continuing beyond death, will take him into the depths of the unknown, always in pursuit of the new, which, by definition, must forever elude him.

## Prose Poems

Baudelaire's *Petits poèmes en prose* was published posthumously in 1869 and was later, as intended by the author, entitled *Le Spleen de Paris* (translated as *The Parisian Prowler*). He did not live long enough to bring these poems together in a single volume, but it is clear from his correspondence that the work he envisaged was both a continuation of, and a radical departure from, *Les Fleurs du mal.* Some of the texts may be regarded as authentic poems in prose, while others are closer to miniature prose narratives. Again the setting is primarily urban, with the focus on crowds and the suffering lives they contain: a broken-down street acrobat (*Le Vieux Saltimbanque*), a hapless street trader (*Le Mauvais Vitrier*), the poor staring at the wealthy in their opulent cafés (*Le Yeux des pauvres*), the deranged (*Mademoiselle Bistouri*) and the derelict (*Assommons les pauvres!*), and, in the final text (*Les Bons Chiens*), the pariah dogs that scurry and scavenge through the streets of Brussels. In its deliberate fragmentation and its merging of the lyrical with the sardonic, *Le Spleen de Paris* may be regarded as one of the earliest and most successful examples of a specifically urban writing, embodying in its poetics of sudden and disorienting encounter that ambiguous "heroism of modern life" that Baudelaire celebrated in his art criticism.

# Fyodor Dostoyevsky

(b. October 30 [November 11, New Style], 1821, Moscow, Russia— d. January 28 [February 9], 1881, St. Petersburg)

Fyodor Dostoyevsky was a Russian novelist and short-story writer whose psychological penetration into the darkest recesses of the human heart, together with his unsurpassed moments of illumination, had an immense influence on 20th-century fiction.

Dostoyevsky is usually regarded as one of the finest novelists who ever lived. Literary modernism, existentialism, and various schools of psychology, theology, and literary criticism have been profoundly shaped by his ideas.

## Background and Early Life

Unlike many other Russian writers of the first part of the 19th century, Dostoyevsky was not born into the landed gentry. He often stressed the difference between his own background and that of Leo Tolstoy or Ivan Turgenev and the effect of that difference on his work. First, Dostoyevsky was always in need of money and had to hurry his works into publication. Although he complained that writing against a deadline prevented him from achieving his full literary powers, it is equally possible that his frenzied style of composition lent his novels an energy that has remained part of their appeal. Second, Dostoyevsky often noted that, unlike writers from the nobility who described the family life of their own class, shaped by "beautiful forms" and stable traditions, he explored the lives of "accidental families" and of "the insulted and the humiliated."

Dostoyevsky's father, a retired military surgeon, served as a doctor at the Mariinsky Hospital for the Poor in Moscow, where he treated charity cases while also conducting a private practice. Though a devoted parent, Dostoyevsky's father was a stern, suspicious, and rigid man. By contrast, his mother, a cultured woman from a merchant family, was kindly and indulgent.

In 1828 Dostoyevsky's father managed to earn the rank of a nobleman (the reforms of Peter I the Great had made such a change in status possible). He bought an estate in 1831, and so young Fyodor spent the summer months in the country. Until 1833 Dostoyevsky was educated at home, before being sent to a day school and then to a boarding school. Dostoyevsky's mother died in 1837, followed by his father in 1839. Dostoyevsky and his older brother Mikhail, who remained his close friend and became his collaborator in publishing journals, were entranced with literature from a young age. Not long after completing his degree (1843) from the Academy of Military Engineering in St. Petersburg and becoming a sublieutenant, Dostoyevsky resigned his commission to commence a hazardous career as a writer living off his pen.

## Early Works

Dostoyevsky did not have to toil long in obscurity. No sooner had he written his first novella, *Bednyye lyudi* (1846;

*Poor Folk*), than he was hailed as the great new talent of Russian literature by the most influential critic of his day, the "furious" Vissarion Belinsky.

*Poor Folk*, the appeal of which has been overshadowed by Dostoyevsky's later works, is cast in the then already anachronistic form of an epistolary novel. Makar Devushkin, a poor copying clerk who can afford to live only in a corner of a dirty kitchen, exchanges letters with a young and poor girl, Varvara Dobrosyolova. Her letters reveal that she has already been procured once for a wealthy and worthless man, whom, at the end of the novel, she agrees to marry. The novel is remarkable for its descriptions of the psychological (rather than just material) effects of poverty.

In the next few years Dostoyevsky published a number of stories, including *Belyye nochi* ("White Nights"), which depicts the mentality of a dreamer, and a novella, *Dvoynik* (1846; *The Double*), a study in schizophrenia. The hero of this novella, Golyadkin, begets a double of himself, who mocks him and usurps his place. Dostoyevsky boldly narrates the story through one of the voices that sounds within Golyadkin's psyche so that the story reads as if it were a taunt addressed directly to its unfortunate hero.

## *Political Activity and Arrest*

In 1847 Dostoyevsky began to participate in the Petrashevsky Circle, a group of intellectuals who discussed utopian socialism. He eventually joined a related, secret group devoted to revolution and illegal propaganda. It appears that Dostoyevsky did not sympathize (as others did) with egalitarian communism and terrorism but was motivated by his strong disapproval of serfdom. On April 23, 1849, he and the other members of the Petrashevsky Circle were arrested. Dostoyevsky spent eight months in prison until, on December 22, the prisoners were led without warning to the Semyonovsky Square. There a sentence of death by firing squad was pronounced, last rites were offered, and three prisoners were led out to be shot first. At the last possible moment, the guns were lowered and a messenger arrived with the information that the tsar had deigned to spare their lives. The mock-execution ceremony was in fact part of the punishment.

Instead of being executed, Dostoyevsky was sentenced to four years in a Siberian prison labour camp, to be followed by an indefinite term as a soldier. After his return to Russia 10 years later, he wrote a novel based on his prison camp experiences, *Zapiski iz myortvogo doma* (1861–62; *The House of the Dead*). Gone was the tinge of Romanticism and dreaminess present in his early fiction. The novel, which was to initiate the Russian tradition of prison camp literature, describes the horrors that Dostoyevsky actually witnessed: the brutality of the guards who enjoyed cruelty for its own sake, the evil of criminals who could enjoy murdering children, and the existence of decent souls amid filth and degradation—all these themes, warranted by the author's own experience, gave the novel the immense power that readers still experience. Tolstoy considered it Dostoyevsky's masterpiece. Above all, *The House of the Dead* illustrates that, more than anything else, it is the need for individual freedom that makes us human. This conviction was to bring Dostoyevsky into direct conflict with the radical determinists and socialists of the intelligentsia.

In Siberia Dostoyevsky experienced what he called the "regeneration" of his convictions. He rejected the condescending attitude of intellectuals, who wanted to impose their political ideas on society, and came to believe in the dignity and fundamental goodness of common people. He describes this change in his sketch *The Peasant Marey* (which appears in *The Diary of a Writer*). Dostoyevsky also became deeply attached to Russian Orthodoxy, as the religion of the common people, although his faith was always at war with his skepticism.

Dostoyevsky suffered his first attacks of epilepsy while in prison. In 1857 Dostoyevsky married a consumptive widow, Mariya Dmitriyevna Isayeva (she died seven years later); the unhappy marriage began with her witnessing one of his seizures on their honeymoon.

## *Works of the 1860s*

Upon his return to Russia, Dostoyevsky plunged into literary activity. With his brother Mikhail, he edited two influential journals, first *Vremya* (1861–63; "Time"), which was closed by the government on account of an objectionable article, and then *Epokha* (1864–65; "Epoch"), which collapsed after the death of Mikhail. After first trying to maintain a middle-of-the-road position, Dostoyevsky began to attack the radicals, who virtually defined the Russian intelligentsia. Dostoyevsky was repulsed by their materialism, their utilitarian morality, their reduction of art to propaganda, and, above all, their denial of individual freedom and responsibility.

In the first part of *Zapiski iz podpolya* (1864; *Notes from the Underground*) an unnamed first-person narrator delivers a brilliant attack on a set of beliefs shared by liberals and radicals: that it is possible to discover the laws of individual psychology, that human beings consequently have no free choice, that history is governed by laws, and that it is possible to design a utopian society based on the laws of society and human nature. Even if such a society could be built, the underground man argues, people would hate it just because it denied them caprice and defined them as utterly predictable. In the novella's second part the underground man recalls incidents from his past, which show him behaving, in answer to determinism, according to sheer spite. Dostoyevsky thus makes clear that the underground man's irrationalist solution is no better than the rationalists' systems.

For several reasons, Dostoyevsky spent much of the 1860s in western Europe: he wanted to see the society that he both admired for its culture and deplored for its materialism, he was hoping to resume an affair with the minor author Appolinariya Suslova, he was escaping his creditors in Russia, and he was disastrously attracted to gambling. An unscrupulous publisher offered him a desperately needed advance on the condition that he deliver a novel by a certain date; the publisher was counting on the forfeit provisions, which would allow him nine years to publish all of Dostoyevsky's works for free. With less than a month remaining, Dostoyevsky hired a stenographer and dictated his novel *Igrok* (1866; *The Gambler*)—based on his relations with Suslova and the psychology of compulsive gambling—which he finished just on time. A few months later (1867) he married the stenographer, Anna Grigoryevna Snitkina. She at last put his life and finances in order and created stable conditions for his work and new family. They had four children, of whom two survived to adulthood.

Written at the same time as *The Gambler*, *Prestupleniye i nakazaniye* (1866; *Crime and Punishment*) describes a young intellectual, Raskolnikov, willing to gamble on ideas. He decides to solve all his problems at a stroke by murdering an old pawnbroker woman. Contradictory motives and theories all draw him to the crime. Utilitarian morality suggests that killing her is a positive good because her money could be used to help many others. On the other hand, Raskolnikov reasons that belief in good and evil is itself sheer prejudice, a mere relic of religion, and that, morally speaking, there is no such thing as crime. Nevertheless, Raskolnikov, despite his denial of morality, sympathizes with the unfortunate and so wants to kill the pawnbroker just because she is an oppressor of the weak. His most famous theory justifying murder divides the world into extraordinary people, such as Solon, Caesar, and Napoleon, and ordinary people, who simply serve to propagate the species. Extraordinary people, he theorizes, must have "the right to transgress," or progress would be impossible. Nothing could be further from Dostoyevsky's own morality, based on the infinite worth of each human soul, than this Napoleonic theory, which Dostoyevsky viewed as the real content of the intelligentsia's belief in its superior wisdom.

After committing the crime, Raskolnikov unaccountably finds himself gripped by "mystic terror" and a horrible sense of isolation. The detective Porfiry Petrovich, who guesses Raskolnikov's guilt but cannot prove it, plays psychological games with him until the murderer at last confesses. Meanwhile, Raskolnikov tries to discover the real motive for his crime but never arrives at a single answer. In a famous commentary, Tolstoy argued that there was no single motive but rather a series of "tiny, tiny alterations" of mood and mental habits.

Quite deliberately, Dostoyevsky made the heroine of the story, Sonya Marmeladova, an unrealistic symbol of pure Christian goodness. Having become a prostitute to support her family, she later persuades Raskolnikov to confess and then follows him to Siberia. In the novel's epilogue, the prisoner Raskolnikov, who has confessed not out of remorse but out of emotional stress, at first continues to maintain his amoral theories but at last is brought to true repentance by a revelatory dream and by Sonya's goodness. Critical opinion is divided over whether the epilogue is artistically successful.

Dostoyevsky's next major novel, *Idiot* (1868–69; *The Idiot*), represents his attempt to describe a perfectly good man in a way that is still psychologically convincing— seemingly an impossible artistic task. If he could succeed, Dostoyevsky believed, he would show that Christ-like goodness is indeed possible; and so the very writing of the work became an attempt at what might be called a novelistic proof of Christianity.

The work's hero, Prince Myshkin, is indeed perfectly generous and so innocent as to be regarded as an idiot; however, he is also gifted with profound psychological insight. Unfortunately, his very goodness seems to bring disaster to all he meets, even to the novel's heroine, Nastasya Filippovna, whom he wishes to save. With a remarkably complex psychology, she both accepts and bitterly defies the world's judgment of her as a fallen woman.

## Dostoyevsky's Last Decade

Dostoyevsky's next novel, *Besy* (1872; *The Possessed*), earned him the permanent hatred of the radicals. Often regarded as one of the most brilliant political novels ever written, it interweaves two plots. One concerns Nikolay Stavrogin, a man with a void at the centre of his being. In his younger years Stavrogin, in a futile quest for meaning, had embraced and cast off a string of ideologies, each of which has been adopted by different intellectuals mesmerized by Stavrogin's personality. Shatov has become a Slavophile who, like Dostoyevsky himself, believes in the "God-bearing" Russian people. Existentialist critics (especially Albert Camus) became fascinated with Kirillov, who adopts a series of contradictory philosophical justifications for suicide. Most famously, Kirillov argues that only an utterly gratuitous act of self-destruction can prove that a person is free because such an act cannot be explained by any kind of self-interest and therefore violates all psychological laws. By killing himself without reason, Kirillov hopes to become the "man-god" and so provide an example for human freedom in a world that has denied Christ (the God-man).

It is the novel's other plot that has earned Dostoyevsky the reputation of a political prophet. It describes a cell of revolutionary conspirators led by Pyotr Stepanovich Verkhovensky, who binds the group together by involving them in murdering Shatov. One of the revolutionaries, Shigalyov, offers his thoughts on the emergence of the perfect society: "Starting with unlimited freedom, I arrive at unlimited despotism." Enforced equality and guaranteed utopia demand the suppression of all individuality and independent thought. In lines that anticipate Soviet and Maoist cultural policy, Pyotr Stepanovich predicts that, when the revolution comes, "Cicero will have his tongue cut out, Copernicus will have his eyes put out, Shakespeare will be stoned," all in the name of "equality."

In 1873 Dostoyevsky assumed the editorship of the conservative journal *Grazhdanin* ("The Citizen"), where he published an irregular column entitled *Dnevnik pisatelya* ("The Diary of a Writer"). He left *Grazhdanin* to write *Podrostok* (1875; *A Raw Youth*, also known as *The Adolescent*), a relatively unsuccessful and diffuse novel describing a young man's relations with his natural father.

In 1876–77 Dostoyevsky devoted his energies to *Dnevnik pisatelya*, which he was now able to bring out in the form he had originally intended. A one-man journal, for which Dostoyevsky served as editor, publisher, and sole contributor, the *Diary* represented an attempt to initiate a new literary genre. Issue by monthly issue, the *Diary* created complex thematic resonances among diverse kinds of material: short stories, plans for possible stories, autobiographical essays, sketches that seem to lie on the boundary between fiction and journalism, psychological analyses of sensational crimes, literary criticism, and political commentary. The *Diary* proved immensely popular and financially rewarding, but as an aesthetic experiment it was less successful, probably because Dostoyevsky, after a few intricate issues, seemed unable to maintain his complex design. Instead, he was drawn into expressing his political views, which, during these two years, became increasingly extreme. He reached his moral nadir with a number of anti-Semitic articles.

Dostoyevsky's last and probably greatest novel, *Bratya Karamazovy* (1879–80; *The Brothers Karamazov*), focuses on his favourite theological and philosophical themes: the origin of evil, the nature of freedom, and the craving for faith. A profligate and vicious father, Fyodor Pavlovich Karamazov, mocks everything noble and engages in unseemly buffoonery at every opportunity. When his sons were infants, he neglected them not out of malice but simply because he "forgot" them. The eldest, Dmitry, a passionate man capable of sincerely loving both "Sodom" and "the Madonna" at the same time, wrangles with his father over money and competes with him for the favours of a "demonic" woman, Grushenka. When the old man is murdered, circumstantial evidence leads to Dmitry's arrest for the crime, which actually has been committed by the fourth, and illegitimate, son, the malicious epileptic Smerdyakov.

The youngest legitimate son, Alyosha, is another of Dostoyevsky's attempts to create a realistic Christ figure. Following the wise monk Zosima, Alyosha tries to put Christian love into practice. The narrator proclaims him the work's real hero, but readers are usually most interested in the middle brother, the intellectual Ivan.

The novel is most famous for two chapters that may be ranked among the greatest pages of Western literature. In

"Rebellion," Ivan indicts God the Father for creating a world in which children suffer. Ivan has also written a "poem," *The Grand Inquisitor,* which represents his response to God the Son. It tells the story of Christ's brief return to earth during the Spanish Inquisition. Recognizing him, the Inquisitor arrests him as "the worst of heretics" because, the Inquisitor explains, the church has rejected Christ. For Christ came to make people free, but, the Inquisitor insists, people do not want to be free, no matter what they say. They want security and certainty rather than free choice, which leads them to error and guilt. And so, to ensure happiness, the church has created a society based on "miracle, mystery, and authority." The Inquisitor is evidently meant to stand not only for medieval Roman Catholicism but also for contemporary socialism. "Rebellion" and "The Grand Inquisitor" contain what many have considered the strongest arguments ever formulated against God, which Dostoyevsky includes so that, in refuting them, he can truly defend Christianity. It is one of the greatest paradoxes of Dostoyevsky's work that his deeply Christian novel more than gives the Devil his due.

In 1880 Dostoyevsky delivered an electrifying speech about the poet Aleksandr Pushkin, which he published in a separate issue of *The Diary of a Writer* (August 1880). After finishing *Karamazov*, he resumed the monthly *Diary* but lived to publish only a single issue (January 1881) before dying of a hemorrhage on January 28 in St. Petersburg.

# GUSTAVE FLAUBERT

(b. December 12, 1821, Rouen, France—d. May 8, 1880, Croisset)

The novelist Gustave Flaubert is regarded as the prime mover of the realist school of French literature and is best known for his masterpiece, *Madame Bovary* (1857). A realistic portrayal of bourgeois life, publication of the work led to a trial on charges of the novel's alleged immorality.

## Early Life and Works

Flaubert's father, Achille Cléophas Flaubert, who was from Champagne, was chief surgeon and clinical professor at the Hôtel-Dieu hospital in Rouen. His mother, a doctor's daughter from Pont l'Évêque, belonged to a family of distinguished magistrates typical of the great provincial bourgeoisie.

Gustave Flaubert began his literary career at school, his first published work appearing in a little review, *Le Colibri*, in 1837. He early formed a close friendship with the young philosopher Alfred Le Poittevin, whose pessimistic outlook had a strong influence on him. No less strong was the impression made by the company of great surgeons and the environment of hospitals, operating theatres, and anatomy classes, with which his father's profession brought him into contact.

Flaubert's intelligence, moreover, was sharpened in a general sense. He conceived a strong dislike of accepted ideas (*idées reçues*), of which he was to compile a "dictionary" for his amusement. He and Le Poittevin invented a grotesque imaginary character, called "le Garçon" (the Boy), to whom they attributed whatever sort of remark seemed to them most degrading. Flaubert came to detest the "bourgeois," by which he meant anyone who "has a low way of thinking."

In November 1841 Flaubert was enrolled as a student at the Faculty of Law in Paris. At age 22, however, he was recognized to be suffering from a nervous disease that was taken to be epilepsy, although the essential symptoms were absent. This made him give up the study of law, with the result that henceforth he could devote all his time to literature. His father died in January 1846, and his beloved sister Caroline died in the following March after giving birth to a daughter. Flaubert then retired with his mother and his infant niece to his estate at Croisset, near Rouen, on the Seine.

On a visit to Paris in July 1846, at the sculptor James Pradier's studio, Flaubert met the poet Louise Colet. She became his mistress, but their relationship did not run smoothly. His self-protecting independence and her jealousy made separation inevitable, and they parted in 1855.

In 1847 Flaubert went on a walking tour along the Loire and the coast of Brittany with the writer Maxime du Camp, whose acquaintance he had made as a law student. The pages written by Flaubert in their journal of this tour "over fields and shores" were published after his death under that title, *Par les champs et par les grèves*. This book contains some of his best writing—e.g., his description of a visit to Chateaubriand's family estate, Combourg.

## Mature Career

Some of the works of Flaubert's maturity dealt with subjects on which he had tried to write earlier. At age 16, for instance, he completed the manuscript of *Mémoires d'un fou* ("Memoirs of a Mad Man"), which recounted his devastating passion for Elisa Schlésinger, 11 years his senior and the wife of a music publisher, whom he had met in 1836. This passion was only revealed to her 35 years later when she was a widow. Elisa provided the model for the character Marie Arnoux in the novel *L'Education sentimentale*. Before receiving its definitive form, however, this work was to be rewritten in two distinct intermediate versions in manuscript: *Novembre* (1842) and a preliminary draft entitled *L'Éducation sentimentale* (1843–45). Stage by stage it was expanded into a vast panorama of France under the July Monarchy—indispensable reading, according to Georges Sorel, for any historian studying the period that preceded the coup d'etat of 1851.

The composition of *La Tentation de Saint Antoine* provides another example of that tenacity in the pursuit of perfection that made Flaubert go back constantly to work on subjects without ever being satisfied with the results. In 1839 he was writing *Smarh*, the first product of his bold ambition to give French literature its *Faust*. He resumed the task in 1846–49, in 1856, and in 1870, and finally published the book as *La Tentation de Saint Antoine* in 1874. The four versions show how the author's ideas changed in the course of time. The version of 1849, influenced by Spinoza's philosophy, is nihilistic in its conclusion. In the second version the writing is less diffuse, but the substance remains the same. The third version shows a respect for religious feeling that was not present in the earlier ones, since in the interval Flaubert had read Herbert Spencer and reconciled the Spencerian notion of the Unknown with his Spinozism. He had come to believe that science and religion, instead of conflicting, are rather the two poles of thought. The published version incorporated a catalog of errors in the field of the Unknown (just as *Bouvard et Pécuchet* was to contain a list of errors in the field of science).

From November 1849 to April 1851 Flaubert was travelling in Egypt, Palestine, Syria, Turkey, Greece, and Italy with Maxime du Camp. Before leaving, however, he wanted to finish *La Tentation* and to submit it to his friend the poet Louis Bouilhet and to du Camp for their sincere opinion. For three days in September 1849 he read his manuscript to them, and they then condemned it mercilessly. "Throw it all into the fire, and let's never mention it again." Bouilhet gave further advice: "Your Muse must be kept on bread and water or lyricism will kill her. Write a down-to-earth novel like Balzac's *Parents pauvres*. The story of Delamare, for instance...."

Eugéne Delamare was a country doctor in Normandy who died of grief after being deceived and ruined by his wife, Delphine (*née* Couturier). The story, in fact that of *Madame Bovary*, is not the only source of that novel. Another was the manuscript *Mémoires de Mme Ludovica*, discovered by Gabrielle Leleu in the library of Rouen in 1946. This is an account of the adventures and misfortunes of Louise Pradier (*née* d'Arcet), the wife of the sculptor James Pradier, as dictated by herself, and, apart from the suicide, it bears a strong resemblance to the story of Emma Bovary. Flaubert, out of kindness as well as out of professional curiosity, had continued to see Louise Pradier when the "bourgeois" were ostracizing her as a fallen woman, and she must have given him her strange document. Even so, when inquisitive people asked him who served as model for his heroine, Flaubert replied, "Madame Bovary is myself." As early as 1837 he had written *Passion et vertu*, a short and pointed story with a heroine, Mazza, resembling Emma Bovary. For *Madame Bovary* he took a commonplace story of adultery and made of it a book that will always be read because of its profound humanity. While working on his novel Flaubert wrote: "My poor Bovary suffers and cries in more than a score of villages in France at this very moment." *Madame Bovary*, with its unrelenting objectivity—by which Flaubert meant the dispassionate recording of every trait or incident that could illuminate the psychology of his characters and their role in the logical development of his story—marks the beginning of a new age in literature.

*Madame Bovary* cost the author five years of hard work. Du Camp, who had founded the periodical *Revue de Paris*, urged him to make haste, but he would not. The novel, with the subtitle *Moeurs de province* ("Provincial Customs"), eventually appeared in installments in the *Revue* from October 1 to December 15, 1856. The French government then brought the author to trial on the ground of his novel's alleged immorality, and he narrowly escaped conviction (January–February 1857). The same tribunal found the poet Charles Baudelaire guilty on the same charge six months later.

To refresh himself after his long application to the dull world of the bourgeoisie in *Madame Bovary*, Flaubert immediately began work on *Salammbô*, a novel about ancient Carthage, in which he set his sombre story of Hamilcar's daughter Salammbô, an entirely fictitious character, against the authentic historical background of the revolt of the mercenaries against Carthage in 240–237 BCE. His transformation of the dry record of Polybius into richly poetic prose is comparable to Shakespeare's treatment of Plutarch's narrative in the lyrical descriptions in *Antony and Cleopatra*. A play, *Le Château des coeurs* (*The Castle of Hearts*, 1904), written in 1863, was not printed until 1880.

## Later Years

The merits of *L'Éducation sentimentale*, which appeared a few months before the outbreak of the Franco-German War of 1870, were not appreciated, and Flaubert was much disappointed. Two plays, *Le Sexe faible* ("The Feeble Sex") and *Le Candidat* (*The Candidate*, 1904), likewise had no success, though the latter was staged for four performances in March 1874. The last years of his life, moreover, were saddened by financial troubles. In 1875 his niece Caroline's husband, Ernest Commanville, a timber importer, found himself heavily in debt. Flaubert sacrificed his own fortune to save him from bankruptcy. Flaubert sought consolation in his work and in the friendship of George Sand, Ivan Turgenev, and younger novelists—Émile Zola, Alphonse Daudet, and, especially, Guy de Maupassant, who was the son of his friend Alfred Le Poittevin's sister Laure and who regarded himself as Flaubert's disciple.

Flaubert temporarily abandoned work on a long novel, *Bouvard et Pécuchet*, in order to write *Trois Contes*, containing the three short stories "Un Coeur simple," a tale about the drab and simple life of a faithful servant; "La Légende de Saint Julien l'Hospitalier"; and "Hérodias." This book, through the diversity of the stories' themes, shows Flaubert's talent in all its aspects and has often been held to be his masterpiece.

The heroes of *Bouvard et Pécuchet* are two clerks who receive a legacy and retire to the country together. Not knowing how to use their leisure, they busy themselves with one abortive experiment after another and plunge successively into scientific farming, archaeology, chemistry, and historiography, as well as taking an abandoned child into their care. Everything goes wrong because their futile book learning cannot compensate for their lack of judgment.

The profound meaning of *Bouvard et Pécuchet*, which was left unfinished by Flaubert and which was not published until after his death, has been seriously misunderstood by those critics who have regarded it as a denial of the value of science. In fact it is "scientism" (and by analogy the confusion of doctrines) that Flaubert is arraigning—i.e., the practice of taking science out of its own domain, of confusing efficient and final causes, and of convincing oneself that one understands fundamentals when one has not even grasped the superficial phenomena. Intoxicated with empty words, Bouvard and Pécuchet awake from their dream only when catastrophe overtakes all of their efforts.

Flaubert has been accused of presenting them as imbeciles, but in fact he expresses his compassion for them: "They acquire a faculty deserving of pity, they recognize stupidity and can no longer tolerate it. Through their inquisitiveness their understanding grows; having had more ideas, they suffered more." Flaubert's satire is thus to some extent the history of his own experience told with a sad humour.

Flaubert died suddenly of an apoplectic stroke. He left on his table an unfinished page and notes for the second volume of his novel. Bouvard and Pécuchet, tired of experimenting, were to go back to the work of transcribing and copying that they had done as clerks. The matter that they chose to transcribe was the subject of the notes: it was to be a selection of quotations, a *sottisier*, or anthology of foolish remarks. There has been much controversy about this bitter conclusion, as the form that it was to take was left undetermined in the notes Flaubert left, though the materials were gathered and have been published.

## MATTHEW ARNOLD

(b. December 24, 1822, Laleham, Middlesex, England—d. April 15, 1888, Liverpool)

The English Victorian poet and literary and social critic Matthew Arnold is noted especially for his classical attacks on the contemporary tastes and manners of the "Barbarians" (the aristocracy), the "Philistines" (the commercial middle class), and the "Populace." He became the apostle of "culture" in such works as *Culture and Anarchy* (1869).

## *Life*

Matthew was the eldest son of the renowned Thomas Arnold, who was appointed headmaster of Rugby School in 1828. Matthew entered Rugby (1837) and then attended Oxford as a scholar of Balliol College; there he won the Newdigate Prize with his poem *Cromwell* (1843) and was graduated with second-class honours in 1844. For Oxford Arnold retained an impassioned affection. His Oxford was the Oxford of John Henry Newman—of Newman just about to be received into the Roman Catholic Church; and although Arnold's own religious thought, like his father's, was strongly liberal, Oxford and Newman always remained for him joint symbols of spiritual beauty and culture.

In 1847 Arnold became private secretary to Lord Lansdowne, who occupied a high cabinet post during Lord John Russell's Liberal ministries. And in 1851, in order to secure the income needed for his marriage (June 1851) with Frances Lucy Wightman, he accepted from Lansdowne an appointment as inspector of schools. This was to be his routine occupation until within two years of his death. He engaged in incessant travelling throughout the British provinces and also several times was sent by the government to inquire into the state of education in France, Germany, Holland, and Switzerland.

## *Poetic Achievement*

The work that gives Arnold his high place in the history of literature and the history of ideas was all accomplished in the time he could spare from his official duties. His first volume of verse was *The Strayed Reveller, and Other Poems. By A.* (1849); this was followed (in 1852) by another under the same initial: *Empedocles on Etna, and Other Poems*. In 1853 appeared the first volume of poems published under

*Matthew Arnold.* Library of Congress, Washington, D.C.

his own name; it consisted partly of poems selected from the earlier volumes and also contained the well-known preface explaining (among other things) why *Empedocles* was excluded from the selection: it was a dramatic poem "in which the suffering finds no vent in action," in which there is "everything to be endured, nothing to be done." This preface foreshadows his later criticism in its insistence upon the classic virtues of unity, impersonality, universality, and architectonic power and upon the value of the classical masterpieces as models for "an age of spiritual discomfort"—an age "wanting in moral grandeur." Other editions followed, and *Merope*, Arnold's classical tragedy, appeared in 1858, and *New Poems* in 1867. After that date, though there were further editions, Arnold wrote little additional verse.

Not much of Arnold's verse will stand the test of his own criteria. Far from being classically poised, impersonal, serene, and grand, it is often intimate, personal, full of romantic regret, sentimental pessimism, and nostalgia.

In 1857, assisted by the vote of his godfather (and predecessor) John Keble, Arnold was elected to the Oxford chair of poetry, which he held for 10 years. It was characteristic of him that he revolutionized this professorship. The keynote was struck in his inaugural lecture: "On the Modern Element in Literature," "modern" being taken to mean not merely "contemporary" (for Greece was "modern"), but the spirit that, contemplating the vast and complex spectacle of life, craves for moral and intellectual "deliverance."

## *Arnold as Critic*

It is said that when the poet in Arnold died, the critic was born; and it is true that from this time onward he turned almost entirely to prose. Some of the leading ideas and phrases were early put into currency in *Essays in Criticism* (First Series, 1865; Second Series, 1888) and *Culture and Anarchy*. The first essay in the 1865 volume, "The Function of Criticism at the Present Time," is an overture announcing briefly most of the themes he developed more fully in later work. It is at once evident that he ascribes to "criticism" a scope and importance hitherto undreamed of. The function of criticism, in his sense, is "a disinterested endeavour to learn and propagate the best that is known and thought in the world, and thus to establish a current of fresh and true ideas." It is in fact a spirit that he is trying to foster, the spirit of an awakened and informed intelligence playing upon not "literature" merely but theology, history, art, science, sociology, and politics, and in every sphere seeking "to see the object as in itself it really is."

In this critical effort, thought Arnold, England lagged behind France and Germany, and the English accordingly remained in a backwater of provinciality and complacency. Even the great Romantic poets, with all their creative energy, suffered from the want of it. The English literary critic must know literatures other than his own and be in touch with European standards. This last line of thought Arnold develops in the second essay, "The Literary Influence of Academies," in which he dwells upon "the note of provinciality" in English literature, caused by remoteness from a "centre" of correct knowledge and correct taste.

The first essay in the 1888 volume, "The Study of Poetry," was originally published as the general introduction to T.H. Ward's anthology, *The English Poets* (1880). It contains many of the ideas for which Arnold is best remembered. In an age of crumbling creeds, poetry will have to replace religion. More and more, we will "turn to poetry to interpret life for us, to console us, to sustain us." Therefore we must know how to distinguish the best poetry from the inferior, the genuine from the counterfeit; and to do this we must steep ourselves in the work of the acknowledged masters, using as "touchstones" passages exemplifying their "high seriousness," and their superiority of diction and movement.

*Culture and Anarchy* is in some ways Arnold's most central work. It is an expansion of his earlier attacks, in "The Function of Criticism" and "Heinrich Heine," upon the smugness, philistinism, and mammon worship of

Victorian England. Culture, as "the study of perfection," is opposed to the prevalent "anarchy" of a new democracy without standards and without a sense of direction. By "turning a stream of fresh thought upon our stock notions and habits," culture seeks to make "reason and the will of God prevail."

Arnold's classification of English society into Barbarians (with their high spirit, serenity, and distinguished manners and their inaccessibility to ideas), Philistines (the stronghold of religious nonconformity, with plenty of energy and morality but insufficient "sweetness and light"), and Populace (still raw and blind) is well known. Arnold saw in the Philistines the key to the whole position; they were now the most influential section of society; their strength was the nation's strength, their crudeness its crudeness: Educate and humanize the Philistines, therefore. Arnold saw in the idea of "the State," and not in any one class of society, the true organ and repository of the nation's collective "best self." No summary can do justice to this extraordinary book; it can still be read with pure enjoyment, for it is written with an inward poise, a serene detachment, and an infusion of mental laughter, which make it a masterpiece of ridicule as well as a searching analysis of Victorian society. The same is true of its unduly neglected sequel, *Friendship's Garland* (1871).

## Religious Writings

Lastly Arnold turned to religion, the constant preoccupation and true centre of his whole life, and wrote *St. Paul and Protestantism* (1870), *Literature and Dogma* (1873), *God and the Bible* (1875), and *Last Essays on Church and Religion* (1877). In these books, Arnold really founded Anglican "modernism." Like all religious liberals, he came under fire from two sides: from the orthodox, who accused him of infidelity, of turning God into a "stream of tendency" and of substituting vague emotion for definite belief; and from the infidels, for clinging to the church and retaining certain Christian beliefs of which he had undermined the foundations. Arnold considered his religious writings to be constructive and conservative. His attitude is best summed up in his own words (from the preface to *God and the Bible*): "At the present moment two things about the Christian religion must surely be clear to anybody with eyes in his head. One is, that men cannot do without it; the other, that they cannot do with it as it is." Convinced that much in popular religion was "touched with the finger of death" and convinced no less of the hopelessness of man without religion, he sought to find for religion a basis of "scientific fact" that even the positive modern spirit must accept.

Arnold died suddenly, of heart failure, in the spring of 1888, in Liverpool. He was buried at Laleham, with the three sons whose early loss had shadowed his life.

# *JULES VERNE*

(b. February 8, 1828, Nantes, France—d. March 24, 1905, Amiens)

J ules Verne was a prolific French author whose writings laid much of the foundation of modern science fiction.

Verne's father, intending that Jules follow in his footsteps as an attorney, sent him to Paris to study law. But the young Verne fell in love with literature, especially theatre. He wrote several plays, worked as secretary of the Théâtre Lyrique (1852–54), and published short stories and scientific essays in the periodical *Musée des familles*. In 1857 Verne married and for several years worked as a broker at the Paris Stock Market. During this period he continued to write, to do research at the Bibliothèque Nationale (National Library), and to dream of a new kind of novel—one that would combine scientific fact with adventure fiction. In September 1862 Verne met Pierre-Jules Hetzel, who agreed to publish the first of Verne's *Voyages extraordinaires* ("Extraordinary Journeys")—*Cinq semaines en balloon* (1863; *Five Weeks in a Balloon*). Initially serialized in Hetzel's *Le Magasin d'éducation et de récréation*, the novel became an international best seller, and Hetzel offered Verne a long-term contract to produce many more works of "scientific fiction." Verne subsequently quit his job at the stock market to become a full-time writer and began what would prove to be a highly successful author-publisher collaboration that lasted for more than 40 years and resulted in more than 60 works in the popular series *Voyages extraordinaires*.

Verne's works can be divided into three distinct phases. The first, from 1862 to 1886, might be termed his positivist period. After his dystopian second novel *Paris au XXe siècle* (1994; *Paris in the 20th Century*) was rejected by Hetzel in 1863, Verne learned his lesson, and for more than two decades he churned out many successful science-adventure novels, including *Voyage au centre de la terre* (1863, expanded 1867; *Journey to the Centre of the Earth*), *De la terre à la lune* (1865; *From the Earth to the Moon*), *Autour de la lune* (1870; *Trip Around the Moon*), *Vingt mille lieues sous les mers* (1870; *Twenty Thousand Leagues Under the Sea*), and *Le Tour du monde en quatre-vingts jours* (1873; *Around the World in Eighty Days*). During these years Verne settled with his family in Amiens and made a brief trip to the United States to visit New York City and Niagara Falls. During this period he also purchased several yachts and sailed to many European countries, collaborated on theatre adaptations of several of his novels, and gained both worldwide fame and a modest fortune.

The second phase, from 1886 until his death in 1905, might be considered Verne's pessimist period. Throughout these years the ideological tone of his *Voyages extraordinaires* began to change. Increasingly Verne turned away from pro-science tales of exploration and discovery in favour of exploring the dangers of technology wrought by hubris-filled scientists in novels such as *Sans dessus dessous* (1889; *Topsy-Turvy*), *L'Île à hélice* (1895; *Floating Island*), *Face au drapeau* (1896; *For the Flag*), and *Maître du monde* (1904; *Master of the World*). This change of focus also paralleled certain adversities in the author's personal life: growing problems with his rebellious son, Michel; financial difficulties that forced him to sell his yacht; the successive deaths of his mother and his mentor Hetzel; and an attack by a mentally disturbed nephew who shot him in the lower leg, rendering him partially crippled. When Verne died he left a drawerful of nearly completed manuscripts in his desk.

The third and final phase of the Jules Verne story, from 1905 to 1919, might be considered the Verne fils period, when his posthumous works were published—after being substantially revamped—by his son, Michel. They include *Le Volcan d'or* (1906; *The Golden Volcano*), *L'Agence Thompson and Co.* (1907; *The Thompson Travel Agency*), *La Chasse au météore* (1908; *The Chase of the Golden Meteor*), *Le Pilote du Danube* (1908; *The Danube Pilot*), *Les Naufragés du Jonathan* (1909; *The Survivors of the Jonathan*), *Le Secret de Wilhelm Storitz* (1910; *The Secret of Wilhelm Storitz*), *Hier et demain* (1910; *Yesterday and Tomorrow*, a collection of short stories), and *L'Étonnante aventure de la mission Barsac* (1919; *The Barsac Mission*). Comparing Verne's original manuscripts with the versions published after his death, modern researchers discovered that Michel Verne did much more than merely edit them. In most cases he entirely rewrote them—among other changes, he recast plots, added fictional characters, and made their style more melodramatic. Scholarly reaction to these discoveries has been mixed. Some critics condemn these posthumous works as contaminated; others view them as a legitimate part of the Verne père et fils collaboration. The debate continues.

With Michel Verne's death in 1925, the final chapter of Jules Verne's literary legacy was more or less complete. The following year American publisher Hugo Gernsback used a representation of Verne's tomb as a logo for his *Amazing Stories*, the first literary magazine featuring tales of "scientifiction." As the term *scientifiction* evolved into *science fiction*, the new genre began to flourish as never before, and Verne became universally recognized as its patron saint.

During the 20th century, Verne's works were translated into more than 140 languages, making him one of the world's most translated authors. A number of successful motion pictures were made from Verne novels, starting in 1916 with *20,000 Leagues Under the Sea* (remade in 1954 by Walt Disney) and including *The Mysterious Island* (1929 and 1961), *From the Earth to the Moon* (1958), *Journey to the Center of the Earth* (1959), and, perhaps the most popular, *Around the World in 80 Days* (1956).

Verne's influence extends beyond literature and film into the world of science and technology, where he inspired generations of scientists, inventors, and explorers. In 1954 the United States Navy launched the world's first nuclear-powered submarine, named for Verne's *Nautilus*. And for more than 130 years, adventurers such as Nellie Bly (1890), Wiley Post (1933), and Steve Fossett (2005) have followed in the footsteps of Verne's fictional hero Phileas Fogg by attempting to circumnavigate the globe in record-breaking times. Verne and his enduringly popular *Voyages extraordinaires* continue to remind us that "What one man can imagine, another will someday be able to achieve."

# HENRIK IBSEN

(b. March 20, 1828, Skien, Norway—d. May 23, 1906, Kristiania
[formerly Christiania; now Oslo])

Henrik Ibsen was a major Norwegian playwright of the late 19th century who introduced to the European stage a new order of moral analysis. The new order was placed against a severely realistic middle-class background and developed with economy of action, penetrating dialogue, and rigorous thought.

## Early Years and First Plays

Ibsen was born at Skien, a small lumbering town of southern Norway. His father was a respected general merchant in the community until 1836, when he suffered the permanent disgrace of going bankrupt. As a result, he sank into a querulous penury, which his wife's withdrawn and sombre religiosity did nothing to mitigate. There was no redeeming the family misfortunes; as soon as he could, aged just 15, Henrik moved to Grimstad, a hamlet of some 800 persons 70 miles (110 km) down the coast. There he supported himself meagerly as an apothecary's apprentice while studying nights for admission to the university. And during this period he used his few leisure moments to write a play.

This work, *Catilina* (1850; *Catiline*), grew out of the Latin texts Ibsen had to study for his university examinations. Though not a very good play, it showed a natural bent for the theatre and embodied themes—the rebellious hero, his destructive mistress—that would preoccupy Ibsen as long as he lived. In 1850 he went to Christiania (known since 1925 by its older name of Oslo), studied for entrance examinations there, and settled into the student quarter—though not, however, into classes. For the theatre was in his blood, and at the age of only 23 he got himself appointed director and playwright to a new theatre at Bergen, in which capacity he had to write a new play every year.

First at Bergen and then at the Norwegian Theatre in Christiania from 1857 to 1862, Ibsen tried to make palatable dramatic fare out of incongruous ingredients. In addition to writing plays which were uncongenial to him and unacceptable to audiences, he did a lot of directing. He was too inhibited to make a forceful director, but too intelligent not to pick up a great deal of practical stage wisdom from his experience. After he moved to Christiania and after his marriage to Suzannah Thoresen in 1858, he began to develop qualities of independence and authority that had been hidden before.

Two of the last plays that Ibsen wrote for the Norwegian stage showed signs of new spiritual energy. *Kjaerlighedens komedie* (1862; *Love's Comedy*), a satire on romantic illusions, was violently unpopular, but it expressed an authentic theme of anti-idealism that Ibsen would soon make his own; and in *Kongsemnerne* (1863; *The Pretenders*) he dramatized the mysterious inner authority that makes a man a man, a king, or a great playwright. This one play was in fact the national drama after which Ibsen had been groping so long, and before long it would be recognized as such. But it came too late; though the play was good, the theatre in Christiania was bankrupt, and Ibsen's career as a stage writer was apparently at an end.

But the death of his theatre was the liberation of Ibsen as a playwright. Without regard for a public he thought petty and illiberal, without care for traditions he found hollow and pretentious, he could now write for himself.

He decided to go abroad, and applied for a small state grant. He was awarded part of it, and in April 1864 he left Norway for Italy. For the next 27 years he lived abroad, mainly in Rome, Dresden, and Munich, returning to Norway only for short visits in 1874 and 1885. For reasons that he sometimes summarized as "small-mindedness," his homeland had left a very bitter taste in his mouth.

## *Mature Career and Major Works*

With him into exile Ibsen brought the fragments of a long semi-dramatic poem to be named *Brand*. Its central figure is a dynamic rural pastor who takes his religious calling with a blazing sincerity that transcends not only all forms of compromise but all traces of human sympathy and warmth as well. "All or nothing" is the demand that his god makes of Brand and that Brand in turn makes of others. Yet in the last scene where Brand stands alone before his god, a voice thunders from an avalanche that, even as it crushes the pastor physically, repudiates his whole moral life as well: "He is the god of love," says the voice from on high. So the play is not only a denunciation of small-mindedness but a tragedy of the spirit that would transcend it. The poem faced its readers not just with a choice but with an impasse; the heroic alternative was also a destructive (and self-destructive) alternative. In Norway *Brand* was a tremendous popular success, even though (and in part because) its central meaning was so troubling.

Hard on the heels of *Brand* (1866) came *Peer Gynt* (1867), another drama in rhymed couplets presenting an utterly antithetical view of human nature. If Brand is a moral monolith, Peer Gynt is a capering will-o'-the-wisp, a buoyant and self-centred opportunist who is aimless, yielding, and wholly unprincipled, yet who remains a lovable and beloved rascal. The wild and mocking poetry of *Peer Gynt* has ended by overshadowing *Brand* in the popular judgment.

With these two poetic dramas, Ibsen won his battle with the world; he paused now to work out his future. He produced a number of moderately successful satires but had not yet found his proper voice; when he did, its effect was not to criticize or reform social life but to blow it up. The explosion came with *Et dukkehjem* (1879; *A Doll's House*).

This play presents a very ordinary family—a bank manager named Torvald Helmer, his wife Nora, and their three little children. Torvald supposes himself the ethical member of the family, while his wife assumes the role of a pretty irresponsible in order to flatter him. Into this snug, not to say stifling, arrangement intrude several hard-minded outsiders, one of whom threatens to expose a fraud that Nora had once committed (without her husband's knowledge) in order to obtain a loan needed to save his life. When Nora's husband finally learns about this dangerous secret, he reacts with outrage and repudiates her out of concern for his own social reputation. Utterly disillusioned about her husband, whom she now sees as a hollow fraud, Nora declares her independence of him and their children and leaves them, slamming the door of the house behind her in the final scene.

Audiences were scandalized at Ibsen's refusal in *A Doll's House* to scrape together (as any other contemporary playwright would have done) a "happy ending," however shoddy or contrived. But that was not Ibsen's way; his play was about knowing oneself and being true to that self. Torvald, who had thought all along that he was a sturdy ethical agent, proves to be a hypocrite and a weak compromiser; his wife is not only an ethical idealist, but a destructive one, as severe as Brand.

Ibsen's next play, *Gengangere* (1881; *Ghosts*), created even more dismay and distaste than its predecessor by showing worse consequences of covering up even more ugly truths. Ostensibly the play's theme is congenital venereal disease, but on another level, it deals with the power of ingrained moral contamination to undermine the most determined idealism. Even after lecherous Captain Alving is in his grave, his ghost will not be laid to rest. In the play, the lying memorial that his conventionally minded widow has erected to his memory burns down even as his son goes insane from inherited syphilis and his illegitimate daughter advances inexorably toward her destiny in a brothel.

A play dealing with syphilis on top of one dealing with a wife's abandonment of her family sealed Ibsen's reputation as a Bad Old Man, but progressive theatres in England and all across the Continent began putting on his plays. His audiences were often small, but there were many of them, and they took his plays very seriously. So did conventionally minded critics; they denounced Ibsen as if he had desecrated all that was sacred and holy. Ibsen's response took the form of a direct dramatic counterattack. Doctor Stockmann, the hero of *En folkefiende* (1882; *An Enemy of the People*), functions as Ibsen's personal spokesman. In the play he is a medical officer, charged with inspecting the public baths on which the prosperity of his native town depends. When he finds their water to be contaminated, he says so publicly, though the town officials and townspeople try to silence him. When he still insists on speaking the truth, he is officially declared an "enemy of the people." Though portrayed as a victim, Doctor Stockmann, like all Ibsen's idealistic truth-tellers after Brand, also carries within him a deep strain of destructiveness.

In *Vildanden* (1884; *The Wild Duck*) Ibsen completely reversed his viewpoint by presenting on stage a gratuitous, destructive truth-teller whose compulsion visits catastrophic misery on a family of helpless innocents. With the help of a number of comforting delusions, Hjalmar

Ekdal and his little family are living a somewhat squalid but essentially cheerful existence. Upon these helpless weaklings descends an infatuated truth-teller, Gregers Werle. He cuts away the moral foundations (delusive as they are) on which the family has lived, leaving them despondent and shattered by the weight of a guilt too heavy to bear. The havoc wrought on the Ekdal family is rather pathetic than tragic; but the working out of the action achieves a kind of mournful poetry that is quite new in Ibsen's repertoire.

Each of this series of Ibsen's classic modern dramas grows by extension or reversal out of its predecessor; they form an unbroken string. The last of the sequence is *Rosmersholm* (1886), in which variants of the destructive saint (Brand) and the all-too-human rogue (Peer) once more strive to define their identities, but this time on a level of moral sensitivity that gives the play a special air of silver serenity. Ex-parson Johannes Rosmer is the ethical personality, while the adventuress Rebecca West is his antagonist. Haunting them both out of the past is the spirit of the parson's late wife, who had committed suicide under the subtle influence, we learn, of Rebecca West, and because of her husband's high-minded indifference to sex. At issue for the future is a choice between bold, unrestricted freedom and the ancient, conservative traditions of Rosmer's house. But even as he is persuaded by Rebecca's emancipated spirit, she is touched by his staid, decorous view of life. Each is contaminated by the other, and for differing but complementary reasons, they tempt one another toward the fatal millpond in which Rosmer's wife drowned. The play ends with a double suicide in which both Rosmer and Rebecca, each for the other's reasons, do justice on themselves.

Ibsen's playwriting career by no means ended with *Rosmersholm*, but thereafter he turned toward a more

*Photographic portrait of Norwegian playwright Henrik Ibsen. His plays examined morality filtered through the lens of his middle-class characters.* Mondadori/Getty Images

self-analytic and symbolic mode of writing that is quite different from the plays that made his world reputation. Among his later plays are *Fruen fra havet* (1888; *The Lady from the Sea*), *Hedda Gabler* (1890), *Bygmester Solness* (1892; *The Master Builder*), *Lille Eyolf* (1894; *Little Eyolf*), *John Gabriel Borkman* (1896), and *Naar vi døde vaagner* (1899; *When We Dead Awaken*). Two of these plays, *Hedda Gabler* and *The Master Builder*, are vitalized by the presence of a demonically idealistic and totally destructive female such as first appeared in *Catiline*. Personal and confessional feelings infuse many of these last dramas; perhaps these resulted from Ibsen's decision in 1891 to return to Norway, or perhaps from the series of fascinated, fearful dalliances he had with young women in his later years. After his return to Norway, Ibsen continued to write plays until a stroke in 1900 and another a year later reduced him to a bedridden invalid. He died in Kristiania in 1906.

## LEO TOLSTOY

(b. August 28 [September 9, New Style], 1828, Yasnaya Polyana, Tula province, Russian Empire—d. November 7 [November 20], 1910, Astapovo, Ryazan province)

L eo Tolstoy was a Russian author, a master of realistic fiction, and one of the world's greatest novelists.

Tolstoy is best known for his two longest works, *War and Peace* and *Anna Karenina*, which are commonly regarded as among the finest novels ever written. *War and Peace* in particular seems virtually to define this form for many readers and critics. Among Tolstoy's shorter works, *The Death of Ivan Ilyich* is usually classed among the best examples of the novella. Especially during his last three decades Tolstoy also achieved world renown as a moral and religious teacher. His doctrine of nonresistance to evil had an important influence on Gandhi. Although Tolstoy's religious ideas no longer command the respect they once did, interest in his life and personality has, if anything, increased over the years.

## Early Years

The scion of prominent aristocrats, Tolstoy was born at the family estate, about 130 miles (210 km) south of Moscow, where he was to live the better part of his life and write his most important works. His mother, Mariya Nikolayevna, née Princess Volkonskaya, died before he was two years old, and his father Nikolay Ilich, Count Tolstoy, followed her in 1837. His grandmother died 11 months later, and then his next guardian, his aunt Aleksandra, in 1841. Tolstoy and his four siblings were then transferred to the care of another aunt in Kazan, in western Russia. Despite the constant presence of death, Tolstoy remembered his childhood in idyllic terms. His first published work, *Detstvo* (1852; *Childhood*), was a fictionalized and nostalgic account of his early years.

Educated at home by tutors, Tolstoy enrolled in the University of Kazan in 1844 as a student of Oriental languages. His poor record soon forced him to transfer to the less demanding law faculty. Interested in literature and ethics, he was drawn to the works of the English novelists Laurence Sterne and Charles Dickens and, especially, to the writings of the French philosopher Jean-Jacques Rousseau; in place of a cross, he wore a medallion with a portrait of Rousseau. But he spent most of his time trying to be comme il faut (socially correct), drinking, gambling, and engaging in debauchery. After leaving the university in 1847 without a degree, Tolstoy returned to Yasnaya

Polyana, where he planned to educate himself, to manage his estate, and to improve the lot of his serfs. Despite frequent resolutions to change his ways, he continued his loose life during stays in Tula, Moscow, and St. Petersburg. In 1851 he joined his older brother Nikolay, an army officer, in the Caucasus and then entered the army himself. He took part in campaigns against the native Caucasian tribes and, soon after, in the Crimean War (1853–56).

In 1847 Tolstoy began keeping a diary, which became his laboratory for experiments in self-analysis and, later, for his fiction. With some interruptions, Tolstoy kept his diaries throughout his life, and he is therefore one of the most copiously documented writers who ever lived. Reflecting the life he was leading, his first diary begins by confiding that he may have contracted a venereal disease. The early diaries record a fascination with rule-making, as Tolstoy composed rules for diverse aspects of social and moral behaviour. They also record the writer's repeated failure to honour these rules, his attempts to formulate new ones designed to ensure obedience to old ones, and his frequent acts of self-castigation. Tolstoy's later belief that life is too complex and disordered ever to conform to rules or philosophical systems perhaps derives from these futile attempts at self-regulation.

## First Publications

Concealing his identity, Tolstoy submitted *Childhood* for publication in *Sovremennik* ("The Contemporary"), a prominent journal edited by the poet Nikolay Nekrasov. Nekrasov was enthusiastic, and the pseudonymously published work was widely praised. During the next few years Tolstoy published a number of stories based on his experiences in the Caucasus, including "Nabeg" (1853; "The Raid") and his three sketches about the Siege of

Sevastopol during the Crimean War: "Sevastopol v dekabre mesyatse" ("Sevastopol in December"), "Sevastopol v maye" ("Sevastopol in May"), and "Sevastopol v avguste 1855 goda" ("Sevastopol in August"; all published 1855–56).

After the Crimean War Tolstoy resigned from the army and was at first hailed by the literary world of St. Petersburg. But his prickly vanity, his refusal to join any intellectual camp, and his insistence on his complete independence soon earned him the dislike of the radical intelligentsia. He was to remain throughout his life an "archaist," opposed to prevailing intellectual trends. In 1857 Tolstoy traveled to Paris and returned after having gambled away his money.

After his return to Russia, he decided that his real vocation was pedagogy, and so he organized a school for peasant children on his estate. After touring western Europe to study pedagogical theory and practice, he published 12 issues of a journal, *Yasnaya Polyana* (1862–63), which included his provocative articles "Progress i opredeleniye obrazovaniya" ("Progress and the Definition of Education"), which denies that history has any underlying laws, and "Komu u kogu uchitsya pisat, krestyanskim rebyatam u nas ili nam u krestyanskikh rebyat?" ("Who Should Learn Writing of Whom: Peasant Children of Us, or We of Peasant Children?"), which reverses the usual answer to the question. Tolstoy married Sofya (Sonya) Andreyevna Bers, the daughter of a prominent Moscow physician, in 1862 and soon transferred all his energies to his marriage and the composition of *War and Peace*. Tolstoy and his wife had 13 children, of whom 10 survived infancy.

Tolstoy's works during the late 1850s and early 1860s experimented with new forms for expressing his moral and philosophical concerns. To *Childhood* he soon added *Otrochestvo* (1854; *Boyhood*) and *Yunost* (1857; *Youth*). A number of stories centre on a single semiautobiographical character, Dmitry Nekhlyudov, who later reappeared as the hero of Tolstoy's novel *Resurrection*.

"Kholstomer" (written 1863; revised and published 1886; "Kholstomer: The Story of a Horse") has become famous for its dramatic use of a favourite Tolstoyan device, "defamiliarization"—that is, the description of familiar social practices from the "naive" perspective of an observer who does not take them for granted. Readers were shocked to discover that the protagonist and principal narrator of "Kholstomer" was an old horse. Like so many of Tolstoy's early works, this story satirizes the artifice and conventionality of human society, a theme that also dominates Tolstoy's novel *Kazaki* (1863; *The Cossacks*).

## The Period of the Great Novels (1863–77)

Happily married and ensconced with his wife and family at Yasnaya Polyana, Tolstoy reached the height of his creative powers. He devoted the remaining years of the 1860s to writing *War and Peace*. Then, after an interlude during which he considered writing a novel about Peter I the Great and briefly returned to pedagogy (bringing out reading primers that were widely used), Tolstoy wrote his other great novel, *Anna Karenina*. These two works share a vision of human experience rooted in an appreciation of everyday life and prosaic virtues.

### War and Peace

*Voyna i mir* (1865–69; *War and Peace*) contains three kinds of material—a historical account of the Napoleonic wars, the biographies of fictional characters, and a set of essays about the philosophy of history. Critics from the 1860s to the present have wondered how these three parts cohere, and many have faulted Tolstoy for including the lengthy essays, but readers continue to respond to them with undiminished enthusiasm.

The work's historical portions narrate the campaign of 1805 leading to Napoleon's victory at the Battle of Austerlitz, a period of peace, and Napoleon's invasion of Russia in 1812. Contrary to generally accepted views, Tolstoy portrays Napoleon as an ineffective, egomaniacal buffoon, Tsar Alexander I as a phrasemaker obsessed with how historians will describe him, and the Russian general Mikhail Kutuzov (previously disparaged) as a patient old man who understands the limitations of human will and planning. Particularly noteworthy are the novel's battle scenes, which show combat as sheer chaos. Generals may imagine they can "anticipate all contingencies," but battle is really the result of "a hundred million diverse chances" decided on the moment by unforeseeable circumstances. In war as in life, no system or model can come close to accounting for the infinite complexity of human behaviour.

Among the book's fictional characters, the reader's attention is first focused on Prince Andrey Bolkonsky, a proud man who has come to despise everything fake, shallow, or merely conventional. Recognizing the artifice of high society, he joins the army to achieve glory, which he regards as truly meaningful. Badly wounded at Austerlitz, he comes to see glory and Napoleon as no less petty than the salons of St. Petersburg. As the novel progresses, Prince Andrey repeatedly discovers the emptiness of the activities to which he has devoted himself. Tolstoy's description of his death in 1812 is usually regarded as one of the most effective scenes in Russian literature.

The novel's other hero, the bumbling and sincere Pierre Bezukhov, oscillates between belief in some philosophical system promising to resolve all questions and a relativism so total as to leave him in apathetic despair. He at last discovers the Tolstoyan truth that wisdom is to be found not in systems but in the ordinary processes of daily life, especially in his marriage to the novel's most memorable heroine, Natasha. When the book stops—it does not really end but just breaks off—Pierre seems to be forgetting this lesson in his enthusiasm for a new utopian plan.

The essays in *War and Peace*, which begin in the second half of the book, satirize all attempts to formulate general laws of history and reject the ill-considered assumptions supporting all historical narratives. In Tolstoy's view, history, like battle, is essentially the product of contingency, has no direction, and fits no pattern. The causes of historical events are infinitely varied and forever unknowable, and so historical writing, which claims to explain the past, necessarily falsifies it. The shape of historical narratives reflects not the actual course of events but the essentially literary criteria established by earlier historical narratives.

## Anna Karenina

In *Anna Karenina* (1875–77) Tolstoy applied these ideas to family life. The novel's first sentence, which indicates its concern with the domestic, is perhaps Tolstoy's most famous: "All happy families resemble each other; each unhappy family is unhappy in its own way." *Anna Karenina* interweaves the stories of three families, the Oblonskys, the Karenins, and the Levins.

The novel begins at the Oblonskys, where the long-suffering wife Dolly has discovered the infidelity of her genial and sybaritic husband Stiva. In her kindness, care for her family, and concern for everyday life, Dolly stands as the novel's moral compass. By contrast, Stiva, though never wishing ill, wastes resources, neglects his family, and regards pleasure as the purpose of life. The figure of Stiva is perhaps designed to suggest that evil, no less than good, ultimately derives from the small moral choices human beings make moment by moment.

Stiva's sister Anna begins the novel as the faithful wife of the stiff, unromantic, but otherwise decent government minister Aleksey Karenin and the mother of a young boy, Seryozha. But Anna, who imagines herself the heroine of a romantic novel, allows herself to fall in love with an officer, Aleksey Vronsky. Schooling herself to see only the worst in her husband, she eventually leaves him and her son to live with Vronsky. Throughout the novel, Tolstoy indicates that the romantic idea of love, which most people identify with love itself, is entirely incompatible with the superior kind of love, the intimate love of good families. As the novel progresses, Anna, who suffers pangs of conscience for abandoning her husband and child, develops a habit of lying to herself until she reaches a state of near madness and total separation from reality. She at last commits suicide by throwing herself under a train. The realization that she may have been thinking about life incorrectly comes to her only when she is lying on the track, and it is too late to save herself.

The third story concerns Dolly's sister Kitty, who first imagines she loves Vronsky but then recognizes that real love is the intimate feeling she has for her family's old friend, Konstantin Levin. Their story focuses on courtship, marriage, and the ordinary incidents of family life, which, in spite of many difficulties, shape real happiness and a meaningful existence. Throughout the novel, Levin is tormented by philosophical questions about the meaning of life in the face of death. Although these questions are never answered, they vanish when Levin begins to live correctly by devoting himself to his family and to daily work. Like his creator Tolstoy, Levin regards the systems of intellectuals as spurious and as incapable of embracing life's complexity.

Both *War and Peace* and *Anna Karenina* advance the idea that ethics can never be a matter of timeless rules applied to particular situations. Rather, ethics depends on a sensitivity, developed over a lifetime, to particular people and specific situations. Tolstoy's preference for particularities over abstractions is often described as the hallmark of his thought.

## Conversion and Religious Beliefs

Upon completing *Anna Karenina*, Tolstoy fell into a profound state of existential despair, which he describes in his *Ispoved* (1884; *My Confession*). All activity seemed utterly pointless in the face of death, and Tolstoy, impressed by the faith of the common people, turned to religion. Drawn at first to the Russian Orthodox church into which he had been born, he rapidly decided that it, and all other Christian churches, were corrupt institutions that had thoroughly falsified true Christianity. Having discovered what he believed to be Christ's message and having overcome his paralyzing fear of death, Tolstoy devoted the rest of his life to developing and propagating his new faith. He was excommunicated from the Russian Orthodox church in 1901.

In the early 1880s he wrote three closely related works, *Issledovaniye dogmaticheskogo bogosloviya* (written 1880; *An Examination of Dogmatic Theology*), *Soyedineniye i perevod chetyrokh yevangeliy* (written 1881; *Union and Translation of the Four Gospels*), and *V chyom moya vera?* (written 1884; *What I Believe*); he later added *Tsarstvo bozhiye vnutri vas* (1893; *The Kingdom of God Is Within You*) and many other essays and tracts. In brief, Tolstoy rejected all the sacraments, all miracles, the Holy Trinity, the immortality of the soul, and many other tenets of traditional religion, all of which he regarded as obfuscations of the true Christian message contained, especially, in the Sermon on the Mount.

# *Fiction After 1880*

Tolstoy's fiction after *Anna Karenina* may be divided into two groups. He wrote a number of moral tales for common people, including "Gde lyubov, tam i bog" (written 1885; "Where Love Is, God Is"), "Chem lyudi zhivy" (written 1882; "What People Live By"), and "Mnogo li cheloveku zemli nuzhno" (written 1885; "How Much Land Does a Man Need"), a story that the Irish novelist James Joyce rather extravagantly praised as "the greatest story that the literature of the world knows." For educated people, Tolstoy wrote fiction that was both realistic and highly didactic. Some of these works succeed brilliantly, especially *Smert Ivana Ilicha* (written 1886; *The Death of Ivan Ilyich*), a novella describing a man's gradual realization that he is dying and that his life has been wasted on trivialities. *Otets Sergy* (written 1898; *Father Sergius*), which may be taken as Tolstoy's self-critique, tells the story of a proud man who wants to become a saint but discovers that sainthood cannot be consciously sought.

In 1899 Tolstoy published his third long novel, *Voskreseniye* (*Resurrection*); he used the royalties to pay for the transportation of a persecuted religious sect, the Dukhobors, to Canada. The novel's most celebrated sections satirize the church and the justice system, but the work is generally regarded as markedly inferior to *War and Peace* and *Anna Karenina*.

Tolstoy's conversion led him to write a treatise and several essays on art. Sometimes he expressed in more extreme form ideas he had always held (such as his dislike for imitation of fashionable schools), but at other times he endorsed ideas that were incompatible with his own earlier novels, which he rejected. In *Chto takoye iskusstvo?* (1898; *What Is Art?*) he argued that true art requires a sensitive appreciation of a particular experience, a highly specific feeling that is communicated to the reader not by propositions but by "infection."

Tolstoy's late works also include a satiric drama, *Zhivoy trup* (written 1900; *The Living Corpse*), and a harrowing play about peasant life, *Vlast tmy* (written 1886; *The Power of Darkness*). After his death, a number of unpublished works came to light, most notably the novella *Khadji-Murat* (1904; *Hadji-Murad*), a brilliant narrative about the Caucasus reminiscent of Tolstoy's earliest fiction.

## Last Years

With the notable exception of his daughter Aleksandra, whom he made his heir, Tolstoy's family remained aloof from or hostile to his teachings. His wife especially resented the constant presence of disciples, led by the dogmatic V.G. Chertkov, at Yasnaya Polyana. Their once happy life had turned into one of the most famous bad marriages in literary history.

Tormented by his domestic situation and by the contradiction between his life and his principles, in 1910 Tolstoy at last escaped incognito from Yasnaya Polyana, accompanied by Aleksandra and his doctor. In spite of his stealth and desire for privacy, the international press was soon able to report on his movements. Within a few days, he contracted pneumonia and died of heart failure at the railroad station of Astapovo.

# EMILY DICKINSON

(b. December 10, 1830, Amherst, Massachusetts, U.S.—d. May 15, 1886, Amherst)

The American lyric poet Emily Dickinson lived in seclusion and commanded a singular brilliance of style and integrity of vision. With Walt Whitman, Dickinson is widely considered to be one of the two leading 19th-century American poets.

Only 10 of Emily Dickinson's nearly 1,800 poems are known to have been published in her lifetime. Devoted to private pursuits, she sent hundreds of poems to friends and correspondents while apparently keeping the greater number to herself. She habitually worked in verse forms suggestive of hymns and ballads, with lines of three or four stresses. Her unusual off-rhymes have been seen as both experimental and influenced by the 18th-century hymnist Isaac Watts. She freely ignored the usual rules of versification and even of grammar, and in the intellectual content of her work she likewise proved exceptionally bold and original. Her verse is distinguished by its epigrammatic compression, haunting personal voice, enigmatic brilliance, and lack of high polish.

## Early Years

The second of three children, Dickinson grew up in moderate privilege and with strong local and religious attachments. For her first nine years she resided in a mansion built by her paternal grandfather, Samuel Fowler Dickinson, who had helped found Amherst College but then went bankrupt shortly before her birth. Her father, Edward Dickinson, was a forceful and prosperous Whig lawyer who served as treasurer of the college and was elected to one term in Congress. Her mother, Emily Norcross Dickinson, from the leading family in nearby Monson, was an introverted wife and hardworking housekeeper; her letters seem equally inexpressive and quirky. Both parents were loving but austere, and Emily became closely attached to her brother, Austin, and sister, Lavinia. Never marrying, the two sisters remained at home, and when their brother married, he and his wife established their own household next door.

As a girl, Emily was seen as frail by her parents and others and was often kept home from school. She attended the coeducational Amherst Academy, where she was recognized by teachers and students alike for her prodigious abilities in composition. She was fond of her teachers, but when she left home to attend Mount Holyoke Female Seminary (now Mount Holyoke College) in nearby South Hadley, she found the school's institutional tone uncongenial. Mount Holyoke's strict rules and invasive religious practices, along with her own homesickness and growing rebelliousness, help explain why she did not return for a second year.

At home as well as at school and church, the religious faith that ruled the poet's early years was evangelical Calvinism, a faith centred on the belief that humans are born totally depraved and can be saved only if they undergo a life-altering conversion in which they accept the vicarious sacrifice of Jesus Christ. Questioning this tradition soon after leaving Mount Holyoke, Dickinson was to be the only member of her family who did not experience conversion or join Amherst's First Congregational Church. Yet she seems to have retained a belief in the soul's immortality or at least to have transmuted it into a Romantic quest for the transcendent and absolute. One reason her mature religious views elude specification is that she took no interest in creedal or doctrinal definition. In this she was influenced by both the Transcendentalism of Ralph Waldo Emerson and the mid-century tendencies of liberal Protestant orthodoxy. These influences pushed her toward a more symbolic understanding of religious truth and helped shape her vocation as poet.

## Development as a Poet

Although Dickinson had begun composing verse by her late teens, few of her early poems are extant. Among them are two of the burlesque "Valentines"—the exuberantly inventive expressions of affection and esteem she sent to friends of her youth. Two other poems dating from the first half of the 1850s draw a contrast between the world as it is and a more peaceful alternative, variously eternity or a serene imaginative order.

Until Dickinson was in her mid-20s, her writing mostly took the form of letters, and a surprising number of those that she wrote from age 11 onward have been preserved. Sent to her brother, Austin, or to friends of her own sex, especially Abiah Root, Jane Humphrey, and Susan Gilbert (who would marry Austin), these generous communications overflow with humour, anecdote, invention, and sombre reflection. In general, Dickinson seems to have given and demanded more from her correspondents than she received. On occasion she interpreted her correspondents' laxity in replying as evidence of neglect or even betrayal.

*Portrait of Emily Dickinson, a reclusive poet known as "the Belle of Amherst," which was her hometown.* **Three Lions/Hulton Archive/ Getty Images**

Indeed, the loss of friends, whether through death or cooling interest, became a basic pattern for Dickinson. Much of her writing, both poetic and epistolary, seems premised on a feeling of abandonment and a matching effort to deny, overcome, or reflect on a sense of solitude.

Dickinson's closest friendships usually had a literary flavour. She was introduced to the poetry of Ralph Waldo Emerson by one of her father's law students, Benjamin F. Newton, and to that of Elizabeth Barrett Browning by Susan Gilbert and Henry Vaughan Emmons, a gifted college student. Two of Barrett Browning's works, *A Vision of Poets,* describing the pantheon of poets, and *Aurora Leigh*, on the development of a female poet, seem to have played a formative role for Dickinson, validating the idea of female greatness and stimulating her ambition.

Always fastidious, Dickinson began to restrict her social activity in her early 20s, staying home from communal functions and cultivating intense epistolary relationships with a reduced number of correspondents. In 1855, leaving the large and much-loved house (since razed) in which she had lived for 15 years, the 25-year-old woman and her family moved back to the dwelling associated with her first decade: the Dickinson mansion on Main Street in Amherst. Her home for the rest of her life, this large brick house, still standing, has become a favourite destination for her admirers. She found the return profoundly disturbing, and when her mother became incapacitated by a mysterious illness that lasted from 1855 to 1859, both daughters were compelled to give more of themselves to domestic pursuits. Various events outside the home—a bitter Norcross family lawsuit, the financial collapse of the local railroad that had been promoted by the poet's father, and a powerful religious revival that renewed the pressure to "convert"—made the years 1857 and 1858 deeply troubling for Dickinson and promoted her further withdrawal.

## *Mature Career*

In summer 1858, at the height of this period of obscure tension, Dickinson began assembling her manuscript-books. She made clean copies of her poems on fine quality stationery and then sewed small bundles of these sheets together at the fold. Over the next seven years she created 40 such booklets and several unsewn sheaves, and altogether they contained about 800 poems. No doubt she intended to arrange her work in a convenient form, perhaps for her own use in sending poems to friends. Perhaps the assemblage was meant to remain private, like her earlier herbarium. Or perhaps, as implied in a poem of 1863, *This is my letter to the world*, she anticipated posthumous publication. Because she left no instructions regarding the disposition of her manuscript-books, her ultimate purpose in assembling them can only be conjectured.

Dickinson sent more poems to her sister-in-law, Susan Gilbert Dickinson, a cultivated reader, than to any other known correspondent. Repeatedly professing eternal allegiance, these poems often imply that there was a certain distance between the two—that the sister-in-law was felt to be haughty, remote, or even incomprehensible. Yet Susan admired the poetry's wit and verve and offered the kind of personally attentive audience Dickinson craved. On one occasion, Susan's dissatisfaction with a poem, *Safe in their alabaster chambers*, resulted in the drafting of alternative stanzas. Susan was an active hostess, and her home was the venue at which Dickinson met a few friends, most importantly Samuel Bowles, publisher and editor of the influential *Springfield Republican*. Gregarious, captivating, and unusually liberal on the question of women's careers,

Bowles had a high regard for Dickinson's poems, publishing (without her consent) seven of them during her lifetime—more than appeared in any other outlet. From 1859 to 1862 she sent him some of her most intense and confidential communications, including the daring poem *Title divine is mine*, whose speaker proclaims that she is now a "Wife," but of a highly unconventional type.

In those years Dickinson experienced a painful and obscure personal crisis, partly of a romantic nature. The abject and pleading drafts of her second and third letters to the unidentified person she called "Master" are probably related to her many poems about a loved but distant person, usually male. Whoever the person was, Master's failure to return Dickinson's affection—together with Susan's absorption in her first childbirth and Bowles's growing invalidism—contributed to a piercing and ultimate sense of distress. In a letter, Dickinson described her lonely suffering as a "terror—since September—[that] I could tell to none." Instead of succumbing to anguish, however, she came to view it as the sign of a special vocation, and it became the basis of an unprecedented creativity. A poem that seems to register this life-restoring act of resistance begins "The zeroes taught us phosphorus," meaning that it is in absolute cold and nothingness that true brilliance originates.

In April 1862 Dickinson sought the critical advice of Thomas Wentworth Higginson, whose witty article of advice to writers, *A Letter to a Young Contributor*, had just appeared in *The Atlantic Monthly*. Higginson was known as a writer of delicate nature essays and a crusader for women's rights. Enclosing four poems, Dickinson asked for his opinion of her verse—whether or not it was "alive." The ensuing correspondence lasted for years, with the poet sending her "preceptor," as she called him, many more samples of her work. In addition to seeking an informed critique from a professional but not unsympathetic man of letters, she was reaching out at a time of accentuated loneliness. "You were not aware that you saved my Life," she confided years later.

In her last 15 years Dickinson averaged 35 poems a year and conducted her social life mainly through her chiselled and often sibylline written messages. Her father's sudden death in 1874 caused a profound and persisting emotional upheaval yet eventually led to a greater openness, self-possession, and serenity. She repaired an 11-year breach with Samuel Bowles and made friends with Maria Whitney, a teacher of modern languages at Smith College, and Helen Hunt Jackson, poet and author of the novel *Ramona* (1884). From about age 50 she conducted a passionate romance with Otis Phillips Lord, an elderly judge on the supreme court of Massachusetts. The letters she apparently sent Lord reveal her at her most playful, alternately teasing and confiding. In declining an erotic advance or his proposal of marriage, she asked, "Dont you know you are happiest while I withhold and not confer—dont you know that 'No' is the wildest word we consign to Language?"

After Dickinson's aging mother was incapacitated by a stroke and a broken hip, caring for her at home made large demands on the poet's time and patience. After her mother died in 1882, Dickinson summed up the relationship in a confidential letter to her Norcross cousins: "We were never intimate Mother and Children while she was our Mother—but...when she became our Child, the Affection came." The deaths of Dickinson's friends in her last years left her feeling terminally alone. But the single most shattering death, occurring in 1883, was that of her eight-year-old nephew next door, the gifted and charming Gilbert Dickinson. Her health broken by this culminating tragedy, she ceased seeing almost everyone, apparently including her sister-in-law. The poet died in 1886, when she was 55 years old.

# LEWIS CARROLL

(b. January 27, 1832, Daresbury, Cheshire, England—d. January 14, 1898, Guildford, Surrey)

Lewis Carroll (a pseudonym of Charles Lutwidge Dodgson) was an English logician, mathematician, photographer, and novelist, especially remembered for *Alice's Adventures in Wonderland* (1865) and its sequel, *Through the Looking-Glass* (1871). His poem *The Hunting of the Snark* (1876) is nonsense literature of the highest order.

Dodgson was the eldest son and third child in a family of seven girls and four boys born to Frances Jane Lutwidge, the wife of the Rev. Charles Dodgson. He was born in the old parsonage at Daresbury. His father was perpetual curate there from 1827 until 1843, when he became rector of Croft in Yorkshire—a post he held for the rest of his life (though later he became also archdeacon of Richmond and a canon of Ripon cathedral).

The Dodgson children, living as they did in an isolated country village, had few friends outside the family but, like many other families in similar circumstances, found little difficulty in entertaining themselves. Charles from the first showed a great aptitude for inventing games to amuse them. With the move to Croft when he was 12 came the beginning of the "Rectory Magazines," manuscript compilations to which all the family were supposed to contribute. In fact, Charles wrote nearly all of those that survive, beginning with *Useful and Instructive Poetry* (1845; published 1954) and following with *The Rectory Magazine* (c. 1850, mostly unpublished), *The Rectory Umbrella* (1850–53), and *Mischmasch* (1853–62; published with *The Rectory Umbrella* in 1932).

Meanwhile, young Dodgson attended Richmond School, Yorkshire (1844–45), and then proceeded to Rugby School (1846–50). He disliked his four years at public school, principally because of his innate shyness, although he was also subjected to a certain amount of bullying; he also endured several illnesses, one of which left him deaf in one ear. After Rugby he spent a further year being tutored by his father, during which time he matriculated at Christ Church, Oxford (May 23, 1850). He went into residence as an undergraduate there on January 24, 1851.

Dodgson excelled in his mathematical and classical studies in 1852; on the strength of his performance in examinations, he was nominated to a studentship (called a scholarship in other colleges). In 1854 he gained a first in mathematical Finals—coming out at the head of the class—and proceeded to a bachelor of arts degree in December of the same year. He was made a "Master of the House" and a senior student (called a fellow in other colleges) the following year and was appointed lecturer in mathematics (the equivalent of today's tutor), a post he resigned in 1881. He held his studentship until the end of his life.

As was the case with all fellowships at that time, the studentship at Christ Church was dependent upon his remaining unmarried, and, by the terms of this particular endowment, proceeding to holy orders. Dodgson was ordained a deacon in the Church of England on December 22, 1861. Had he gone on to become a priest he could have married and would then have been appointed to a parish by the college. But he felt himself unsuited for parish work and, though he considered the possibility of marriage, decided that he was perfectly content to remain a bachelor.

Dodgson's association with children grew naturally enough out of his position as an eldest son with eight younger brothers and sisters. He also suffered from a bad stammer (which he never wholly overcame, although he was able to preach with considerable success in later life) and, like many others who suffer from the disability, found that he was able to speak naturally and easily to children. It is therefore not surprising that he should begin to entertain the children of Henry George Liddell, dean of Christ Church. Alice Liddell and her sisters Lorina and Edith were not, of course, the first of Dodgson's child friends. They had been preceded or were overlapped by the children of the writer George Macdonald, the sons of the poet Alfred, Lord Tennyson, and various other chance acquaintances. But the Liddell children undoubtedly held an especially high place in his affections—partly because they were the only children in Christ Church, since only heads of houses were free both to marry and to continue in residence.

Properly chaperoned by their governess, Miss Prickett (nicknamed "Pricks"—"one of the thorny kind," and so the prototype of the Red Queen in *Through the Looking-Glass*), the three little girls paid many visits to the young mathematics lecturer in his college rooms. As Alice remembered in 1932, they

> *used to sit on the big sofa on each side of him, while he told us stories, illustrating them by pencil or ink drawings as he went along.... He seemed to have an endless store of these fantastical tales, which he made up as he told them, drawing busily on a large sheet of paper all the time. They were not always entirely new. Sometimes they were new versions of old stories; sometimes they started on the old basis, but grew into new tales owing to the frequent interruptions which opened up fresh and undreamed-of possibilities.*

On July 4, 1862, Dodgson and his friend Robinson Duckworth, fellow of Trinity, rowed the three children up the Thames from Oxford to Godstow, picnicked on the bank, and returned to Christ Church late in the evening: "On which occasion," wrote Dodgson in his diary, "I told them the fairy-tale of *Alice's Adventures Underground*, which I undertook to write out for Alice." Much of the story was based on a picnic a couple of weeks earlier when they had all been caught in the rain; for some reason, this inspired Dodgson to tell so much better a story than usual that both Duckworth and Alice noticed the difference, and Alice went so far as to cry, when they parted at the door of the deanery, "Oh, Mr. Dodgson, I wish you would write out Alice's adventures for me!" Dodgson himself recollected in 1887

> *how, in a desperate attempt to strike out some new line of fairy-lore, I had sent my heroine straight down a rabbit-hole, to begin with, without the least idea what was to happen afterwards.*

Dodgson was able to write down the story more or less as told and added to it several extra adventures that had been told on other occasions. He illustrated it with his own crude but distinctive drawings and gave the finished product to Alice Liddell, with no thought of hearing of it again. But the novelist Henry Kingsley, while visiting the deanery, chanced to pick it up from the drawing-room table, read it, and urged Mrs. Liddell to persuade the author to publish it. Dodgson, honestly surprised, consulted his friend George Macdonald, author of some of the best children's stories of the period. Macdonald took it home to be read to his children, and his son Greville, aged six, declared that he "wished there were 60,000 volumes of it."

Accordingly, Dodgson revised it for publication. He cut out the more particular references to the previous picnic (they may be found in the facsimile of the original manuscript, later published by him as *Alice's Adventures*

*Underground* in 1886) and added some additional stories, told to the Liddells at other times, to make up a volume of the desired length. At Duckworth's suggestion he got an introduction to John Tenniel, the *Punch* magazine cartoonist, whom he commissioned to make illustrations to his specification. The book was published as *Alice's Adventures in Wonderland* in 1865. (The first edition was withdrawn because of bad printing, and only about 21 copies survive—one of the rare books of the 19th century—and the reprint was ready for publication by Christmas of the same year, though dated 1866.)

The book was a slow but steadily increasing success, and by the following year Dodgson was already considering a sequel to it, based on further stories told to the Liddells. The result was *Through the Looking-Glass and What Alice Found There* (dated 1872; actually published December 1871), a work as good as, or better than, its predecessor.

By the time of Dodgson's death, *Alice* (taking the two volumes as a single artistic triumph) had become the most popular children's book in England: by the time of his centenary in 1932 it was one of the most popular and perhaps the most famous in the world.

There is no answer to the mystery of *Alice*'s success. Many explanations have been suggested, but, like the Mad Hatter's riddle ("The riddle, as originally invented, had no answer at all"), they are no more than afterthoughts. The book is not an allegory; it has no hidden meaning or message, either religious, political, or psychological, as some have tried to prove; and its only undertones are some touches of gentle satire—on education for the children's special benefit and on familiar university types, whom the Liddells may or may not have recognized. Various attempts have been made to solve the "riddle of Lewis Carroll" himself; these include the efforts to prove that his friendships with little girls were some sort of subconscious substitute for a married life, that he showed symptoms of jealousy when his favourites came to tell him that they were engaged to be married, that he contemplated marriage with some of them—notably with Alice Liddell. But there is little or no evidence to back up such theorizing. He in fact dropped the acquaintance of Alice Liddell when she was 12, as he did with most of his young friends. In the case of the Liddells, his friendship with the younger children, Rhoda and Violet, was cut short at the time of his skits on some of Dean Liddell's Christ Church "reforms." For besides children's stories, Dodgson also produced humorous pamphlets on university affairs, which still make good reading. The best of these were collected by him as *Notes by an Oxford Chiel* (1874).

Besides writing for them, Dodgson is also to be remembered as a fine photographer of children and of adults as well (notable portraits of the actress Ellen Terry, the poet Alfred, Lord Tennyson, the poet-painter Dante Gabriel Rossetti, and many others survive and have been often reproduced). Dodgson had an early ambition to be an artist: failing in this, he turned to photography. He photographed children in every possible costume and situation, finally making nude studies of them. But in 1880 Dodgson abandoned his hobby altogether, feeling that it was taking up too much time that might be better spent. Suggestions that this sudden decision was reached because of an impurity of motive for his nude studies have been made, but again without any evidence.

Before he had told the original tale of *Alice's Adventures*, Dodgson had, in fact, published a number of humorous items in verse and prose and a few inferior serious poems. The earliest of these appeared anonymously, but in March 1856 a poem called "Solitude" was published over the pseudonym Lewis Carroll. Dodgson arrived at this pen name by taking his own names Charles Lutwidge, translating them into Latin as Carolus Ludovicus, then reversing and retranslating them into English. He used the name afterward for all his nonacademic works. As Charles L. Dodgson, he was the author of a fair number of books on mathematics, none of enduring importance, although *Euclid and His Modern Rivals* (1879) is of some historical interest.

His humorous and other verses were collected in 1869 as *Phantasmagoria and Other Poems* and later separated (with additions) as *Rhyme? and Reason?* (1883) and *Three Sunsets and Other Poems* (published posthumously, 1898). The 1883 volume also contained *The Hunting of the Snark*, a narrative nonsense poem that is rivalled only by the best of Edward Lear.

Later in life, Dodgson had attempted a return to the *Alice* vein but only produced *Sylvie and Bruno* (1889) and its second volume, *Sylvie and Bruno Concluded* (1893), which has been described aptly as "one of the most interesting failures in English literature." This elaborate combination of fairy-tale, social novel, and collection of ethical discussions is unduly neglected and ridiculed. It presents the truest available portrait of the man. *Alice*, the perfect creation of the logical and mathematical mind applied to the pure and unadulterated amusement of children, was struck out of him as if by chance; while making full use of his specialized knowledge, it transcends his weaknesses and remains unique.

# *Louisa May Alcott*

(b. November 29, 1832, Germantown, Pennsylvania, U.S.—d. March 6, 1888, Boston, Massachusetts)

The American author Louisa May Alcott is known for her children's books, especially the classic *Little Women*.

A daughter of the transcendentalist Bronson Alcott, Louisa spent most of her life in Boston and Concord,

Massachusetts, where she grew up in the company of Ralph Waldo Emerson, Theodore Parker, and Henry David Thoreau. Her education was largely under the direction of her father, for a time at his innovative Temple School in Boston and, later, at home. Alcott realized early that her father was too impractical to provide for his wife and four daughters; after the failure of Fruitlands, a utopian community that he had founded, Louisa Alcott's lifelong concern for the welfare of her family began. She taught briefly, worked as a domestic, and finally began to write.

Alcott produced potboilers at first and many of her stories—notably those signed "A.M. Barnard"—were lurid and violent tales. The latter works are unusual in their depictions of women as strong, self-reliant, and imaginative. She volunteered as a nurse after the American Civil War began, but she contracted typhoid from unsanitary hospital conditions and was sent home. She was never completely well again. The publication of her letters in book form, *Hospital Sketches* (1863), brought her the first taste of fame.

Alcott's stories began to appear in *The Atlantic Monthly*, and, because family needs were pressing, she wrote the autobiographical *Little Women* (1868–69), which was an immediate success. Based on her recollections of her own childhood, *Little Women* describes the domestic adventures of a New England family of modest means but optimistic outlook. The book traces the differing personalities and fortunes of four sisters as they emerge from childhood and encounter the vicissitudes of employment, society, and marriage. *Little Women* created a realistic but wholesome picture of family life with which younger readers could easily identify. In 1869 Alcott was able to write in her journal: "Paid up all the debts...thank the Lord!" She followed *Little Women*'s success with further domestic narratives drawn from her early experiences: *An Old-Fashioned Girl* (1870);

*Louisa May Alcott.* Encyclopædia Britannica, Inc.

*Aunt Jo's Scrap Bag*, 6 vol. (1872–82); *Little Men* (1871); *Eight Cousins* (1875); *Rose in Bloom* (1876); and *Jo's Boys* (1886).

Except for a European tour in 1870 and a few briefer trips to New York, she spent the last two decades of her life in Boston and Concord, caring for her mother, who died in 1877 after a lengthy illness, and her increasingly helpless father. Late in life she adopted her namesake, Louisa May Nieriker, daughter of her late sister, May. Her own health, never robust, also declined, and she died in Boston two days after her father's death.

Alcott's books for younger readers have remained steadfastly popular, and the republication of some of her lesser-known works late in the 20th century aroused renewed critical interest in her adult fiction. *A Modern Mephistopheles*, which was published pseudonymously in 1877 and republished in 1987, is a Gothic novel about a failed poet who makes a Faustian bargain with his tempter. *Work: A Story of Experience* (1873), based on Alcott's own struggles, tells the story of a poor girl trying to support herself by a succession of menial jobs. The Gothic tales and thrillers that Alcott published pseudonymously between 1863 and 1869 were collected and republished as *Behind a Mask* (1975) and *Plots and Counterplots* (1976), and an unpublished Gothic novel written in 1866, *A Long Fatal Love Chase*, was published in 1995.

# MARK TWAIN

(b. November 30, 1835, Florida, Missouri, U.S.—d. April 21, 1910, Redding, Connecticut)

The American humorist, journalist, lecturer, and novelist Mark Twain (a pseudonym of Samuel Langhorne Clemens) acquired international fame for his travel narratives, especially *The Innocents Abroad* (1869), *Roughing It* (1872), and *Life on the Mississippi* (1883), and for his adventure stories of boyhood, especially *The Adventures of Tom Sawyer* (1876) and *Adventures of Huckleberry Finn* (1885). A gifted raconteur, distinctive humorist, and irascible moralist, he transcended the apparent limitations of his origins to become a popular public figure and one of America's best and most beloved writers.

## Youth

Samuel Clemens, the sixth child of John Marshall and Jane Lampton Clemens, was born two months prematurely and was in relatively poor health for the first 10 years of his life. His mother tried various allopathic and hydropathic remedies on him during those early years, and his recollections of those instances (along with other memories of his growing up) would eventually find their way into *Tom Sawyer* and other writings. Because he was sickly, Clemens was often coddled, particularly by his mother, and he developed early the tendency to test her indulgence through mischief, offering only his good nature as bond for the domestic crimes he was apt to commit.

It was the diminishing fortunes of the Clemens family that led them in 1839 to move 30 miles (50 km) east from Florida, Missouri, to the Mississippi River port town of Hannibal, where there were greater opportunities. John Clemens opened a store and eventually became a justice of the peace, which entitled him to be called "Judge" but not to a great deal more. In the meantime, the debts accumulated.

Perhaps it was the romantic visionary in him that caused Clemens to recall his youth in Hannibal with such fondness. As he remembered it in *Old Times on the Mississippi* (1875), the village was a "white town drowsing in the sunshine of a summer's morning," until the arrival of a riverboat suddenly made it a hive of activity. The gamblers, stevedores, and pilots, the boisterous raftsmen and elegant travelers, all bound for somewhere surely glamorous and exciting, would have impressed a young boy and stimulated his already active imagination.

After the death of his father in 1847, Sam Clemens worked at several odd jobs in town, and in 1848 he became a printer's apprentice for Joseph P. Ament's *Missouri Courier*. He lived sparingly in the Ament household but was allowed to continue his schooling and, from time to time, indulge in boyish amusements. Nevertheless, by the time Clemens was 13, his boyhood had effectively come to an end.

## *Apprenticeships*

In 1850 the oldest Clemens boy, Orion, returned from St. Louis, Missouri, and began to publish a weekly newspaper. A year later he bought the Hannibal *Journal*, and Sam and his younger brother Henry worked for him. Sam became more than competent as a typesetter, but he also occasionally contributed sketches and articles to his brother's paper. Some of those early sketches, such as *The Dandy Frightening the Squatter* (1852), appeared in Eastern newspapers and periodicals.

Having acquired a trade by age 17, Clemens left Hannibal in 1853 with some degree of self-sufficiency. For almost two decades he would be an itinerant labourer, trying many occupations. And Clemens continued to write, though without firm literary ambitions, occasionally publishing letters in his brother's newspaper. Restless and ambitious, he booked passage in 1857 on a steamboat bound for New Orleans, planning to find his fortune in South America. Instead, he saw a more immediate opportunity and persuaded the accomplished riverboat captain Horace Bixby to take him on as an apprentice, with an eye toward obtaining a pilot's license.

His experience as a cub and then as a full-fledged pilot gave him a sense of discipline and direction he might never have acquired elsewhere. Before this period his had been a directionless knockabout life; afterward he had a sense of determined possibility. He continued to write occasional pieces throughout these years and, in one satirical sketch, *River Intelligence* (1859), lampooned the self-important senior pilot Isaiah Sellers, whose observations of the Mississippi were published in a New Orleans newspaper. Clemens had no particular use for this nonunion man, but he did envy what he later recalled to be Sellers's delicious pen name, Mark Twain.

The Civil War severely curtailed river traffic, and, fearing that he might be impressed as a Union gunboat pilot, Clemens brought his years on the river to a halt a mere two years after he had acquired his license. He returned to Hannibal, where he joined the prosecessionist Marion Rangers, a ragtag lot of about a dozen men. After only two uneventful weeks, during which the soldiers mostly retreated from Union troops rumoured to be in the vicinity, the group disbanded. A few of the men joined other Confederate units, and the rest, along with Clemens, scattered. Twain would recall this experience, a bit fuzzily and with some fictional embellishments, in *The Private History of the Campaign That Failed* (1885). Clemens then lit out for the Nevada Territory, accompanying his brother Orion.

Clemens's own political sympathies during the war are obscure. It is known at any rate that Orion Clemens was deeply involved in Republican Party politics and in Abraham Lincoln's campaign for the U.S. presidency, and it was as a reward for those efforts that he was appointed territorial secretary of Nevada. Upon their arrival in

Carson City, the territorial capital, Sam Clemens's association with Orion did not provide him the sort of livelihood he might have supposed, and, once again, he had to shift for himself—mining and investing in timber and silver and gold stocks, oftentimes "prospectively rich," but that was all. Clemens submitted several letters to the Virginia City *Territorial Enterprise*, and these attracted the attention of the editor, Joseph Goodman, who offered him a salaried job as a reporter.

In February 1863 Clemens covered the legislative session in Carson City and wrote three letters for the *Enterprise*. He signed them "Mark Twain." Apparently the mistranscription of a telegram misled Clemens to believe that the pilot Isaiah Sellers had died and that his cognomen was up for grabs. Clemens seized it. It would be several years before this pen name would acquire the firmness of a full-fledged literary persona, however. In the meantime, he was discovering by degrees what it meant to be a "literary person."

In 1864, after challenging the editor of a rival newspaper to a duel and then fearing the legal consequences for this indiscretion, he left

**American humorists** (from left) *Josh Billings, Mark Twain, and Petroleum V. Nasby, 1868.* Library of Congress, Washington, D.C. (neg. no. LC-USZ62-57976)

Virginia City for San Francisco and became a full-time reporter for the *Call*. Finding that work tiresome, he began contributing to the *Golden Era* and the new literary magazine the *Californian*, edited by Bret Harte. He went to the Tuolumne foothills to do some mining. It was there that he heard the story of a jumping frog. The story was widely known, but it was new to Clemens, and he took notes for a literary representation of the tale. When the humorist Artemus Ward invited him to contribute something for a book of humorous sketches, Clemens decided to write up the story. *Jim Smiley and His Jumping Frog* arrived too late to be included in the volume, but it was published in the New York *Saturday Press* in November 1865 and was subsequently reprinted throughout the country. "Mark Twain" had acquired sudden celebrity, and Sam Clemens was following in his wake.

## Literary Maturity

The next few years were important for Clemens. After he had finished writing the jumping-frog story but before it was published, he declared in a letter to Orion that he had a " 'call' to literature of a low order—i.e., humorous. It is nothing to be proud of," he continued, "but it is my strongest suit." However much he might deprecate his calling, it appears that he was committed to making a professional career for himself. He continued to write for newspapers, traveling to Hawaii for the Sacramento *Union* and also writing for New York newspapers, but he apparently wanted to become something more than a journalist. He went on his first lecture tour, speaking mostly on the Sandwich Islands (Hawaii) in 1866. It was a success, and for the rest of his life, though he found touring grueling, he knew he could take to the lecture platform when he needed money. Meanwhile, he tried, unsuccessfully, to publish a book made up of his letters from Hawaii. His first book was in fact *The Celebrated Jumping Frog of Calaveras County and Other Sketches* (1867), but it did not sell well. That same year, he moved to New York City, serving as the traveling correspondent for the San Francisco *Alta California* and for New York newspapers. He had ambitions to enlarge his reputation and his audience, and the announcement of a transatlantic excursion to Europe and the Holy Land provided him with just such an opportunity. The *Alta* paid the substantial fare in exchange for some 50 letters he would write concerning the trip. Eventually his account of the voyage was published as *The Innocents Abroad* (1869). It was a great success.

The trip abroad was fortuitous in another way. He met on the boat a young man named Charlie Langdon, who invited Clemens to dine with his family in New York and introduced him to his sister Olivia; the writer fell in love with her. Clemens's courtship of Olivia Langdon, the daughter of a prosperous businessman from Elmira, New York, was an ardent one, conducted mostly through correspondence. They were married in February 1870. With financial assistance from Olivia's father, Clemens bought a one-third interest in the *Express* of Buffalo, New York, and began writing a column for a New York City magazine, the *Galaxy*. A son, Langdon, was born in November 1870, but the boy was frail and would die of diphtheria less than two years later. Clemens came to dislike Buffalo and hoped that he and his family might move to the Nook Farm area of Hartford, Connecticut. In the meantime, he worked hard on a book about his experiences in the West. *Roughing It* was published in February 1872 and sold well. The next month, Olivia Susan (Susy) Clemens was born in Elmira. Later that year, Clemens traveled to England. Upon his return, he began work with his friend Charles Dudley Warner on a satirical novel about political and financial corruption in the United States. *The Gilded Age* (1873) was remarkably well received, and a play based on the most amusing character from the novel, Colonel Sellers, also became quite popular.

*The Gilded Age* was Twain's first attempt at a novel, and the experience was apparently congenial enough for him to begin writing *Tom Sawyer*, along with his reminiscences about his days as a riverboat pilot. He also published *A True Story*, a moving dialect sketch told by a former slave, in the prestigious *Atlantic Monthly* in 1874. A second daughter, Clara, was born in June, and the Clemenses moved into their still-unfinished house in Nook Farm later the same year. *Old Times on the Mississippi* appeared in the *Atlantic* in installments in 1875. The highly episodic narrative of *Tom Sawyer*, which recounts the mischievous adventures of a boy growing up along the Mississippi River, was coloured by a nostalgia for childhood and simplicity that would permit Twain to characterize the novel as a "hymn" to childhood. The continuing popularity of *Tom Sawyer* (it sold well from its first publication, in 1876, and has never gone out of print) indicates that Twain could write a novel that appealed to young and old readers alike. The antics and high adventure of Tom Sawyer and his comrades continue to delight children, while the book's comedy, narrated by someone who vividly recalls what it was to be a child, amuses adults with similar memories.

In the summer of 1876, while staying with his in-laws Susan and Theodore Crane on Quarry Farm overlooking Elmira, Clemens began writing what he called in a letter to his friend William Dean Howells "Huck Finn's Autobiography." Huck had appeared as a character in *Tom Sawyer*, and Clemens decided that the untutored boy had his own story to tell. He soon discovered that it had to be told in Huck's own vernacular voice. *Huckleberry Finn* was written in fits and starts over an extended period and would not be published until 1885.

He published *A Tramp Abroad* (1880), about his travels with his friend Joseph Twichell in Europe's Black Forest and Swiss Alps, and *The Prince and the Pauper* (1881), a fanciful tale set in 16th-century England and written for "young people of all ages." In 1882 he traveled up the Mississippi with Horace Bixby, taking notes for the book that became *Life on the Mississippi* (1883). All the while, he continued to make often ill-advised investments, the most disastrous of which was the continued financial support of an inventor, James W. Paige, who was perfecting an automatic typesetting machine. In 1884 Clemens founded his own publishing company, bearing the name of his nephew and business agent, Charles L. Webster, and embarked on a

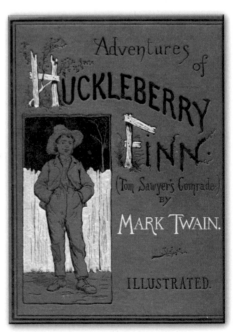

four-month lecture tour with fellow author George W. Cable, both to raise money for the company and to promote the sales of *Huckleberry Finn*. Not long after that, Clemens began the first of several Tom-and-Huck sequels. None of them would rival *Huckleberry Finn*. What distinguishes *Huckleberry Finn* from the others is the moral dilemma Huck faces in aiding the runaway slave Jim while at the same time escaping from the unwanted

*Front cover of an 1885 edition of Mark Twain's* Adventures of Huckleberry Finn. *Project Gutenberg (Text 76)*

influences of so-called civilization. Through Huck, the novel's narrator, Twain was able to address the shameful legacy of chattel slavery prior to the Civil War and the persistent racial discrimination and violence after. That he did so in the voice and consciousness of a 14-year-old boy, a character who shows the signs of having been trained to accept the cruel and indifferent attitudes of a slaveholding culture, gives the novel its affecting power, which can elicit genuine sympathies in readers but can also generate controversy and debate and can affront those who find the book patronizing toward African Americans, if not perhaps much worse.

For a time, Clemens's prospects seemed rosy. After

"MARK TWAIN,"
AMERICA'S BEST HUMORIST.

working closely with Ulysses S. Grant, he watched as his company's publication of the former U.S. president's memoirs in 1885–86 became an overwhelming success. It was in a generally sanguine mood that he began to write *A Connecticut Yankee in King Arthur's Court*, about the exploits of a practical and democratic factory superintendent who is magically transported to Camelot and attempts to transform

*Mark Twain, lithograph from Puck, 1885.* Library of Congress, Washington, D.C. LC-USZC4-4294

the kingdom according to 19th-century republican values and modern technology.

Things did not go according to plan, however. His publishing company was floundering, and cash flow problems meant he was drawing on his royalties to provide capital for the business. Clemens was suffering from rheumatism in his right arm, but he continued to write for magazines out of necessity. Still, he was getting deeper and deeper in debt, and by 1891 he had ceased his monthly payments to support work on the Paige typesetter, effectively giving up on an investment that over the years had cost him some $200,000 or more. He closed his beloved house in Hartford, and the family moved to Europe, where they might live more cheaply and, perhaps, where his wife, who had always been frail, might improve her health. Debts continued to mount, and the financial panic of 1893 made it difficult to borrow money. Luckily, he was befriended by a Standard Oil executive, Henry Huttleston Rogers, who undertook to put Clemens's financial house in order. In 1894, approaching his 60th year, Samuel Clemens was forced to repair his fortunes and to remake his career.

## *Later Works*

Late in 1894 *The Tragedy of Pudd'nhead Wilson and the Comedy of Those Extraordinary Twins* was published. Set in the antebellum South, *Pudd'nhead Wilson* concerns the fates of transposed babies, one white and the other black, and is a fascinating, if ambiguous, exploration of the social and legal construction of race. It also reflects Twain's thoughts on determinism, a subject that would increasingly occupy his thoughts for the remainder of his life.

Clemens published his next novel, *Personal Recollections of Joan of Arc* (serialized 1895–96), anonymously in hopes that the public might take it more seriously than a book bearing the Mark Twain name. The strategy did not work, for it soon became generally known that he was the author; when the novel was first published in book form, in 1896, his name appeared on the volume's spine but not on its title page. However, in later years he would publish some works anonymously, and still others he declared could not be published until long after his death, on the largely erroneous assumption that his true views would scandalize the public. Clemens's sense of wounded pride was necessarily compromised by his indebtedness, and he embarked on a lecture tour in July 1895 that would take him around the world. Clemens was in London when he was notified of the death of his daughter Susy, of spinal meningitis. A pall settled over the Clemens household; they would not celebrate birthdays or holidays for the next several years. As an antidote to his grief as much as anything else, Clemens threw himself into work. He wrote a great deal he did not intend to publish during those years, but he did publish *Following the Equator* (1897), a relatively serious account of his world lecture tour. By 1898 the revenue generated from the tour and the subsequent book, along with Henry Huttleston Rogers's shrewd investments of his money, had allowed Clemens to pay his creditors in full. Rogers was shrewd as well in the way he publicized and redeemed the reputation of "Mark Twain" as a man of impeccable moral character.

Clemens had acquired the esteem and moral authority he had yearned for only a few years before, and the writer made good use of his reinvigorated position. He began writing *The Man That Corrupted Hadleyburg* (1899), a devastating satire of venality in small-town America, and the first of three manuscript versions of *The Mysterious Stranger*. (None of the manuscripts was ever completed, and they were posthumously combined and published in 1916.) He also started *What Is Man?* (published anonymously in

1906), a dialogue in which a wise "Old Man" converts a resistant "Young Man" to a brand of philosophical determinism. He began to dictate his autobiography, which he would continue to do until a few months before he died. Some of Twain's best work during his late years was not fiction but polemical essays in which his earnestness was not in doubt: an essay against anti-Semitism, *Concerning the Jews* (1899); a denunciation of imperialism, *To the Man Sitting in Darkness* (1901); an essay on lynching, *The United States of Lyncherdom* (posthumously published in 1923); and a pamphlet on the brutal and exploitative Belgian rule in the Congo, *King Leopold's Soliloquy* (1905).

## Old Age

The family, including Clemens himself, had suffered from one sort of ailment or another for a very long time. In 1896 his daughter Jean was diagnosed with epilepsy, and by 1901 his wife's health was seriously deteriorating. She was violently ill in 1902, and for a time Clemens was allowed to see her for only five minutes a day. Removing to Italy seemed to improve her condition, but that was only temporary. She died on June 5, 1904. Something of his affection for her and his sense of personal loss after her death is conveyed in the moving piece *Eve's Diary* (1906). The story chronicles in tenderly comic ways the loving relationship between Adam and Eve. After Eve dies, Adam comments at her grave site, "Wheresoever she was, there was Eden." Clemens had written a commemorative poem on the anniversary of Susy's death, and *Eve's Diary* serves the equivalent function for the death of his wife. He would have yet another occasion to publish his grief. His daughter Jean died on December 24, 1909. *The Death of Jean* (1911) was written beside her deathbed. He was writing, he said, "to keep my heart from breaking."

It is true that Clemens was bitter and lonely during his last years. He moved into his new house in Redding, Connecticut, in June 1908. *Extracts from Captain Stormfield's Visit to Heaven* was published in installments in *Harper's Magazine* in 1907–08. *Little Bessie* and *Letters from the Earth* (both published posthumously) were also written during this period, and, while they are sardonic, they are antically comic as well. Clemens thought *Letters from the Earth* was so heretical that it could never be published. However, it was published in a book by that name, along with other previously unpublished writings, in 1962, and it reinvigorated public interest in Twain's serious writings. The letters did present unorthodox views — that God was something of a bungling scientist and human beings his failed experiment, that Christ, not Satan, devised hell, and

*Mark Twain.* Library of Congress, Washington, D.C. LC-USZ62-112728

that God was ultimately to blame for human suffering, injustice, and hypocrisy. Twain was speaking candidly in his last years but still with a vitality and ironic detachment that kept his work from being merely the fulminations of an old and angry man.

Perhaps as an escape from painful memories, he traveled to Bermuda in January 1910. By early April he was having severe chest pains. His biographer Albert Bigelow Paine joined him, and together they returned home. Clemens died on April 21. Clemens was buried in the family plot in Elmira, New York, alongside his wife, his son, and two of his daughters. Only Clara survived him.

# *Samuel Butler*

(b. December 4, 1835, Langar Rectory, Nottinghamshire, England—d. June 18, 1902, London)

Samuel Butler was an English novelist, essayist, and critic whose satire *Erewhon* (1872) foreshadowed the collapse of the Victorian illusion of eternal progress. *The Way of All Flesh* (1903), his autobiographical novel, is generally considered his masterpiece.

Butler was the son of the Reverend Thomas Butler and grandson of Samuel Butler, headmaster of Shrewsbury School and later bishop of Lichfield. After six years at Shrewsbury, the young Samuel went to St. John's College, Cambridge, and was graduated in 1858. His father wished him to be a clergyman, and young Butler actually went as far as to do a little "slumming" in a London parish by way of preparation for holy orders. But the whole current of his highly independent and heretical nature was carrying him away from everything his father stood for: home, church, and Christianity itself—or what Christianity had appeared to mean at Langar Rectory. Butler returned to Cambridge and continued his musical studies and drawing, but after an unpleasant altercation with his father he left Cambridge, the church, and home and emigrated to New Zealand, where (with funds advanced by his father) he set up a sheep run in the Canterbury settlement.

When Darwin's *Origin of Species* (1859) came into his hands soon after his arrival in New Zealand, it took him by storm; he became "one of Mr. Darwin's many enthusiastic admirers," and a year or two later he told a friend that he had renounced Christianity altogether. Yet, as it proved, Christianity had by no means finished with him. For the next 25 years it was upon religion and evolution that Butler's attention was mainly fixed. At first he welcomed Darwinism because it enabled him to do without God (or rather, without his father's God). Later, having found a God of his own, he rejected Darwinism itself because it left God out. Thus, he antagonized both the church and the orthodox Darwinians and spent his life as a lonely outsider, or as Butler called himself after the biblical outcast, "an Ishmael." To the New Zealand *Press* he contributed several articles on Darwinian topics, of which two— "Darwin Among the Machines" (1863) and "Lucubratio Ebria" (1865)—were later worked up in *Erewhon*. Both show him already grappling with the central problem of his later thought: the relationship between mechanism and life. In the former he tries out the consequences of regarding machines as living organisms competing with man in the struggle for existence. In the "Lucubratio" he takes the opposite view that machines are extracorporeal limbs and that the more of these a man can tack on to himself the more highly evolved an organism he will be.

Having doubled his capital in New Zealand, Butler returned to England (1864) and took the apartment in

Clifford's Inn, London, which was to be his home for the rest of his life. In 1865 his *Evidence for the Resurrection of Jesus Christ...Critically Examined* appeared anonymously. For a few years he studied painting at Heatherley's art school and tried to convince himself that this was his vocation. Until 1876 he exhibited occasionally at the Royal Academy. One of his oil paintings, "Mr. Heatherlcy's Holiday" (1874), is in the Tate Gallery, London, and his "Family Prayers," in which the ethos of Langar Rectory is satirically conveyed, is at St. John's College, Cambridge. Later he tried his hand at musical composition, publishing *Gavottes, Minuets, Fugues and Other Short Pieces for the Piano* (1885), and *Narcissus*, a comic cantata in the style of Handel—whom he rated high above all other composers—in 1888; *Ulysses: An Oratorio* appeared in 1904. It was typical of Butler to use his native gifts and mother wit in such exploits, and even in literature, his rightful territory, much of his work is that of the shrewd amateur who sets out to sling pebbles at the Goliaths of the establishment. "I have never," he said, "written on any subject unless I belicved that the authorities on it were hopelessly wrong"; hence his assault on the citadels of orthodox Darwinism and orthodox Christianity; hence, later, his attempt to prove that the *Odyssey* was written in Sicily by a woman (*The Authoress of the Odyssey*, 1897); and hence his new interpretation of Shakespeare's sonnets (*Shakespeare's Sonnets Reconsidered, and in Part Rearranged*, 1899).

*Erewhon* (1872) made whatever reputation as a writer Butler enjoyed in his lifetime; it was the only one of his many books on which he made any profit worth mentioning, and he made only £69 3s. 10d. on that. Yet *Erewhon* ("nowhere" rearranged) was received by many as the best thing of its kind since *Gulliver's Travels*—that is to say, as a satire on contemporary life and thought conveyed by the time-honoured convention of travel in an imaginary

country. The opening chapters, based upon Butler's recollections of the upper Rangitoto Mountains in New
Zealand, are in an excellent narrative style; and a description of the hollow statues at the top of the pass, vibrating
in the wind with unearthly chords, makes a highly effective transition to the strange land beyond. The landscape
and people of Erewhon are idealized from northern Italy;
its institutions are partly utopian and partly satiric inversions of our own world. Butler's two main themes, religion
and evolution, appear respectively in "The Musical Banks"
(churches) and in chapters called "Some Erewhonian Trials"
and "The Book of the Machines." The Erewhonians have
long ago abolished machines as dangerous competitors in
the struggle for existence, and by punishing disease as a
crime they have produced a race of great physical beauty
and strength.

   *The Fair Haven* (1873) is an ironical defense of
Christianity, which under the guise of orthodox zeal
undermines its miraculous foundations. Butler was dogged
all through life by the sense of having been bamboozled
by those who should have been his betters; he had been
taken in by his parents and their religion; he was taken in
again by friends, who returned neither the money nor the
friendship they accepted from Butler for years; life itself,
and the world, sometimes seemed to him a hollow sham.
Was Darwin himself, his saviour from the world of Langar
Rectory, now to prove a fraud as well? This was the suspicion that dawned upon him while writing *Life and Habit*
(1878) and envenomed the series of evolutionary books
that followed: *Evolution, Old and New* (1879), *Unconscious
Memory* (1880), and *Luck or Cunning* (1887). Darwin had
not really explained evolution at all, Butler reasoned,
because he had not accounted for the variations on which
natural selection worked. Where Darwin saw only chance,
Butler saw the effort on the part of creatures to respond

to felt needs. He conceived creatures as acquiring necessary habits (and organs to perform them) and transmitting these to their offspring as unconscious memories. He thus restored teleology to a world from which purpose had been excluded by Darwin, but instead of attributing the purpose to God he placed it within the creatures themselves as the life force.

Many regard *The Way of All Flesh*, published in 1903, the year after Butler's death, as his masterpiece. It certainly contains much of the quintessence of Butlerism. This largely autobiographical novel tells, with ruthless wit, realism, and lack of sentiment, the story of Butler's escape from the suffocating moral atmosphere of his home circle. In it, the character Ernest Pontifex stands for Butler's early self and Overton for his mature self; Theobald and Christina are his parents; Towneley and Alethea represent "nice" people who "love God" in Butler's special sense of having "good health, good looks, good sense, experience, and a fair balance of cash in hand." The book was influential at the beginning of the anti-Victorian reaction and helped turn the tide against excessive parental dominance and religious rigidity.

# BANKIM CHANDRA CHATTERJEE

(b. June 26/27, 1838, near Naihati, Bengal, India—
d. April 8, 1894, Calcutta)

Bankim Chandra Chatterjee (also spelled Catterji) was an Indian author whose novels firmly established prose as a literary vehicle for the Bengali language and helped create in India a school of fiction on the European model.

Bankim Chandra was a member of an orthodox Brahman family and was educated at Hooghly College, at Presidency College, Calcutta, and at the University of Calcutta, of which he was one of the first graduates. From 1858, until his retirement in 1891, he served as a deputy magistrate in the Indian civil service.

Some of Bankim Chandra's youthful compositions appeared in the newspaper *Sambad Prabhakar*, and in 1858 he published a volume of poems entitled *Lalita O Manas*. For a while he wrote in English, and his novel *Rajmohan's Wife* appeared serially in *Indian Field* in 1864. His first notable Bengali work was the novel *Durges'nandinī*, which features a Rajput hero and a Bengali heroine. In itself it is of indifferent quality, but in the philosopher Debendranath Tagore's words, it took "the Bengali heart by storm," and with it the Bengali novel was full born. *Kapālkuṇḍalā*, a love story against a gruesome background of Tantric rites, was published in 1866; and *Mṛnalinī*, which was set at the time of the first Muslim invasion of Bengal, in 1869.

*Baṅgadarśan*, Bankim Chandra's epochmaking newspaper, commenced publication in 1872, and in it some of his later novels were serialized. *Biśabṛksa*, which poses the problem of widow remarriage, and *Indira* were published in 1873; *Yugalanguriya* in 1874; *Radharani* and *Candraśekhar* in 1875; *Rājanī* in 1877; *Kṛṣṇakānter Uil*, which the author considered his greatest novel, in 1878; *Rājsiṃha*, a story of Rajput heroism and Muslim oppression, in 1881; *Ānandamaṭh*, a patriotic tale of the revolt of the sannyasis against the Muslim forces of the East India company, in 1882; *Debī Caudhurānī*, a domestic novel with a background of dacoity, in 1884; and finally, in 1886, *Sītārām*, a marital tangle and a struggle of Hindus against Muslim tyranny.

Bankim Chandra's novels are considered exciting to read but structurally faulty. Serial publication was partly responsible for imperfect integration of the various episodes. Evolution of plot depends too frequently on chance or supernatural intervention, and characterization is often subordinated to an overriding didactic purpose. His achievements, however, outweigh these technical imperfections. To his contemporaries his voice was that of a prophet; his valiant Hindu heroes aroused their patriotism and pride of race. In him nationalism and Hinduism merged as one; and his creed was epitomized in the song "Bande Mātaram" ("Hail to thee, Mother")—from his novel *Ānandamaṭh*—which later became the *mantra* ("hymn") and slogan of Hindu India in its struggle for independence.

# ÉMILE ZOLA

(b. April 2, 1840, Paris, France—d. September 28, 1902, Paris)

The French novelist, critic, and political activist Émile-Édouard-Charles-Antoine Zola was the most prominent French novelist of the late 19th century. He was noted for his theories of naturalism, which underlie his monumental 20-novel series *Les Rougon-Macquart*, and for his intervention in the Dreyfus Affair through his famous open letter, "J'accuse."

## Life

Though born in Paris in 1840, Zola spent his youth in Aix-en-Provence in southern France, where his father, a civil engineer, was involved in the construction of a municipal water system. The senior Zola died in 1847, leaving Madame Zola and her young son in dire financial straits.

In Aix, Zola was a schoolmate of the painter Paul Cézanne, who would later join him in Paris and introduce him to Édouard Manet and the Impressionist painters.

Although Zola completed his schooling at the Lycée Saint-Louis in Paris, he twice failed the *baccalauréat* exam, which was a prerequisite to further studies, and in 1859 he was forced to seek gainful employment. Zola spent most of the next two years unemployed and living in abject poverty. He subsisted by pawning his few belongings and, according to legend, by eating sparrows trapped outside his attic window. Finally, in 1862 he was hired as a clerk at the publishing firm of L.-C.-F. Hachette, where he was later promoted to the advertising department. To supplement his income and make his mark in the world of letters, Zola began to write articles on subjects of current interest for various periodicals; he also continued to write fiction, a pastime he had enjoyed since boyhood. In 1865 Zola published his first novel, *La Confession de Claude* (*Claude's Confession*), a sordid, semiautobiographical tale that drew the attention of the public and the police and incurred the disapproval of Zola's employer. Having sufficiently established his reputation as a writer to support himself and his mother, albeit meagerly, as a freelance journalist, Zola left his job at Hachette to pursue his literary interests.

In the following years Zola continued his career in journalism while publishing two novels: *Thérèse Raquin* (1867), a grisly tale of murder and its aftermath that is still widely read, and *Madeleine Férat* (1868), a rather unsuccessful attempt at applying the principles of heredity to the novel. It was this interest in science that led Zola, in the fall of 1868, to conceive the idea of a large-scale series of novels similar to Honoré de Balzac's *La Comédie humaine* (*The Human Comedy*), which had appeared earlier in the century. Zola's project, originally involving 10 novels, each featuring a different member of the same family, was

*Émile Zola.* Encyclopædia Britannica, Inc.

gradually expanded to comprise the 20 volumes of the *Rougon-Macquart* series.

*La Fortune des Rougon* (*The Rougon Family Fortune*), the first novel in the series, began to appear in serial form in 1870, was interrupted by the outbreak of the Franco-German War in July, and was eventually published in book form in October 1871. Zola went on to produce these 20 novels—most of which are of substantial length—at the rate of nearly one per year, completing the series in 1893. In 1870 Zola married Gabrielle-Alexandrine Meley, who had been his companion and lover for almost five years, and the young couple assumed the care of Zola's mother. In the early '70s Zola expanded his literary contacts, meeting frequently with Gustave Flaubert, Edmond Goncourt, Alphonse Daudet, and Ivan Turgenev. Beginning in 1878 the Zola home in Médan, on the Seine River not far from Paris, served as a gathering spot for a group of the novelist's disciples, the best-known of whom were Guy de Maupassant and Joris-Karl Huysmans, and together they published a collection of short stories, *Les Soirées de Médan* (1880; *Evenings at Médan*).

As the founder and most celebrated member of the naturalist movement, Zola published several treatises to explain his theories on art, including *Le Roman expérimental* (1880; *The Experimental Novel*) and *Les Romanciers naturalistes* (1881; *The Naturalist Novelists*). Naturalism involves the application to literature of two scientific principles: determinism, or the belief that character, temperament, and, ultimately, behaviour are determined by the forces of heredity, environment, and historical moment; and the experimental method, which entails the objective recording of precise data in controlled conditions.

If Zola's penchant for polemics and publicity led him to exaggerate his naturalist principles in his early writings, in later years, it can be said, rather, that controversy sought out the reluctant novelist. His publication of a particularly grim and sordid portrait of peasant life in *La Terre* in 1887 led a group of five so-called disciples to repudiate Zola in a manifesto published in the important newspaper *Le Figaro*. His novel *La Débâcle* (1892), which was openly critical of the French army and government actions during the Franco-German War (1870–71), drew vitriolic criticism from French and Germans alike.

Although Zola's marriage to Alexandrine endured until his death, the author had a fourteen-year affair with Jeanne Rozerot, one of his wife's housemaids, beginning in 1888. Jeanne bore him his only children—Denise and Jacques—who were "recognized" by Madame Zola after her husband's death.

In 1898 Zola intervened in the Dreyfus Affair—that of a Jewish French army officer whose wrongful conviction for treason in 1894 sparked a 12-year controversy that deeply divided French society. At an early stage in the proceedings Zola had decided rightly that Alfred Dreyfus was innocent. On January 13, 1898, in the newspaper *L'Aurore*, Zola published a fierce denunciation of the French general staff in an open letter beginning with the words "J'accuse" ("I accuse"). He charged various high-ranking military officers and, indeed, the War Office itself of concealing the truth in the wrongful conviction of Dreyfus for espionage. Zola was prosecuted for libel and found guilty. In July 1899, when his appeal appeared certain to fail, he fled to England. He returned to France the following June when he learned that the Dreyfus case was to be reopened with a possible reversal of the original verdict. Zola's intervention in the controversy helped to undermine anti-Semitism and rabid militarism in France.

*Front page of the newspaper* L'Aurore, *January 13, 1898, with the open letter "J'accuse" written by Émile Zola about the Dreyfus affair.* From L'Aurore, January 13, 1898

Zola's final series of novels, *Les Trois Villes* (1894–98; *The Three Cities*) and *Les Quatre Évangiles* (1899–1903; *The Four Gospels*) are generally conceded to be far less forceful than his earlier work. However, the titles of the novels in the latter series reveal the values that underlay his entire life and work: *Fécondité* (1899; *Fecundity*), *Travail* (1901; *Work*), *Vérité* (1903; *Truth*), and *Justice* (which, ironically, remained incomplete).

Zola died unexpectedly in September 1902, the victim of coal gas asphyxiation resulting from a blocked chimney flue. Officially, the event was determined to be a tragic accident, but there were—and still are—those who believe that fanatical anti-Dreyfusards arranged to have the chimney blocked.

At the time of his death, Zola was recognized not only as one of the greatest novelists in Europe but also as a man of action—a defender of truth and justice, a champion of the poor and the persecuted. At his funeral he was eulogized by Anatole France as having been not just a great man, but "a moment in the human conscience," and crowds of mourners, prominent and poor alike, lined the streets to salute the passing casket.

# Les Rougon-Macquart

Although he produced some 60 volumes of fiction, theory, and criticism, in addition to numerous pieces of journalism, during his 40-year career, Zola is best known for his 20-volume series *Les Rougon-Macquart*, which is "the natural and social history of a family under the Second Empire." As the subtitle suggests, the naturalist goal of demonstrating the deterministic influence of heredity is fulfilled by tracing the lives of various members of the three branches of the Rougon-Macquart family. At the same time, the weight of historical moment is shown by limiting the action of the novels to one historical period, that of the Second Empire (1852–70), which was the reign of Napoleon III, the nephew and pale imitation of Napoleon Bonaparte. Finally, Zola examines the impact of environment by varying the social, economic, and professional milieu in which each novel takes place.

*La Curée* (1872; *The Kill*), for example, explores the land speculation and financial dealings that accompanied the renovation of Paris during the Second Empire. *Le Ventre de Paris* (1873; *The Belly of Paris*) examines the structure of the Halles, the vast central marketplace of Paris, and its influence on the lives of its workers.

*Son Excellence Eugène Rougon* (1876; *His Excellency Eugène Rougon*) traces the machinations and maneuverings of cabinet officials in Napoleon III's government.

*L'Assommoir* (1877; "The Club"; Eng. trans. *The Drunkard*), which is among the most successful and enduringly popular of Zola's novels, shows the effects of alcoholism in a working-class neighbourhood by focusing on the rise and decline of a laundress, Gervaise Macquart. Zola's use of slang, not only by the characters but by the narrator, and his vivid paintings of crowds in motion lend authenticity and power to his portrait of the working class. *Nana* (1880) follows the life of Gervaise's daughter as her economic circumstances and hereditary penchants lead her to a career as an actress, then a courtesan, professions underscored by a theatrical metaphor that extends throughout the novel, revealing the ceremonial falseness of the Second Empire. *Au Bonheur des Dames* (1883; *Ladies' Delight*) depicts the mechanisms of a new economic entity, the department store, and its impact on smaller merchants.

*Germinal* (1885), which is generally acknowledged to be Zola's masterpiece, depicts life in a mining community by highlighting relations between the bourgeoisie and the working class. At the same time, the novel weighs the events of a miners' strike and its aftermath in terms of those contemporary political movements (Marxism, anarchism, trade unionism) that purport to deal with the problems of the proletariat. Zola's comparison of the coal mine to a devouring monster and his use of animal and botanical imagery to characterize the workers create a novel of epic scope that replicates, in modern terms, ancient myths of damnation and resurrection. A quite different work, *L'Oeuvre* (1886), explores the milieu of the art world and the interrelationship of the arts by means of the friendship between an Impressionist painter, Claude Lantier, and a naturalist novelist, Pierre Sandoz. Zola's verbal style mirrors the visual techniques of Impressionism in word-pictures of Paris transformed by varying effects of colour, light, and atmosphere.

In *La Terre* (1887; *Earth*) Zola breaks with the tradition of rustic, pastoral depictions of peasant life to show what he considered to be the sordid lust for land among the French peasantry. In *La Bête humaine* (1890; *The Human Beast*) he analyzes the hereditary urge to kill that haunts the Lantier branch of the family, set against the background of the French railway system, with its powerful machinery and rapid movement. *La Débâcle* (1892; *The Debacle*) traces both the defeat of the French army by the Germans at the Battle of Sedan in 1870 and the anarchist uprising of the Paris Commune. Finally, in *Le Docteur Pascal* (1893) he uses the main character, the doctor Pascal Rougon, armed with a genealogical tree of the Rougon-Macquart family published with the novel, to expound the theories of heredity underlying the entire series.

The *Rougon-Macquart* series thus constitutes a family saga while providing a valuable sociological document of the events, institutions, and ideas that marked the rise of modern industrialism and the cultural changes it entailed. However, if the novels continue to be widely read today, it is largely due to Zola's unique artistry, a poetry of machine and motion, vitalized by the individual viewpoint, yet structured by vast networks of imagery that capture the intense activity and alienation of modern industrial society. Above all, Zola's writings endure on account of his forthright portrayal of social injustice, his staunch defence of the downtrodden, and his unwavering belief in the betterment of the human condition through individual and collective action.

# THOMAS HARDY

(b. June 2, 1840, Higher Bockhampton, Dorset, England—d. January 11, 1928, Dorchester, Dorset)

The English novelist and poet Thomas Hardy set much of his work in Wessex, his name for the counties of southwestern England.

Hardy was the eldest of the four children of Thomas Hardy, a stonemason and jobbing builder, and his wife, Jemima (née Hand). He grew up in an isolated cottage on the edge of open heathland. Though he was often ill as a child, his early experience of rural life, with its seasonal rhythms and oral culture, was fundamental to much of his later writing. He spent a year at the village school at age eight and then moved on to schools in Dorchester, the nearby county town, where he received a good grounding in mathematics and Latin. In 1856 he was apprenticed to John Hicks, a local architect, and in 1862, shortly before his 22nd birthday, he moved to London and became a draftsman in the busy office of Arthur Blomfield, a leading ecclesiastical architect. Driven back to Dorset by ill health in 1867, he worked for Hicks again and then for the Weymouth architect G.R. Crickmay.

## Early Works

Though architecture brought Hardy both social and economic advancement, it was only in the mid-1860s that lack of funds and declining religious faith forced him to abandon his early ambitions of a university education and eventual ordination as an Anglican priest. His habits of intensive private study were then redirected toward the reading of poetry and the systematic development of his own poetic skills. The verses he wrote in the 1860s would emerge in revised form in later volumes (e.g., "Neutral Tones," "Retty's Phases"), but when none of them achieved immediate publication, Hardy reluctantly turned to prose.

In 1867–68 he wrote the class-conscious novel *The Poor Man and the Lady*, which was sympathetically considered by three London publishers but never published. George Meredith, as a publisher's reader, advised Hardy to write a more shapely and less opinionated novel. The result was the densely plotted *Desperate Remedies* (1871), which was influenced by the contemporary "sensation" fiction of Wilkie Collins. In his next novel, however, the brief and affectionately humorous idyll *Under the Greenwood Tree* (1872), Hardy found a voice much more distinctively his own. In this book he evoked, within the simplest of marriage plots, an episode of social change (the displacement of a group of church musicians) that was a direct reflection of events involving his own father shortly before Hardy's own birth.

In March 1870 Hardy had been sent to make an architectural assessment of the lonely and dilapidated Church of St. Juliot in Cornwall. There—in romantic circumstances later poignantly recalled in prose and verse—he first met the rector's vivacious sister-in-law, Emma Lavinia Gifford, who became his wife four years later. She actively encouraged and assisted him in his literary endeavours, and his next novel, *A Pair of Blue Eyes* (1873), drew heavily upon the circumstances of their courtship for its wild Cornish setting and its melodramatic story of a young woman (somewhat resembling Emma Gifford) and the two men, friends become rivals, who successively pursue, misunderstand, and fail her.

Hardy's break with architecture occurred in the summer of 1872, when he undertook to supply *Tinsley's*

*Magazine* with the 11 monthly installments of *A Pair of Blue Eyes*—an initially risky commitment to a literary career that was soon validated by an invitation to contribute a serial to the far more prestigious *Cornhill Magazine*. The resulting novel, *Far from the Madding Crowd* (1874), introduced Wessex for the first time and made Hardy famous by its agricultural settings and its distinctive blend of humorous, melodramatic, pastoral, and tragic elements. The book is a vigorous portrayal of the beautiful and impulsive Bathsheba Everdene and her marital choices among Sergeant Troy, the dashing but irresponsible soldier; William Boldwood, the deeply obsessive farmer; and Gabriel Oak, her loyal and resourceful shepherd.

## Middle Period

Hardy and Emma Gifford were married, against the wishes of both their families, in September 1874. At first they moved rather restlessly about, living sometimes in London, sometimes in Dorset. His record as a novelist during this period was somewhat mixed. *The Hand of Ethelberta* (1876), an artificial social comedy turning on versions and inversions of the British class system, was poorly received and has never been widely popular. *The Return of the Native* (1878), on the other hand, was increasingly admired for its powerfully evoked setting of Egdon Heath, which was based on the sombre countryside Hardy had known as a child. The novel depicts the disastrous marriage between Eustacia Vye, who yearns romantically for passionate experiences beyond the hated heath, and Clym Yeobright, the returning native, who is blinded to his wife's needs by a naively idealistic zeal for the moral improvement of Egdon's impervious inhabitants. Hardy's next works were *The Trumpet-Major* (1880), set in the Napoleonic period, and two more novels generally considered "minor"—*A Laodicean* (1881) and *Two on a Tower* (1882). The serious illness which hampered completion of *A Laodicean* decided the Hardys to move to Wimborne in 1881 and to Dorchester in 1883.

It was not easy for Hardy to establish himself as a member of the professional middle class in a town where his humbler background was well known. He signaled his determination to stay by accepting an appointment as a local magistrate and by designing and building Max Gate, the house just outside Dorchester in which he lived until his death. Hardy's novel *The Mayor of Casterbridge* (1886) incorporates recognizable details of Dorchester's history and topography. The busy market-town of Casterbridge becomes the setting for a tragic struggle, at once economic and deeply personal, between the powerful but unstable Michael Henchard, who has risen from workman to mayor by sheer natural energy, and the more shrewdly calculating Donald Farfrae, who starts out in Casterbridge as Henchard's protégé but ultimately dispossesses him of everything that he had once owned and loved. In Hardy's next novel, *The Woodlanders* (1887), socioeconomic issues again become central as the permutations of sexual advance and retreat are played out among the very trees from which the characters make their living, and Giles Winterborne's loss of livelihood is integrally bound up with his loss of Grace Melbury and, finally, of life itself.

*Wessex Tales* (1888) was the first collection of the short stories that Hardy had long been publishing in magazines. His subsequent short-story collections are *A Group of Noble Dames* (1891), *Life's Little Ironies* (1894), and *A Changed Man* (1913). Hardy's short novel *The Well-Beloved* (serialized 1892, revised for volume publication 1897) displays a hostility to marriage that was related to increasing frictions within his own marriage.

*Thomas Hardy, c. 1890.* © Photos.com/Thinkstock

## *Late Novels*

The closing phase of Hardy's career in fiction was marked by the publication of *Tess of the d'Urbervilles* (1891) and *Jude the Obscure* (1895), which are generally considered his finest novels. Though *Tess* is the most richly "poetic" of Hardy's novels, and *Jude* the most bleakly written, both books offer deeply sympathetic representations of working-class figures: Tess Durbeyfield, the erring milkmaid, and Jude Fawley, the studious stonemason. In powerful, implicitly moralized narratives, Hardy traces these characters' initially hopeful, momentarily ecstatic, but persistently troubled journeys toward eventual deprivation and death.

Though technically belonging to the 19th century, these novels anticipate the 20th century in regard to the nature and treatment of their subject matter. *Tess* profoundly questions society's sexual mores by its compassionate portrayal and even advocacy of a heroine who is seduced, and perhaps raped, by the son of her employer. She has an illegitimate child, suffers rejection by the man she loves and marries, and is finally hanged for murdering her original seducer. In *Jude the Obscure* the class-ridden educational system of the day is challenged by the defeat of Jude's earnest aspirations to knowledge, while conventional morality is affronted by the way in which the sympathetically presented Jude and Sue change partners, live together, and have children with little regard for the institution of marriage. Both books encountered some brutally hostile reviews, and Hardy's sensitivity to such attacks partly precipitated his long-contemplated transition from fiction to poetry.

## *Poetry*

Hardy seems always to have rated poetry above fiction, and *Wessex Poems* (1898), his first significant public appearance as a poet, included verse written during his years as a novelist as well as revised versions of poems dating from the 1860s. As a collection it was often perceived as miscellaneous and uneven—an impression reinforced by the author's own idiosyncratic illustrations—and acceptance of Hardy's verse was slowed, then and later, by the persistence of his reputation as a novelist. *Poems of the Past and the Present* (1901) contained nearly twice as many poems as its predecessor, most of them newly written. Some of the poems are explicitly or implicitly grouped by subject or theme. There are, for example, 11 "War Poems" prompted by the South African War (e.g., "Drummer Hodge," "The Souls of the Slain") and a sequence of disenchantedly "philosophical" poems (e.g., "The Mother Mourns," "The Subalterns," "To an Unborn Pauper Child"). In *Time's Laughingstocks* (1909), the poems are again arranged under headings, but on principles that often remain elusive. Indeed, there is no clear line of development in Hardy's poetry from immaturity to maturity; his style undergoes no significant change over time. His best poems can be found mixed together with inferior verse in any particular volume, and new poems are often juxtaposed to reworkings of poems written or drafted years before. The range of poems within any particular volume is also extremely broad—from lyric to meditation to ballad to satirical vignette to dramatic monologue or dialogue—and Hardy persistently experiments with different, often invented, stanza forms and metres.

In 1903, 1905, and 1908 Hardy successively published the three volumes of *The Dynasts*, a huge poetic drama that is written mostly in blank verse and subtitled "an epic-drama of the War with Napoleon"—though it was not intended for actual performance. The sequence of major historical events—Trafalgar, Austerlitz, Waterloo, and so on—is diversified by prose episodes involving ordinary soldiers and civilians and by an ongoing cosmic commentary from such personified "Intelligences" as the "Spirit of the Years" and the "Spirit of the Pities." Hardy, who once described his poems as a "series of seemings" rather than expressions of a single consistent viewpoint, found in the contrasted moral and philosophical positions of the various Intelligences a means of articulating his own intellectual ambiguities. *The Dynasts* as a whole served to project his central vision of a universe governed by the purposeless movements of a blind, unconscious force that he called the Immanent Will. Though subsequent criticism has tended to find its structures cumbersome and its verse inert, *The Dynasts* remains an impressive—and highly readable—achievement, and its publication certainly reinforced both Hardy's "national" image (he was appointed to the Order of Merit in 1910) and his enormous fame worldwide.

The sudden death of Emma Hardy in 1912 brought to an end some 20 years of domestic estrangement. It also stirred Hardy to profundities of regret and remorse and to the composition of "After a Journey," "The Voice," and the other "Poems of 1912–13," which are by general consent regarded as the peak of his poetic achievement. In 1914 Hardy married Florence Emily Dugdale, who was 38 years his junior. While his second wife sometimes found her situation difficult—as when the inclusion of "Poems of 1912–13" in the collection *Satires of Circumstance* (1914) publicly proclaimed her husband's continuing devotion to her predecessor—her attention to Hardy's health, comfort, and privacy made a crucial contribution to his remarkable productivity in old age. Late in his eighth decade he published a fifth volume of verse, *Moments of Vision* (1917), and wrote in secret an official "life" of himself for posthumous publication under the name of his widow. In his ninth decade Hardy published two more poetry collections, *Late*

*Lyrics and Earlier* (1922) and *Human Shows* (1925), and put together the posthumously published *Winter Words* (1928). Following his death, on January 11, 1928, his cremated remains were interred with national pomp in Westminster Abbey, while his separated heart was buried in the churchyard of his native parish.

# STÉPHANE MALLARMÉ

(b. March 18, 1842, Paris, France—d. September 9, 1898, Valvins, near Fontainebleau)

The French poet Stéphane Mallarmé was an originator (with Paul Verlaine) and leader of the Symbolist movement in poetry.

Mallarmé enjoyed the sheltered security of family life for only five brief years, until the early death of his mother in August 1847. This traumatic experience was echoed 10 years later by the death of his younger sister Maria, in August 1857, and by that of his father in 1863. These tragic events would seem to explain much of the longing Mallarmé expressed, from the very beginning of his poetic career, to turn away from the harsh world of reality in search of another world; and the fact that this remained the enduring theme of his poetry may be explained by the comparative harshness with which adult life continued to treat him. After spending the latter part of 1862 and the early months of 1863 in London so as to acquire a knowledge of English, he began a lifelong career as a schoolteacher, first in provincial schools (Tournon, Besançon, and Avignon) and later in Paris. He was not naturally gifted in this profession, however, and found the work decidedly uncongenial. Furthermore, his financial situation was by no means comfortable, particularly after his marriage in 1863 and after the birth of his children, Geneviève (in 1864) and Anatole (in 1871). To try to improve matters he engaged in part-time activities, such as editing a magazine for a few months at the end of 1874, writing a school textbook in 1877, and translating another textbook in 1880. In October 1879, after a six-month illness, his son Anatole died.

Despite these trials and tribulations, Mallarmé made steady progress with his parallel career as a poet. His early poems, which he began contributing to magazines in 1862, were influenced by Charles Baudelaire, whose recently published collection *Les Fleurs du mal* ("The Flowers of Evil") was largely concerned with the theme of escape from reality, a theme by which Mallarmé was already becoming obsessed. But Baudelaire's escapism had been of an essentially emotional and sensual kind—a vague dream of tropical islands and peaceful landscapes where all would be "*luxe, calme et volupté*" ("luxury, calm, and voluptuousness"). Mallarmé was of a much more intellectual bent, and his determination to analyze the nature of the ideal world and its relationship with reality is reflected in the two dramatic poems he began to write in 1864 and 1865, respectively, *Hérodiade* ("Herodias") and *L'Après-midi d'un faune* ("The Afternoon of a Faun"), the latter being the work that inspired Claude Debussy to compose his celebrated *Prélude* a quarter of a century later.

By 1868 Mallarmé had come to the conclusion that, although nothing lies beyond reality, within this nothingness lie the essences of perfect forms. The poet's task is to perceive and crystallize these essences. In so doing, the poet becomes more than a mere descriptive versifier, transposing into poetic form an already existent reality; he becomes a veritable God, creating something from nothing, conjuring up for the reader, as Mallarmé himself put it, *"l'absente de tous bouquets"*—the ideal flower that is absent from all real bouquets. But to crystallize essences in this way, to create the notion of floweriness, rather than to describe an actual flower, demands an extremely subtle and complex use of all the resources of language, and Mallarmé devoted himself during the rest of his life to putting his theories into practice in what he called his *Grand Oeuvre* ("Great Work"), or *Le Livre* ("The Book"). He never came near to completing this work, however, and the few preparatory notes that have survived give little or no idea of what the end result might have been.

On the other hand, Mallarmé did complete a number of poems related to his projected *Grand Oeuvre*, both in their themes and in their extremely evocative use of language. Among these are several elegies—the principal ones being to Charles Baudelaire, Edgar Allan Poe, Richard Wagner, Théophile Gautier, and Paul Verlaine—that Mallarmé was commissioned to write at various times in his career. He no doubt agreed to do them because the traditional theme of the elegy—the man is dead but he lives on in his work— is clearly linked to the poet's own belief that, although beyond reality there is nothing, poetry has the power to transcend this annihilation. In a second group of poems, Mallarmé wrote about poetry itself, reflecting evocatively on his aims and achievements.

In addition to these two categories of poems, he also wrote some poems that run counter to his obsession with the ideal world, though they, too, display that magical use of language of which Mallarmé had made himself such a master. These are the dozen or so sonnets he addressed to his mistress, Méry Laurent, between 1884 and 1890, in which he expressed his supreme satisfaction with reality. At that time, life was becoming much happier for him, not only because his liaison was agreeable but also because a review of him in the series of articles entitled *Les Poètes maudits* ("The Accursed

Poets") published by Verlaine in 1883 and the praise lavished on him by J.-K. Huysmans in his novel *À rebours* ("The Wrong Way") in 1884 led to his wide recognition as the most eminent French poet of the day. A series of celebrated Tuesday evening meetings at his tiny flat in Paris were attended by well-known writers, painters, and musicians of the time. All this perhaps decreased his need to seek refuge in an ideal world, and in *Un Coup de dés jamais n'abolira le hasard, poème* ("A Throw of Dice Will Never Abolish the Hazard, Poem"), the work that appeared in 1897, the year before his death, he found consolation in the thought that he had met with some measure of success in giving poetry a truly creative function.

Mallarmé died in 1898, at his cottage at Valvins, a village on the Seine near Fontainebleau, his main residence after retirement.

# *HENRY JAMES*

(b. April 15, 1843, New York, New York, U.S. — d. February 28, 1916, London, England)

H enry James was an American novelist and, as a naturalized English citizen from 1915, a great figure in the transatlantic culture. His fundamental theme was the innocence and exuberance of the New World in clash with the corruption and wisdom of the Old, as illustrated in such works as *Daisy Miller* (1879), *The Portrait of a Lady* (1881), *The Bostonians* (1886), and *The Ambassadors* (1903).

## *Early Life and Works*

Henry James was named for his father, a prominent social theorist and lecturer, and was the younger brother of the pragmatist philosopher William James. The young Henry was a shy, book-addicted boy who assumed the role of quiet observer beside his active elder brother. They were taken abroad as infants, were schooled by tutors and governesses, and spent their preadolescent years in Manhattan. Returned to Geneva, Paris, and London during their teens, the James children acquired languages and an awareness of Europe vouchsafed to few Americans in their times. On the eve of the American Civil War, the James family settled at Newport, Rhode Island, and there, and later in Boston, Henry came to know New England intimately. When he was 19 years of age he enrolled at the Harvard Law School, but he devoted his study time to reading Charles-Augustin Sainte-Beuve, Honoré de Balzac, and Nathaniel Hawthorne. His first story appeared anonymously two years later in the New York *Continental Monthly* and his first book reviews in the *North American Review*. When William Dean Howells became editor of *The Atlantic Monthly*, James found in him a friend and mentor who published him regularly. Between them, James and Howells inaugurated the era of American "realism."

## *Establishment of a Career in Europe*

Recognizing the appeal of Europe, given his cosmopolitan upbringing, James made a deliberate effort to discover whether he could live and work in the United States. Two years in Boston, two years in Europe, mainly in Rome, and a winter of unremitting hackwork in New York City convinced him that he could write better and live more cheaply abroad. Thus began his long expatriation—heralded by publication in 1875 of the novel *Roderick Hudson*, the story of an American sculptor's struggle by the banks of the Tiber between his art and his passions; *Transatlantic Sketches*, his first collection of travel writings; and a collection of tales. With these three substantial books, he inaugurated a career that saw about 100 volumes through the press during the next 40 years.

During 1875–76 James lived in Paris, writing literary and topical letters for the *New York Tribune* and working on his novel *The American* (1877), the story of a self-made American millionaire whose guileless and forthright character contrasts with that of the arrogant and cunning family of French aristocrats whose daughter he unsuccessfully attempts to marry. In Paris James sought out the Russian novelist Ivan Turgenev, whose work appealed to him, and through Turgenev was brought into Gustave Flaubert's coterie, where he got to know Edmond de Goncourt, Émile Zola, Alphonse Daudet, and Guy de Maupassant. From Turgenev he received confirmation of his own view that a novelist need not worry about "story" and that, in focusing on character, he would arrive at the life experience of his protagonist.

Much as he liked France, James felt that he would be an eternal outsider there, and late in 1876 he crossed to London. There, in small rooms in Bolton Street off Piccadilly, he wrote the major fiction of his middle years. In 1878 he achieved international renown with his story of an American flirt in Rome, *Daisy Miller*, and further advanced his reputation with *The Europeans* that same year. In England he was promptly taken up by the leading Victorians and became a regular at Lord Houghton's breakfasts, where he consorted with Alfred Tennyson, William Gladstone, Robert Browning, and others. He was elected to London clubs, published his stories simultaneously in English and American periodicals, and mingled with George Meredith, Robert Louis Stevenson, Edmund Gosse, and other writers, thus establishing himself as a significant figure in Anglo-American literary and artistic relations.

James's reputation was founded on his versatile studies of "the American girl." In a series of witty tales, he pictured the "self-made" young woman, the bold and brash American innocent who insists upon American standards in European society. James ended this first phase of his career by producing his masterpiece, *The Portrait of a Lady* (1881), a study of a young woman from Albany who brings to Europe her narrow provincialism and pretensions but also her sense of her own sovereignty, her "free spirit," her refusal to be treated, in the Victorian world, merely as a marriageable object. As a picture of Americans moving in the expatriate society of England and of Italy, this novel has no equal in the history of modern fiction. It is a remarkable study of a band of egotists while at the same time offering a shrewd appraisal of the American character. James's understanding of power in personal relations was profound, as evinced in *Washington Square* (1881), the story of a young American heroine whose hopes for love and marriage are thwarted by her father's callous rejection of a somewhat opportunistic suitor.

## Changes in Artistic Style

In the 1880s James wrote two novels dealing with social reformers and revolutionaries, *The Bostonians* (1886) and *The Princess Casamassima* (1886). In the novel of Boston life, James analyzed the struggle between conservative masculinity embodied in a Southerner living in the North and an embittered man-hating suffragist. *The Bostonians* remains the fullest and most rounded American social novel of its time in its study of cranks, faddists, and "do-gooders." In *The Princess Casamassima* James exploited the anarchist violence of the decade and depicted the struggle of a man who toys with revolution and is destroyed by it. These novels were followed by *The Tragic Muse* (1890), in which James projected a study of the London and Paris art studios and the stage, the conflict between art and "the world."

The latter novel raised the curtain on his own "dramatic years," 1890–95, during which he tried to win success writing for the stage. His dramatization of *The American* in 1891 was a modest success, but an original play, *Guy Domville*, produced in 1895, was a failure, and James was booed at the end of the first performance. Crushed and feeling that he had lost his public, he spent several years seeking to adapt his dramatic experience to his fiction. The result was a complete change in his storytelling methods. In *The Spoils of Poynton* (1897), *What Maisie Knew* (1897), *The Turn of the Screw* and *In the Cage* (1898), and *The Awkward Age* (1899), James began to use the methods of alternating "picture" and dramatic scene, close adherence to a given angle of vision, a withholding of information from the reader, making available to him only that which the characters see. The subjects of this period are the developing consciousness and moral education of children—in reality James's old international theme of innocence in a corrupting world, transferred to the English setting.

## Late Years

The experiments of this "transition" phase led James to the writing of three grandiose novels at the beginning of the new century, which represent his final—his "major"—phase, as it has been called. In these novels James pointed the way for the 20th-century novel. He had begun as a realist who describes minutely his crowded stage. He ended by leaving his stage comparatively bare, and showing a small group of characters in a tense situation, with a retrospective working out, through multiple angles of vision, of their drama. In addition to these technical devices he

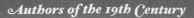

*Novelist and American expatriate Henry James drew upon themes of innocence and corruption in his works.* Time & Life Pictures/ Getty Images

resorted to an increasingly allusive prose style, which became dense and charged with symbolic imagery. His late "manner" derived in part from his dictating directly to a typist and in part from his unremitting search for ways of projecting subjective experience in a flexible prose.

The first of the three novels was *The Ambassadors* (1903). This is a high comedy of manners, of a middle-aged American who goes to Paris to bring back to a Massachusetts industrial town a wealthy young man who, in the view of his affluent family, has lingered too long abroad. The "ambassador" in the end is captivated by civilized Parisian life. The novel is a study in the growth of perception and awareness in the elderly hero, and it balances the relaxed moral standards of the European continent against the parochial rigidities of New England. The second of this series of novels was *The Wings of the Dove*, published in 1902, before *The Ambassadors*, although written after it. This novel, dealing with a melodramatic subject of great pathos, that of an heiress doomed by illness to die, avoids its cliche subject by focusing upon the characters surrounding the unfortunate young woman. They intrigue to inherit her millions. Told in this way, and set in London and Venice, it becomes a powerful study of well-intentioned humans who, with dignity and reason, are at the same time also birds of prey. In its shifting points of view and avoidance of scenes that would end in melo-drama, *The Wings of the Dove* demonstrated the mastery with which James could take a tawdry subject and invest it with grandeur. His final novel was *The Golden Bowl* (1904), a study of adultery, with four principal characters. The first part of the story is seen through the eyes of the aris-tocratic husband and the second through the developing awareness of the wife.

While many of James's short stories were potboil-ers written for the current magazines, he achieved high mastery in the ghostly form, notably in *The Turn of the Screw* (1898), and in such remarkable narratives as "The Aspern Papers" (1888) and "The Beast in the Jungle" (1903)—his prophetic picture of dissociated 20th-century man lost in an urban agglomeration. As a critic James tended to explore the character and personality of writers as revealed in their creations; his essays are a brilliant series of studies, moral portraits, of the most famous novelists of his century, from Balzac to the Edwardian realists. His travel writings, *English Hours* (1905), *Italian Hours* (1909), and *A Little Tour in France* (1884), portray the backgrounds James used for his fictions.

In his later years, James lived in retirement in an 18th-century house at Rye in Sussex, though on completion of *The Golden Bowl* he revisited the United States in 1904–05. James had lived abroad for 20 years, and in the interval America had become a great industrial and political power. His observation of the land and its people led him to write, on his return to England, a poetic volume of rediscovery and discovery, *The American Scene* (1907), prophetic in its vision of urban doom, spoliation, and pollution of resources and filled with misgivings over the anomalies of a "melting pot" civilization. The materialism of American life deeply troubled James, and on his return to England he set to work to shore up his own writings, and his own career, against this ephemeral world. He devoted three years to rewriting and revising his principal novels and tales for the highly selective "New York Edition," published in 24 volumes. For this edition James wrote 18 significant prefaces, which contain both reminiscence and exposition of his theories of fiction.

Throwing his moral weight into Britain's struggle in World War I, James became a British subject in 1915 and received the Order of Merit from King George V.

# BENITO PÉREZ GALDÓS

(b. May 10, 1843, Las Palmas, Canary Islands, Spain—d. January 4, 1920, Madrid)

B enito Pérez Galdós was a writer who was often regarded as the greatest Spanish novelist since Miguel de Cervantes. His enormous output of short novels chronicling the history and society of 19th-century Spain earned him comparison with Honoré de Balzac and Charles Dickens.

Born into a middle-class family, Pérez Galdós went to Madrid in 1862 to study law but soon abandoned his studies and took up journalism. After the success of his first novel, *La fontana de oro* (1870; "The Fountain of Gold"), he began a series of novels retelling Spain's history from the Battle of Trafalgar (1805) to the restoration of the Bourbons in Spain (1874). The entire cycle of 46 novels would come to be known as the *Episodios nacionales* (1873–1912; "National Episodes"). In these works Galdós perfected a unique type of historical fiction that was based on meticulous research using memoirs, old newspaper articles, and eyewitness accounts. The resulting novels are vivid, realistic, and accurate accounts of historical events as they must have appeared to those participating in them. The Napoleonic occupation of Spain and the struggles between liberals and absolutists preceding the death of Ferdinand VII in 1833 are respectively treated in the first two series of 10 novels each, all composed in the 1870s.

In the 1880s and '90s Pérez Galdós wrote a long series of novels dealing with contemporary Spain, beginning with *Doña Perfecta* (1876). Known as the *Novelas españolas*

*The works of author Benito Pérez Galdós chronicle the culture and mores of 19th-century Spanish society.* Hulton Archive/Getty Images

*contemporáneas* ("Contemporary Spanish Novels"), these books were written at the height of the author's literary maturity and include some of his finest works, notably *La desheredada* (1881; *The Disinherited Lady*) and his masterpiece, the four-volume novel *Fortunata y Jacinta* (1886–87), a study of two unhappily married women from different social classes. Pércz Galdós' earlier novels in the series show a reforming liberal zeal and an intransigent opposition to Spain's ubiquitous and powerful clergy, but after the 1880s he displayed a newly tolerant acceptance of Spain's idiosyncracies and a greater sympathy for his country. He demonstrated a phenomenal knowledge of Madrid, of which he showed himself the supreme chronicler. He also displayed a deep understanding of madness and abnormal psychological states. Pérez Galdós gradually came to admit more elements of spirituality into his work, eventually accepting them as an integral part of reality, as evident in the important late novels *Nazarín* (1895) and *Misericordia* (1897; *Compassion*).

Financial difficulties prompted Pérez Galdós in 1898 to begin a third series of novels (covering the Carlist wars of the 1830s) in the *Episodios nacionales,* and he eventually went on to write a fourth series (covering the period from 1845 to 1868) and begin a fifth, so that by 1912 he had brought his history of Spain down to 1877 and retold events of which he himself had been a witness. The books of the fifth series, however, and his last works showed a decline in mental powers compounded by the blindness that overtook him in 1912.

Pérez Galdós also wrote plays, some of which were immensely popular, but their succcss was largely owing to the political views presented in them rather than to their artistic value.

# PAUL VERLAINE

(b. March 30, 1844, Metz, France — d. January 8, 1896, Paris)

P aul-Marie Verlaine was a French lyric poet first associated with the Parnassians and later known as a leader of the Symbolists. With Stéphane Mallarmé and Charles Baudelaire he formed the so-called Decadents.

Verlaine was the only child of an army officer in comfortable circumstances. He was undoubtedly spoiled by his mother. At the Lycée Bonaparte (now Condorcet) in Paris, he showed both ability and indolence and at 14 sent his first extant poem ("La Mort") to the "master" poet Victor Hugo. Obtaining the *baccalauréat* in 1862, with distinction in translation from Latin, he became a clerk in an insurance company, then in the Paris city hall. All the while he was writing verse and frequenting literary cafés and drawing rooms, where he met the leading poets of the Parnassian group and other talented contemporaries, among them Mallarmé, Villiers de L'Isle-Adam, and Anatole France. His poems began to appear in their literary reviews; the first, "Monsieur Prudhomme," in 1863. Three years later the first series of *Le Parnasse contemporain*, a collection of pieces by contemporary poets (hence the term Parnassian), contained eight contributions by Verlaine.

The same year, his first volume of poetry appeared. Besides virtuoso imitations of Baudelaire and Leconte de Lisle, *Poèmes saturniens* included poignant expressions of love and melancholy supposedly centred on his cousin Élisa, who married another and died in 1867 (she had paid for this book to be published). In *Fêtes galantes* personal sentiment is masked by delicately clever evocations of

402

scenes and characters from the Italian commedia dell'arte and from the sophisticated pastorals of 18th-century painters, such as Watteau and Nicolas Lancret, and perhaps also from the contemporary mood-evoking paintings of Adolphe Monticelli. In June 1869 Verlaine fell in love with Mathilde Mauté, aged 16, and they married in August 1870. In the delicious poems written during their engagement (*La Bonne Chanson*), he fervently sees her as his long hoped-for saviour from erring ways. When insurrectionists seized power and set up the Paris Commune, Verlaine served as press officer under their council. His fear of resultant reprisals from the Third Republic was one factor in his later bohemianism. Incompatibility in his marriage was soon aggravated by his infatuation for the younger poet Arthur Rimbaud, who came to stay with the Verlaines in September 1871.

Verlaine abandoned his wife and infant son, Georges, in July 1872, to wander with Rimbaud in northern France and Belgium and write "impressionist" sketches for his next collection, *Romances sans paroles* ("Songs Without Words"). The pair reached London in September and found, besides exiled Communard friends, plenty of interest and amusement and also inspiration: Verlaine completed the *Romances*, whose opening pages, especially, attain a pure musicality rarely surpassed in French literature and embody some of his most advanced prosodic experiments; the subjects are mostly landscape or regret or vituperation of his estranged wife. The collection was published in 1874 by his friend Edmond Lepelletier; the author himself was then serving a two-year sentence at Mons for wounding Rimbaud with a revolver during an emotional storm in Brussels on July 10, 1873.

Contrition, prison abstinence, and pious reading (some in English, along with admiring study of Shakespeare and Dickens) seem to have produced a sincere return to Roman Catholicism in the summer of 1874, after his wife had obtained a separation. Leaving prison in January 1875, he tried a Trappist retreat, then hurried to Stuttgart to meet Rimbaud, who apparently repulsed him with violence. He took refuge in England and, for over a year, taught French and drawing at Stickney and Boston in Lincolnshire, then at Bournemouth, Hampshire, impressing all by his dignity and piety and gaining an appreciation of English authors as diverse as Tennyson, Swinburne, and the Anglican hymn writers. In 1877 he returned to France.

From this period (1873–78) date most of the poems in *Sagesse* ("Wisdom"), which was published in October 1880 at the author's expense (as were his previous books). They include outstanding poetical expressions of simple Catholic Christianity as well as of his emotional odyssey. Literary recognition now began. In 1882 his famous "Art poétique" (probably composed in prison eight years earlier) was enthusiastically adopted by the young Symbolists. He later disavowed the Symbolists, however, chiefly because they went further than he in abandoning traditional forms: rhyme, for example, seemed to him an unavoidable necessity in French verse.

In 1880 Verlaine made an unsuccessful essay at farming with his favourite pupil, Lucien Létinois, and the boy's parents. Lucien's death in April 1883, as well as that of the poet's mother (to whom he was tenderly attached) in January 1886, and the failure of all attempts at reconciliation with his wife broke down whatever will to "respectability" remained, and he relapsed into drink and debauchery. Now both famous and notorious, he was still writing in an attempt to earn a living but seldom with the old inspiration.

*Jadis et naguère* ("Yesteryear and Yesterday") consists mostly of pieces like "Art poétique," written years before but not fitting into previous carefully grouped collections. Similarly, *Parallèlement* comprises bohemian and erotic pieces often contemporary with, and technically equal to, his "respectable" ones. Verlaine frankly acknowledged the parallel nature of both his makeup and his muse. In *Amour* new poems still show the old magic, notably passages of his lament for Lucien Létinois, no doubt intended to emulate Tennyson's *In Memoriam*, but lacking its depth. Prose works such as *Les Poètes maudits*, short biographical studies of six poets, among them Mallarmé and Rimbaud; *Les Hommes d'aujourd'hui*, brief biographies of contemporary writers, most of which appeared in 1886; *Mes Hôpitaux,* accounts of Verlaine's stays in hospitals; *Mes Prisons,* accounts of his incarcerations, including the story of his "conversion" in 1874; and *Confessions, notes autobiographiques* helped attract notice to ill-recognized contemporaries as well as to himself (he was instrumental in publishing Rimbaud's *Illuminations* in 1886 and making him famous). There is little of lasting value, however, in the rest of the verse and prose that Verlaine turned out in an unsuccessful effort to keep the wolf from a door shared usually with aging prostitutes such as Philomène Boudin and Eugénie Krantz, prominent among the muses of his decadence. During frequent spells in hospitals, doctors gave him devoted care and friendship. He was feted in London, Oxford, and Manchester by young sympathizers, among them the critic Arthur Symons, who arranged a lecture tour in England in November 1893. Frank Harris and Cranmer Byng published articles and poems by Verlaine in *The Fortnightly Review* and *The Senate*. Relief pensions from admirers (1894) and the state (1895) were also recognition, however tardy or insufficient, of the esteem he attracted as a poet and a friend. He died in Eugénie Krantz's lodgings in January 1896.

# Anatole France

(b. April 16, 1844, Paris, France — d. October 12, 1924,
Saint-Cyr-sur-Loire)

The writer and ironic, skeptical, and urbane critic Anatole France (a pseudonym of Jacques-Anatole-François Thibault) was considered in his day to be the ideal French man of letters. He was elected to the French Academy in 1896 and was awarded the Nobel Prize for Literature in 1921.

The son of a bookseller, he spent most of his life around books. At school he received the foundations of a solid humanist culture and decided to devote his life to literature. His first poems were influenced by the Parnassian revival of classical tradition, and, though scarcely original, they revealed a sensitive stylist who was already cynical about human institutions.

This ideological skepticism appeared in his early stories: *Le Crime de Sylvestre Bonnard* (1881), a novel about a philologist in love with his books and bewildered by everyday life; *La Rôtisserie de la Reine Pédauque* (1893; *At the Sign of the Reine Pédauque*), which discreetly mocks belief in the occult; and *Les Opinions de Jérome Coignard* (1893), in which an ironic and perspicacious critic examines the great institutions of the state. His personal life underwent considerable turmoil. His marriage in 1877 to Marie-Valérie Guérin de Sauville ended in divorce in 1893. He had met Madame Arman de Caillavet in 1888, and their liaison inspired his novels *Thaïs* (1890), a tale set in Egypt of a courtesan who becomes a saint, and *Le Lys rouge* (1894; *The Red Lily*), a love story set in Florence.

*Colorized portrait of French writer Anatole France, whose works are noted more for their wit and turn of phrase than they are for substance of plot.* RDA/Hulton Archive/Getty Images

A marked change in France's work first appears in four volumes collected under the title *L'Histoire contemporaine* (1897–1901). The first three volumes—*L'Orme du mail* (1897; *The Elm-Tree on the Mall*), *Le Mannequin d'osier* (1897; *The Wicker Work Woman*), and *L'Anneau d'améthyste* (1899; *The Amethyst Ring*)—depict the intrigues of a provincial town. The last volume, *Monsieur Bergeret à Paris* (1901; *Monsieur Bergeret in Paris*), concerns the participation of the hero, who had formerly held himself aloof from political strife, in the Alfred Dreyfus affair. This work is the story of Anatole France himself, who was diverted from his role of an armchair philosopher and detached observer of life by his commitment to support Dreyfus. After 1900 he introduced his social preoccupations into most of his stories. *Crainquebille* (1903), a comedy in three acts adapted by France from an earlier short story, dramatizes the unjust treatment of a small tradesman and proclaims the hostility toward the bourgeois order that led France eventually to embrace socialism. Toward the end of his life, his sympathies were drawn to communism. However, *Les Dieux ont soif* (1912; *The Gods are Athirst*) and *L'Île des Pingouins* (1908; *Penguin Island*) show little belief in the ultimate arrival of a fraternal society. World War I reinforced his profound pessimism and led him to seek refuge from his times in childhood reminiscences. *Le Petit Pierre* (1918; *Little Pierre*) and *La Vie en fleur* (1922; *The Bloom of Life*) complete the cycle started in *Le Livre de mon ami* (1885; *My Friend's Book*).

France has been faulted for the thinness of his plots and for his lack of a vital creative imagination. His works are, however, considered remarkable for their wide-ranging erudition, their wit and irony, their passion for social justice, and their classical clarity, qualities that mark France as an heir to the tradition of Denis Diderot and Voltaire.

# GERARD MANLEY HOPKINS

(b. July 28, 1844, Stratford, Essex, England—d. June 8, 1889, Dublin, Ireland)

G erard Manley Hopkins was an English poet, a Jesuit priest, and one of the most individual of Victorian writers. His work was not published in collected form until 1918, but it influenced many leading 20th-century poets.

Hopkins was the eldest of the nine children of Manley Hopkins, an Anglican, who had been British consul general in Hawaii and had himself published verse. Hopkins won the poetry prize at the Highgate grammar school and in 1863 was awarded a grant to study at Balliol College, Oxford, where he continued writing poetry while studying classics. In 1866, in the prevailing atmosphere of the Oxford Movement, which renewed interest in the relationships between Anglicanism and Roman Catholicism, he was received into the Roman Catholic Church by John Henry (later Cardinal) Newman. The following year, he left Oxford with such a distinguished academic record that Benjamin Jowett, then a Balliol lecturer and later master of the college, called him "the star of Balliol." Hopkins decided to become a priest. He entered the Jesuit novitiate in 1868 and burned his youthful verses, determining "to write no more, as not belonging to my profession."

Until 1875, however, he kept a journal recording his vivid responses to nature as well as his expression of a philosophy for which he later found support in Duns Scotus, the medieval Franciscan thinker. Hopkins' philosophy emphasized the individuality of every natural thing, which he called "inscape." To Hopkins, each sensuous impression had its own elusive "selfness"; each scene was to him a "sweet especial scene."

In 1874 Hopkins went to St. Beuno's College in North Wales to study theology. There he learned Welsh, and, under the impact of the language itself as well as that of the poetry and encouraged by his superior, he began to write poetry again. Moved by the death of five Franciscan nuns in a shipwreck in 1875, he broke his seven-year silence to write the long poem "The Wreck of the Deutschland," in which he succeeded in realizing "the echo of a new rhythm" that had long been haunting his ear. It was rejected, however, by the Jesuit magazine *The Month*. He also wrote a series of sonnets strikingly original in their richness of language and use of rhythm, including the remarkable "The Windhover," one of the most frequently analyzed poems in the language. He continued to write poetry, but it was read only in manuscript by his friends and fellow poets, Robert Bridges (later poet laureate), Coventry Patmore, and the Rev. Richard Watson Dixon. Their appreciation of the strangeness of the poems (for the times) was imperfect, but they were, nevertheless, encouraging.

Ordained to the priesthood in 1877, Hopkins served as missioner, occasional preacher, and parish priest in various Jesuit churches and institutions in London, Oxford, Liverpool, and Glasgow and taught classics at Stonyhurst College, Lancashire. He was appointed professor of Greek literature at University College, Dublin, in 1884. But Hopkins was not happy in Ireland; he found the environment uncongenial, and he was overworked and in poor health. From 1885 he wrote another series of sonnets, beginning with "Carrion Comfort." They show a sense of desolation produced partly by a sense of spiritual aridity and partly by a feeling of artistic frustration. These poems, known as the "terrible sonnets," reveal strong tensions between his delight in the sensuous world and his urge to express it and his equally powerful sense of religious vocation.

While in Dublin, Hopkins developed another of his talents, musical composition; the little he composed shows the same daring originality as does his poetry. His skill in drawing, too, allowed him to illustrate his journal with meticulously observed details of flowers, trees, and waves.

His friends continually urged him to publish his poems, but Hopkins resisted; all that he saw in print in his lifetime were some immature verses and original Latin poems, in which he took particular pleasure.

Hopkins died of typhoid fever and was buried in the Glasnevin Cemetery, Dublin. Among his unfinished works was a commentary on the *Spiritual Exercises* of St. Ignatius of Loyola, founder of the Jesuit order.

After Hopkins's death, Robert Bridges began to publish a few of the Jesuit's most mature poems in anthologies, hoping to prepare the way for wider acceptance of his style. By 1918, Bridges, then poet laureate, judged the time opportune for the first collected edition. It appeared but sold slowly. Not until 1930 was a second edition issued, and thereafter Hopkins's work was recognized as among the most original, powerful, and influential literary accomplishments of his century; it had a marked influence on such leading 20th-century poets as T.S. Eliot, Dylan Thomas, W.H. Auden, Stephen Spender, and C. Day Lewis.

Hopkins sought a stronger "rhetoric of verse." His exploitation of the verbal subtleties and music of English, of the use of echo, alliteration, and repetition, and a highly compressed syntax were all in the interest of projecting deep personal experiences, including his sense of God's mystery, grandeur, and mercy, and his joy in "all things counter, original, spare, strange," as he wrote in "Pied

Beauty." He called the energizing prosodic element of his verse "sprung rhythm," in which each foot may consist of one stressed syllable and any number of unstressed syllables, instead of the regular number of syllables used in traditional metre. The result is a muscular verse, flexible, intense, vibrant, and organic, that combines accuracy of observation, imaginative daring, deep feeling, and intellectual depth.

Hopkins's letters reveal a brilliant critical faculty, scrupulous self-criticism, generous humanity, and a strong will. His friends paid tribute to his personal integrity and to his rare "chastity of mind." Coventry Patmore wrote of him: "There was something in all his words and manners which were at once a rebuke and an attraction to all who could only aspire to be like him."

# HENRYK SIENKIEWICZ

(b. May 5, 1846, Wola Okrzejska, Poland—d. November 15, 1916, Vevey, Switzerland)

Henryk Sienkiewicz was a Polish novelist and the winner of the Nobel Prize for Literature in 1905.

Sienkiewicz's family owned a small estate but lost everything and moved to Warsaw, where Sienkiewicz studied literature, history, and philology at Warsaw University. He left the university in 1871 without taking a degree. He had begun to publish critical articles in 1869 that showed the influence of Positivism, a system of philosophy—popular in Poland and elsewhere at the time—emphasizing in particular the achievements of science. His first novel, *Na marne* (*In Vain*), was published in 1872, and his first short story, "Stary sługa" ("An Old Retainer"), in 1875.

Sienkiewicz traveled in the United States (1876–78) and, upon his return to Poland after a prolonged stay in Paris, published a number of successful short stories, among them "Janko muzykant" (1879; "Yanko the Musician"), "Latarnik" (1882; "The Lighthouse Keeper"), and "Bartek zwyciezca" (1882; "Bartek the Conqueror"). The last story appears in a volume of his stories entitled *Charcoal Sketches and Other Tales* (1990), and there is also a volume of his stories entitled *Selected Tales* (1976).

From 1882 to 1887 Sienkiewicz was coeditor of the daily *Słowo* ("The Word"). In 1900, to celebrate the 30th year of his career as a writer, the Polish people presented him with the small estate of Oblęgorek, near Kielce in south-central Poland, where he lived until 1914. At the outbreak of World War I he went to Switzerland, where, together with the famous politician and pianist Ignacy Paderewski, he promoted the cause of Polish independence and organized relief for Polish war victims.

Sienkiewicz's great trilogy of historical novels began to appear in *Słowo* in 1883. It comprises *Ogniem i mieczem* (1884; *With Fire and Sword*; filmed 1999), *Potop* (1886; *The Deluge*; filmed 1974), and *Pan Wołodyjowski* (1887–88; *Pan Michael*, also published as *Fire in the Steppe*; filmed 1969). Set in the later 17th century, the trilogy describes Poland's struggles against Cossacks, Tatars, Swedes, and Turks, stressing Polish heroism with epic range and with clarity and simplicity. The finest of the three works, *With Fire and Sword*, describes the Poles' attempts to halt the rebellion of the Zaporozhian Cossacks led by Bohdan Khmelnytsky.

Sienkiewicz's other novels include the widely translated *Quo vadis?* (1896; Eng. trans. *Quo vadis*; filmed 1909, 1913, 1951, 2001), a historical novel set in Rome under Nero, which established Sienkiewicz's international reputation. Although Sienkiewicz's major novels have been criticized for their theatricality and lack of historical accuracy, they display great narrative power and contain vivid characterizations.

# JORIS-KARL HUYSMANS

(b. February 5, 1848, Paris, France—d. May 12, 1907, Paris)

Joris-Karl Huysmans was a French writer whose major novels epitomize successive phases of the aesthetic, spiritual, and intellectual life of late 19th-century France.

Huysmans was the only son of a French mother and a Dutch father. At 20 he began a long career in the Ministry of the Interior, writing many of his novels on official time (and notepaper). His early work, influenced by contemporary naturalist novelists, include a novel, *Marthe, histoire d'une fille* (1876; *Marthe*), about his liaison with a soubrette, and a novella, *Sac au dos* (1880; "Pack on Back"), based on his experience in the Franco-German War. The latter was published in *Les Soirées de Médan* (1881), war stories written by members of Émile Zola's "Médan" group of naturalist writers. Huysmans soon broke with the group, however, publishing a series of novels too decadent in content and violent in style to be considered examples of naturalism.

The first was *À vau-l'eau* (1882; *Down Stream*), a tragi-comic account of the misfortunes, largely sexual, of a humble civil servant, Folantin. *À rebours* (1884; *Against the Grain*), Huysmans's best-known novel, relates the experiments in aesthetic decadence undertaken by the bored survivor of a noble line. The ambitious and controversial *Là-bas* (1891; *Down There*) tells of the occultist revival that occurred in France in the 1880s. A tale of 19th-century Satanists interwoven with a life of the medieval Satanist Gilles de Rais, the book introduced what was clearly an autobiographical protagonist, Durtal, who reappeared in Huysmans's last three novels: *En route* (1895), an account of Huysmans-Durtal's religious retreat in the Trappist monastery of Notre-Dame d'Igny and his return to Roman Catholicism; *La Cathédrale* (1898; *The Cathedral*), basically a study of Nôtre-Dame de Chartres with a thin story attached; and *L'Oblat* (1903; *The Oblate*), set in the Benedictine abbey of Ligugé, near Poitiers, in the neighbourhood in which Huysmans lived in 1899–1901 as an oblate (lay monk).

The chief fascination of Huysmans's work lies in its autobiographical content. Together his novels tell the story of a protracted spiritual odyssey. In each the hero tries to find happiness in some kind of spiritual and physical escapism; each ends on a note of disappointment and revolt until, in *L'Oblat*, Huysmans and his hero acknowledge that escapism is not only futile but wrong. Huysmans exemplified his hard-won belief in the value of suffering in his courageous bearing during the months of pain that preceded his death from cancer.

Also a perceptive art critic, Huysmans helped win public recognition of the Impressionist painters (*L'Art moderne*, 1883; *Certains*, 1889). He was the first president of the Goncourt Academy, which annually awards a prestigious French literary prize.

# AUGUST STRINDBERG

(b. January 22, 1849, Stockholm, Sweden—d. May 14, 1912, Stockholm)

The Swedish playwright, novelist, and short-story writer Johan August Strindberg combined psychology and Naturalism in a new kind of European drama that evolved into Expressionist drama. His chief works include *The Father* (1887), *Miss Julie* (1888), *Creditors* (1888), *A Dream Play* (1902), and *The Ghost Sonata* (1907).

## Early Years

Strindberg's father, Carl Oskar Strindberg, was a bankrupt aristocrat who worked as a steamship agent, and his mother was a former waitress. His childhood was marred by emotional insecurity, poverty, his grandmother's religious fanaticism, and neglect, as he relates in his remarkable autobiography *Tjänstekvinnans son* (1886–87; *The Son of a Servant*). He studied intermittently at the University of Uppsala, preparing in turn for the ministry and a career in medicine but never taking a degree. To earn his living, he worked as a freelance journalist in Stockholm, as well as at other jobs that he almost invariably lost. Meanwhile he struggled to complete his first important work, the historical drama *Mäster Olof* (published in 1872), on the theme of the Swedish Reformation, influenced by Shakespeare and by Henrik Ibsen's *Brand*. The Royal Theatre's rejection of *Mäster Olof* deepened his pessimism and sharpened his contempt for official institutions and traditions. For several years he continued revising the play—later recognized as the first modern Swedish drama—thus delaying his development as a dramatist of contemporary problems.

In 1874 he became a librarian at the Royal Library, and in 1875 he met the Finno-Swedish Siri von Essen, then the unhappy wife of an officer of the guards; two years later they married. Their intense but ultimately disastrous relationship ended in divorce in 1891, when Strindberg, to his great grief, lost the custody of their four children. At first, however, marriage stimulated his writing, and in 1879 he published his first novel, *The Red Room*, a satirical account of abuses and frauds in Stockholm society: this

*Swedish dramatist and author August Strindberg strikes an austere pose in the late 1890s, near the end of the early period wherein he wrote his most inspired works.* Hulton Archive/Getty Images

was something new in Swedish fiction and made its author nationally famous.

He also wrote more plays, of which *Lucky Peter's Travels* (1881) contains the most biting social criticism. In 1883, the year after he published *Det nya riket* ("The New Kingdom"), a withering satire on contemporary Sweden, Strindberg left Stockholm with his family and for six years moved restlessly about the Continent. Although he was then approaching a state of complete mental breakdown, he produced a great number of plays, novels, and stories. The publication in 1884 of the first volume of his collected stories, *Married*, led to a prosecution for blasphemy. He was acquitted, but the case affected his mind, and he imagined himself persecuted, even by Siri.

He returned to drama with new intensity, and the conflict between the sexes inspired some of the outstanding works written at this time, such as *The Father*, *Miss Julie*, and *The Creditors*. All of these were written in total revolt against contemporary social conventions. In these bold and concentrated works, he combined the techniques of dramatic Naturalism—including unaffected dialogue, stark rather than luxurious scenery, and the use of stage props as symbols—with his own conception of psychology, thereby inaugurating a new movement in European drama. *The People of Hemsö*, a vigorous novel about the Stockholm skerries (rocky islands), always one of Strindberg's happiest sources of inspiration, was also produced during this intensively creative phase.

The years after his return to Sweden in 1889 were lonely and unhappy. Even though revered as a famous writer who had become the voice of modern Sweden, he was by now an alcoholic unable to find steady employment. In 1892 he went abroad again, to Berlin. His second marriage, to a young Austrian journalist, Frida Uhl, followed in 1893; they finally parted in Paris in 1895.

Due to a period of emotional stress and physical strain that left him unable to produce any new literary works, Strindberg underwent a kind of religious conversion; the crisis that he described in *Inferno*. During these years he devoted considerable time to experiments in alchemy and to the study of theosophy.

## Late Years

His new faith, coloured by mysticism, re-created him as a writer. The immediate result was a drama in three parts, *To Damascus*, in which he depicts himself as "the Stranger," a wanderer seeking spiritual peace and finding it with another character, "the Lady," who resembles both Siri and Frida.

By this time Strindberg had again returned to Sweden, settling first in Lund and then, in 1899, in Stockholm, where he lived until his death. The summers he often spent among his beloved skerries. His view that life is ruled by the "Powers," punitive but righteous, was reflected in a series of historical plays that he began in 1889. Of these, *Gustav Vasa* is the best, masterly in its firmness of construction, characterization, and its vigorous dialogue. In 1901 he married the young Norwegian actress Harriet Bosse; in 1904 they parted, and again Strindberg lost the child, his fifth.

Yet his last marriage, this "spring in winter," as he called it, inspired, among other works, the plays *The Dance of Death* and *A Dream Play*, as well as the charming autobiography *Ensam* ("Alone") and some lyrical poems. Renewed bitterness after his parting from his last wife provoked the grotesquely satirical novel *Svarta Fanor* (1907; "Black Banners"), which attacked the vices and follies of Stockholm's literary coteries, as Strindberg saw them. *Kammarspel* ("Chamber Plays"), written for the little

Intima Theatre, which Strindberg ran for a time with a young producer, August Falck, embody further developments of his dramatic technique: of these, *The Ghost Sonata* is the most fantastic, anticipating much in later European drama. His last play, *The Great Highway*, a symbolic presentation of his own life, appeared in 1909.

# GUY DE MAUPASSANT

(b. August 5, 1850, Château de Miromesnil?, near Dieppe, France — d. July 6, 1893, Paris)

The French naturalist writer of short stories and novels Henry-René-Albert-Guy de Maupassant is by general agreement the greatest French short-story writer.

Maupassant was the elder of the two children of Gustave and Laure de Maupassant. His mother's claim that he was born at the Château de Miromesnil has been disputed. The couple's second son, Hervé, was born in 1856.

Both parents came of Norman families, the father's of the minor aristocracy, but the marriage was a failure, and the couple separated permanently when Guy was 11 years old. Although the Maupassants were a free-thinking family, Guy received his first education from the church and at age 13 was sent to a small seminary at Yvetot that took both lay and clerical pupils. He felt a decided antipathy for this form of life and deliberately engineered his own expulsion for some trivial offense in 1868. He moved to the lycée at Le Havre and passed his baccalaureate the following year. In the autumn of 1869 he began law studies in Paris, which were interrupted by the outbreak of the Franco-German War. Maupassant volunteered, served first as a private in the field, and was later transferred through his father's intervention to the quartermaster corps. His firsthand experience of war was to provide him with the material for some of his finest stories.

Maupassant was demobilized in July 1871 and resumed his law studies in Paris. His father came to his assistance again and obtained a post for him in the Ministry of Marine, which was intended to support him until he qualified as a lawyer. He did not care for the bureaucracy but was not unsuccessful and was several times promoted. His father managed to have him transferred, at his own wish, to the Ministry of Public Instruction in 1879.

## Apprenticeship with Flaubert

Maupassant's mother, Laure, was the sister of Alfred Le Poittevin, who had been a close friend of Gustave Flaubert, and she herself remained on affectionate terms with the novelist for the rest of his life. Laure sent her son to make Flaubert's acquaintance at Croisset in 1867, and when he returned to Paris after the war, she asked Flaubert to keep an eye on him. This was the beginning of the apprenticeship that was the making of Maupassant the writer. Whenever Flaubert was staying in Paris, he used to invite Maupassant to lunch on Sundays, lecture him on prose style, and correct his youthful literary exercises. He also introduced him to some of the leading writers of the time, such as Émile Zola, Ivan Turgenev, Edmond Goncourt, and Henry James. "He's my disciple and I love him like a son," Flaubert said of Maupassant. It was a concise description of a twofold relationship: if Flaubert was the inspiration for Maupassant the writer, he also provided the child of a broken marriage with a foster father. Flaubert's sudden and unexpected death in 1880 was a grievous blow to Maupassant.

Zola described the young Maupassant as a "terrific oarsman able to row fifty miles on the Seine in a single day for pleasure." Maupassant was a passionate lover of the sea and of rivers, which accounts for the setting of much of his fiction and the prevalence in it of nautical imagery. In spite of his lack of enthusiasm for the bureaucracy, his years as a civil servant were the happiest of his life. He devoted much of his spare time to swimming and to boating expeditions on the Seine. One can see from a story like *Mouche* (1890; *Fly*) that the latter were more than merely boating expeditions and that the girls who accompanied Maupassant and his friends were usually prostitutes or prospective prostitutes. Indeed, there can be little doubt that the early years in Paris were the start of his phenomenal promiscuity.

When Maupassant was in his early 20s, he discovered that he was suffering from syphilis, one of the most frightening and widespread maladies of the age. The fact that his brother died at an early age of the same disease suggests that it might have been congenital. Maupassant was adamant in refusing to undergo treatment, with the result that the disease was to cast a deepening shadow over his mature years and was accentuated by neurasthenia, which had also afflicted his brother.

During his apprenticeship with Flaubert, Maupassant published one or two stories under a pseudonym in obscure provincial magazines. The turning point came in April 1880, the month before Flaubert's death. Maupassant was one of six writers, led by Zola, who each contributed a short story on the Franco-German War to a volume called *Les Soirées de Médan*. Maupassant's story, *Boule de suif* ("Ball of Fat"), was not only by far the best of the six, it is probably the finest story he ever wrote. In it, a prostitute traveling by coach is companionably treated by her fellow French passengers, who are anxious to share her provisions of food, but then a German officer stops the coach and refuses to let it proceed until he has possessed her; the other passengers induce her to satisfy him, and then ostracize her for the rest of the journey. *Boule de suif* epitomizes Maupassant's style in its economy and balance.

## *Mature Life and Works*

As soon as *Boule de suif* was published, Maupassant found himself in demand by newspapers. He left the ministry and spent the next two years writing articles for *Le Gaulois* and the *Gil Blas*. Many of his stories made their first appearance in the latter newspaper. The 10 years from 1880 to 1890 were remarkable for their productivity; he published some 300 short stories, six novels, three travel books, and his only volume of verse.

*La Maison Tellier* (1881; "The Tellier House"), a book of short stories on various subjects, is typical of Maupassant's achievement as a whole, both in his choice of themes and in his determination to present men and women objectively in the manifold aspects of life. His concern was with *l'humble vérité*—words which he chose as the subtitle to his novel *Une Vie* (1883; *A Woman's Life*). This book, which sympathetically treats its heroine's journey from innocent girlhood through the disillusionment of an unfortunate marriage and ends with her subsequent widowhood, records what Maupassant had observed as a child, the little dramas and daily preoccupations of ordinary people. He presents his characters dispassionately, foregoing any personal moral judgment on them but always noting the word, the gesture, or even the reticence that betrays each one's essential personality, all the while enhancing the effect by describing the physical and social background against which his characters move. Concision, vigour, and the most rigorous economy are the characteristics of his art.

Collections of short stories and novels followed one another in quick succession until illness struck Maupassant down. Two years saw six new books of short stories: *Mademoiselle Fifi* (1883), *Contes de la bécasse* (1883; "Tales of the Goose"), *Clair de lune, Les Soeurs Rondoli* ("The Rondoli Sisters"), *Yvette*, and *Miss Harriet* (all 1884). The stories can be divided into groups: those dealing with the Franco-German War, the Norman peasantry, the bureaucracy, life on the banks of the Seine River, the emotional problems of the different social classes, and—somewhat ominously in a late story such as *Le Horla* (1887)—hallucination. Together, the stories present a comprehensive picture of French life from 1870 to 1890.

Maupassant's most important full-length novels are *Une Vie, Bel-Ami* (1885; "Good Friend"), and *Pierre et Jean* (1888). *Bel-Ami* is drawn from the author's observation of the world of sharp businessmen and cynical journalists in Paris, and it is a scathing satire on a society whose members let nothing stand in the way of their ambition to get rich quick. Bel-Ami, the amiable but amoral hero of the novel, has become a standard literary personification of an ambitious opportunist. *Pierre et Jean* is the tale of a man's tragic jealousy of his half-brother, who is the child of their mother's adultery.

Maupassant prospered from his best-sellers and maintained an apartment in Paris with an annex for clandestine meetings with women, a house at Étretat, a couple of residences on the Riviera, and several yachts. He began to travel in 1881, visiting French Africa and Italy, and in 1889 he paid his only visit to England. While lunching in a restaurant there as Henry James's guest, he shocked his host profoundly by pointing to a woman at a neighbouring table and asking James to "get" her for him.

The French critic Paul Léautaud called Maupassant a "complete erotomaniac." His extraordinary fascination with brothels and prostitution is reflected not only in *Boule de suif* but also in stories such as *La Maison Tellier.* It is significant, however, that as the successful writer became more closely acquainted with women of the nobility there was a change of angle in his fiction: a move from the peasantry to the upper classes, from the brothel to the boudoir. Maupassant's later books of short stories include *Toine* (1886), *Le Horla* (1887), *Le Rosier de Madame Husson* (1888; "The Rose-Bush of Madame Husson"), and *L'Inutile Beauté* (1890; "The Useless Beauty"). Four more novels also appeared: *Mont-Oriol* (1887), on the financing of a fashionable watering place; *Pierre et Jean; Fort comme la mort* (1889; "As Strong as Death"); and *Notre coeur* (1890; "Our Heart").

Although Maupassant appeared outwardly a sturdy, healthy, athletic man, his letters are full of lamentations about his health, particularly eye trouble and migraine headaches. With the passing of the years he had become more and more sombre. He had begun to travel for pleasure, but what had once been carefree and enjoyable holidays gradually changed, as a result of his mental state, into compulsive, symptomatic wanderings until he felt a constant need to be on the move.

A major family crisis occurred in 1888. Maupassant's brother was a man of minimal intelligence—today one would call it arrested development—and could work at nothing more demanding than nursery gardening. In 1888 he suddenly became violently psychotic, and he died in an asylum in 1889. Maupassant was reduced to despair by his brother's death; but though his grief was genuine, it cannot have been unconnected with his own advanced case of syphilis. On January 2, 1892, when he was staying near his mother, he tried to commit suicide by cutting his throat. Doctors were summoned, and his mother agreed reluctantly to his commitment. Two days later he was removed, according to some accounts in a straitjacket, to

Dr. Blanche's nursing home in Paris, where he died one month before his 43rd birthday.

Maupassant's work is thoroughly realistic. His characters inhabit a world of material desires and sensual appetites in which lust, greed, and ambition are the driving forces, and any higher feelings are either absent or doomed to cruel disappointment. The tragic power of many of the stories derives from the fact that Maupassant presents his characters, poor people or rich bourgeois, as the victims of ironic necessity, crushed by a fate that they have dared to defy yet still struggling against it hopelessly.

Because so many of his later stories deal with madness, it has been suggested that Maupassant himself was already mentally disturbed when he wrote them. Yet these stories are perfectly well balanced and are characterized by a clarity of style that betrays no sign of mental disorder. The lucid purity of Maupassant's French and the precision of his imagery are in fact the two features of his work that most account for its success.

By the second half of the 20th century, it was generally recognized that Maupassant's popularity as a short-story writer had declined and that he was more widely read in the English-speaking countries than in France. This does not detract from his genuine achievement—the invention of a new, high-quality, commercial short story, which has something to offer to all classes of readers.

# HARISHCHANDRA

(b. September 9, 1850, Vārānasi, India—d. January 6, 1885, Vārānasi)

Harishchandra (also called Bhartendu) was an Indian poet, dramatist, critic, and journalist and was commonly referred to as the "father of modern Hindi." His great contributions in founding a new tradition of Hindi prose were recognized even in his short lifetime, and he was admiringly called Bhartendu ("Moon of India"), an honorific that has taken precedence over his own name.

Harishchandra was born into a distinguished family that traced its descent from Aminchand, the prosperous banker whose intrigues against his master, the Nawab of Bengal, and deception by Robert Clive is a celebrated incident of modern Indian history. His father, Gopalachandra (pen name Giridharadaja), was a poet who composed a considerable amount of traditional Braj Bhasa (a dialect of Hindi) verse of technical virtuosity but with little poetic feeling.

Harishchandra began his own literary career at the age of 17, when he established (1867) the first literary magazine in Hindi, the *Kavi-vachana-sudha*, followed in 1872 by *Harishchandra Magazine*, later called *Harishchandra Chandrika*. A circle of distinguished poets and litterateurs whom he generously patronized gathered around him, and their work resulted in a radical transformation of Hindi language and literature in the pages of his magazine.

Harishchandra's influence was deep and far-reaching: his works mark the end of the Rīti period of Hindi literature (*c.* 1650–1850) and usher in what is called the Bhartendu epoch, which in turn leads into the modern period. His advocacy of the development of the Hindi language and his opposition to the undue importance given to Urdu in official circles had important political results, leading ultimately to the establishment of modern Hindi as the state language of India.

Harishchandra's poetry, in contrast to the rather dry poetry of the Rīti period, was simple, deeply felt, and filled with devotional ardour and emotional lyricism. His numerous plays, written partly in modern Hindi and partly in Braj Bhasa verse, are among the first in the language and concern themselves with a wide range of themes. They include satirical farces and several dramas in which the poet expresses his intense grief at the stultifying poverty of India and the decline of its civilization under centuries of foreign domination and colonialism.

Harishchandra's passionate participation in social and educational activities did not, however, prevent him from taking delight in the world around him. He was known also as an accomplished actor, a keen and witty polemicist, and, within the circle of his own caste and religious community, an outrageous practical joker.

# JOSÉ JULIÁN MARTÍ

(b. January 28, 1853, Havana, Cuba—d. May 19, 1895, Dos Ríos)

José Julián Martí y Pérez was a poet and essayist, patriot and martyr, who became the symbol of Cuba's struggle for independence from Spain. His dedication to the goal of Cuban freedom made his name a synonym for liberty throughout Latin America. As a patriot, Martí organized and unified the movement for Cuban independence and died on the battlefield fighting for it. As a writer, he was distinguished for his personal prose and deceptively simple, sincere verse on themes of a free and united America.

Educated first in Havana, Martí had published several poems by the age of 15, and at age 16 he founded a newspaper, *La Patria Libre* ("The Free Fatherland"). During a revolutionary uprising that broke out in Cuba in 1868, he sympathized with the patriots, for which he was sentenced to six months of hard labour and, in 1871, deported to Spain. There he continued his education and his writing, receiving both an M.A. and a degree in law from the University of Zaragoza in 1874 and publishing political essays. He spent the next few years in France, in Mexico, and in Guatemala, writing and teaching, and returned to Cuba in 1878.

Because of his continued political activities, however, Martí was again exiled from Cuba to Spain in 1879. From there he went to France, to New York City, and, in 1881, to Venezuela, where he founded the *Revista Venezolana* ("Venezuelan Review"). The politics of his journal, however, provoked Venezuela's dictator, Antonio Guzmán Blanco, and Martí returned that year to New York City, where he remained, except for occasional travels, until the year of his death.

Martí continued to write and publish newspaper articles, poetry, and essays. His regular column in *La Nación* of Buenos Aires made him famous throughout Latin America. His poetry, such as the collection *Versos libres* (1913; "Free Verses"), written between 1878 and 1882 on the theme of freedom, reveals a deep sensitivity and an original poetic vision. Martí's essays, which are considered by most critics his greatest contribution to Spanish American letters, helped to bring about innovations in Spanish prose and to promote better understanding among the American nations. In essays such as *Emerson* (1882), *Whitman* (1887), *Nuestra América* (1881; "Our America"), and *Bolívar* (1893), Martí expressed his original thoughts about Latin America and the United States in an intensely personal style that is still considered a model of Spanish prose. His writings reflect his exemplary life, his kindness, his love of liberty and justice, and his deep understanding of human nature. Collections of English translations of Martí's writings are *Inside the Monster: Writings on the United States and*

*American Imperialism* (1975), *Our America: Writings on Latin America and the Cuban Struggle for Independence* (1978), and *On Education* (1979)—all edited by Philip Foner.

In 1892 Martí was elected *delegado* ("delegate"; he refused to be called president) of the Partido Revolucionario Cubano ("Cuban Revolutionary Party") that he had helped to form. Making New York City the centre of operations, he began to draw up plans for an invasion of Cuba. He left New York for Santo Domingo on January 31, 1895, accompanied by the Cuban revolutionary leader Máximo Gómez and other compatriots. They arrived in Cuba to begin the invasion on April 11. Martí's death a month later in battle on the plains of Dos Ríos, Oriente province, came only seven years before his lifelong goal of Cuban independence was achieved.

# OSCAR WILDE

(b. October 16, 1854, Dublin, Ireland—d. November 30, 1900, Paris, France)

O scar Wilde was an Irish wit, poet, and dramatist whose reputation rests on his only novel, *The Picture of Dorian Gray* (1891), and on his comic masterpieces *Lady Windermere's Fan* (1892) and *The Importance of Being Earnest* (1895). He was a spokesman for the late 19th-century Aesthetic movement in England, which advocated art for art's sake, and he was the object of celebrated civil and criminal suits involving homosexuality and ending in his imprisonment (1895–97).

Wilde was born of professional and literary parents. His father, Sir William Wilde, was Ireland's leading ear and eye surgeon, who also published books on archaeology, folklore, and the satirist Jonathan Swift. His mother,

*Oscar Wilde, 1882.* Encyclopædia Britannica, Inc.

who wrote under the name Speranza, was a revolutionary poet and an authority on Celtic myth and folklore.

After attending Portora Royal School, Enniskillen (1864–71), Wilde went, on successive scholarships, to Trinity College, Dublin (1871–74), and Magdalen College, Oxford (1874–78), which awarded him a degree with honours. During these four years, he distinguished himself not only as a Classical scholar, a poseur, and a wit but also as a poet by winning the coveted Newdigate Prize in 1878 with a long poem, *Ravenna*. He was deeply impressed by the teachings of the English writers John Ruskin and Walter Pater on the central importance of art in life and particularly by the latter's stress on the aesthetic intensity by which life should be lived. Like many in his generation, Wilde was determined to follow Pater's urging "to burn always with [a] hard, gemlike flame." But Wilde also delighted in affecting an aesthetic pose; this, combined with rooms at Oxford decorated with objets d'art, resulted in his famous remark, "Oh, would that I could live up to my blue china!"

In the early 1880s, when Aestheticism was the rage and despair of literary London, Wilde established himself in social and artistic circles by his wit and flamboyance. Soon the periodical *Punch* made him the satiric object of its antagonism to the Aesthetes for what was considered their unmasculine devotion to art. And in their comic opera *Patience*, Gilbert and Sullivan based the character Bunthorne, a "fleshly poet," partly on Wilde. Wishing to reinforce the association, Wilde published, at his own expense, *Poems* (1881), which echoed, too faithfully, his discipleship to the poets Algernon Swinburne, Dante Gabriel Rossetti, and John Keats. Eager for further acclaim, Wilde agreed to lecture in the United States and Canada in 1882, announcing on his arrival at customs in New York City that he had "nothing to declare but his genius." Despite widespread hostility in the press to his languid poses and aesthetic costume of velvet jacket, knee breeches, and black silk stockings, Wilde for 12 months exhorted the Americans to love beauty and art; then he returned to Great Britain to lecture on his impressions of America.

In 1884 Wilde married Constance Lloyd, daughter of a prominent Irish barrister; two children, Cyril and Vyvyan, were born, in 1885 and 1886. Meanwhile, Wilde was a reviewer for the *Pall Mall Gazette* and then became editor of *Woman's World* (1887–89). During this period of apprenticeship as a writer, he published *The Happy Prince and Other Tales* (1888), which reveals his gift for romantic allegory in the form of the fairy tale.

In the final decade of his life, Wilde wrote and published nearly all of his major work. In his only novel, *The Picture of Dorian Gray* (published in *Lippincott's Magazine*, 1890, and in book form, revised and expanded by six chapters, 1891), Wilde combined the supernatural elements of the Gothic novel with the unspeakable sins of French decadent fiction. Critics charged immorality despite Dorian's self-destruction; Wilde, however, insisted on the amoral nature of art regardless of an apparently moral ending. *Intentions* (1891), consisting of previously published essays, restated his aesthetic attitude toward art by borrowing ideas from the French poets Théophile Gautier and Charles Baudelaire and the American painter James McNeill Whistler. In the same year, two volumes of stories and fairy tales also appeared, testifying to his extraordinary creative inventiveness: *Lord Arthur Savile's Crime, and Other Stories* and *A House of Pomegranates*.

But Wilde's greatest successes were his society comedies. Within the conventions of the French "well-made play" (with its social intrigues and artificial devices to resolve conflict), he employed his paradoxical, epigrammatic wit to create a form of comedy new to the 19th-century English theatre. His first success, *Lady Windermere's Fan*, demonstrated that this wit could revitalize the rusty machinery of French drama. In the same year, rehearsals of his macabre play *Salomé*, written in French and designed, as he said, to make his audience shudder by its depiction of unnatural passion, were halted by the censor because it contained biblical characters. It was published in 1893, and an English translation appeared in 1894 with Aubrey Beardsley's celebrated illustrations.

A second society comedy, *A Woman of No Importance* (produced 1893), convinced the critic William Archer that Wilde's plays "must be taken on the very highest plane of modern English drama." In rapid succession, Wilde's final plays, *An Ideal Husband* and *The Importance of Being Earnest*, were produced early in 1895. In the latter, his greatest achievement, the conventional elements of farce are transformed into satiric epigrams — seemingly trivial but mercilessly exposing Victorian hypocrisies:

> *I suppose society is wonderfully delightful. To be in it is merely a bore. But to be out of it simply a tragedy.*
> *I never travel without my diary. One should always have something sensational to read in the train.*
> *All women become like their mothers. That is their tragedy. No man does. That's his.*
> *I hope you have not been leading a double life, pretending to be wicked and being really good all the time. That would be hypocrisy.*

In many of his works, exposure of a secret sin or indiscretion and consequent disgrace is a central design. If life imitated art, as Wilde insisted in his essay "The Decay of Lying" (1889), he was himself approximating the pattern in his reckless pursuit of pleasure. In addition, his close friendship with Lord Alfred Douglas, whom he had met in 1891, infuriated the marquess of Queensberry, Douglas's father. Accused, finally, by the marquess of being a sodomite, Wilde, urged by Douglas, sued for criminal libel. Wilde's case collapsed, however, when the evidence went against him, and he dropped the suit. Urged to flee to France by his friends, Wilde refused, unable to believe that his world was at an end. He was arrested and ordered to stand trial.

Wilde testified brilliantly, but the jury failed to reach a verdict. In the retrial he was found guilty and sentenced, in May 1895, to two years at hard labour. Most of his sentence was served at Reading Gaol, where he wrote a long letter to Douglas (published in 1905 in a drastically cut version as *De Profundis*) filled with recriminations against the younger man for encouraging him in dissipation and distracting him from his work.

In May 1897 Wilde was released, bankrupt, and immediately went to France, hoping to regenerate himself as a writer. His only remaining work, however, was *The Ballad of Reading Gaol* (1898), revealing his concern for inhumane prison conditions. Despite constant money problems, he maintained, as George Bernard Shaw said, "an unconquerable gaiety of soul" that sustained him, and he was visited by such loyal friends as Max Beerbohm and Robert Ross, later his literary executor; he was also reunited with Douglas. He died suddenly of acute meningitis brought on by an ear infection. In his semiconscious final moments, he was received into the Roman Catholic Church, which he had long admired.

# ARTHUR RIMBAUD

(b. October 20, 1854, Charleville, France—d. November 10, 1891, Marseille)

The French poet and adventurer Jean-Nicolas-Arthur Rimbaud won renown among the Symbolist movement and markedly influenced modern poetry.

Rimbaud grew up at Charleville in the Ardennes region of northeastern France. He was the second son of an army captain and a local farmer's daughter. Outwardly pious and obedient, he was a child prodigy and a model pupil who astonished the teachers at the Collège de Charleville by his brilliance in all subjects, especially literature. Rimbaud was a voracious reader who soon familiarized himself with the major French writers of both the past and present. He had a particular talent for Latin verse, and in August 1870 he won the first prize for a Latin poem at the Concours Académique. Rimbaud seemed obsessed with poetry, spending hours juggling with rhyme. This firm grounding in the craft of versification gave him a complete, even arrogant confidence and an ambition to be acknowledged by the currently fashionable Parnassian poets, of whom he was soon producing virtuoso pastiches.

In his 16th year Rimbaud found his own distinctive voice in poems whose sentiments swing between two extremes: revolt against a repressive hometown environment, and a passionate desire for freedom and adventure. All of the unhappy adolescent's loathing and longing are in these poems, which are already remarkable works. The cliches of sentimentality, and, increasingly, religion itself become the targets of fierce cynicism. Equally ringing is the lyrical language that voices Rimbaud's yearning for freedom and transcendence. Based on exquisitely perceived sense impressions, the imagery in these poems expresses a longing for sensual union with the natural world.

Rimbaud had begun taking a keen interest in politics by the time the Franco-German War began in July 1870. The war served to intensify Rimbaud's rebelliousness; the elements of blasphemy and scatology in his poetry grew more intense, the tone more strident, and the images more grotesque and even hallucinatory. Reading widely in the town library, Rimbaud soon became involved with revolutionary socialist theory. In an impulsive attempt to put his hopes for revolution into practice, he ran away to Paris that August but was arrested at the station for traveling without a ticket. His mother had him brought back to Charleville by the police, but in February 1871 he again ran off to Paris as a volunteer in the forces of the Paris Commune, which was then under siege by regular French troops. After a frustrating three weeks there, he returned home just before the Paris Commune was mercilessly suppressed.

The collapse of his passionately felt political ideals seems to have been a turning point for Rimbaud. From now on, he declares in two important letters (May 13 and 15, 1871), he has given up the idea of "work" (i.e., action) and, having acknowledged his true vocation, will devote himself with all his energy to his role as a poet.

## Poetic Vision

Rimbaud wanted to serve as a prophet, a visionary, or, as he put it, a *voyant* ("seer"). He had come to believe in a universal life force that informs or underlies all matter. This spiritual force, which Rimbaud referred to simply as "l'inconnu" ("the unknown"), can be sensed only by a chosen few. Rimbaud set himself the task of striving to "see" this spiritual unknown and allowing his individual consciousness to be taken over and used by it as a mere instrument. He should then be able to transmit (by means of poetry) this music of the universe to his fellow men, awakening them spiritually and leading them forward to social progress. Rimbaud had not given up his social ideals, but now intended to realize them through poetry. First, though, he had to qualify himself for the task, and he coined a now-famous phrase to describe his method:

"le dérèglement de tous les sens" ("the derangement of all the senses"). Rimbaud intended to systematically undermine the normal functioning of his senses so that he could attain visions of the "unknown." In a voluntary martyrdom he would subject himself to fasting and pain, imbibe alcohol and drugs, and even cultivate hallucination and madness in order to expand his consciousness.

## Major Works

At the end of August 1871, on the advice of a literary friend in Charleville, Rimbaud sent to the poet Paul Verlaine samples of his new poetry. Verlaine, impressed by their brilliance, summoned Rimbaud to Paris and sent the money for his fare. In a burst of self-confidence, Rimbaud composed "Le Bateau ivre" ("The Drunken Boat"). This is perhaps his finest poem, and one that clearly demonstrates what his method could achieve. Ostensibly, "Le Bateau ivre" describes the journey of the *voyant* in a tipsy boat that has been freed from all constraints and launched headlong into a world of sea and sky that is heaving with the erotic rhythms of a universal dynamic force. The *voyant* himself is on an ecstatic search for some unnamed ideal that he seems to glimpse through the aquatic tumult. But monsters threaten, the dream breaks up in universal cataclysm, weariness and self pity take over, and both boat and *voyant* capitulate. Here Rimbaud succeeded in his aim of matching form to vision. A pounding rhythm drives the poem forward through enjambment across the verses, with internal rhymes and excited repetitions mounting on alliteration as with the swell of the envisioned sea.

Rimbaud was already a marvelous poet, but his behaviour in Paris was atrocious. He arrived there in September 1871, stayed for three months with Verlaine and his wife, and met most of the well-known poets of the day, but he antagonized them all—except Verlaine himself—by his rudeness, arrogance, and obscenity. Embarking upon a life of drink and debauchery, he became involved in a homosexual relationship with Verlaine that gave rise to scandal. The two men were soon being seen in public as lovers, and Rimbaud was blamed for breaking up Verlaine's marriage. In March 1872, while tormented by violent passion, jealousy, and guilt and in a state of physical dissolution, Rimbaud returned to Charleville so that Verlaine could attempt a reconciliation with his wife.

Rimbaud would later suggest that he was near death at this time, and the group of delicate, tenuous poems he then wrote—now known as *Derniers Vers* ("Last Verses")—express his yearning for purification through all this suffering. Still trying to match form to vision, he expresses his longing for spiritual regeneration in pared-down verse forms that are almost abstract patterns of musical and symbolic allusiveness. These poems clearly show the influence of Verlaine. Rimbaud now virtually abandoned verse composition; henceforth most of his literary production would consist of prose poems.

In May 1872 Rimbaud was recalled to Paris by Verlaine, who said that he could not live without him. That July Verlaine abandoned his wife and child and fled with Rimbaud to London, where they spent the following winter. During this winter Rimbaud composed a series of 40 prose poems to which he gave the title *Illuminations*. These are his most ambitious attempt to develop new poetic forms from the content of his visions. The *Illuminations* consist of a series of theatrical tableaux in which Rimbaud creates a primitive fantasy world, an imaginary universe complete with its own mythology, its own quasi-divine beings, its own cities, all depicted in kaleidoscopic images that have the vividness of hallucinations.

In the *Illuminations* Rimbaud reached the height of his originality and found the form best suited to his elliptical and esoteric style. He stripped the prose poem of its anecdotal, narrative, and descriptive content and used words for their evocative and associative power, divesting them of their logical or dictionary meaning. The hypnotic rhythms, the dense musical patterns, and the visual pyrotechnics of the poems work in counterpoint with Rimbaud's playful mastery of juggled syntax, ambiguity, etymological and literary references, and bilingual puns. A unique achievement, the *Illuminations'* innovative use of language greatly influenced the subsequent development of French poetry.

In real life the two poets' relationship was growing so tense and violent that Verlaine became physically ill and mentally disturbed. In April 1873 Rimbaud left him to return to his family, and it was at their farm at Roche, near Charleville, that he began to apply himself to another major work, *Une Saison en enfer* (1873; *A Season in Hell*). A month later Verlaine persuaded Rimbaud to accompany him to London. Rimbaud treated Verlaine with sadistic cruelty, and after more wanderings and quarrels, he rejoined Verlaine in Brussels only to make a last farewell. As he was leaving Verlaine shot him, wounding him in the wrist. Rimbaud was hospitalized, and Verlaine was arrested and sentenced to two years' imprisonment. Rimbaud soon returned to Roche, where he finished *Une Saison en enfer*.

*Une Saison en enfer*, which consists of nine fragments of prose and verse, is a remarkable work of self-confession and psychological examination. It is quite different from the *Illuminations* and in fact repudiates the aesthetic they represent. Rimbaud was going through a spiritual and moral crisis, and in *Une Saison en enfer* he retrospectively examines the hells he had entered in search of experience, his guilt-ridden and unhappy passion for Verlaine, and the failure of his own overambitious aesthetic. The poem consists of a series of scenes in which the narrator acts out various roles, seemingly a necessary therapy for a young man still searching for some authentic, unified identity. In the book's final section, "Adieu" ("Goodbye"), Rimbaud takes a nostalgic backward look at his past life and then moves on, declaring that his spiritual battle has been won. He contemplates a future in which he can "possess the truth in a soul and a body." The enigmatic ambiguity of this concluding statement is characteristic of Rimbaud. Perhaps it implies both a saner, more realistic stance towards life and a healing of the split between body and soul that had so plagued him.

"Adieu" has sometimes been read as Rimbaud's farewell to creative writing. It was certainly a farewell to the visionary, apocalyptic writing of the *voyant*. His last encounter with Verlaine, early in 1875, ended in a violent quarrel, but it was at this time that he gave Verlaine the manuscript of the *Illuminations*.

## Later Life

The rest of Rimbaud's life, from the literary point of view, was silence. In 1875 he set out to see the world, and by 1879 he had crossed the Alps on foot, joined and deserted the Dutch colonial army in the East Indies, visited Egypt, and worked as a labourer in Cyprus, in every instance suffering illness or other hardships. In 1880 he found employment in the service of a coffee trader at Aden (now in Yemen), who sent him to Hārer (now in Ethiopia).

In time Rimbaud set up as an explorer and trader in Ethiopia, traveling in the interior and at one point selling arms to Menilek II, king of Shewa (Shoa), who became that country's emperor in 1889. Rimbaud's gift for languages and his humane treatment of the Ethiopians made him popular with them. All trace of his amazing literary gift had disappeared; his ambition now was simply to amass as much money as possible and then return home to live at leisure.

During this period of expatriation, Rimbaud had become known as a poet in France. Verlaine had written about him in *Les Poètes maudits* (1884) and had published a selection of his poems. These had been enthusiastically received, and in 1886, unable to discover where Rimbaud was or to get an answer from him, Verlaine published the prose poems, under the title *Illuminations*, and further verse poems, in the Symbolist periodical *La Vogue*, as the work of "the late Arthur Rimbaud."

Rimbaud did make a considerable fortune in Ethiopia, but in February 1891 he developed a tumour on his knee. He was sent back to France, and shortly after he arrived at Marseille his right leg had to be amputated. In July he returned to the family farm at Roche, where his health grew steadily worse. In August 1891 he set out on a nightmarish journey to Marseille, where his disease was diagnosed as cancer. He endured agonizing treatment at the hospital there and died, according to his sister Isabelle, after having made his confession to a priest.

# GLOSSARY

**aesthetic** Pleasing to the senses; appreciative of, responsive to, or zealous about the beautiful.

**canto** One of the major divisions of a long poem.

**dissertation** An extended, usually written treatment of a subject.

**ecclesiastical** Of or relating to a church.

**existential** Grounded in existence or the experience of existence.

**folio** Referring to a book printed on paper cut two pages to a sheet.

**lyricism** An intense personal quality expressive of feeling or emotion in an art, especially poetry.

**manuscript** A written document submitted for publication.

**melancholy** An abnormal state characterized by easy anger or depression.

**metaphysics** A division of philosophy concerned with the fundamental nature of reality and being.

**motif** A recurring theme or dominant idea in a work of art.

**ode** A lyric poem usually marked by intense feeling and style, as well as a variety of line lengths and a complexity of stanza forms.

**pastoral** Of or relating to the countryside, marked by an often idealized state of peace and innocence.

**philology** The study of literature, or of disciplines relevant to or language as used therein.

**polemic** An aggressive attack on or refutation of the opinions or principles of another.

**protagonist** The principal character in a literary work.

**pseudonym** A fictitious name, especially used by writers as a name under which they publish their works.

**quintessence** The essence of a thing in its purest and most concentrated form.

**Romantic movement** A period marked by the celebration of nature and imagination in the arts during the late 18th and early 19th centuries.

**syllogism** A logical, well-conceived argument containing major and minor premises and a conclusion.

**treatise** A written argument comprised of a methodical discussion of the facts and principles involved and conclusions reached.

**vocation** A strong inclination, or calling, to take a particular course of action.

# BIBLIOGRAPHY

Noteworthy studies of some of the Romantic authors covered in this volume include Nicholas Boyle, *Goethe: The Poet and the Age*, containing the volumes *The Poetry of Desire (1749–1790)* (1991) and *Revolution and Renunciation (1790–1803)* (2000); Northrop Frye, *Fearful Symmetry: A Study of William Blake* (1947), an enormously persuasive work by one of the most influential literary critics of the 20th century; Peter Ackroyd, *Blake* (1996); Tom Conner, *Chateaubriand's Mémoires d'outre-tombe: A Portrait of the Artist as Exile* (1995); Stephen Gill, *William Wordsworth: A Life* (1989); Richard Holmes, *Coleridge: Early Visions* (1990), and *Coleridge: Darker Reflections* (1998), which together create a comprehensive biography; Robert M. Adams, *Stendhal: Notes on a Novelist* (1959, reissued 1969); Robert F. Gleckner (ed.), *Critical Essays on Lord Byron* (1991); Richard Holmes, *Shelley: The Pursuit* (1974, reprinted 1987 and 2003); Janko Lavrin, *Pushkin and Russian Literature* (1947, reprinted 1969), which discusses Pushkin's place and significance in the development of Russian literature; Victor Brombert, *Victor Hugo and the Visionary Novel* (1984); Arthur H. Quinn, *Edgar Allan Poe: A Critical Biography* (1941, reprinted 1969); Elizabeth C. Gaskell, *The Life of Charlotte Brontë*, 2 vol. (1857), which raised controversy and was modified in the third edition (1857, reprinted in 1 vol., 1978); and Rebecca Fraser, *The Brontës: Charlotte Brontë and Her Family* (1988).

Authors of the latter half of the 19th century are surveyed in Edgar Johnson, *Charles Dickens: His Tragedy and*

*Triumph*, 2 vol. (1952, reprinted 1965); Duane DeVries (ed.), *General Studies of Charles Dickens and His Writings and Collected Editions of His Works: An Annotated Bibliography* (2004– ); Michael Slater, *Charles Dickens* (2007); William E. Sedgwick, *Herman Melville: The Tragedy of Mind* (1944, reissued 1972), one of the best studies of Melville's ideas as they appear in his novels; Joseph Frank, *Dostoevsky: The Seeds of Revolt, 1821–1849* (1976), *Dostoevsky: The Years of Ordeal, 1850–1859* (1983), *Dostoevsky: The Stir of Liberation, 1860–1865* (1986), *Dostoevsky: The Miraculous Years, 1865–1871* (1995), and *Dostoevsky: The Mantle of the Prophet, 1871–1881* (2002); Mikhail Bakhtin, *Problems of Dostoevsky's Poetics*, ed. and trans. by Caryl Emerson (1984; originally published in Russian, 2nd ed., rev. and enlarged, 1963); Halvdan Koht, *Life of Ibsen* (1971); Maxim Gorky, *Reminiscences of Leo Nicolaevich Tolstoy* (1920, reprinted 1977; originally published in Russian, 1919); Hugh McLean (ed.), *In the Shade of the Giant: Essays on Tolstoy* (1989); Wendy Barker, *Lunacy of Light: Emily Dickinson and the Experience of Metaphor* (1987), which applies a feminist perspective to illuminate patterns of figurative language in Dickinson's poetry; Gladys Carmen Bellamy, *Mark Twain as a Literary Artist* (1950, reissued 1969); Ron Powers, *Mark Twain: A Life* (2005); F.W.J. Hemmings, *The Life and Times of Émile Zola* (1977); J. Hillis Miller, *Thomas Hardy: Distance and Desire* (1970); F.O. Matthiessen, *Henry James: The Major Phase* (1944, reprinted 1970); Richard Ellmann, *Oscar Wilde* (1988); and W.M. Frohock, *Rimbaud's Poetic Practice: Image and Theme in the Major Poems* (1963).

# INDEX

# G

*Germinal*, 378
*Ghosts*, 320–321
Goethe, Johann Wolfgang
 von, 1–15, 65, 69, 86, 111,
 133, 167, 278
Gogol, Nikolay, 190–196, 256, 257
Goncourt, Edmond, 259, 374,
 393, 421, 422
*Great Expectations*, 209, 216,
 219–221
Grillparzer, Franz, 108–111
Grimm, Jacob, 80–87
Grimm, Wilhelm, 80–87
*Grimm's Fairy Tales*, 80, 83, 84
Guiccioli, Teresa Gamba,
 95–96
*Guldbornene*, 68, 69

# H

Hallam, Arthur, 197–198, 199, 200
Hardy, Thomas, 380–388
Harvard, 162, 166, 167, 180, 181,
 243, 246, 248, 392
Harishchandra, 426–428
Hawthorne, Nathaniel, 168–174,
 270, 272, 392
Hazlitt, William, 65–68
Heine, Heinrich, 131–137
*He Knew He Was Right*, 233
Herder, Johann Gottfried, 4, 6,
 11, 81
*Hero of Our Time, A*, 227, 230
Hidemith, Paul, 62
Higginson, Thomas Wentworth,
 340–341
Hoffmann, E.T.A., 60–62, 176
Hogg, Thomas Jefferson, 112, 113
Hölderlin, Friedrich, 31–35

Hopkins, Gerard Manley, 409–412
*House of the Dead*, 293
*House of the Seven Gables, The*, 168,
 171, 174
*Household Words*, 216–217
Hugo, Victor, 126, 127, 151–159, 402
Hunt, Leigh, 96, 97, 118, 119, 125
Huysmans, Joris-Karl, 374, 391,
 414–415
*Hyperion* (Holderlin), 32, 33
*Hyperion* (Keats), 124–125

# I

Ibsen, Henrik, 110, 317–324, 416
*Idiot, The*, 297
*Idylls of the King*, 201
*Illuminations*, 405, 439, 440, 441
*Importance of Being Earnest, The*,
 430, 434
*In Memoriam*, 199, 200, 405
Irving, Washington, 77–80, 180

# J

"J'accuse," 371, 375
James, Henry, 259, 391–398,
 421, 424
*Jane Eyre*, 235–236, 239–240,
 241, 252
*Jude the Obscure*, 385

# K

Kabuki, 235–235
Kant, Immanuel, 63
Kawatake, Mokuami, 234–235
Keats, John, 41, 66, 117, 118–125,
 185, 432
Kleist, Heinrich von, 62–65